CHILTON'S
REPAIR & TUNE-UP GUIDE

BLAZER JIMMY 1969-82

Blazer 1969-82 • Jimmy 1970-82

Managing Editor KERRY A. FREEMAN, S.A.E.
Senior Editor RICHARD J. RIVELE, S.A.E.
Editor RON WEBB

President WILLIAM A. BARBOUR
Executive Vice President JAMES A. MIADES
Vice President and General Manager JOHN P. KUSHNERICK

CHILTON BOOK COMPANY
Radnor, Pennsylvania
19089

SAFETY NOTICE

Proper service and repair procedures are vital to the safe, reliable operation of all motor vehicles, as well as the personal safety of those performing repairs. This book outlines procedures for servicing and repairing vehicles using safe, effective methods. The procedures contain many NOTES, CAUTIONS and WARNINGS which should be followed along with standard safety procedures to eliminate the possibility of personal injury or improper service which could damage the vehicle or compromise its safety.

It is important to note that repair procedures and techniques, tools and parts for servicing motor vehicles, as well as the skill and experience of the individual performing the work vary widely. It is not possible to anticipate all of the conceivable ways or conditions under which vehicles may be serviced, or to provide cautions as to all of the possible hazards that may result. Standard and accepted safety precautions and equipment should be used when handling toxic or flammable fluids, and safety goggles or other protection should be used during cutting, grinding, chiseling, prying, or any other process that can cause material removal or projectiles.

Some procedures require the use of tools specially designed for a specific purpose. Before substituting another tool or procedure, you must be completely satisfied that neither your personal safety, nor the performance of the vehicle will be endangered.

Although information in this guide is based on industry sources and is as complete as possible at the time of publication, the possibility exists that the manufacturer made later changes which could not be included here. While striving for total accuracy, Chilton Book Company cannot assume responsibility for any errors, changes, or omissions that may occur in the compilation of this data.

PART NUMBERS

Part numbers listed in this reference are not recommendations by Chilton for any product by brand name. They are references that can be used with interchange manuals and aftermarket supplier catalogs to locate each brand supplier's discrete part number.

ACKNOWLEDGMENTS

Chilton Book Company wishes to express appreciation to the Chevrolet Motor Division, General Motors Corporation, Detroit, Michigan; GMC Truck and Coach Division, General Motors Corporation, Detroit, Michigan; and Macpherson RTV, MacHoward Auto and Truck Leasing Santa Ana, California for their generous assistance in the preparation of this book.

Information has been selected from Chevrolet and GMC shop manuals, owners manuals, data books, brochures, service bulletins, and technical training manuals.

Manufactured in the United States of America
1234567890   1098765432

Chilton's Repair & Tune-Up Guide: Blazer and Jimmy 1969–82
ISBN 0-8019-7203-5 pbk.
Library of Congress Catalog Card No. 81-70234

CONTENTS

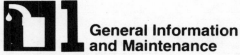

Quick Reference Specifications For Your Vehicle

Fill in this chart with the most commonly used specifications for your vehicle. Specifications can be found in Chapters 1 through 3 or on the tune-up decal under the hood of the vehicle.

 ## Tune-Up

Firing Order_____

Spark Plugs:

    Type_____

    Gap (in.)_____

Point Gap (in.)_____

Dwell Angle (°)_____

Ignition Timing (°)_____

    Vacuum (Connected/Disconnected)_____

Valve Clearance (in.)

    Intake_____   Exhaust_____

Capacities

Engine Oil (qts)

    With Filter Change_____

    Without Filter Change_____

Cooling System (qts)_____

Manual Transmission (pts)_____

    Type_____

Automatic Transmission (pts)_____

    Type_____

Front Differential (pts)_____

    Type_____

Rear Differential (pts)_____

    Type_____

Transfer Case (pts)_____

    Type_____

FREQUENTLY REPLACED PARTS

Use these spaces to record the part numbers of frequently replaced parts.

PCV VALVE

Manufacturer_____

Part No._____

OIL FILTER

Manufacturer_____

Part No._____

AIR FILTER

Manufacturer_____

Part No._____

General Information and Maintenance

HOW TO USE THIS BOOK

This book has been written to help the Blazer or Jimmy owner perform maintenance, tune-ups and repairs on his automobile. It is intended for both the novice and for those more familiar with auto repairs. Since this book contains information on very simple operations (Chapters 1 and 2) and the more involved ones (Chapters 3–10), the user will not outgrow the book as he masters simple repairs and is ready to progress to more difficult operations. Chapter 11 contains helpful Troubleshooting information for all systems on the vehicle.

Several things were assumed of you while the repair procedures were being written. They are mentioned here so that you will be aware of them. It was assumed that you own, or are willing to purchase, a basic set of hand tools and equipment. A skeletal listing of tools and equipment has been drawn up for you.

For many repair operations, the factory has suggested a special tool to perform the repairs. If it was at all possible, a conventional tool was substituted for the special tool in these cases. However, there are some operations which cannot be done without the use of these tools. To perform these jobs cor-rectly, it will be necessary to order the tool through your local dealer's parts department.

Two basic rules of automobile mechanics deserve mentioning here. Whenever the left-side of the vehicle is referred to, it is meant to specify the driver's side. Likewise, the right-side of the vehicle means the passenger's side. Also, most screws, nuts, and bolts are removed by turning counterclockwise and tightened by turning clockwise.

Before performing any repairs, read the entire section of the book that deals with that job. In many places a description of the system is provided. By reading this first, and then reading the entire repair procedure, you will understand the function of the system you will be working on and what will be involved in the repair operation, prior to starting the job. This will enable you to avoid problems and also to help you learn about your vehicle while you are working on it.

While every effort was made to make the book as simple, yet as detailed as possible, there is no substitute for personal experience. You can gain the confidence and feel for mechanical things needed to make auto repairs only by doing them yourself. If you take your time and concentrate on what you are doing, you will be amazed at how fast you can learn.

TOOLS AND EQUIPMENT

Naturally, without the proper tools and equipment it is impossible to properly service your vehicle. It would be impossible to catalog each tool that you would need to perform each operation in this book. It would also be unwise for the amateur to rush out and buy an expensive set of tools on the theory that he may need one or more of them at sometime.

The best approach is to proceed slowly, putting together a good set of those tools which are used most frequently. Don't be misled by the low cost of bargain tools. It is far better to spend a little more for better quality. Forged wrenches, 12 point sockets and fine tooth ratchets are far preferable to their less expensive counterparts.

Begin accumulating those tools that are used most frequently; those associated with routine maintenance and tune-up.

In addition to the normal assortment of screwdrivers and pliers you should have the following tools for routine maintenance jobs:

1. SAE or SAE/Metric wrenches—sockets and combination open end/box end wrenches in sizes from ⅛ in. (3 mm) to ¾ in. (19mm) and a spark plug socket ($^{13}/_{16}$ or ⅝ in. depending on plug type).

If possible, buy various length socket drive extensions. One break in this department is that the metric sockets available in the U.S. will all fit the ratchet handles and extensions you may already have.

2. Jackstands—for support and safety;
3. Oil filter wrench;
4. Oil filter spout—for pouring oil;
5. Grease gun—for chassis lubrication.

The second list of tools is for tune-ups. While the tools here are slightly more sophisticated, they're not necessarily expensive. There are several inexpensive tach/dwell meters available that are every bit as good for the average mechanic as the expensive professional model. Just be sure that it goes to at least 1,200–1,500 rpm on the tach scale and that it works on 4, 6, or 8 cylinder engines. Tune-up equipment could include:

1. Tach-dwell meter;
2. Spark plug wrench;
3. Timing light (a DC light that works from the battery is best, although an AC light that plugs into 110V house current will suffice at some sacrifice in brightness);
4. Wire spark plug gauge;
5. Set of feeler blades.

Here again, be guided by your own needs. A feeler blade will set the point gap as easily as a dwell meter will read dwell, but slightly less accurately.

In addition to these basic tools, there are several other tools and gauges you may find useful. These include:

1. A compression gauge. The screw-in type is slower to use, but eliminates the possibility of a faulty reading due to escaping pressure.
2. A manifold vacuum gauge.
3. A test light.
4. An induction meter. This is used for determining whether or not there is current in a wire. These are handy for use if a wire is broken somewhere in a wiring harness.

As a final note, you will probably find a torque wrench necessary for all but the most basic work. The beam type models are perfectly adequate, although the newer click type are more precise.

Special Tools

Normally, the use of special factory tools is avoided for repair procedures, since these are not readily available for the do-it-yourself mechanic. When it is possible to perform the job with more commonly available tools, it will be pointed out, but occasionally, a special tool which was designed to perform a specific function should be used. Before substituting another tool, you should be convinced that neither your safety nor the performance of the vehicle will be compromised.

Some special tools are available commercially from major tool manufacturers. Others can be purchased from your car dealer or by contacting:

Kent-Moore Corporation
Service Tool Division
1501 South Jackson St.
Jackson, Michigan 49203

SERVICING YOUR VEHICLE SAFELY

It is virtually impossible to anticipate all of the hazards involved with automotive maintenance and service but care and common sense will prevent most accidents.

The rules of safety for mechanics range from "don't smoke around gasoline," to "use the proper tool for the job." The trick to avoiding injuries is to develop safe work habits and take every possible precaution.

Do's

• Do keep a fire extinguisher and first aid kit within easy reach.

• Do wear safety glasses or goggles when cutting, drilling, grinding or prying.

• Do shield your eyes whenever you work around the battery. Batteries contain sulphuric acid. In case of contact with the eyes or skin, flush the area with water or a mixture of water and baking soda and get medical attention immediately.

• Do use safety stands for any under-car service. Jacks are for raising vehicles; safety stands are for making sure the vehicle stays raised until you want it to come down. Whenever the vehicle is raised, block the wheels remaining on the ground and set the parking brake.

• Do disconnect the negative battery cable when working on the electrical system. The primary ignition system can contain up to 40,000 volts.

• Do properly maintain your tools. Loose hammerheads, mushroomed punches and chisels, frayed or poorly grounded electrical cords, excessively worn screwdrivers, spread wrenches (open end), cracked sockets, slipping ratchets, or faulty droplight sockets can cause accidents and injuries.

• Do use the proper size and type of tool for the job being done.

• Do when possible, pull on a wrench handle rather than push on it, and adjust your stance to prevent a fall.

• Do be sure that adjustable wrenches are tightly adjusted on the nut or bolt and pulled so that the face is on the side of the fixed jaw.

• Do select a wrench or socket that fits the nut or bolt. The wrench or socket should sit straight, not cocked.

• Do strike squarely with a hammer—avoid glancing blows.

• Do set the parking brake and block the drive wheels if the work requires that the engine be running.

Dont's

• Don't run an engine in a garage or anywhere else without proper ventilation—EVER! Carbon monoxide is poisonous; it takes a long time to leave the human body and you can build up a deadly supply of it in your system by simply breathing in a little every day. Always use power vents, windows, fans or open the garage doors.

• Don't work around moving parts while wearing a necktie or other loose clothing. Short sleeves are much safer than long, loose sleeves and hard-toed shoes with neoprene soles protect your toes and give a better grip on slippery surfaces. Jewelry is not safe when working around a car. Long hair should be hidden under a hat or cap.

• Don't use pockets for toolboxes. A fall or bump can drive a screwdriver deep into your body. Even a wiping cloth hanging from the back pocket can wrap around a spinning shaft or fan.

• Don't smoke when working around gasoline, cleaning solvent or other flammable material.

• Don't smoke when working around the battery. When the battery is being charged, it gives off explosive hydrogen gas.

• Don't use gasoline to wash your hands; there are excellent soaps available. Gasoline may contain lead, and lead can enter the body through a cut, accumulating in the body until you are very ill. Gasoline also removes all the natural oils from the skin so that bone dry hands will absorb oil and grease.

• Don't service the air conditioning system unless you are equipped with the necessary tools and training. The refrigerant, R-12, is extremely cold and when exposed to the air will instantly freeze any surface it comes in contact with, including your eyes. Although the refrigerant is normally non-toxic, R-12 becomes a deadly poisonous gas in the presence of an open flame. One good whiff of the vapors from burning refrigerant can be fatal.

HISTORY

The Blazer was introduced during the 1969 model year in both six-cylinder and V8, two and four wheel drive models. Chevrolet's new utility vehicle was designed to use proven components from the Chevrolet/GMC light truck line in a new size and body style. The GMC Jimmy was introduced in 1970.

There are three notably different Blazer/Jimmy body styles. The first, from 1969 through 1972, is easily identified by the rounded wheelwells. The second, from 1973 through 1975, has a high flat hood and rectangular wheelwells, as well as a generally squared-off shape. The third, from 1976, adds a fixed steel cab roof with rollover protection and replaces the frameless-glass doors with doors similar to those used on pickup trucks and Suburbans.

All four wheel drive Blazers and Jimmys have leaf springs at all four wheels. All two wheel drive models have coil spring independent from suspension with coil spring rear suspension through 1972, and rear leaf springs starting 1973. Numerous GVW packages have been offered to suit the suspension to the job. Vacuum assisted front disc brakes were introduced in 1971; earlier models had 11 inch diameter front drum brakes. All four wheel drive Blazers and Jimmys through 1972 use a conventional two-speed transfer case and all 1973–74 V8s and 1975–80 four wheel drive automatic transmission models use full time four wheel drive. Full time four wheel drive was dropped from manual transmission models early in the 1975 model year, and from automatic transmission models in 1981.

SERIAL NUMBER IDENTIFICATION

Vehicle

The vehicle identification number (VIN) is on a plate fastened to the left door frame. It also appears in several other places on the vehicle. The gross vehicle weight (GVW) or maximum safe total weight of the vehicle, cargo, and passengers is also given on the plate.

MFD. BY GENERAL MOTORS CORPORATION

GVWR

GAWR FRONT   GAWR REAR

VIN

CAMPER LOADING DATA

CWR   DIM A   DIM B

INFLATION DATA FOR TIRES FURNISHED WITH VEHICLE
FRONT   PRESSURE
REAR   PRESSURE

WARRANTY VOIDED IF LOADED IN EXCESS OF RATINGS
SEE OWNERS MANUAL FOR OTHER LOADING AND INFLATION DATA

One of the several types of V.I.N. and GVW plates which may be found on the left door frame

1969

The first letter is B. The second letter is the chassis type. C is conventional, or two wheel drive; K is four wheel drive. The third letter identifies the engine; S for six and E for V8. The first number gives the load capacity range; 1 for ½ ton. The second and third numbers indicate the cab to axle measure-

ment; 07 for 42–47 in. The fourth and fifth numbers are 14 for Blazer utility body. The sixth number is the last digit of the model year; 9 for 1969. The next letter indicates the assembly plant. The remaining numbers are the vehicle's individual serial number.

1970–71

The first letter is the chassis type. C is conventional, or two wheel drive; K is four wheel drive. The second letter identifies the engine; S for six and E for V8. The first number gives the load capacity range; 1 for ½ ton. The second number is 8 for Blazer/Jimmy utility body. The third number is the last digit of the model year, as 1 for 1971. The next letter indicates the assembly plant. The remaining numbers are the vehicle's individual serial number.

1972–80

The first letter indicates a Chevrolet (C) or GMC (T) vehicle. The second letter is the chassis type; C is conventional, or two wheel drive, K is four wheel drive. The third letter identifies the engine. For 1972, it was S for six and E for V8. For 1973–80, it is:

- Q   250 six through 1975
- D   250 six from 1976
- U   305 V8
- X   307 V8
- V, M   350 2 bbl V8
- Y, L   350 4 bbl V8
- U   400 V8 through 1976
- R   400 V8, 1977–79

The first number gives the load capacity range; 1 for ½ ton. The second number is 8 for Blazer/Jimmy utility body. The third number is the last digit of the model year, as 6 for 1976. The next letter indicates the assembly plant. The remaining numbers are the vehicle's individual serial number.

From 1981

A seventeen number/letter "world" identification was introduced in 1981. See the illustration for an explanation of the VIN number.

Engine

The six cylinder engine number is on a pad at the right side of the cylinder block behind the distributor. On V8s, the number is on the right front bank of the engine block. The last three letters of the engine number are a code identifying the engine as a truck engine (T), and two letters identifying the engine dis-

Typical VIN Number From 1981

1GCEC14D9BF123456

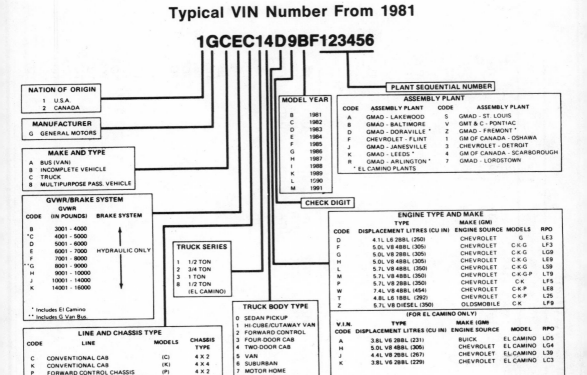

NATION OF ORIGIN	
1	U.S.A.
2	CANADA

MANUFACTURER	
G	GENERAL MOTORS

MAKE AND TYPE	
A	BUS (VAN)
B	INCOMPLETE VEHICLE
C	TRUCK
8	MULTIPURPOSE PASS. VEHICLE

GVWR/BRAKE SYSTEM

CODE	GVWR (IN POUNDS)	BRAKE SYSTEM
B	3001 - 4000	
*C	4001 - 5000	
D	5001 - 6000	
E	6001 - 7000	HYDRAULIC ONLY
F	7001 - 8000	
**G	8001 - 9000	
H	9001 - 10000	
J	10001 - 14000	
K	14001 - 16000	

* Includes El Camino
** Includes G Van Bus.

MODEL YEAR

CODE	YEAR
B	1981
C	1982
D	1983
E	1984
F	1985
G	1986
H	1987
I	1988
K	1989
L	1590
M	1991

CHECK DIGIT

PLANT SEQUENTIAL NUMBER

ASSEMBLY PLANT

CODE	ASSEMBLY PLANT	CODE	ASSEMBLY PLANT
A	GMAD - LAKEWOOD	S	GMAD - ST. LOUIS
B	GMAD - BALTIMORE	V	GMT & C - PONTIAC
D	GMAD - DORAVILLE *	Z	GMAD - FREMONT *
F	CHEVROLET - FLINT	1	GM OF CANADA - OSHAWA
J	GMAD - JANESVILLE	3	CHEVROLET - DETROIT
K	GMAD - LEEDS *	4	GM OF CANADA - SCARBOROUGH
R	GMAD - ARLINGTON *	7	GMAD - LORDSTOWN
* EL CAMINO PLANTS			

ENGINE TYPE AND MAKE

CODE	TYPE DISPLACEMENT LITRES (CU IN)	MAKE (GM) ENGINE SOURCE	MODELS	RPO
D	4.1L L6 2BBL (250)	CHEVROLET	G	LE3
F	5.0L V8 4BBL (305)	CHEVROLET	C-K-G	LF3
G	5.0L V8 2BBL (305)	CHEVROLET	C-K-G	LG9
H	5.0L V8 4BBL (305)	CHEVROLET	C-K-G	LE9
L	5.7L V8 4BBL (350)	CHEVROLET	C-K-G	LS9
M	5.7L V8 4BBL (350)	CHEVROLET	C-K-G-P	LT9
P	5.7L V8 2BBL (350)	CHEVROLET	C-K	LF5
W	7.4L V8 4BBL (454)	CHEVROLET	C-K-P	LE8
T	4.8L L6 1BBL (292)	CHEVROLET	C-K-P	L25
Z	5.7L V8 DIESEL (350)	OLDSMOBILE	C-K	LF9

(FOR EL CAMINO ONLY)

V.I.N. CODE	TYPE DISPLACEMENT LITRES (CU IN)	MAKE (GM) ENGINE SOURCE	MODEL	RPO
A	3.8L V6 2BBL (231)	BUICK	EL CAMINO	LD5
H	5.0L V8 4BBL (305)	CHEVROLET	EL CAMINO	LG4
J	4.4L V8 2BBL (267)	CHEVROLET	EL CAMINO	L39
K	3.8L V6 2BBL (229)	CHEVROLET	EL CAMINO	LC3

TRUCK SERIES

	SERIES TYPE
1	1/2 TON
2	3/4 TON
3	1 TON
8	1/2 TON (EL CAMINO)

TRUCK BODY TYPE

0	SEDAN PICKUP
1	HI-CUBE/CUTAWAY VAN
2	FORWARD CONTROL
3	FOUR-DOOR CAB
4	TWO-DOOR CAB
5	VAN
6	SUBURBAN
7	MOTOR HOME
8	BLAZER
9	STAKE/PLATFORM

LINE AND CHASSIS TYPE

CODE	LINE	MODELS	CHASSIS TYPE
C	CONVENTIONAL CAB	(C)	4 X 2
K	CONVENTIONAL CAB	(K)	4 X 4
P	FORWARD CONTROL CHASSIS	(P)	4 X 2
G	VAN, SPORT VAN & CUTAWAY VAN	(G)	4 X 2
W	EL CAMINO	(APU)	4 X 2

placement, model year, special equipment, and transmission type. The T is not used on 1969 models. These codes are listed in the Engine Identification Code Chart. They can also be found in more detail in dealer parts books.

Transmission

The Muncie or Saginaw three speed manual transmission serial number is on the left side of the case next to the rear of the cover. The three speed top-cover Tremec transmission (1976 and later) has the number on the upper forward mounting flange. The four speed transmission is numbered on the rear of the case, near the output shaft. The Turbo Hydra-Matic unit number is on the right rear surface of the fluid pan. The unit number on 700R4 transmissions is stamped on the right side of the transmission. See Chapter 6 for transmission and transfer case identification.

Axles

The rear axle serial number is on the bottom flange of the differential carrier housing for

Six cylinder engine serial number location

V8 engine serial number location

Engine Identification Code Chart

Engine	'69	'70	'71–'72	'73	'74	'75	'76	'77	'78	'79	'80	'81	'82
6—250	PC PD PE	TAA TAB TAD TCK	TPL TPY TPT TPW TPS* TPR*	TAA TAB TAC TBL* TBM TAC* TAD*	TAA TAB TAC TAD* TAL* TBL* TDB TDC TDD* TDF* TDU	TTK TTL TTM* TTR* TTS* TTU TTW	TBA TBB TBC* TBD* TAS TAT TAA	TAS TAT	TAR TAM	TAK TAJ TAX* TAW* TAD* TAA*	TCJ TCA TAB TCC* TAF*	TUA TUB TUF* TUH*	TLA TLB TLC TLD TLF TLH TLJ TLK TLL TLM TLR TLS TLT TLU TLW
8—305	—	—	—	—	—	—	—	UTF UTH	UTW UTX	UTB UYR UTA UTS TYR TYS	UTF UTJ UTL UTH	UAA UAB UAC UAD UAZ*	TBJ TBK TBM TBR TBS TBT TBU TBV TBW TBZ TCA TCB TCC TCD TCF TCL TCM TCR TCS TCT TCU TCW TCX TCY

8—307

UA	TAK	TDA	TCH	—	—	—	—	—	—
UM	TAO	TDB	TCJ						
UO	TAS	TDL	TCX						
	TAT	TDP	TCY*						
		TRA*							
		TAD*							
		TAH*							
		TAJ*							

8—350 2 bbl

—	—	—	—	TMM	TYC	—	—	—	—
				TMR	TJG				
					TJN				
					TKF				

8—350 4 bbl

XA	TAX	TBL*	TJB	TJA	TYD*	TWJ*	TYX	TWY	TBC
XW	TAY	TFD*	TJZ	TJB	TYW*	TJK*	TYZ	TWZ	TJS
	TBA	TFH*	TJY*	TJD*	TYX	TKA	TYW*		TMH
	TBB	TFJ*	TDY*	TJY*	TYY*	TKB	TYY*		TBA
	TBC	TDD	TJH	TKT	TYZ	TKH	TJR		TBB
	TBD	TDG	TJX	TKU	TKN	TYX			TMF
		TDJ		TWS*	TME*	TYZ			TBT*
		TDR			TZA	TYW*			TBR*
					TZC	TYY*			TBS*
					TZD				TRR
					TZJ*				TMC
					TZK*				TBF
									TJT
									TBD
									TBX*
									TBY*
									TBU*
									TBW*
									TFT
									TRS

TDA	UHA	TBL
TKM	UHB	TFA
TKL	UHC	TFB
TFA	UHD	TFC
TKA	UHK*	TFD
TKD**	UHL*	TFF
TDB	UHM*	TFJ
TDM**	UHR	TFK
TDR*	UHS*	TFL
TKM**	UJU	TFM
TKL**	UJW	TFU
TDW**	UZA	TFS
TKT**	UZB	TGH
TKK**	UZC	TGJ
TKY	UZD	TGK
TDU		TGM
TKH		TSC
TKZ		TSD
		TSF
		TSH
		TSJ
		TSK

8—400

—	—	—	—	—	TLR*	TLR*	TLS	TLK	—
					TLS*	TLS	TLR*		
TLD									
TLH									
TTR									
TLS*									
TLR*									

* With California emission control system
** Used also with California as well as Federal emission equipment
— Not available that year

1969–73, and on the front of the right axle tube for 1974 and later models. Front axles are marked on the front of the left axle tube.

ROUTINE MAINTENANCE

The Maintenance Intervals Chart gives the recommended maintenance intervals for the components covered here.

Air Cleaner

Paper Element Type

Loosen the wing nut on top of the cover and remove the cover. If the filter element has a foam wrapper, remove the wrapper and wash it in a safe solvent. Shake or blot dry. Saturate the wrapper in engine oil and squeeze it tightly in an absorbent towel or rag to remove the excess. Leave the wrapper moist. Clean the dirt from the filter element by rapping it against a flat surface. Replace the element if necessary. Clean the housing and the cover. Replace the crankcase ventilation filter in the housing if it appears excessively dirty. These sometimes can be disassembled and washed in solvent. Replace the oiled wrapper on the element and reinstall the element in the housing, repositioning it 180° from its original position.

NOTE: *Inverting the air cleaner cover for increased intake air volume is not recommended. This causes an increase in intake noise, faster element dirt buildup, and poor cold weather driveability.*

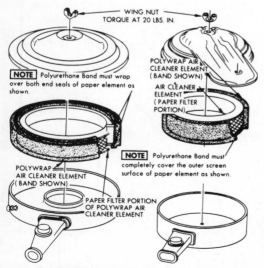

WING NUT
TORQUE AT 20 LBS. IN.

NOTE Polyurethane Band must wrap over both end seals of paper element as shown.

POLYWRAP AIR CLEANER ELEMENT (BAND SHOWN)

AIR CLEANER ELEMENT (PAPER FILTER PORTION)

NOTE Polyurethane Band must completely cover the outer screen surface of paper element as shown.

POLYWRAP AIR CLEANER ELEMENT (BAND SHOWN)

PAPER FILTER PORTION OF POLYWRAP AIR CLEANER ELEMENT

A Polywrap foam wrapper over a paper element is the heavy duty option air cleaner starting 1972

Oil Bath Type

To service the optional oil bath type air cleaner, remove the wing nut at the top and remove the cover and element. Remove the reservoir. Drain all of the oil from the reservoir. Clean all parts with kerosene or a safe solvent and dry thoroughly, but don't use compressed air on the element. Reinstall the reservoir and fill to the mark with SAE 50 engine oil above freezing temperatures, and SAE 20 below freezing. Install the element, replace the cover, and tighten the wing nut.

Positive Crankcase Ventilation (PCV) Valve

The PCV valve is a plunger assembly inserted into a grommet in the valve (rocker arm) cover. Check it by pulling it out and shaking it. You should be able to hear a rattle, showing the plunger is free. If there is no sound, install a new valve. Check the connecting hoses for stoppage or leaks. The plastic T-fittings used in this system break easily, so be careful.

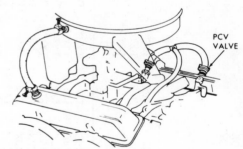

PCV VALVE

Typical PCV valve location

Evaporative Canister

The only maintenance that need be performed on the evaporative emission canister is to change the filter and check the condition of the hoses. If any hoses need replacement, use only hoses which are marked "EVAP."

The canister is in the left front of the engine compartment, with a filter in its bottom. Not all Blazers and Jimmys have one.

To replace the canister filter:

1. Note the installed positions of the hoses, tagging them as necessary, in case any have to be removed.
2. Loosen the clamps and remove the canister.
3. Pull the filter out and throw it away.
4. Install a new filter.
5. Check the hoses.

Heat Riser

The heat riser is a thermostatically or vacuum operated valve in the exhaust manifold. Not all engines have one. It closes when the engine is warming up, to direct hot exhaust gases to the intake manifold, in order to preheat the incoming fuel/air mixture. If it sticks open, the result will be frequent stalling during warmup, especially in cold and damp weather. If it sticks shut, the result will be a rough idle after the engine is warm. There is only one heat riser on a V8. The heat riser should move freely. If it sticks, apply GM Manifold Heat Control Solvent or something similar (engine cool) to the ends of the shaft. Sometimes rapping the end of the shaft sharply with a hammer (engine hot) will break it loose. If this fails, components must be removed for further repairs.

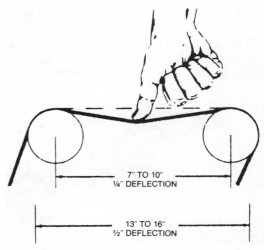

7" TO 10"
1/4" DEFLECTION

13" TO 16"
1/2" DEFLECTION

Checking belt tension

Typical V8 heat riser, shown here with the exhaust pipe removed

Belt Tension Adjustment

Any engine V-belt is correctly tensioned when the longest span of belt between pulleys can be depressed about ½ in. in the middle by moderate thumb pressure. To adjust, loosen the accessory's slotted adjusting bracket bolt. If the hinge bolt is very tight, it may be necessary to loosen it to move the item.

CAUTION: *Be careful not to overtighten belts, as this will damage the bearings, particularly in air or water pumps and alternators.*

Cooling System

At least once every 2 years, the engine cooling system should be inspected, flushed, and refilled with fresh coolant. If the coolant is left in the system too long, it loses its ability to prevent rust and corrosion. If the coolant has too much water, it won't protect against freezing.

The pressure cap should be looked at for signs of age or deterioration. Fan belt and other drive belts should be inspected and adjusted to the proper tension. (See "Belt Tension Adjustment").

Hose clamps should be tightened, and soft or cracked hoses replaced. Damp spots, or accumulations of rust or dye near hoses, water pump or other areas, indicate possible leakage, which must be corrected before filling the system with fresh coolant.

CHECK THE RADIATOR CAP

While you are checking the coolant level, check the radiator cap for a worn or cracked gasket. If the cap doesn't seal properly, fluid will be lost and the engine will overheat.

Worn caps should be replaced with a new one.

CLEAN RADIATOR OF DEBRIS

Periodically clean any debris—leaves, paper, insects, etc.—from the radiator fins. Pick the large pieces off by hand. The smaller pieces can be washed away with water pressure from a hose.

Carefully straighten any bent radiator fins with a pair of needle nose pliers. Be careful—

HOW TO SPOT WORN V-BELTS

V-Belts are vital to efficient engine operation—they drive the fan, water pump and other accessories. They require little maintenance (occasional tightening) but they will not last forever. Slipping or failure of the V-belt will lead to overheating. If your V-belt looks like any of these, it should be replaced.

Cracking or weathering

This belt has deep cracks, which cause it to flex. Too much flexing leads to heat build-up and premature failure. These cracks can be caused by using the belt on a pulley that is too small. Notched belts are available for small diameter pulleys.

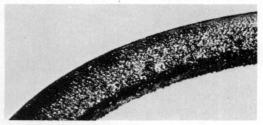

Softening (grease and oil)

Oil and grease on a belt can cause the belt's rubber compounds to soften and separate from the reinforcing cords that hold the belt together. The belt will first slip, then finally fail altogether.

Glazing

Glazing is caused by a belt that is slipping. A slipping belt can cause a run-down battery, erratic power steering, overheating or poor accessory performance. The more the belt slips, the more glazing will be built up on the surface of the belt. The more the belt is glazed, the more it will slip. If the glazing is light, tighten the belt.

Worn cover

The cover of this belt is worn off and is peeling away. The reinforcing cords will begin to wear and the belt will shortly break. When the belt cover wears in spots or has a rough jagged appearance, check the pulley grooves for roughness.

Separation

This belt is on the verge of breaking and leaving you stranded. The layers of the belt are separating and the reinforcing cords are exposed. It's just a matter of time before it breaks completely.

HOW TO SPOT BAD HOSES

Both the upper and lower radiator hoses are called upon to perform difficult jobs in an inhospitable environment. They are subject to nearly 18 psi at under hood temperatures often over 280°F., and must circulate nearly 7500 gallons of coolant an hour—3 good reasons to have good hoses.

Swollen hose

A good test for any hose is to feel it for soft or spongy spots. Frequently these will appear as swollen areas of the hose. The most likely cause is oil soaking. This hose could burst at any time, when hot or under pressure.

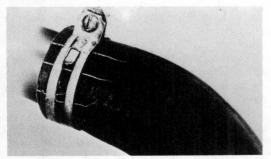

Cracked hose

Cracked hoses can usually be seen but feel the hoses to be sure they have not hardened; a prime cause of cracking. This hose has cracked down to the reinforcing cords and could split at any of the cracks.

Frayed hose end (due to weak clamp)

Weakened clamps frequently are the cause of hose and cooling system failure. The connection between the pipe and hose has deteriorated enough to allow coolant to escape when the engine is hot.

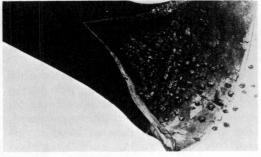

Debris in cooling system

Debris, rust and scale in the cooling system can cause the inside of a hose to weaken. This can usually be felt on the outside of the hose as soft or thinner areas.

the fins are very soft. Don't wiggle the fins back and forth too much. Straighten them once and try not to move them again.

DRAIN AND REFILL THE COOLING SYSTEM

Completely draining and refilling the cooling system every two years at least will remove accumulated rust, scale and other deposits. Coolant in late model trucks is a 50–50 mixture of ethylene glycol and water for year round use. Use a good quality antifreeze with water pump lubricants, rust inhibitors and other corrosion inhibitors along with acid neutralizers.

1. Remove the radiator cap. Drain the existing coolant by opening the radiator and engine drain petcocks, or disconnecting the bottom radiator hose at the radiator outlet.

NOTE: *Before opening the radiator petcock, spray it with some penetrating lubricant.*

2. Close the petcock or re-connect the lower hose and fill the system with water.

3. Add a can of quality radiator flush.

4. Idle the engine until the upper radiator hose gets hot.

5. Drain the system again.

6. Repeat this process until the drained water is clear and free of scale.

7. Close all petcocks and connect all the hoses.

8. If equipped with a coolant recovery system, flush the reservoir with water and leave empty.

9. Determine the capacity of your cooling system (see capacities specifications). Add a 50/50 mix of quality antifreeze (ethylene glycol) and water to provide the desired protection.

10. Run the engine to operating temperature.

11. Stop the engine and check the coolant level.

12. Check the level of protection with an anti-freeze tester, replace the cap and check for leaks.

Air Conditioning System Check

CAUTION: *Do not attempt to charge or discharge the refrigerant system unless you are thoroughly familiar with its operation and the hazards involved. The compressed refrigerant used in the air conditioning system expands and evaporates into the atmosphere at a temperature of* $-21.7°F$ *or*

less. This will freeze any surface, including your eyes, that it contacts. In addition, the refrigerant decomposes into a poisonous gas in the presence of flame.

1969–72

These units have a sight glass for checking the refrigerant charge. This is on top of the receiver dehydrator, alongside the radiator.

1. Start the engine and set it on fast idle.

2. Set the controls for maximum cold with the blower on high.

3. If bubbles are present in the sight glass, the system is low on charge. If no bubbles are present, the system is either fully charged or empty.

4. Feel the high or low pressure lines at the compressor. The high pressure line should be warm and the low pressure line should be cool. If no appreciable temperature difference is felt, the system is empty or nearly empty.

Even though there is a noticeable temperature difference, there is a possibility of overcharge. Disconnect the compressor clutch wire. If the refrigerant in the sight glass remains clear for more than 45 seconds before foaming and then settling away from the sight glass, an overcharge is indicated. If the refrigerant foams and then settles away from the sight glass in less than 45 seconds, it can be assumed that the system is properly charged.

From 1973

These systems have no sight glass.

1. Warm the engine to normal operating temperature.

2. Open the hood and doors.

3. Set the selector lever at A/C.

4. Set the temperature lever at the first detent to the right of COLD (outside air).

5. Set the blower at HI.

6. Idle the engine at 1,000 rpm.

7. Feel the temperature of the evaporator inlet and the accumulator outlet lines with the compressor engaged.

Both lines should be cold. If the inlet pipe is colder than the outlet pipe the system is low on charge.

NOTE: *This system has an internal filter combined with the expansion tube at the evaporator inlet (the lower line). If the filter is clogged, the result will be poor cooling and occasional external icing at this point on system startup, even though system pressures will be near normal.*

Windshield Wipers

Intense heat from the sun, snow and ice, road oils and the chemicals used in windshield washer solvents combine to deteriorate the rubber wiper refills. The refills should be replaced about twice a year or whenever the blades begin to streak or chatter.

WIPER REFILL REPLACEMENT

Normally, if the wipers are not cleaning the windshield properly, only the refill has to be replaced. The blade and arm usually require replacement only in the event of damage. It is not necessary to remove the arm or the blade to replace the refill (rubber part), though you may have to position the arm

higher on the glass. You can do this by turning the key on and operating the wipers. When they are positioned where they are accessible, turn the key off. Do not move the wipers by hand, which will damage the drive mechanism.

There are several types of refills and your vehicle could have any kind, since aftermarket blades and arms may not use exactly the same type refill as the original equipment.

Most Trico styles use a release button that is pushed down to allow the refill to slide out of the yoke jaws. The new refill slides in and locks in place. Some Trico refills are removed by locating where the metal backing strip or the refill is wider and inserting a small screw-

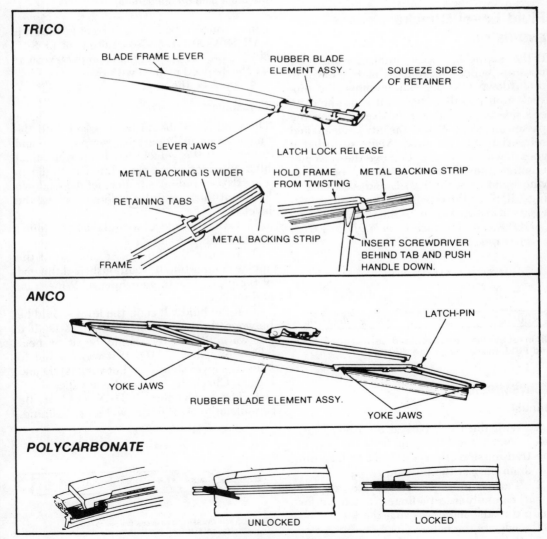

Windshield wiper blade refills

driver blade between the frame and metal backing strip. Press down to release the refill from the retaining tab.

The Anco style is unlocked at one end by squeezing 2 metal tabs, and the refill is slid out of the frame jaws. When the new refill is installed, the tabs will click into place, locking the refill.

The polycarbonate type is held in place by a locking lever that is pushed downward out of the groove in the arm to free the refill. When the new refill is installed, it will lock in place automatically.

No matter which type of refill you use, be sure that all of the frame claws engage the refill. Before operating the wipers, be sure that no part of the metal frame is contacting the windshield.

Fluid Level Checks

ENGINE OIL

If the engine has been running, wait a few minutes before checking the oil to allow it to drain down into the pan. Remove the dipstick from its tube. On V8s it is on the driver's side of the engine; on sixes it is on the passenger side. Wipe the stick clean and reinsert it into the tube. Make sure that it goes down all the way. Remove the stick and examine the oil level. It should be somewhere between the FULL and ADD markings. Replace the dipstick and add oil as necessary at the rocker cover filler cap.

NOTE: *The distance from ADD to FULL is one quart.*

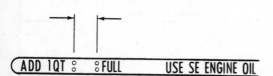

Oil level should be maintained between the ADD and FULL markings on the dipstick

TRANSMISSION

Manual

1. With the truck parked on a level surface, remove the filler plug from the side of the transmission. Be careful not to take out the drain plug at the bottom.

2. If lubricant seeps out, there is enough. If not, carefully insert a finger (watch out for sharp threads) and check that the level is up to the edge of the hole.

3. Lubricant may be added with a suction

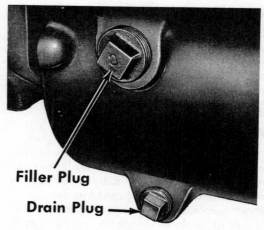

Filler Plug

Drain Plug ➤

Typical manual transmission fill and drain plugs. The three speed is shown here; the four speed has the drain plug on the bottom

gun or squeeze bulb. The correct lubricant is SAE 80W-90 GL-5 Gear Lubricant or SAE 80W GL-5 for cold climates and Dexron II for the 4-speed manual with overdrive.

4. Replace the plug.

Automatic

The fluid level should be checked with the engine at normal operating temperature and running. If the vehicle has been running at high speed for a long period, in city traffic on a hot day, or pulling a trailer, let it cool down for about thirty minutes before checking the level.

1. Park on the level with the engine idling and the shift lever in Park.

2. Remove the dipstick at the rear of the engine compartment. Cautiously feel the end of the dipstick with your fingers. Wipe it off and replace it.

3. If the fluid felt cool, the level should be between the two dimples below ADD. If it felt warm, the level should be at or near (above or below) ADD. If it was too hot to hold, the level should be between ADD and FULL. Check the level on the dipstick.

4. The correct fluid is DEXRON® II. Be careful not to overfill; this will cause foaming,

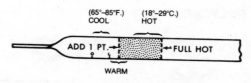

(65°–85°F.) COOL   (18°–29°C.) HOT

ADD 1 PT. ➤   ◄ FULL HOT

WARM

NOTE: DO NOT OVERFILL. It takes only one pint to raise level from ADD to FULL with a hot transmission.

Automatic transmission dipstick

fluid loss, and slippage. Add fluid through the dipstick tube.

NOTE: *The distance from ADD to FULL is one pint.*

TRANSFER CASE

1. With the truck parked on a level surface, remove the filler plug from the rear of the transfer case (behind the transmission). Be careful not to take out the drain plug at the bottom.

2. If lubricant seeps out, there is enough. If not, carefully insert a finger (watch out for sharp threads) and check that the level is up to the edge of the hole (½ in. below for full time four wheel drive).

3. Lubricant may be added with a suction gun or squeeze bulb. Conventional transfer cases require SAE 80 or 90 GL-5 Gear Lubricant; full time systems use 10W-30 or 10W-40 engine oil through 1980. Dexron II is used in transfer cases from 1981.

BRAKE MASTER CYLINDER

Check the brake fluid level by removing the retaining clip which holds the top on the master cylinder reservoirs at the left rear of the engine compartment. The fluid level should be ¼ in. from the top rear of each reservoir. Replacement fluid should be Delco Supreme No. 11, DOT 3, or its equivalent.

NOTE: *It is normal for the fluid level to fall as the disc brake pads wear.*

CAUTION: *Brake fluid dissolves paint. Be very careful not to spill any on a painted surface. If this happens wipe it off right away and rinse the area with water. It also absorbs moisture from the air; never leave a container or the master cylinder uncovered any longer than necessary.*

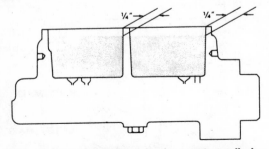

Correct brake fluid level in the master cylinder

COOLANT

Since the cooling system is pressurized, the radiator cap must not be removed unless the engine has cooled. To do otherwise involves the risk of being scalded by steam. To check the coolant level:

Without Coolant Recovery System

1. Allow the engine to cool.

2. Turn the cap counterclockwise to the detent. It is a fine idea to wear a glove or use a thick rag for protection.

3. If there is still pressure in the system, its escape will make a hissing sound.

4. When there is no further hissing, press down on the cap and continue turning it counterclockwise to remove.

5. The coolant level should be 1¼ in. below the bottom of the filler neck hot, and 3 in. below cold. Overfilling will result in coolant loss due to heat expansion.

6. If the coolant needs to be replenished, add equal amounts of anti-freeze and water.

CAUTION: *Never add large quantities of cold water to a hot engine. A cracked engine block may result.*

Anti-freeze solution should be used, even in summer, to prevent rust and to take advantage of the solution's higher boiling point compared to plain water. This is imperative on air conditioned trucks; the heater core can freeze if it isn't protected.

7. If the coolant level is frequently low, refer to the "Troubleshooting" section in Chapter 2 for diagnosis of the problem. See Chapter 3 for coolant draining and refilling.

8. Replace the radiator cap.

With Coolant Recovery System

If you have a coolant recovery system, coolant level checking is easy. The level in the plastic catch tank alongside the radiator should be between the FULL COLD and FULL HOT marks with the engine idling at normal operating temperature. The radiator will be full. Add coolant only to the tank; don't remove the radiator cap. If you do remove the cap, you will allow air into the system. Steps 6 and 7 "Without Coolant Recovery System" apply to this type, too.

AXLES

Locking front hubs should be run in the lock position for at least 10 miles each month so that the front drive axle gets proper lubrication.

1. Park on the level.

2. Remove the filler plug from the differential housing cover.

3. If lubricant seeps out, there is enough.

WARNING
ENGINE COOLANT ONLY

Coolant Recovery Tank

One of the several types of coolant recovery tanks—this one doesn't have the FULL HOT marking

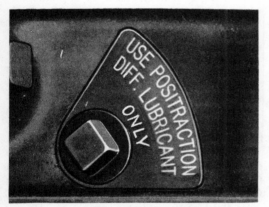

The Positraction® axle filler plug has an identification tag which must be heeded

If not, carefully insert a finger (watch out for sharp threads) and check that the level is up to the level of the hole. Front axles should be full up to the level of the hole when warm and ½ in. below cold.

4. Lubricant may be added with a suction gun or squeeze bulb. Front axles use SAE 90; in cold climates, SAE 80. Rear axles use SAE 80 in cold climates, SAE 90 normally, and SAE 140 in very hot climates. 1969–73 Positraction® limited slip axles must use special lubricant available from dealers. If the special fluid is not used, noise, uneven operation, and damage will result. There is also a Positraction additive to cure noise and slippage. Positraction axles have an identifying tag, as well as a warning sticker near the jack or on the rear wheel well.

NOTE: *Since 1974, the locking differential does not require special lubricant.*

MANUAL STEERING GEAR

The only maintenance check required on the steering gear is to occasionally check for leakage of grease. An oily film is not considered to be leakage.

POWER STEERING RESERVOIR

The reservoir is part of the belt-driven power steering pump at the front of the engine.
1. Wipe off the cap and surrounding area, after stopping the engine with the wheels straight (1969–71 models, the wheels should be all the way to the left).
2. Remove the cap and attached dipstick.
3. Wipe the dipstick off with a clean, lint-free rag, replace the cap, remove and take a reading. If the fluid is hot, the level should be between HOT and COLD; if it is cold, it should be between COLD and ADD.
4. Either GM Power Steering Fluid or DEXRON® Automatic Transmission Fluid may be used.

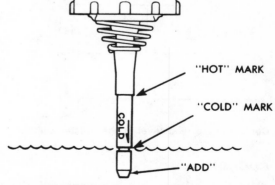

"HOT" MARK

"COLD" MARK

"ADD"

Typical power steering pump reservoir cap and dipstick

The second cap from the left is the Delco eye

BATTERY ELECTROLYTE

No battery fluid level checking is required on models with the sealed Freedom battery. If the battery is equipped with the Delco Eye in one cell cap, the Eye is supposed to glow when the electrolyte in that cell is low. The Eye does not indicate level in the other cells, so it is better to look into each cell. If the surface of the electrolyte in the cell looks flat instead of distorted around the edges, water should be added. Only colorless, odorless, preferably distilled, water should be added. It is a good idea to add the water with a squeeze bulb device to avoid having sulfuric acid electrolyte splash out, as sometimes happens when attempting to pour in water. If water is frequently needed, the most likely cause is overcharging, caused by a faulty voltage regulator. If any acid solution should escape, it can be neutralized with a baking soda and water solution, but don't let the stuff get in the battery. When replacing a battery, it is important that the replacement have an output rating equal to or greater than original equipment. See Chapter Three for details on battery replacement.

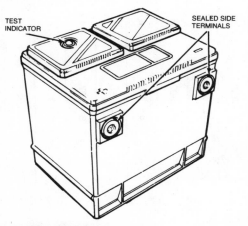

TEST INDICATOR

SEALED SIDE TERMINALS

Sealed Freedom battery

CAUTIONS: Avoid sparks and smoking around the battery. A battery gives off explosive hydrogen gas. If you get acid on your skin and eyes, rinse it off immediately with lots of water. See a doctor if it gets in your eyes. In winter, add water only before driving to prevent the battery from freezing and cracking.

Tires and Wheels

General Motors does not give recommended tire pressures, as such, for the Blazer and Jimmy. They do give very specific load limits for factory-installed tire sizes at specific pressures. Late models have the maximum load pressures listed on the V.I.N. plate on the left door frame. In general, pressures of 28–32 psi would be suitable for highway use with moderate loads and passenger car type tires (load range B, non-flotation) of original equipment size. Pressures should be checked before driving, since pressure can increase as much as 6 psi due to heat. It is a good idea to have an accurate gauge and to check pressures weekly. A good gauge only costs a dollar or two. Not all gauges on service station air pumps are to be trusted. In general, truck-type tires require higher pressures and flotation-type tires, lower pressures.

When buying new tires, give some thought to these points, especially if you are switching to larger tires or to another profile series (50, 60, 70, 78):

1. All four tires should be of the same construction type. Radial, bias, or bias-belted tires should not be mixed. Four wheel drive requires that all tires be the same size, type, and tread pattern to provide even traction on loose surfaces, to prevent driveline bind when conventional four wheel drive is used, and to prevent excessive wear on the center differential with full time four wheel drive.

2. The wheels must be the correct width for the tire. Tire dealers have charts of tire and rim compatibility. A mismatch can cause sloppy handling and rapid tread wear. The

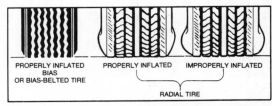

PROPERLY INFLATED BIAS OR BIAS-BELTED TIRE   PROPERLY INFLATED   IMPROPERLY INFLATED

RADIAL TIRE

Proper tire inflation should be checked with a gauge; appearances can be misleading

Capacities

| Year | Engine No. Cyl Displacement (cu in.) | Engine Crankcase (qts) Add 1 Qt For New Filter | Transmission Pts To Refill After Draining | | | Transfer Case (Pts) | Drive Axle (pts) Front/Rear | Gasoline Tank (gals) Std/Opt | Cooling System ■ (qts) | | |
| | | | Manual | | Automatic ▲ | | | | With Heater | A/C | With HD Cooling |
			3-Speed	4-Speed							
'69–'70	6—250	4	3	8	5	2¾①	5/4½	23½	12.2	12.9	12.8
	8—307	4	3	8	5	2¾①	5/4½	23½	15.8	18.1	18.1
	8—350	4	—	8	5	2¾①	5/4½	23½	15.8	18.1	18.1
'71	6—250	4	3	8	5	2¾②	5/4½	21	12.2	—	12
	8—307	4	3	8	5	2¾②	5/4½	21	15.8	17	17
	8—350	4	—	8	5	5	5/4½	21	16.2	18	16
'72	6—250	4	3	8	5	2¾②	5/4½	21	12.1	—	12.1
	8—307	4	3	8	5	2¾②	5/4½	21	15.5/16.2	15.9/16.2	15.5/15.8
	8—350	4	—	8	5	5	5/4½	21	15.5/15.9	17.5/17.8	15.7/16
'73	6—250	4	3	8	5	5④	5/4½	24/30	14.6	—	14.6
	8—307	4	3	8	5	5④	5/4½	24/30	17.8	18	18/17.8
	8—350	4	—	8	5	5④	5/4½	24/30	17.8	18.2	18
'74	6—250	4	3	8	5	5④	5/4½	24/30	15	—	15

Year	Engine										
'75	8—350 2 bbl	4	3	8	5	5④	5/4½	24/30	18	18	18
	8—350 4 bbl	4	—	8	5	5④	5/4½	24/30	18	18	18
'76	6—250	4	3	8	5	—	—/3½	25/30	14.8	15.6	14.8
	8—350 2 bbl	4	3	—	5	—	—/3½	25/30	17.6	18	18
	8—350 4 bbl	4	—	8	5	5④	5/3½	25/30	17.6	18	18
	8—400	4	—	—	5	5④	5/3½	25/30	19.6	20.4	20.4
'77	6—250	4	3③	8	5	5④	5/3½	25/31	14.8	15.6	14.8
	8—350	4	3③	8	5	5④	5/3½	25/31	17.6	18	18
	8—400	4	—	—	5	5④	5/3½	25/31	19.6	20.4	20.4
'78	6—250	4	3.5	8.3	5	5④	5/3½	25/31	14.8	15.6	14.8
	8—305	4	3.5	8.3	5	5④	5/3½	25/31	17.6	18	18
	8—350	4	3.5	8.3	5	5④	5/3½	25/31	17.6	18	18
	8—400	4	—	—	5	5④	5/3½	25/31	19.6	20.4	20.4
'79	6—250	4	3	8	5	5④	5/3.5⑤	25/31	15	15.6	15.6
	8—305	4	3	8	5	5④	5/3.5⑤	25/31	17.5	18	18.4
	8—350	4	3	8	5	5④	5/3.5⑤	25/31	17.6	17.6	17.6
	8—400	4	—	—	5	5④	5/3.5⑤	25/31	19.7	20.4	20.4
	6—250	4	3	8	5	5④	5/3.5⑤	25/31	15	15.5	15.5

Capacities (cont.)

Year	Engine No. Cyl Displacement (cu in.)	Engine Crankcase ● (qts) Add 1 Qt For New Filter	Transmission Pts To Refill After Draining — Manual 3-Speed	4-Speed	Automatic ▲	Transfer Case (Pts)	Drive Axle (pts) Front/Rear	Gasoline Tank (gals) Std/Opt	Cooling System ■ (qts) With Heater	A/C	With HD Cooling
'79	8—305	4	3	8	5	5④	5/3.5⑤	25/31	17.5	17.5	17.5
	8—350	4	3	8	5	5④	5/3.5⑤	25/31	17.5	18	18
	8—400	4	—	—	5	5④	5/3.5⑤	25/31	18	19	19
'80–'81	6—250	5	3	8	5	5	5/3.5⑤	25/31	15	15.5	15.5
	8—305	5	3	8	5	5	5/3.5⑤	25/31	17.5	17.5	17.5
	8—350	5	3	8	5	5	5/3.5⑤	25/31	17.5	18	18
'82	6—250	5	2	8	6	5	5/⑦	25/31	15	15.5	—
	8—305	5	2	8	6	5	5/⑦	25/31	17.5	18	—
	8—350	5	2	8	6⑥	5	5/⑦	25/31	17.5	18	—
	8—379	7	—	8	6⑥	5	5/⑦	27/32	24.8	24.8	—

● More with optional (1973 and later) engine oil cooler
▲ More with dealer-installed transmission fluid cooler
① 5 with automatic transmission
② 5 with automatic or 4-speed transmission
③ 3½ with top-cover Tremec three-speed
④ 8¼ with full-time 4 wheel drive
⑤ 8.5 ring gear—4.2
⑥ with TH-M 400: 7.0
   with TH-M 700-R4: 10.0
⑦ 8¼″ ring gear: 4.25
   8⅞″ ring gear: 3.5
   9¾″ ring gear (Dana): 6.0
   10½″ ring gear (Dana): 7.2
                (Chev.): 6.5
■ Automatic transmission models have either the A/C or HD radiator; capacity may be increased on trucks with 4.11:1 axle ratios; when two figures are separated by a slash, the first is for 2 wheel drive

old rule of thumb is that the tread width should match the rim width (inside bead to inside bead) within an inch. For radial tires, the rim width should be 80% or less of the tire (not tread) width.

3. The height (mounted diameter) of the new tires can greatly change speedometer accuracy, engine speed at a given road speed, fuel mileage, acceleration, and ground clearance. Tire manufacturers furnish full measurement specifications. Speedometer drive gears are available for correction.

NOTE: *Dimensions of tires marked the same size may vary significantly, even among tires from the same manufacturer.*

4. The spare tire should be usable, at least for low speed operation, with the new tires.

5. There shouldn't be any body interference when loaded, on bumps, or in turning.

The best way to keep out of major trouble with these points is to stick to tire and wheel sizes available as factory options.

TIRE ROTATION

Tire rotation is recommended to obtain maximum tire wear. The pattern you use depends on personal preference, and whether or not you have a usable spare. Radial tires should not be cross-switched; they last longer if their direction of rotation is not changed. Truck type tires sometimes have directional tread indicated by arrows on the sidewalls; the arrow shows the direction of rotation. They will wear very rapidly if reversed. Studded snow tires will lose their studs if their direction of rotation is reversed.

NOTE: *Mark the wheel position or direction of rotation on radial tires or studded snow tires before removing them.*

CAUTION: *Avoid overtightening the lug nuts or the brake disc or drum may be permanently distorted. Alloy wheels can also*

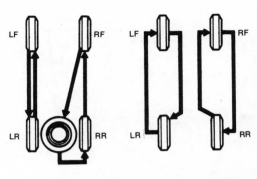

5 WHEEL ROTATION   4 WHEEL ROTATION

This rotation pattern is for radial tires, bias or bias-belted tires. The radial spare can be used on the left side, too, but don't change its direction of rotation once it has been used

be cracked by overtightening. Use of a torque wrench is highly recommended. Tighten the lug nuts in a criss-cross pattern. Recommended torques are:

Year	Model	Torque (ft. lbs.)
'69–'70	All	55–75
'71–'73	2WD	65–90
'71–'73	4WD	55–75
'74–'82	2WD	75–100
'74–'82	4WD	70–90

Fuel Filter Replacement
GASOLINE ENGINE

A clogged filter can cause the engine to die out on acceleration or at high speeds. All engines have the filter in the carburetor fuel inlet.

1. Let the engine cool.

2. Remove the air cleaner for access.

3. Place an absorbent rag under the fuel line connection.

4. Hold the large nut to keep it from turning. Unscrew the small fuel line nut, preferably with a special line flare wrench.

5. Move the fuel line aside and unscrew the large nut, being careful to catch the filter and spring.

6. If you want to, you can test the old filter by blowing through it. Air should pass freely. Most engines have a paper filter, but a few older ones have a bronze unit.

7. Insert the spring, then the filter, with the opening toward the fuel line.

8. Screw in the large nut and tighten it gently.

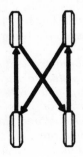

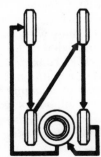

BIAS PLY TIRE 4 WHEEL ROTATION   BIAS PLY TIRE 5 WHEEL ROTATION

This rotation pattern is for bias or bias-belted tires only

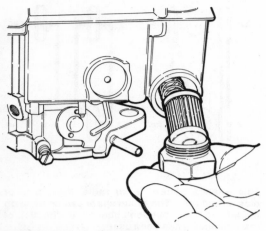

Paper fuel filter element in the fuel inlet line

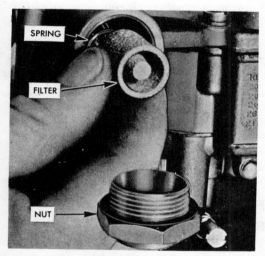

The bronze fuel filter found in the fuel inlet of some earlier models

NOTE: *Repair kits are available at auto parts stores, if the carburetor threads are damaged.*

9. Screw in the fuel line nut and tighten gently.

10. Remove and safely discard the rag.

11. Start the engine and check for leaks. Stop the engine and replace the air cleaner.

DIESEL ENGINE

This engine uses two fuel filters; a primary, located on the firewall, and a secondary, mounted on the inlet manifold.

Removal and Installation

Both the primary and secondary fuel filters are serviced in the same manner.

1. Disconnect the inlet and outlet fuel lines at the adapter.

2. Unscrew mounting bolts and remove adapter from the inlet/firewall.

3. Unscrew filter from adapter.

4. Anytime either of the filters are removed or replaced, refill with clean diesel fuel to prevent stalling after start up, and to avoid long engine cranking time.

5. Screw the filter onto the adapter.

6. Remount the adapter and install the fuel lines.

7. Run engine and check for leaks.

Water Drain

Water can be drained from the primary fuel filter only.

1. Open the petcock on top of the primary filter housing.

2. Place a drain pan below the filter and open the petcock on the bottom of the filter.

NOTE: *A length of hose can be attached to the petcock to direct the drained fuel below the frame.*

3. When all water is drained, close both petcocks tightly. If all fuel in the filter has been drained, remove the filter and fill it with clean diesel fuel.

4. Start the engine and let it run briefly. It may run rough at first until all air is purged from the system. If roughness continues, check that both petcocks are closed tightly.

LUBRICATION

Fuel and Oil Recommendations

GASOLINE ENGINES

Fuel

All engines through 1971 are designed to use fuel of 91 research octane or higher. All 1972 and later engines, except those with a catalytic converter, use unleaded or low-lead fuel. All engines with a catalytic converter must use unleaded fuel.

NOTE: *Your engine's fuel requirement can change with time, mainly due to carbon buildup changing the compression ratio. If your engine pings, knocks, or runs on, switch to a higher grade of fuel and check the ignition timing as soon as possible. If it is necessary to retard timing from specifications, don't change it more than about four degrees. Retarded timing will reduce power output and fuel mileage and increase engine temperature.*

Should you plan to operate your Blazer or Jimmy in a foreign country, you can contact the Chevrolet or GMC Owner Relations Department to obtain information on required engine modifications or adjustments and the quality of the fuels available there. Be sure to supply your vehicle's VIN number and the engine's compression ratio if available.

Oil

Only oils labeled SE/SF are approved under warranty for use in 1972 and later models. Oils labeled SD were approved for 1971 and earlier models, since the higher quality SE rated oils were not generally available at that time. SE/SF oils should now be used in all models. Non-detergent oils are specifically not recommended. You can find the SE/SF marking either on the top or on the side of the oil container; the viscosity rating should be in the same place. Select the viscosity rating to be used by your type of driving and the temperature range anticipated before the next oil change.

The multi-viscosity oils offer the important advantage of being adaptable to temperature extremes. They can allow easy starts at low temperatures, yet still give good protection at high speeds and warm temperatures. This is a decided advantage in changeable climates or in long distance touring.

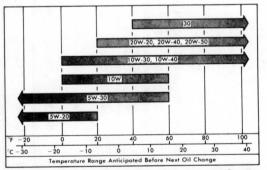

Engine oil viscosity chart—the lower viscosity oils should not be used for high speed driving

DIESEL ENGINES

Fuel

Fuel makers produce two grades of diesel fuel, No. 1 and No. 2, for use in diesel engines. Generally speaking, No. 2 fuel is recommended over No. 1 for driving in temperatures above 20°F. In fact, in many areas, No. 2 diesel is the only fuel available. By comparison, No. 2 diesel fuel is less volatile than No.

1 fuel, and gives better fuel economy. No. 2 fuel is also a better injection pump lubricant.

Two important characteristics of diesel fuel are its cetane number and its viscosity.

The cetane number of a diesel fuel refers to the ease with which a diesel fuel ignites. High cetane numbers mean that the fuel will ignite with relative ease or that it ignites well at low temperatures. Naturally, the lower the cetane number, the higher the temperature must be to ignite the fuel. Most commercial fuels have cetane numbers that range from 35 to 65. No. 1 diesel fuel generally has a higher cetane rating than No. 2 fuel.

Viscosity is the ability of a liquid, in this case diesel fuel, to flow. Using straight No. 2 diesel fuel below 20° can cause problems, because this fuel tends to become cloudy, meaning wax crystals begin forming in the fuel. In extreme cold weather, No. 2 fuel can stop flowing altogether. In either case, fuel flow is restricted, which can result in a "no start" condition or poor engine performance. Fuel manufacturers often "winterize" No. 2 diesel fuel by using various fuel additivies and blends (No. 1 diesel fuel, kerosene, etc.) to lower its winter-time viscosity. Generally speaking, though, No. 1 diesel fuel is more satisfactory in extremely cold weather.

NOTE: *No. 1 and No. 2 diesel fuels will mix and burn with no ill effects, although the engine manufacturer will undoubtedly recommend one or the other. Consult the owner's manual for information.*

Depending on local climate, most fuel manufacturers make winterized No. 2 fuel available seasonally.

Many automobile manufacturers publish pamphlets giving the locations of diesel fuel stations nationwide. Contact the local dealer for information.

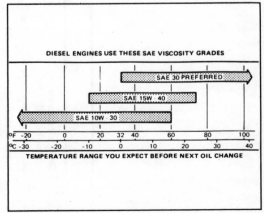

Diesel engine, oil viscosity chart

Maintenance Intervals in Thousands of Miles*

Item	'69-'70	'71	'72-'73	'74	'75	'76	'77	'78	'79-'80	'81-'82
Clean air cleaner element or oil bath	12	12	12	12	15	—	—	—	—	—
Replace air cleaner paper element	24	24	12 six/ 24 V8	12 six/ 24 V8	15 six/ 30 V8	30	30	30	30	30
Replace or clean air cleaner PCV element or flame arrestor	12	12	24	24	30	30	30	30	30	30
Replace PCV valve	12/12 mo	24/24 mo	24/24 mo	24/24 mo	30/24 mo	30/24 mo	30	30	30	30
Replace evaporative canister filter	—	12/12 mo	24/24 mo	24/24 mo	30/24 mo	30/24 mo	30	30/24 mo	30/24 mo	30/24 mo
Lubricate heat riser if sticking	as needed	as needed	6/4 mo	12/12 mo	8/6 mo	8/6 mo	12	12	12	12
Rotate tires	6	as needed	as needed	as needed	8/15 radial	as needed	8 ①	6 ②	6 ②	7 ②
Replace fuel filter	12	24	12/12 mo	12/12 mo	15/12 mo	15/12 mo	15	15/12 mo	15/12 mo	15/12 mo

Change engine oil	6/4 mo	6/4 mo	6/4 mo	6/4 mo	7/6 mo	7/6 mo	7/12 mo	7/12 mo	7/12 mo	7/12 mo ④
Change engine oil filter	12/8 mo	12/8 mo	12/8 mo	12/8 mo	14/12 mo	14/12 mo	Every 2nd oil change	Every 2nd oil change	Every 2nd oil change	Every 2nd oil change ④
Change automatic transmission fluid and filter	24	24	24	30	60	60	60	60	100	100 ③
Check manual transmission, transfer case, and axle fluid levels	6	6/4 mo	6/4 mo	8/6 mo	8/6 mo	7	7	7	7	7
Grease chassis	6	6	6/4 mo	8/6 mo	8/6 mo	8/12 mo	7/12 mo	7/12 mo	7/12 mo	7/12 mo
Grease front wheel bearings	30	30	30	24	30 2WD/12 4WD	30	30	30	30	30
Change engine coolant	24 mo	24 mo	24 mo	30/24 mo	30/24 mo	30/24 mo	30/24 mo	30/24 mo	30	30/24 mo

* Minimum intervals for a truck driven the average 12,000 miles per year under ideal conditions. Intervals given only in thousands of miles can be roughly converted to months: 12,000 mi = 12 mo. Halve service intervals for severe use such as trailer towing or off-road driving. If both miles and months are given, use whichever interval elapses first.

① 15,000 miles for radial tires
② 12,000 miles for radial tires
③ 15,000 miles under heavy duty conditions
④ Change the engine oil and oil filter every 5000 miles on vehicles equipped with a diesel engine.

Do not substitute home heating oil for automotive diesel fuel. While in some cases, home heating oil refinement levels equal those of diesel fuel, many times they are far below diesel engine requirements. The result of using "dirty" home heating oil will be a clogged fuel system, in which case the entire system may have to be dismantled and cleaned.

One more word on diesel fuels. Don't thin diesel fuel with gasoline in cold weather. The lighter gasoline, which is more explosive, will cause rough running at the very least, and may cause extensive engine damage if enough is used.

Oil

Use ONLY engine oils labeled with the A.P.I. (American Petroleum Institute) designation "SF/CD" or "SF/CC". Do not use any other type of oil. The A.P.I. designations are listed somewhere on the oil can, usually on the top or label. The A.P.I. has several designations, such as: SC, SD, SE, CB, CC, CD.

Several different designations may appear on the can. Be sure the oil used has either "SF/CD" or "SF/CC" designations, regardless of the order in which they appear on the oil can.

Using any type of oil other than "SF/CD" or "SF/CC" may affect warranty.

CAUTION: *Do not use engine oils labeled only SE or only CC. These oils will not give the protection and lubrication of diesel engine needs. When reading the can, be sure not to confuse the SE designation with the letters "SAE", which may also appear on the can.*

ENGINE OIL ADDITIVES

Do not use any supplemental additives. Using oil additives may cause engine damage and may affect warranty.

OIL VISCOSITY

Engine oil viscosity (thickness) has an effect on fuel economy. Lower viscosity engine oils can provide increased fuel economy; however, higher temperature weather conditions require higher viscosity engine oils for satisfactory lubrication. The chart on page 23 lists the engine oil viscosities that will provide the best balance of fuel economy, engine life, and oil economy.

Lubricant Changes
ENGINE OIL AND FILTER

Assuming that the recommended oils are used, the oil and filter should be changed at the intervals shown in the "Maintenance Intervals" chart. This interval should be halved under severe usage such as dusty conditions, trailer towing, prolonged high-speeds, off-road driving, or repeated short trips in freezing temperatures. Although it isn't required by the factory, it is a good idea to change the filter with each oil change. A filter can hold a quart of dirty oil.

To change the oil and filter:

1. Operate the truck until the engine is at normal operating temperature. If you don't, most of the contaminants will stay in your engine. Stop the engine.

2. Slide a pan of at least six quarts capacity under the oil pan. Throw-away aluminum roasting pans work well.

3. Remove the drain plug from the engine oil pan, after wiping the plug area clean. If this is your first attempt at oil changing, make sure that you have the engine drain plug and not the one of the transmission or something else. It's the plug at the lowest point of the oil pan.

CAUTION: *When the oil comes out of the drain hole, it's going to be hot enough to burn you. While you're unscrewing the drain plug, keep an inward pressure on it until you feel it come loose, then pull it away quickly. Don't worry if you drop it into the drain pan. You can always fish it out later.*

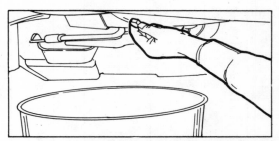

Press up against the threads when removing the drain plug

4. Allow the oil to drain into the pan. Do not replace the plug before the oil has completely stopped draining.

5. Clean off the plug, particularly the threads, and replace it.

6. The filter is at the left rear on the V8, and the right front on the six. Use a filter

Remove the oil filter with a strap wrench

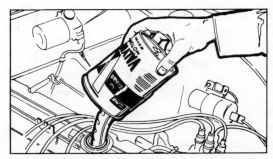

Add oil through the capped opening in the valve cover

wrench to loosen it. These are available at discount and auto supply stores and they're not very expensive. Place a drain pan under the filter. Unscrew and discard the old filter after wiping the area clean.

CAUTION: *Watch it! The filter may be full of hot oil and is probably too hot to hold for long.*

7. If the filter has been overtightened and collapses when you use the filter wrench on it, drive a long punch or a screwdriver through the cartridge as near the base as possible and use this as a lever to unscrew it.

8. Lubricate the new filter gasket with a few drops of clean engine oil, smeared on with a finger.

9. Screw the filter on by hand until the gasket makes contact. Then tighten the filter one half a full turn by hand. If you overtighten the filter, you may have to resort to the methods of Step 7 to get it off the next time. Just be sure it makes a good seal.

10. Remove the filler cap on the rocker (valve) cover, after wiping the area clean.

11. Add the correct number of quarts of the oil specified under "Fuel and Oil Recommendations." If you don't have an oil can spout, you will need a funnel. If you are adding oil from a bulk container (other than 1 qt cans), keep track of the number of quarts

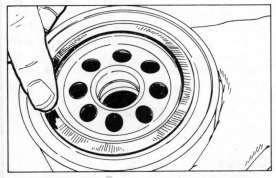

Coat the new filter gasket with clean oil before installation to prevent the gasket from tearing

added. Overfilling could cause damage to the engine seals. Replace the cap.

12. Check the oil level on the dipstick. It is normal for the level to be a bit above FULL. Start the engine and look for leaks around the drain plug and the filter.

13. Stop the engine and recheck the level.

TRANSMISSION
Manual

No intervals are specified for changing transmission lubricant, but it is a good idea on a used vehicle, one that has been worked hard, or if you have driven in deep water. The transmission should be at normal operating temperature.

1. Slide a drain pan under the transmission.

2. Remove the filler plug from the side of the transmission and the drain plug from the bottom. The 1976 and later Tremec topcover three speed is drained by removing the lower extension housing bolt.

3. Wipe the area clean and replace the drain plug.

4. Add lubricant with a suction gun or squeeze bulb. The correct lubricant is SAE 80W-90 GL-5 Gear Lubricant, or SAE 80W GL-5 for cold climates.

5. When the lubricant level is up to the bottom of the filler hole, replace the plug.

Automatic

The fluid should be drained with the transmission warm.

1. Prepare a pan to catch the transmission fluid (about 5 pts).

2. Loosen all the pan bolts, then pull one-corner down to drain most of the fluid. You can buy aftermarket drain plug kits that make this operation a bit less messy, once installed. Some early models already have a plug.

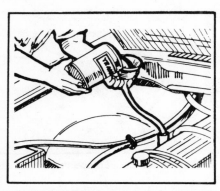

Add transmission fluid through the dipstick tube with the aid of a funnel and hose

NOTE: *If the fluid removed smells burnt, serious transmission troubles, probably due to overheating, should be suspected.*

3. Remove the pan screws and empty out the pan. On some models there isn't much room to get at the screws at the front of the pan. The pan can be cleaned out with solvent but it must be dried thoroughly before replacement. Be very careful not to leave any lint or threads from rags in the pan.

4. Remove the filter or strainer retaining bolts. A reusable strainer may be found on some models. The strainer may be cleaned in solvent and air dried thoroughly or replaced. The filter and gasket are to be replaced.

5. Install the new gasket and filter.

6. Install the pan with a new gasket. Tighten the bolts evenly to 12 ft. lbs. in a crisscross pattern.

7. Add DEXRON® or DEXRON II® transmission fluid through the dipstick tube. The correct amount is in the Capacities Chart.

8. Start the engine and let it idle. Do not race it. Shift through all the indicator positions, holding the brakes. Check the fluid level with the engine idling, in Park. The level should be between the two dimples on the dipstick, about ¼ in. above the ADD mark. Add fluid as necessary.

9. Check the fluid level after the truck has been driven enough to thoroughly warm up the transmission. Details are given under Fluid Level Checks earlier in the chapter. If the Transmission is overfilled, the excess must be drained off. Overfilling causes aerated fluid, resulting in transmission slippage and probable damage.

TRANSFER CASE

No intervals are specified for changing transfer case lubricant, but it is a good idea for trucks that are worked hard or driven in deep water.

1. With the transfer case warmed up, park on a level surface.

2. Slide a pan of at least 6 pts. capacity under the case drain plug.

3. Remove the filler plug from the rear of the transfer case (behind the transmission). Remove the drain plug from the bottom and allow the fluid to drain completely.

4. Wipe the area clean and replace the drain plug.

5. Add lubricant with a suction gun or squeeze bulb. Conventional transfer cases require SAE 80 or 90 GL-5 Gear Lubricant; full time systems use 10W-30 or 10W-40 engine oil through 1980. Dexron II is used in transfer cases from 1981.

6. When the lubricant level is up to the bottom of the filler hole (½ in. below for full time four wheel drive), replace the plug.

AXLES

No intervals are specified for changing axle lubricant, but it is a good idea, especially if you have driven in water over the axle vents.

1. Park the vehicle on level ground with the axles at normal operating temperature.

2. Place a pan of at least 6 pints capacity under the differential housing.

3. Remove the filler plug.

4. If you have a drain plug, remove it. If not, unbolt and remove the differential cover.

5. Replace the drain plug, or differential cover with a new gasket.

6. Lubricant may be added with a suction gun or squeeze bulb. Front axles use SAE 90 GL-5 Gear Lubricant; in cold climates, SAE 80. Fill front axles to ½ in. below the filler plug opening. Rear axles use SAE 80 in cold climates, SAE 90 normally, and SAE 140 in very hot climates. 1969–73 Positraction limited slip axles must use special lubricant available from dealers. If the special fluid is not used, noise, uneven operation, and damage will result. There is also a Positraction additive used to cure noise and slippage. Positraction axles have an identifying tag, as well as a warning sticker near the jack or on the rear wheel well. Rear axle lubricant level should be up to the bottom of the filler plug opening.

NOTE: *From 1974 the locking differential does not require special lubricant.*

Chassis Greasing

The lubrication charts show the points to be lubricated. Not all vehicles have all the fittings illustrated. For example, most trucks

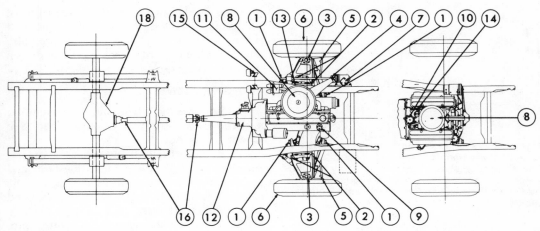

1. Lower control arms
2. Upper control arms
3. Upper and lower ball joints
4. Intermediate steering shaft —not on Blazers
5. Tie rod ends
6. Wheel bearings
7. Steering gear
8. Air cleaner
9. Distributor cam lubricator, six
10. Distributor cam lubricator, V8
11. Master cylinder
12. Transmission
13. Throttle bellcrank, six
14. Carburetor linkage, V8
15. Brake and clutch pedal springs
16. Universal joints
18. Rear axle

Two wheel drive chassis lubrication chart

don't have grease fittings on the driveshaft universal joints; the fittings on the shafts are for lubricating the sliding splines.

The four wheel drive front driveshaft requires special attention for lubrication. The large constant velocity joint at the front of the transfer case has a special grease fitting in the centering ball; a special needle nose adapter for a flush type fitting is required, as well as a special lubricant, GM part no. 1050679 or 1052497. You can only get at this fitting when it is facing up toward the floorboards, so you

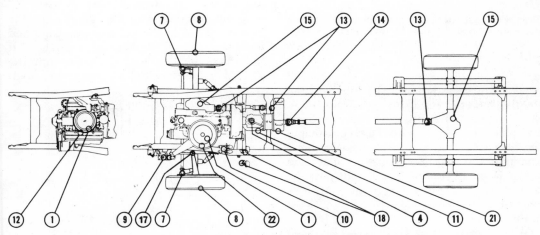

1. Air cleaner
2. Distributor cam lubricator, six—not shown on diagram
3. Distributor cam lubricator, V8—not shown on diagram
4. Transmission and transfer case linkage
5. Not used on diagram
6. Not used on diagram
7. Tie rod ends
8. Wheel bearings and spindle bearings
9. Steering gear
10. Master cylinder
11. Transmission
12. Carburetor linkage, V8
13. Universal joints, front constant velocity joint
14. Driveshaft slip joints (splines)
15. Front and rear axle
16. Not used on diagram
17. Drag link
18. Brake and clutch pedal springs
19. Not used on diagram
20. Not used on diagram
21. Transfer case
22. Throttle bellcrank, six

Four wheel drive chassis lubrication chart

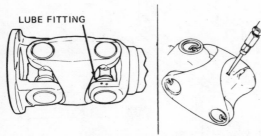

LUBE FITTING

One of these types of constant velocity joints is located at the transfer case end of the driveshaft. The illustration shows how the joint may be lubricated from above using a special adapter at the end of a flex hose. Use water resistant EP chassis lubricant

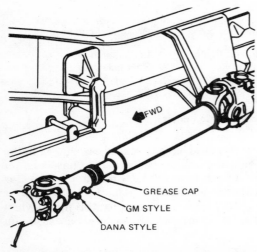

FWD

GREASE CAP

GM STYLE

DANA STYLE

The grease cap, or spline seal collar indicated on the front driveshaft must be unscrewed to lubricate the Dana type front driveshaft splines properly

need a flexible hose, too. To lubricate the sliding splines in the Dana type front driveshaft properly, first unscrew and slide back the spline seal collar. Pump chassis grease into the fitting until it oozes out the vent hole, then plug the vent hole with your finger and pump in grease until it comes out past the seal. This isn't necessary on the GM style driveshaft, which has the grease fitting closer to the seal collar.

Water resistant EP chassis lubricant (grease) conforming to GM specification 6031-M should be used for all chassis grease points.

Wheel Bearing Lubrication and Adjustment

Only front wheel bearings require periodic service. A premium high melting point grease

must be used. Long fiber type greases must not be used. This service is recommended at the intervals in the "Maintenance Intervals" chart or whenever the truck has been driven in water up to the hubs.

Two Wheel Drive

1. Remove the wheel and tire assembly, and the brake drum or brake caliper. See Chapter 9 for details.

2. Remove the hub and disc as an assembly. Remove the caliper mounting bolts and insert a block between the brake pads as the caliper is removed. Remove the caliper and wire it out of the way.

3. Pry out the grease cap, cotter pin, spindle nut, and washer, then remove the hub. Do not drop the wheel bearings.

4. Remove the outer roller bearing assembly from the hub. The inner bearing assembly will remain in the hub and may be removed after prying out the inner seal. Discard the seal.

5. Clean all parts in solvent (air dry) and check for excessive wear or damage.

6. Using a hammer and drift, remove the bearing cups from the hub. When installing new cups, make sure that they are not cocked and that they are fully seated against the hub shoulder.

7. Pack both wheel bearings using high melting point wheel bearing grease made for disc brakes. Ordinary grease will melt and ooze out, ruining the pads. Place a healthy glob of grease in the palm of one hand and force the edge of the bearing into it so that the grease fills the bearing. Do this until the whole bearing is packed. Grease packing tools

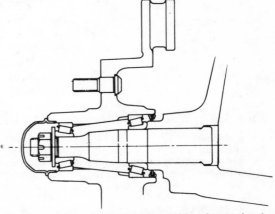

Cutaway view of the two wheel drive front wheel bearings. The dust cap is on the left and the grease seal is on the right

are available to make this job a lot less messy. There are also tools which make it possible to grease the inner bearing without removing it or the disc from the spindle.

8. Place the inner bearing in the hub and install a new inner seal, making sure that the seal flange faces the bearing cup.

9. Carefully install the wheel hub over the spindle.

10. Using your hands, firmly press the outer bearing into the hub. Install the spindle washer and nut.

11. To adjust the bearings on 1969 through 1971 models, tighten the adjusting nut to 15 ft. lbs. while rotating the hub. Back the nut off one flat ($^1/_6$ turn) and insert a new cotter pin. If the nut and spindle hole do not align, back the nut off slightly. There should be 0.001–0.008 in. end play in the bearing. This can be measured with a dial indicator, if you wish. Install the dust cap, wheel, and tire.

12. To adjust the bearings on 1972 and later models, spin the wheel hub by hand and tighten the nut until it is just snug (12 ft. lbs.). Back off the nut until it is loose, then tighten it finger tight. Loosen the nut until either hole in the spindle lines up with a slot in the nut and insert a new cotter pin. There should be 0.001–0.008 in. end play in the bearing through 1973, and 0.001–0.010 in. from 1974. This can be measured with a dial indicator, if you wish.

13. Replace the dust cap, wheel and tire.

Four Wheel Drive

NOTE: *This procedure requires snap ring pliers and a special hub nut wrench. It isn't very easy without them.*

1. Remove the wheel and tire. If you have locking front hubs, lock them. Remove the outer retaining plate Allen head bolts and take off the plate, O-ring, and knob. Take out the large snap ring inside the hub and remove the outer clutch retaining ring and actuating cam body. This is a lot easier with snap ring pliers. Relieve pressure on the axle shaft snap ring and remove it. Take out the axle shaft sleeve and clutch ring assembly and the inner clutch ring and bushing assembly. Remove the spring and retainer plate.

NOTE: *You will have to modify this procedure if you have locking hubs other than the factory installed type.*

2. If you don't have locking front hubs, remove the hub cap and snap ring. Remove the drive gear by prying out with a prybar.

Special four wheel drive bearing wrench—these are available at four wheel drive suppliers and truck parts stores

Watch it, there is a spring behind the gear. Remove the spring.

3. Remove the wheel bearing outer lock nut, lock ring, and wheel bearing inner adjusting nut. A special wrench is required.

4. Remove the brake disc assembly and outer wheel bearing. Remove the spring retainer plate if you don't have locking hubs. See Chapter 9 for details on brake drum or disc and caliper removal.

5. Remove the oil seal and inner bearing cone from the hub using a brass drift and hammer. Discard the oil seal. Use the drift to remove the inner and outer bearing cups.

6. Check the condition of the spindle bearing. If you have drum brakes, remove the grease retainer, gasket, and backing plate after removing the bolts. Unbolt the spindle and tap it with a soft hammer to break it loose. Remove the spindle and check the condition of the thrust washer, replacing it if worn. Now you can remove the oil seal and spindle roller bearing.

NOTE: *The spindle bearings must be greased each time the wheel bearings are serviced.*

Drive out the bearing cups

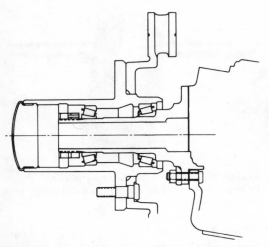

Cutaway view of the four wheel drive front wheel bearings

Removing the spindle

7. Clean all parts in solvent, dry, and check for wear or damage.

8. Pack both wheel bearings (and the spindle bearing) using wheel bearing grease. Place a healthy glob of grease in the palm of one hand and force the edge of the bearing into it so that grease fills the bearing. Do this until the whole bearing is packed. Grease packing tools are available to make this job a lot less messy.

9. To reassemble the spindle: drive the repacked bearing into the spindle and install the grease seal onto the slinger with the lip toward the spindle. It would be best to replace the axle shaft slinger when the spindle seal is replaced. See Axle Shaft Removal and Overhaul in Chapter 7 for details.

10. To reassemble the wheel bearings: drive the outer bearing cup into the hub, replace the inner bearing cup, and insert the repacked bearing.

11. Install the disc or drum and outer wheel bearing to the spindle.

12. Adjust the bearings by rotating the hub and torquing the inner adjusting nut to 50 ft. lbs., then loosening it and retorquing to 35 ft. lbs., still rotating the hub. Next, back the nut off ⅜ turn or less. Turn the nut to the nearest hole in the lockwasher. Install the outer locknut and torque to a minimum of 50

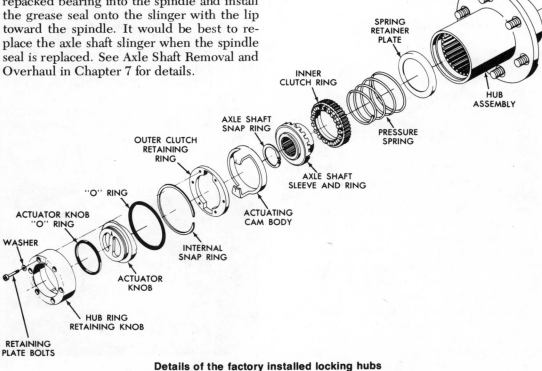

Details of the factory installed locking hubs

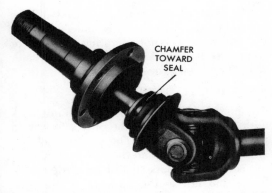

Replacing the spindle thrust washer and spindle. The components are removed here for clarity

ft. lbs. through 1978 and 80 ft. lbs. for 1979 and later models. There should be 0.001–0.010 in. bearing end play. This can be measured with a dial indicator.

13. Replace the brake components.

14. Lubricate the locking hub components with high temperature grease. Install the spring retainer plate with the flange side to the bearing and seat it against the outer bearing cup. Install the pressure spring with the large end against the retainer plate. Place the inner clutch ring and bushing assembly into the axle shaft sleeve and clutch ring assembly. Push in the assembly and install the axle shaft snap ring. If there are two axle shaft snap ring grooves use the inner one.

NOTE: *You can install a 7/16 in. bolt in the axle end and pull to aid in seating the snap ring.*

Install the actuating cam body with the cams out, the outer clutch retaining ring, and the internal snap ring. Install a new O-ring, then install the actuating knob and retaining plate into the lock position. The grooves in the knob must fit into the actuator cam body. Install the cover bolts and seals.

15. Without locking hubs, replace the snap ring and hub cap. If there are two axle shaft snap ring grooves use the inner one.

PUSHING AND TOWING

Pushing

Trucks with automatic transmission may not be started by pushing or towing. Manual

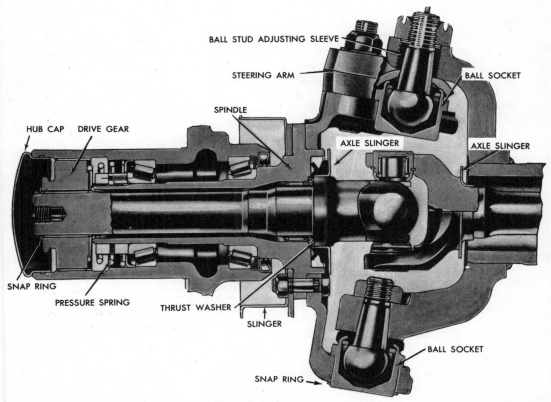

Cutaway view of the four wheel drive front wheel bearings. The spindle bearing is to the left of the thrust washer. The axle shown here does not have locking hubs

transmission trucks may be started by pushing. The truck need not be pushed very fast to start.

To push start a manual transmission truck:

1. Make sure that the bumpers of the two trucks align so as not to damage either one. It would be a good idea to put an old tire between the two bumpers.

2. Turn on the ignition switch in the pushed truck. Place the transmission in second gear and hold down the clutch pedal.

3. Have the truck pushed to a speed of 10 mph and stop the pushing vehicle, allowing the pushed vehicle to roll on.

4. Release the clutch and press down on the accelerator slightly at the same time.

The truck should not be towed to start, since there is a good chance of the towed vehicle ramming the towing truck.

Towing

TWO WHEEL DRIVE

Two wheel drive Blazers and Jimmys can be towed on all four wheels (flat towed) at speeds of less than 35 mph for distances less than 50 miles, providing that the axle, driveline, and transmission are normally operable. The transmission should be in Neutral, the steering column unlocked, and the parking brake released. Power steering and brake assists will not work with the engine off, so the only safe way to tow is with a tow bar. Do not attach chains to the bumpers or bracketing. All attachments must be made to the frame. Safety chains should be used.

The rear wheels must be raised off the ground or the driveshaft disconnected when the transmission is not operating properly, or when speeds over 35 mph or distances greater than 50 miles will be encountered.

FOUR WHEEL DRIVE

The power steering and brakes will not work with the engine off, so the only safe way to tow is with a tow bar. The steering column should be unlocked and the parking brake released. Attachments should be made to the frame and not to the bumper or brackets. Safety chains are also required.

Details on towing procedures are given in the "Towing Four Wheel Drive Chart."

NOTE: *When towing a full time four wheel drive manual transmission vehicle with all four wheels on the ground, the transfer case must be in Neutral and the transmission in high gear. There is no speed restriction.*

JACKING AND HOISTING

The jack supplied with the truck should never be used to support the truck for any service operation other than tire changing. NEVER get under the truck while it is supported only by the jack. It may slip or topple over. Always block the wheels when changing tires.

Some of the service operations in this book require that one or both ends of the truck be raised and supported safely. The best arrangement is a grease pit or a vehicle lift. It is understood that these items are not often

FRONT WHEELS OFF THE GROUND	
FULL TIME (4 X 4) AUTOMATIC TRANSMISSION	PART TIME (4 X 4)
1. TRANSFER CASE IN NEUTRAL 2. TRANSMISSION IN PARK 3. MAXIMUM SPEED 35 MPH 4. MAXIMUM DISTANCE 50 MILES NOTE: For distances over 50 miles, disconnect rear propshaft at rear axle carrier and secure in safe position.	1. TRANSFER CASE IN 2 H 2. TRANSMISSION IN NEUTRAL 3. MAXIMUM SPEED 35 MPH 4. MAXIMUM DISTANCE 50 MILES NOTE: For distances over 50 miles, disconnect the rear propshaft at rear axle carrier and secure in safe position.
REAR WHEELS OFF THE GROUND	
CAUTION: When towing a vehicle in this position, the steering wheel should be secured to keep the front wheels in a straight ahead position.	
FULL TIME (4 X 4)	PART TIME (4 X 4)
1. TRANSFER CASE IN NEUTRAL 2. TRANSMISSION IN PARK 3. MAXIMUM SPEED 35 MPH 4. MAXIMUM DISTANCE 50 MILES NOTE: For distances over 50 miles, disconnect front propshaft at front axle carrier and secure in safe position.	1. TRANSFER CASE IN 2 H 2. TRANSMISSION IN NEUTRAL 3. MAXIMUM SPEED 35 MPH 4. MAXIMUM DISTANCE 50 MILES NOTE: For distances over 50 miles, disconnect the front propshaft at front axle carrier and secure in safe position.
ALL FOUR WHEELS ON GROUND	
FULL TIME (4 X 4)	PART TIME (4 X 4)
1. TRANSFER CASE IN NEUTRAL 2. TRANSMISSION IN PARK NOTE: Do not exceed speed as per State laws for towing vehicles.	1. TRANSFER CASE IN 2 H 2. TRANSMISSION IN NEUTRAL 3. MAXIMUM SPEED 35 MPH 4. MAXIMUM DISTANCE 50 MILES NOTE: For speeds or distances greater than above, both propshafts must be disconnected at the axle carrier end and secured in a safe position. It is recommended that both propshafts be removed and stored in the vehicle. NOTE: Do not exceed speeds as per State laws for towing vehicles.

Towing Four Wheel Drive

JUMP STARTING A DEAD BATTERY

The chemical reaction in a battery produces explosive hydrogen gas. This is the safe way to jump start a dead battery, reducing the chances of an accidental spark that could cause an explosion.

Jump Starting Precautions

1. Be sure both batteries are of the same voltage.
2. Be sure both batteries are of the same polarity (have the same grounded terminal).
3. Be sure the vehicles are not touching.
4. Be sure the vent cap holes are not obstructed.
5. Do not smoke or allow sparks around the battery.
6. In cold weather, check for frozen electrolyte in the battery.
7. Do not allow electrolyte on your skin or clothing.
8. Be sure the electrolyte is not frozen.

Jump Starting Procedure

1. Determine voltages of the two batteries; they must be the same.
2. Bring the starting vehicle close (they must not touch) so that the batteries can be reached easily.
3. Turn off all accessories and both engines. Put both cars in Neutral or Park and set the handbrake.
4. Cover the cell caps with a rag—do not cover terminals.
5. If the terminals on the run-down battery are heavily corroded, clean them.
6. Identify the positive and negative posts on both batteries and connect the cables in the order shown.
7. Start the engine of the starting vehicle and run it at fast idle. Try to start the car with the dead battery. Crank it for no more than 10 seconds at a time and let it cool off for 20 seconds in between tries.
8. If it doesn't start in 3 tries, there is something else wrong.
9. Disconnect the cables in the reverse order.
10. Replace the cell covers and dispose of the rags.

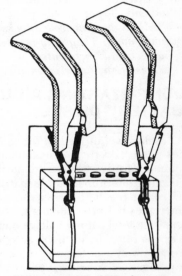

Side terminal batteries occasionally pose a problem when connecting jumper cables. There frequently isn't enough room to clamp the cables without touching sheet metal. Side terminal adaptors are available to alleviate this problem and should be removed after use.

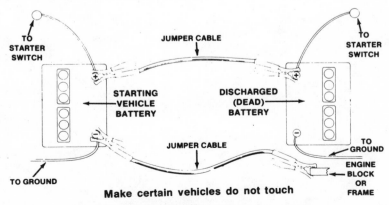

TO STARTER SWITCH

JUMPER CABLE

TO STARTER SWITCH

STARTING VEHICLE BATTERY

DISCHARGED (DEAD) BATTERY

JUMPER CABLE

TO GROUND

TO GROUND

ENGINE BLOCK OR FRAME

Make certain vehicles do not touch

This hook-up for negative ground cars only

found in the home garage, but there are reasonable and safe substitutes. Small hydraulic, screw, or scissors jacks are satisfactory for raising the truck.

Heavy wooden blocks or adjustable jackstands should be used to support the truck while it is being worked on. Drive-on trestles, or ramps, are also a handy and safe way to raise the truck. These can be bought or constructed from suitable heavy timbers or steel.

In any case, it is always best to spend a little extra time to make sure that the truck is lifted and supported safely.

CAUTION: *Concrete blocks are not recommended. They may break if the load is not evenly distributed. Boxes and milk crates of any description must not be used.*

JUMP-STARTING A DUAL BATTERY DIESEL

Diesels are equipped with two 12 volt batteries. The batteries are connected in parallel circuit (positive terminal to positive terminal, negative terminal to negative terminal). Hooking the batteries up in parallel circuit increases battery cranking power without increasing total battery voltage output (12 volts). On the other hand, hooking two 12 volt batteries up in a series circuit (positive terminal to negative terminal, positive terminal to negative terminal) increases total battery output to 24 volts (12 volts + 12 volts).

CAUTION: *NEVER hook the batteries up in a series circuit or the entire electrical system will go up in smoke.*

In the event that a dual battery diesel must be jumped started, use the following procedure.

1. Open the hood and locate the batteries. The manufacturer usually suggests using the battery on the driver's side to make the connection.

2. Position the donor car so that the jumper cables will reach from its battery (must be 12 volt, negative ground) to the appropriate battery in the diesel. Do not allow the cars to touch.

3. Shut off all electrical equipment on both vehicles. Turn off the engine of the donor car, set the parking brakes on both vehicles and block the wheels. Also, make sure both vehicles are in Neutral (manual transmission models) or Park (automatic transmission models).

4. Using the jumper cables, connect the positive (+) terminal of the donor car battery to the positive terminal of one (not both) of the diesel batteries.

5. Using the second jumper cable, connect the negative (−) terminal of the donor battery to a solid, stationary, metallic point on the diesel (alternator bracket, engine block, etc.). Be very careful to keep the jumper cables away from moving parts (cooling fan, alternator belt, etc.) on both vehicles.

6. Start the engine of the donor car and run it at moderate speed.

7. Start the engine of the diesel.

8. When the diesel starts, disconnect the battery cables in the reverse order of attachment.

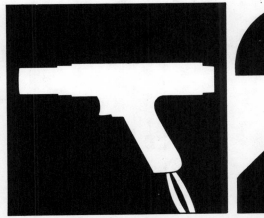

Tune-Up

TUNE-UP PROCEDURES

The following are specific procedures to be used in performing each tune-up step. Refer to Chapter Eleven for troubleshooting and diagnosis of engine problems.

The manufacturer's recommended tune-up interval is every 12,000 miles or one year, whichever comes first, for 1969–74 models. For 1975–80, it is every 22,500 miles or 18 months, 1981 and later models—every 30,000 miles. Naturally, this interval should be shortened if the vehicle is subjected to severe operating conditions such as trailer towing or off-road driving or if starting and running problems are noted. It is assumed that the routine maintenance described in Chapter 1 has been kept up, as this will have an effect on the results of the tune-up. All the applicable tune-up steps should be followed, as each adjustment complements the effects of the others. If the tune-up (emission control) sticker in the engine compartment disagrees with the "Tune-Up Specifications" chart in this chapter, the sticker figures must be followed. The sticker often reflects running changes made in production. The sticker is usually on the underhood sheet metal above the grille or on top of the air cleaner.

The light duty emission control (tune-up) sticker is usually on the underhood sheet metal above the grille (© Chevrolet Motor Division)

Spark Plugs

1. Disconnect each spark plug wire by twisting and pulling on the rubber cap, not on the wire. Carbon core wires can be internally broken rather easily. Label the wires so you won't get them mixed up. Labeling them now is a lot easier than tracing them later.

2. If the wires are dirty or oily, wipe them clean with a cloth dampened in kerosene and then wipe them dry. If the wires are cracked, they should be replaced. Make sure to get the radio noise suppression type.

3. Blow or brush the dirt away from each of the spark plugs. This can be done by loosening the plugs and cranking the engine with the starter.

4. Remove each spark plug with a spark plug socket; ⅝ in. for plug designations with a T, ¹³⁄₁₆ for the rest. Make sure that the socket is all the way down on the plug to pre-

Tune-Up Specifications

When analyzing compression test results, look for uniformity among cylinders rather than specific pressures.

| Year | Engine No. Cyl Displacement | Spark Plugs | | Distributor | | Ignition Timing (deg) | | Fuel Pump Pressure (psi) | Idle Speed (rpm) | |
		Orig Type •	Gap (in.)	Point Dwell (deg)	Point Gap* (in.)	Man Trans	Auto Trans •		Man Trans	Auto Trans ▲ •
'69	6—250	R46N	.035	31–34	.019	TDC	4B	3–4½	700	550①/400
	8—307	R44	.035	28–32	.019	2B	2B	5–6½	700	600
	8—350	R44	.035	28–32	.019	TDC	4B	5–6½	700	600
'70	6—250	R46T	.035	31–34	.019	TDC	4B	3½–4½	750/400	600/400
	8—307	R45	.035	28–32	.019	2B	8B	5–6½	700	600/450
	8—350	R44	.035	28–32	.019	TDC	4B	7–8½	600	500
'71	6—250	R46TS	.035	31–34	.019	4B	4B	3½–4½	550	500
	8—307	R45TS	.035	28–32	.019	4B	8B	5–6½	600	550①
	8—350	R44TS	.035	28–32	.019	4B	8B	7–8½	600	550①
'72	6—250	R46T	.035	31–34	.019	4B	4B	3½–4½	700/450	600/450
	8—307	R44T	.035	29–31	.019	4B	8B	5–6½	900(950)②/450	600/450
	8—350	R44T	.035	29–31	.019	4B	8B	7–8½	800②/450	600/450
'73	6—250	R46T	.035	31–34	.019	6B	6B	3½–4½	700/450	600/450
	8—307	R44T	.035	29–31	.019	4B	8B	5–6½	900/450	600/450

Year	Engine	Spark Plug	Gap	Dwell	Point Gap	Timing (1)	Timing (2)	Fuel Pump Press.	Idle (1)	Idle (2)
'74	8—350	R44T	.035	29—31	.019	8B	12B	7—8½	900/450	600/450
	6—250	R46T	.035	31—34	.019	8B	8B	3½—4½	850/450	600/450
	8—350 2 bbl	R44T	.035	29—31	.019	TDC	8B	7—8½	900/450	600/450
	8—350 4 bbl	R44T	.035	29—31	.019	TDC(4B)	8B	7—8½	900/450	600/450
'75	6—250	R46TX	.060	Electronic		10B	10B	3½—4½	900/425①	550(600)/425①
	8—350 2 bbl	R44TX	.060	Electronic		③	6B	7—8½	③	600
	8—350 4 bbl, 2WD	R44TX	.060	Electronic		6B	6B	7—8½	800/450	600/450
	8—350 4 bbl, 4WD	R44TX	.060	Electronic		8B(2B)	8B(2B)	7—8½	600(700)①	600(700)①
	8—400	R44TX	.060	Electronic		—	4B(2B)	7—8½	—	700①
'76	6—250	R46T	.035	Electronic		6B	6B	3½—4½	600①	600①N
	8—350	R44TX	.060	Electronic		8B(2B)	8B(2B)	7—8½	600(700)	600(700)N
	8—400	R44TX	.060	Electronic		—	4B	7—8½	—	700N
'77–'78	6—250	R46T	.035	Electronic		6B	6B	3½—4½	600/450	600/450
	8—305	R44T	.045	Electronic		6B	6B	7—8½	700	700
	8—350	R44T (R44TX)	.045 (.060)	Electronic		8B(2B)	8B(2B)	7—8½	700	700
	8—400	R44T	.045	Electronic		—	4B(2B)	7—8½	—	700

Tune-Up Specifications (cont.)

When analyzing compression test results, look for uniformity among cylinders rather than specific pressures.

Year	Engine No. Cyl Displacement	Spark Plugs Orig Type •	Spark Plugs Gap (in.)	Distributor Point Dwell (deg)	Distributor Point Gap* (in.)	Ignition Timing (deg) Man Trans •	Ignition Timing (deg) Auto Trans	Fuel Pump Pressure (psi)	Idle Speed (rpm) Man Trans •	Idle Speed (rpm) Auto Trans ▲
'79	6—250	R46TS	.035	Electronic		10B	10B	4½–6	750	600
	8—305	R45TS	.045	Electronic		6B	6B	④	600	500
	8—350	R45TS	.045	Electronic		8B	8B	④	700	500
	8—400	R45TS	.060	Electronic		—	4B	④	—	500
'80–81	6—250	R46TS	.035	Electronic		10B	10B	3.5–4.5	750	650(D)
	8—305	R45TS	.045	Electronic		4B	2B	7.0–8.5	700	500(D)
	8—350	R45TS	.045	Electronic		8B	8B	7.0–8.5	700	500(D)
'82	See underhood specifications sticker									

● Figures in parentheses are for California, and are given only when they differ from the 49 State models. When two idle speeds separated by a slash are given, the lower figure is with the solenoid disconnected.

* Decrease setting to .016 in. for used points.

▲ Automatic transmission idle speed set in Drive unless otherwise indicated

B Before Top Dead Center
TDC Top Dead Center
N Neutral
2WD Two wheel drive
4WD 4 wheel drive

① Air conditioning on
② 600 rpm without transmission controlled spark (TCS) system
③ See the underhood specification sticker
④ With vapor return line—5½–7
  Without vapor return line—7½–9

NOTE: *The underhood specifications sticker often reflects tune-up specification changes made in production. Sticker figures must be used if they disagree with those in this chart. Part numbers in this chart are not recommendations by Chilton for any product name.*

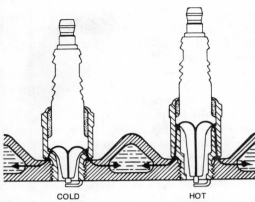

Checking the spark plug gap with a wire gauge

The plug with the higher heat range is on the right; it has a longer heat flow path and thus operates at a higher temperature. It should be used for slower driving and light loads as these promote carbon accumulation

Adjusting the gap with the tool on the gauge

vent it from slipping and cracking the porcelain insulator. On some V8s, the plugs are more accessible from under the truck.

5. Refer to the economy tip section on evaluating plug condition. In general, a tan or medium gray color on the business end of the plugs indicates normal combustion conditions. A spark plug's useful life is about 12,000 miles (22,500–30,000 with HEI electronic ignition). Thus it would make sense to throw away the plugs if it has been 12,000 miles or more since the last tune-up. Most professional mechanics won't waste their time cleaning used plugs; there is too much chance of unsatisfactory performance and a customer

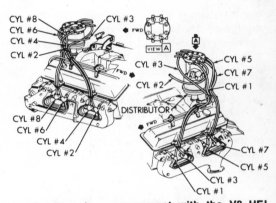

Spark plug wire arrangement with the V8 HEI system

comeback. Refer to the "Tune-Up Specifications" chart for the proper spark plug type.

The letter codes on the General Motors original equipment type plugs are read this way:

- R resistor
- S extended tip
- T tapered seat
- X wide gap

The numbers indicate heat range; hotter running plugs have higher numbers.

6. If the plugs are to be reused, file the center and side electrodes flat with a small, fine file. Heavy or baked on deposits can be carefully scraped off with a small knife blade or the scraper tool on a combination spark plug tool. A wire brush will help loosen deposits, also. It is often suggested that plugs be tested and cleaned on a service station

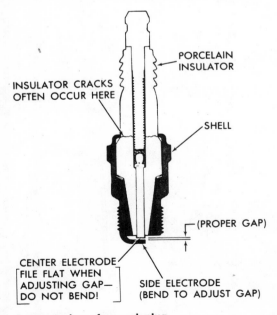

Cutaway view of a spark plug

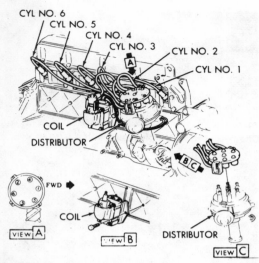

CYL NO. 6
CYL NO. 5
CYL NO. 4
CYL NO. 3
CYL NO. 2
CYL NO. 1
COIL
DISTRIBUTOR
FWD
COIL
DISTRIBUTOR
VIEW A
VIEW B
VIEW C

Spark plug wire arrangement with the six cylinder HEI system

sandblasting machine; however, this piece of equipment is becoming rare. Check the gap between the two electrodes with a spark plug gap gauge. The round wire type is the most accurate. If the gap is not as specified, use the adjusting device on the gap gauge to bend the outside electrode to correct.

NOTE: *Check the gap on new plugs.*

Be careful not to bend the electrode too far or too often, because excessive bending may cause it to break off and fall into the combus-

tion chamber. This would require cylinder head removal to reach the broken piece, and could easily result in cylinder wall, ring, or valve damage.

7. Clean the plug threads with a wire brush. If you choose to lubricate the threads, use only one drop of engine oil.

8. Screw the plugs in finger-tight. Tighten them with the plug socket. If a torque wrench is available, tighten them to 15 ft. lbs. for plug designations with a T, and 25 ft. lbs. for the rest.

9. Reinstall the wires. If there is any doubt as to their proper locations, refer to the "Firing Order" illustrations in Chapter 3.

Glow Plugs [Diesel Engine]

Eight glow plugs are used to preheat the chamber as an aid to starting. They are essentially small 12 volt heaters that turn on when the ignition switch is turned to the "Run" position prior to starting the engine. They remain on for a short time after starting and then automatically shut off.

REMOVAL AND INSTALLATION

NOTE: *Use extreme care when removing the glow plugs as the tip may break off; requiring cylinder head removal to retrieve it.*

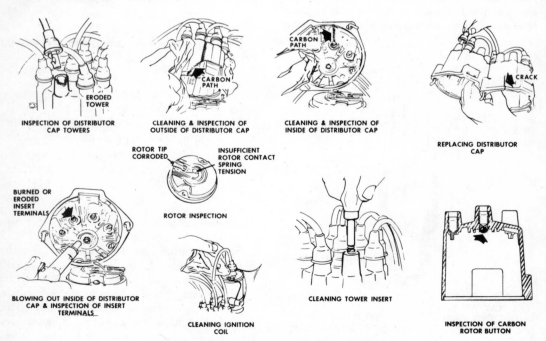

INSPECTION OF DISTRIBUTOR CAP TOWERS

CLEANING & INSPECTION OF OUTSIDE OF DISTRIBUTOR CAP

CLEANING & INSPECTION OF INSIDE OF DISTRIBUTOR CAP

REPLACING DISTRIBUTOR CAP

BURNED OR ERODED INSERT TERMINALS

ROTOR TIP CORRODED

INSUFFICIENT ROTOR CONTACT SPRING TENSION

ROTOR INSPECTION

BLOWING OUT INSIDE OF DISTRIBUTOR CAP & INSPECTION OF INSERT TERMINALS

CLEANING IGNITION COIL

CLEANING TOWER INSERT

INSPECTION OF CARBON ROTOR BUTTON

Inspecting the distributor cap and rotor

1. Tag and disconnect the electrical connectors.

2. Using the large hex nut, loosen the plug and carefully pull it out of the cylinder head.

3. Installation is in the reverse order.

Breaker Points, Condenser and Dwell Angle

1969–74

The usual procedure is to replace the condenser each time the point set is replaced. Although this is not always necessary, it is easy to do at this time and the cost is negligible. Every time you adjust or replace the breaker points, the ignition timing must be checked and, if necessary, adjusted. No special equipment other than a feeler gauge is required for point replacement or adjustment, but a dwell meter is strongly advised.

1. Push down on the spring-loaded V8 distributor cap retaining screws and give them a half-turn to release. Unscrew the captive six-cylinder cap retaining screws. Remove the cap. You might have to unclip or detach some or all of the plug wires to remove the cap.

2. Clean the cap inside and out with a clean rag. Check for cracks and carbon paths. A carbon path shows up as a dark line, usually from one of the cap sockets or inside terminals to a ground. Check the condition of the carbon button inside the center of the cap and the inside terminals. Replace the cap as necessary.

3. Pull the six-cylinder rotor up and off the shaft. Remove the two screws and lift the round V8 rotor off. There is less danger of losing the screws if you just back them out all the way and lift them off with the rotor. Clean off the metal outer tip if it is burned or corroded. Don't file it. Replace the rotor as necessary or if one came with your tune-up kit.

4. Remove the radio frequency interference shield if your distributor has one. Watch out for those little screws! The factory says that the points don't need to be replaced if they are only slightly rough or pitted. However, sad experience shows that it is more economical and reliable in the long run to replace the point set while the distributor is open, than to have to do this at a later (and possibly more inconvenient) time.

5. Pull off the two wire terminals from the point assembly. One wire comes from the condenser and the other comes from within the distributor. The terminals are usually held in place by spring tension only. There might

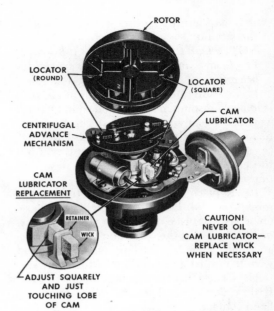

Details of the V8 distributor showing the cam lubricator and the square peg in the square hole arrangement that prevents incorrect installation of the rotor

be a clamp screw securing the terminals on some older versions. There is also available a one-piece point/condenser assembly for V8s. The radio frequency interference shield isn't needed with this set. Loosen the point set hold-down screw(s). Be very careful not to drop any of these little screws inside the distributor. If this happens, the distributor will probably have to be removed to get at the screw. If the hold-down screw is lost elsewhere, it must be replaced with one that is no longer than the original to avoid interference with the distributor workings. Remove the point set, even if it is to be reused.

6. If the points are to be reused, clean them with a few strokes of a special point file. This is done with the points removed to prevent tiny metal filings getting into the distributor. Don't use sandpaper or emery cloth; they will cause rapid point burning.

7. Loosen the condenser hold-down screw and slide the condenser out of the clamp. This will save you a struggle with the clamp, condenser, and the tiny screw when you install the new one. If you have the type of clamp that is permanently fastened to the condenser, remove the screw and the condenser. Don't lose the screw.

8. Attend to the distributor cam lubricator. If you have the round kind, turn it around on its shaft at the first tune-up and replace it at the second. If you have the long kind,

switch ends at the first tune-up and replace it at the second.

NOTE: *Don't oil or grease the lubricator. The foam is impregnated with a special lubricant.*

If you didn't get any lubricator at all, or if it looks like someone took it off, don't worry. You don't really need it. Just rub a match-head size dab of grease on the cam lobes.

9. Install the new condenser. If you left the clamp in place, just slide the new condenser into the clamp.

10. Replace the point set and tighten the screws on a V8. Leave the screw slightly loose on a six. Replace the two wire terminals, making sure that the wires don't interfere with anything. Some V8 distributors have a ground wire that must go under one of the screws.

11. Check that the contacts meet squarely. If they don't, bend the tab supporting the fixed contact.

NOTE: *If you are installing preset points on a V8, go ahead to Step 16. If they are preset, it will say so on the package. It would be a good idea to make a quick check on point gap, anyway. Sometimes those preset points aren't.*

12. Turn the engine until a high point on the cam that opens the points contacts the rubbing block on the point arm. You can turn the engine by hand if you can get a wrench on the crankshaft pulley nut, or you can grasp the fan belt and turn the engine with the spark plugs removed.

CAUTION: *If you try turning the engine by hand, be very careful not to get your fingers pinched in the pulleys.*

On a stick-shift you can push it forward in High gear. Another alternative is to bump the starter switch or use a remote starter switch.

13. On a six, there is a screwdriver slot near the contacts. Insert a screwdriver and lever the points open or closed until they ap-

ADJUST DWELL
ANGLE SETTING OR
POINT OPENING

Six cylinder breaker point adjustment

pear to be at about the gap specified in the "Tune-Up Specifications." On a V8, simply insert a ⅛ in. allen wrench into the adjustment screw and turn. The wrench sometimes comes with a tune-up kit.

14. Insert the correct size feeler gauge and adjust the gap until you can push the gauge in and out between the contacts with a slight drag, but without disturbing the point arm. This operation takes a bit of experience to obtain the correct feel. Check by trying the gauges 0.001–0.002 larger and smaller than the setting size. The larger one should disturb the point arm, while the smaller one should not drag at all. Tighten the six-cylinder point set hold-down screw. Recheck the gap, because it often changes when the screw is tightened.

15. After all the point adjustments are complete, pull a white business card through (between) the contacts to remove any traces of oil. Oil will cause rapid contact burning.

NOTE: *You can adjust six-cylinder dwell at this point, if you wish. Refer to Step 18.*

16. Replace the radio frequency interference shield, if any. You don't need it if you are installing the one-piece point/condenser set. Push the rotor firmly down into place. It will only go on one way. Tighten the V8 rotor screws. If the rotor is not installed properly, it will probably break when the starter is operated.

17. Replace the distributor cap.

18. If a dwell meter is available, check the dwell. The dwell meter hookup is shown in the "Tune-up" Sections.

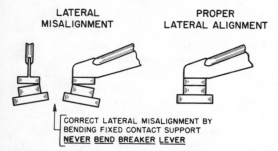

LATERAL
MISALIGNMENT

PROPER
LATERAL ALIGNMENT

CORRECT LATERAL MISALIGNMENT BY
BENDING FIXED CONTACT SUPPORT
NEVER BEND BREAKER LEVER

Point misalignment can be corrected by gentle bending

V8 dwell adjustment

NOTE: *This hookup may not apply to electronic, capacitive discharge, or other special ignition systems. Some dwell meters won't work at all with such systems.*

Dwell can be checked with the engine running or cranking. Decrease dwell by increasing the point gap; increase by decreasing the gap. Dwell angle is simply the number of degrees of distributor shaft rotation during which the points stay closed. Theoretically, if the point gap is correct, the dwell should also be correct or nearly so. Adjustment with a dwell meter produces more exact, consistent results since it is a dynamic adjustment. If dwell varies more than 3 degrees from idle speed to 1,750 engine rpm, the distributor is worn.

19. To adjust dwell on a six, trial and error point adjustments are required. On a V8, simply open the metal window on the distributor and insert a ⅛ in. allen wrench. Turn until the meter shows the correct reading. Be sure to snap the window closed.

20. An approximate dwell adjustment can be made without a meter on a V8. Turn the adjusting screw clockwise until the engine begins to misfire, then turn it out ½ turn.

21. If the engine won't start, check:

a. That all the spark plug wires are in place.

b. That the rotor has been installed.

c. That the two (or three) wires inside the distributor are connected.

d. That the points open and close when the engine turns.

e. That the gap is correct and the hold-down screw (on a six) is tight.

22. After the first 200 miles or so on a new set of points, the point gap often closes up due to initial rubbing block wear. For best performance, recheck the dwell (or gap) at this time. This quick initial wear is the reason why the factory recommends 0.003 in. more gap on new points.

23. Since changing the gap affects the ignition timing, the timing should be checked and adjusted as necessary after each point replacement or adjustment.

From 1975

These engines use the breakerless HEI (High Energy Ignition) system. Since there is no mechanical contact, there is no wear or need for periodic service.

High Energy Ignition (HEI) System

The General Motors HEI system is a pulse-triggered, transistored-controlled, inductive discharge ignition system. Except on early inline six-cylinder models, the entire HEI system is contained within the distributor cap. Inline six-cylinder engines through 1977 have an external coil. Otherwise, the system are the same.

The distributor, in addition to housing the mechanical and vacuum advance mechanisms, contains the ignition coil (except on early inline six engines), the electronic control module, and the magnetic triggering device. The magnetic pick-up assembly contains a permament magnet, a pole piece with internal "teeth," and a pick-up coil (not to be confused with the ignition coil).

In the HEI system, as in other electronic ignition systems, the breaker points have been replaced with an electronic switch—a transistor—which is located *within* the control module. This switching transistor per-

The toothed wheel is the pole piece

HEI distributor components. The module is still in the distributor

forms the same function the points did in a conventional ignition system; it simply turns coil primary current on and off at the correct time. Essentially then, electronic and conventional ignition systems operate on the same principle.

The module which houses the switching transistor is controlled (turned on and off) by a magnetically generated impulse induced in the pick-up coil. When the teeth of the rotating timer align with the teeth of the pole piece, the induced voltage in the pick-up coil signals the electronic module to open the coil primary circuit. The primary current then decreases, and a high voltage is induced in the ignition coil secondary windings which is then directed through the rotor and high voltage leads (speark plug wires) to fire the spark plugs.

In essence then, the pick-up coil module system simply replaces the conventional breaker points and condenser. The condenser found within the distributor is for radio suppression purposes only and has nothing to do with the ignition process. The

module automatically controls the dwell period, increasing it with increasing engine speed. Since dwell is automatically controlled, it cannot be adjusted. The module itself is non-adjustable and non-repairable and must be replaced if found defective.

HEI SYSTEM PRECAUTIONS

Before going on to troubleshooting, it might be a good idea to take note of the following precautions:

Timing Light Use

Inductive pick-up timing lights are the best kind to use if your truck is equipped with HEI. Timing lights which connect between the spark plug and the spark plug wire occasionally (not always) give false readings.

Spark Plug Wires

The plug wires used with HEI systems are of a different construction than conventional wires. When replacing them, make sure you get the correct wires, since conventional wires won't carry the voltage. Also, handle them carefully to avoid cracking or splitting them and *never* pierce them.

Tachometer Use

Not all tachometers will operate or indicate correctly when used on a HEI system. While some tachometers may give a reading, this does not necessarily mean the reading is correct. In addition, some tachometers hook up differently from others. If you can't figure out whether or not your tachometer will work on your truck, check with the tachometer manufacturer. Dwell readings, of course, have no significance at all.

HEI System Testers

Instruments designed specifically for testing HEI systems are available from several tool manufacturers. Some of these will even test the module itself. However, the tests given in the following section will require only an ohmmeter and a voltmeter.

TROUBLESHOOTING THE HEI SYSTEM

The symptoms of a defective component within the HEI system are exactly the same as those you would encounter in a conventional system. Some of these symptoms are:
- Hard or no Starting
- Rough Idle
- Poor Fuel Economy

The coil is inside the distributor cap in most models. Check all wiring connections when troubleshooting

• Engine misses under load or while accelerating

If you suspect a problem in your ignition system, there are certain preliminary checks which you should carry out before you begin to check the electronic portions of the system. First, it is extremely important to make sure the vehicle battery is in a good state of charge. A defective or poorly charged battery will cause the various components of the ignition system to read incorrectly when they are being tested. Second, make sure all wiring connections are clean and tight, not only at the battery, but also at the distributor cap,

The module connectors are of two different sizes and will connect only one way. Later models have a slightly different module and connector design

ignition coil, and at the electronic control module.

Since the only change between electronic and conventional ignition systems is in the distributor component area, it is imperative to check the secondary ignition circuit first. If the secondary circuit checks out properly, then the engine condition is probably not the fault of the ignition system. To check the secondary ignition system, perform a simple spark test. Remove one of the plug wires and insert some sort of extension in the plug socket. An old spark plug with the ground electrode removed makes a good extension. Hold the wire and extension about ¼ in. away from the block and crank the engine. If a normal spark occurs, then the problem is most likely *not* in the ignition system. Check for fuel system problems, or fouled spark plugs.

If, however, there is no spark or a weak spark, then further ignition system testing will have to be done. Troubleshooting techniques fall into two categories, depending on the nature of the problem. The categories are (1) Engine cranks, but won't start or (2) Engine runs, but runs rough or cuts out. To begin with, let's consider the first case.

Engine Fails to Start

If the engine won't start, perform a spark test as described earlier. This will narrow the problem area down considerably. If no spark occurs, check for the presence of normal battery voltage at the battery (BAT) terminal in the distributor cap. The ignition switch must be in the "on" position for this test. Either a voltmeter or a test light may be used for this test. Connect the test light wire to ground and the probe end to the BAT terminal at the distributor. If the light comes on, you have voltage to the distributor. If the light fails to come on, this indicates an open circuit in the ignition primary wiring leading to the distributor. In this case, you will have to check wiring continuity back to the ignition switch using a test light. If there is battery voltage at the BAT terminal, but no spark at the plugs, then the problem lies within the distributor assembly. Go on to the distributor components test section.

Engine Runs, But Runs Rough or Cuts Out

1. Make sure the plug wires are in good shape first. There should be no obvious cracks or breaks. You can check the plug wires with an ohmmeter, but *do not* pierce the wires with a probe. Check the chart for the correct plug wire resistance.

HEI Plug Wire Resistance Chart

Wire Length	Minimum	Maximum
0–15 inches	3000 ohms	10,000 ohms
15–25 inches	4000 ohms	15,000 ohms
25–35 inches	6000 ohms	20,000 ohms
Over 35 inches		25,000 ohms

2. If the plug wires are OK, remove the cap assembly, and check for moisture, cracks, chips, or carbon tracks, or any other high voltage leaks or failures. Replace the cap if you find any defects. Make sure the timer wheel rotates when the engine is cranked. If everything is all right so far, go on to the distributor components test section.

Distributor Components Testing

If the trouble has been narrowed down to the units within the distributor, the following tests can help pinpoint the defective component. An ohmmeter with both high and low ranges should be used. These tests are made with the cap assembly removed and the battery wire disconnected.

1. Connect an ohmmeter between the Tach and Bat terminals in the distributor cap.

One ohmmeter lead connects to the rotor button in the center of the distributor cap when checking coil secondary resistance

The primary coil resistance should be less than one ohm.

2. To check the coil secondary resistance, connect an ohmmeter between the rotor button and the BAT terminal. Then connect the ohmmeter between the rotor button and the Tach terminal. The resistance should be between 6,000 and 30,000 ohms in both cases.

3. Replace the coil *only* if the readings in step one and two are infinite.

NOTE: *These resistance checks will not disclose shorted coil windings. This condition can only be detected with scope analysis or a suitably designed coil tester. If these instruments are unavailale, replace the coil with a known good coil as a final coil test.*

4. To test the pick-up coil, first disconnect the white and green module leads. Set the ohmmeter on the high scale and connect it between a ground and either the white or green lead. Any resistance measurement *less* than infinity requires replacement of the pick-up coil.

5. Pick-up coil continuity is tested by connecting the ohmmeter (on low range) between the white and green leads. Normal resistance is between 650 and 850 ohms. Move the vacuum advance arm while performing this test. This will detect any break in coil continuity. Such a condition can cause intermittent misfiring. Replace the pick-up coil if the reading is outside the specified limits.

6. If no defects have been found at this time, and you still have a problem, then the module will have to be checked. If you do not have access to a module tester, the only pos-

sible alternative is a substitution test. If the module fails the substitution test, replace it.

COMPONENT REPLACEMENT

Internal Ignition Coil

1. Disconnect the feed and module wire terminal connectors from the distributor cap.
2. Remove the ignition wire set retainer.
3. Remove the 4 coil cover-to-distributor cap screws and the coil cover.
4. Remove the 4 coil-to-distributor cap screws.
5. Using a blunt drift, press the coil wire spade terminals up out of distributor cap.
6. Lift the coil up out of the distributor cap.
7. Remove and clean the coil spring, rubber seal washer and coil cavity of the distributor cap.
8. Reverse the above procedures to install.

Distributor Cap—All Engines

1. Remove the feed and module wire terminal connectors from the distributor cap.
2. Remove the retainer and spark plug wires from the cap.
3. Depress and release the 4 distributor cap-to-housing retainers and lift off the cap assembly.
4. If the cap has an internal coil, remove the coil from the old cap and install into the new cap.
5. Using a new distributor cap, reverse the above procedures to assemble.

Rotor–all Engines

1. Disconnect the feed and module wire connectors from the distributor.
2. Depress and release the 4 distributor cap to housing retainers and lift off the cap assembly.
3. Remove the two rotor attaching screws and rotor.
4. Reverse the above procedure to install.

Vacuum Advance Unit—All Engines So Equipped

1. Remove the distributor cap and rotor as previously described.
2. Disconnect the vacuum hose from the vacuum advance unit. Remove the module.
3. Remove the two vacuum advance retaining screws, pull the advance unit outward, rotate and disengage the operating rod from its tang.
4. Reverse the above procedure to install.

Module—All Engines

1. Remove the distributor cap and rotor as previously described.
2. Disconnect the harness connector and pick-up coil spade connectors from the module (note their positions).
3. Remove the two screws and module from the distributor housing.
4. Coat the bottom of the new module with silicone lubricant.
   NOTE: *The lubricant is required for proper module cooling.*
Reverse the above procedure to install. Be sure that the leads are installed correctly.

Ignition Timing

Timing should be checked at each tune-up and any time the points are adjusted or replaced. It isn't likely to change much with HEI. The timing marks consist of a notch on the rim of the crankshaft pulley or vibration damper and a graduated scale attached to the engine front (timing) cover. A stroboscopic flash (dynamic) timing light must be used, as a static light is too inaccurate for emission controlled engines.

There are three basic types of timing light available. The first is a simple neon bulb with two wire connections. One wire connects to the spark plug terminal and the other plugs into the end of the spark plug wire for the No. 1 cylinder, thus connecting the light in series with the spark plug. This type of light is pretty dim and must be held very closely to the timing marks to be seen. Sometimes a dark corner has to be sought out to see the flash at all. This type of light is very inexpensive. The second type operates from the vehicle battery—two alligator clips connect to the battery terminals, while an adapter enables a third clip to be connected to the No. 1 spark plug and wire. This type is a bit more expensive, but it provides a nice bright flash that you can see even in bright sunlight. It is the type most often seen in professional shops. The third type replaces the battery power source with 110 volt current.

To check and adjust the timing:
1. Warm up the engine to normal operating temprature. Stop the engine and connect the timing light. Clean off the timing marks and mark the pulley or damper notch and timing scale with white chalk.
2. Disconnect and plug the vacuum lines at the distributor.

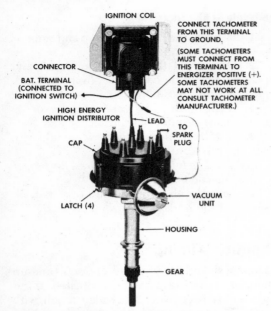

Six cylinder HEI system, showing the test tachometer hookup

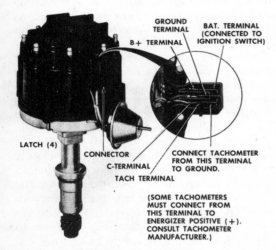

V8 HEI system, showing the test tachometer hookup

3. Start the engine and adjust the idle speed to that specified in the "Tune-Up Specifications" chart. With automatic transmission, set the specified idle speed in Park. It will be too high, since it is normally (in most cases) adjusted in Drive. You can disconnect the idle solenoid, if any, to get the speed down. Otherwise, adjust the idle speed screw. This is done to prevent any centrifugal (mechanical) advance. The tachometer hookup for 1969–74 models is the same as the dwell meter hookup shown in the "Tune-Up

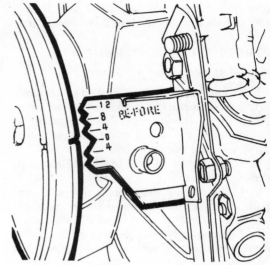

Typical ignition timing marks

and Troubleshooting" sections. On 1975–77 HEI systems, the tachometer connects to the TACH terminal on the distributor (V8) or on the coil (six) and to a ground. On all 1978 and later systems, the tachometer connects to the TACH terminal and to a ground. Some tachometers must connect to the TACH terminal and to the positive battery terminal. Some tachometers won't work with HEI.

CAUTION: *Never ground the HEI TACH terminal; serious system damage will result.*

4. Aim the timing light at the pointer marks. Be careful not to touch the fan, because it may appear to be standing still. If the pulley or damper notch isn't aligned with the proper timing mark (see the "Tune-Up Specifications" chart), the timing will have to be adjusted.

NOTE: *TDC or Top Dead Center corre-*

Aiming the timing light at the timing marks

sponds to 0 degrees. *B, or BTDC, or Before Top Dead Center may be shown as BEFORE. A, or ATDC, or After Top Dead Center may be shown as AFTER.*

5. Loosen the distributor base clamp locknut. You can buy wrenches which make this task a lot easier on V8s. Turn the distributor slowly to adjust the timing, holding it by the body and not the cap. Turn the distributor in the direction of rotor rotation (found in the "Firing Order" illustration in Chapter 3) to retard, and against the direction of rotation to advance.

6. Tighten the locknut. Check the timing again, in case the distributor moved slightly as you tightened it.

7. Replace the distributor vacuum line. Correct the idle speed.

8. Stop the engine and disconnect the timing light.

Valve Adjustment

All of the engines used in the Blazer and Jimmy use hydraulic valve lifters which require no periodic adjustment. The valves must be adjusted whenever they are disturbed, such as after cylinder head removal and installation; this procedure is covered in Chapter 3.

Carburetor

See Chapter 4 for other carburetor adjustments.

IDLE SPEED AND MIXTURE ADJUSTMENT

Gasoline Engines

These procedures require the use of a tachometer. Tachometer hookup was explained earlier under Ignition Timing, Step 3. In some cases, the degree of accuracy required is greater than that available on a hand-held unit; a shop tachometer would be required to follow the instructions exactly. If the idle speed screws have plastic limiter caps (1971 and later), it is not recommended that they be removed unless a satisfactory idle cannot be obtained with them in place. If the caps are removed, exhaust emissions may go beyond the specified legal limits. This should be checked on an exhaust gas analyzer.

Idle speed and mixture are set with the engine at normal running temperature. The automatic transmission should be in Drive, except when specified in Neutral. The air conditioner should be off for adjusting mixture and off unless specified for setting idle speed.

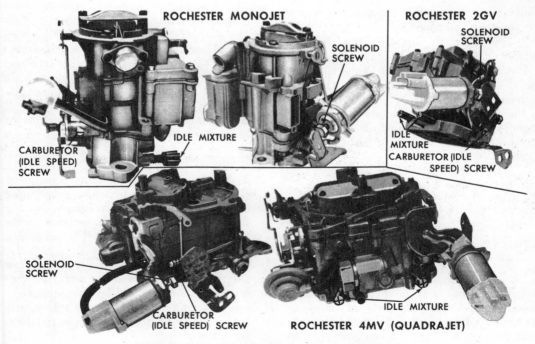

Typical idle speed and mixture screws, 1971 shown

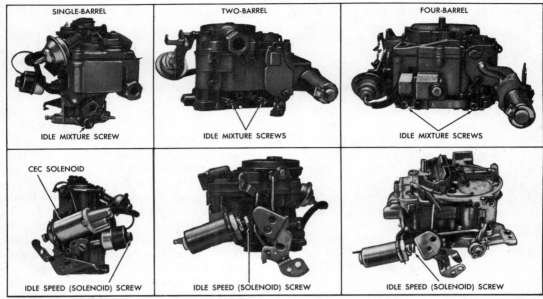

SINGLE-BARREL	TWO-BARREL	FOUR-BARREL
IDLE MIXTURE SCREW	IDLE MIXTURE SCREWS	IDLE MIXTURE SCREWS
CEC SOLENOID		
IDLE SPEED (SOLENOID) SCREW	IDLE SPEED (SOLENOID) SCREW	IDLE SPEED (SOLENOID) SCREW

Typical idle speed and mixture screws, 1972–74 shown

CAUTION: *Block the wheels, set the parking brake, and don't stand in front of the truck.*

1969

1. With the engine off, turn the idle mixture screw or screws in until they seat lightly, then back them out three turns.
2. With the air cleaner in place and the choke open, adjust the idle speed screw to get the specified speed.
3. Now adjust the mixture screw or screws equally to get the highest steady idle speed.
4. Correct the idle speed to the specified speed with the idle speed screw. On sixes with an idle speed solenoid, adjust the speed by turning the solenoid plunger hex nut. Disconnect the solenoid and adjust the low idle speed as necessary, using the carburetor idle speed screw.
5. Adjust one mixture screw in to get a 20 rpm drop in speed.
6. Turn the mixture screw out ¼ turn.
7. On V8s, repeat Steps 5 and 6 for the second mixture screw.
8. Correct the idle speed.

1970

1. Disconnect and plug the distributor vacuum line. Detach the fuel tank line from the evaporative canister. Turn the mixture screw or screws in until lightly seated, then back out four turns.

2. On sixes, adjust the solenoid hexnut to get 800 rpm—manual, 630 rpm—automatic in Drive. Adjust the mixture screw in to get the specified idle speed. Disconnect the solenoid and adjust the low idle speed as necessary, using the carburetor idle speed screw.
3. On 307 V8s, adjust the idle speed screw to get 800 rpm—manual; adjust the solenoid hexnut to get 630 rpm—automatic in Drive. Adjust the mixture screws in equally to get the specified idle speed. Disconnect the solenoid and adjust the low idle speed as necessary, using the carburetor idle speed screw.
4. On 350 V8s, adjust the idle speed screw to get 650 rpm—manual, 550—automatic in Drive. Adjust the mixture screws in equally to get the specified idle speed.
5. Reconnect the solenoid, distributor vacuum line, and evaporative canister line.

1971 IDLE SPEED ADJUSTMENT

1. Disconnect the distributor vacuum line and the fuel tank line from the evaporative canister. Plug the distributor vacuum line.
2. Use the carburetor idle speed screw to get the specified idle speed. Do not adjust the solenoid hexnut.

CAUTION: *If the Combination Emission Control (CEC) solenoid hex nut is used to set idle speed, you will be able to accelerate, but not decelerate. Details and adjustment of the CEC system are given in Chapter 4.*

3. Reconnect the hoses.

1972–74 IDLE SPEED ADJUSTMENT

1. Be sure the ignition timing is correct.
2. Disconnect the fuel tank vapor hose at the vapor canister.
3. Disconnect the vacuum advance hose at the distributor. Plug the hose. A golf tee is handy for this.
4. Start the engine.
5. On the 1 bbl carburetor:
   a. Turn the solenoid (clockwise to increase, counterclockwise to decrease) to obtain the curb idle speed as specified in the "Tune-Up" chart.
   b. Disconnect the wire at the solenoid.
   c. Using a ⅛ in. allen wrench, turn the allen wrench fitting at the end of the solenoid to adjust the idle to 450 rpm.
   d. Connect the wire.
6. On the 2 and 4 bbl carburetors:
   a. Disconnect the wire at the solenoid.
   b. With the idle speed adjusting screw on the low step of the cam, adjust the idle to 450 rpm with the screw.
   c. Connect the wire at the solenoid.
   d. Rev the engine momentarily to fully extend the solenoid plunger. Adjust the solenoid screw to obtain the curb idle speed listed in the "Tune-Up" chart.

1975 IDLE SPEED ADJUSTMENT

Six cylinder: Do not disconnect the distributor vacuum line. Disconnect the vapor canister "FUEL TANK" hose. With automatic transmission in Drive and manual in Neutral, adjust the solenoid to get the specified idle speed. Use a ⅛ in. Allen wrench in the end of the solenoid body to set the low idle speed to 450 rpm with the solenoid wire disconnected. Reset the idle speed with the air conditioning on, except on the 250 engine.

V8 with two barrel carburetor: Disconnect the vapor canister "FUEL TANK" hose. Leave the distributor vacuum advance hose in place. Adjust the idle speed screw to get the specified idle speed with automatic in Drive and manual in Neutral.

Light duty V8 with four barrel carburetor: Disconnect the vapor canister "FUEL TANK" hose. Leave the distributor vacuum advance hose in place. Disconnect the solenoid wire. Place automatic in Drive and manual in Neutral. Turn the low idle speed screw on the carburetor to get about 450 rpm. Connect the solenoid wire and open the throttle slightly, so that the solenoid plunger can extend. Turn the plunger screw to get the specified idle speed.

Heavy duty V8 with four barrel carburetor: This adjustment is the same as for 1976. Reset the idle speed with the air conditioner on.

1976 IDLE SPEED ADJUSTMENT

Six cylinder: Disconnect and plug the "CARBURETOR" and "PCV" vapor canister hoses on the 250. Disconnect the canister "FUEL TANK" hose on the 292. If the engine has a vacuum advance hose running directly from the vacuum source to the distributor vacuum advance unit, disconnect and plug it.
   NOTE: *Automatic transmission models should be in Drive with parking brake on and safety methods applied.*
Turn the solenoid to get the specified idle speed. Disconnect the solenoid wire and turn off the air conditioner. Use a ⅛ in. Allen wrench in the end of the solenoid body to set the low idle speed to 450 rpm.

V8 with two barrel carburetor: This procedure is the same as 1975, except that the canister hose can be left in place.

Light duty V8 with four barrel carburetor: Place the automatic in Drive and manual in Neutral. Set the idle speed screw on the carburetor to obtain the specified rpm.

Heavy duty V8 with four barrel carburetor: Disconnect the vapor canister "FUEL TANK" hose on California models. Leave the vacuum advance hose in place. Turn the air conditioner on. Set the automatic in Park and manual in Neutral. Set the idle speed screw on the carburetor to obtain the specified rpm.

1977 IDLE SPEED ADJUSTMENT

See the underhood emission sticker for any hoses or wires that may need to be disconnected.

1 bbl: Start the engine and allow it to run until it reaches normal operating temperature. Be sure the choke is fully open and the cam follower is off the steps of the cam. Turn the nut on the end of the solenoid to obtain the specified rpm. See the Tune-Up chart. Disconnect the wire from the solenoid and turn the ⅛ in. allen head screw in the end of the solenoid to set the base idle to specification. Refer to the Tune-Up chart or the underhood emission sticker. Reconnect the wire.

2 and 4 bbl: Be sure the ignition timing is correct. Refer to the underhood emission sticker in order to prepare the vehicle for adjustment.

On carburetors without a solenoid: Be sure the idle speed screw is on the low step of the fast idle cam. Turn the screw to obtain the idle specified in the Tune-Up chart.

On carburetors with a solenoid: Turn the idle screw to obtain the idle speed specified in the Tune-Up chart. Disconnect the electrical lead from between the solenoid and the A/C compressor at the compressor and turn the A/C On. Place the automatic transmission in Drive. Open the throttle momentarily to fully extend the solenoid plunger. Turn the solenoid screw to obtain the base idle speed as specified in the Tune-Up chart or on the emission sticker. Reconnect the electrical lead at the compressor.

1978 IDLE SPEED ADJUSTMENT

1 bbl: The idle speed adjusting procedure is the same as 1977. Refer to the Tune-Up chart for the correct idle speed.

2 bbl: Be sure the ignition timing is correct. Refer to the underhood emission sticker in order to prepare the vehicle for adjustment.

On carburetors without a solenoid: This procedure is the same as 1977. See the Tune-Up chart for the correct idle speed.

On models with a solenoid and without air conditioning: Rev the engine momentarily to fully extend the solenoid plunger. Turn the solenoid screw to obtain the curb idle speed listed in the Tune-Up chart. Disconnect the wire from the solenoid. Turn the idle speed screw to obtain the solenoid idle speed listed on the underhood emission sticker. Reconnect the wire at the solenoid.

On models with air conditioning: Turn the idle speed screw to obtain the idle speed listed in the Tune-Up chart. Disconnect the wire at the A/C compressor and turn the A/C On. Rev the engine momentarily to fully extend the solenoid plunger. Turn the solenoid screw to obtain the solenoid idle speed listed on the underhood emission sticker. Reconnect the wire at the compressor.

4 bbl: Refer to the underhood emission sticker and prepare the vehicle for adjustment as specified on the sticker. On models without a solenoid, turn the idle speed screw to obtain the idle speed listed in the Tune-Up chart. On models with a solenoid, turn the idle speed screw to obtain the idle speed listed in the Tune-Up chart. Disconnect the wire at the A/C compressor and turn the A/C On. Rev the engine momentarily to fully extend the solenoid plunger. Turn the solenoid screw to obtain the solenoid idle speed listed

on the underhood emission sticker. Reconnect the A/C wire at the compressor.

1979–82 IDLE SPEED ADJUSTMENT

1 bbl: This procedure is the same as 1977. Refer to the Tune-Up chart for the correct idle speed.

2 bbl (six cylinder): Be sure the ignition timing is correct. Refer to the underhood emission sticker and prepare the engine for adjustment as specified on the sticker. Rev the engine momentarily to fully extend the solenoid plunger. Turn the solenoid screw to obtain the curb idle speed as listed in the Tune-Up chart. Disconnect the wire at the solenoid and turn the idle speed screw to adjust the base idle. Refer to the Tune-Up chart or the underhood emission sticker. Reconnect the wire at the solenoid.

2 bbl (V8): Be sure the engine timing is correct. Refer to the underhood emission label in order to prepare the vehicle for adjustment. Turn the idle speed screw to adjust the curb idle speed. Disconnect the wire from the solenoid to the A/C compressor at the compressor and turn the A/C On. Open the throttle momentarily to fully extend the solenoid plunger. Turn the solenoid screw to obtain the base idle speed. Refer to the Tune-Up chart or the underhood emission sticker for the correct speeds.

4 bbl: This procedure is the same as for 1977.

1971–73 IDLE MIXTURE ADJUSTMENT

1. Break off the idle mixture screw limiter cap or caps. Detach the distributor vacuum line and the fuel tank line from the evaporative canister. Plug the distributor vacuum line. Turn the mixture screw or screws in until they seat lightly, then back them out four turns.

2. Adjust the idle stop solenoid or carburetor idle speed screw to obtain the speed shown in the "Initial Idle Speed Setting Chart."

3. If the initial idle speed setting didn't specify Lean Drop, adjust the idle mixture screws in equally to obtain the idle speed specified in the "Tune-Up Specifications Chart."

4. If the initial idle speed setting specified Lean Drop, turn the idle speed screws in equally to get a speed decrease of 20 rpm, then turn them out ¼ turn. Adjust the idle stop solenoid or carburetor idle speed screw

to obtain the idle speed specified in the "Tune-Up Specifications Chart."

NOTE: *Most 1973 and later four barrel carburetors have an internal idle fuel passage restriction; beyond a certain limited point, turning the idle mixture screws out has no further richening effect.*

5. Install new limiter caps. Replace the hoses.

1974–76 IDLE MIXTURE ADJUSTMENT

1. Apply the parking brake and block the wheels.

2. Be sure the ignition timing and the idle speed are set correctly. These adjustments must be made before the mixture can be adjusted. The engine must be warmed up.

3a. On 1974 models, disconnect the fuel tank vapor hose from the evaporative canister and disconnect and plug the vacuum advance hose at the distributor. Place the transmission in Neutral.

b. On 1975 models, disconnect the fuel tank vapor hose at the evaporative canister. Place the automatic transmission in Drive and the manual transmission in Neutral.

c. On the 1976 models, disconnect the fuel tank vapor hose at the evaporative canister. If the vehicle is equipped with a vacuum hose which runs uninterrupted from BELOW the carburetor to the distributor, leave that hose connected. On all other models, disconnect and plug the vacuum advance hose at the distributor. Place the transmission in Neutral.

4. Remove the air cleaner and carefully cut or break off the idle mixture screw limiter cap. Install the air cleaner.

5. Turn the air conditioning Off.

6. On 1976 models, turn the idle mixture screw or screws to obtain the maximum possible rpm. If there are two mixture screws, be sure to adjust them equally, about ⅛ turn at a time.

7. Set the idle speed to the rpm listed in the "Initial Idle Speed Chart" by turning the solenoid screw. If the carburetor is not equipped with a solenoid, use the idle speed screw.

8. On 1974–75 models, perform Step 6.

9. Equally turn in the mixture screw or screws to obtain the idle speed listed in the "Tune-Up" chart.

10. Connect all hoses.

1977 IDLE MIXTURE ADJUSTMENT

1. Apply the parking brake and block the wheels.

2. Remove the air cleaner for access to the carburetor but leave all the hoses attached.

3. Be sure the idle speed and ignition timing is adjusted correctly. These must be correct before the mixture can be set.

4. Remove the plastic limiter caps from the mixture screws.

5. Lightly seat the screw(s), then back it out so the engine will just barely run. If equipped with two mixture screws, always adjust them equally.

6. Place the transmission in Neutral.

7. Back out the mixture screw(s) ⅛ turn at a time to obtain the maximum possible rpm. Turn the idle speed solenoid or screw to obtain the rpm listed in the "Initial Idle Speed Chart."

8. Turn the mixture screw(s) in to obtain 600 rpm for the 1 bbl and 700 rpm for the 2 bbl and 4 bbl.

9. Reset the idle speed solenoid or the idle speed screw to obtain the idle speed listed in the "Tune-Up" chart.

10. Connect all hoses and replace the air cleaner.

1978–82 IDLE MIXTURE ADJUSTMENT

A change has been made in GM carburetors which limits the effect of the mixture screw for rich adjustment. In other words, backing out the screw will have little or no effect. Artificial enrichment by means of propane is necessary for proper mixture adjustment. The equipment necessary for this procedure is not readily available to the general public.

Diesel Engine

SLOW IDLE ADJUSTMENT

1. Run the engine until it reaches normal operating temperature.

2. Set the parking brake and block the drive wheels.

3. Remove the air cleaner and turn all accessories off.

4. Install a diesel tachometer.

5. Turn the low idle speed screw on the injection pump until the proper idle is obtained. Automatic transmissions should be in Drive and manual transmissions should be in Neutral.

6. Disconnect the tachometer and install the air cleaner.

FAST IDLE SPEED ADJUSTMENT

1. Run the engine until it reaches normal operating temperature.

2. Set the parking brake and block the drive wheels.

3. Disconnect the connector from the fast idle solenoid. Connect an insulated jumper wire between the positive battery terminal and the solenoid terminal. This will energize the terminal.

4. Open the throttle momentarily to ensure that the fast idle solenoid plunger is energized and fully extended.

5. Adjust the extended plunger by turning the hex head until the proper fast idle is obtained. The transmission should be in Neutral.

6. Remove the jumper wire, reinstall the solenoid connector and disconnect the tachometer.

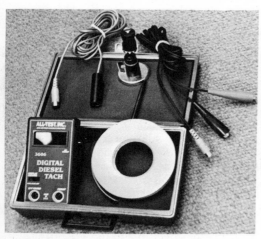

A typical diesel tachometer "kit"

Magnetic tape is placed at least 6 inches apart on the crankshaft balancer

The sensor unit is mounted to face the crankshaft balancer

The leads from the unit are connected to the battery and sensor. After the engine is started the idle rpm will show on the display of the unit if the sensor is aimed correctly at the crankshaft balancer

Engine and Engine Rebuilding

ENGINE ELECTRICAL

Distributor

REMOVAL AND INSTALLATION

1969–74

1. Remove the distributor cap and position it out of the way.

2. Disconnect the primary coil wire (the thin wire) and the vacuum advance line(s).

3. Scribe a mark on the distributor body and the engine block showing their relationship. Mark the distributor housing to show the direction in which the rotor is pointing. Note the positioning of the vacuum advance unit.

4. Remove the distributor hold-down bolt.

5. Slowly pull the distributor up. The rotor will turn a little bit as it is removed. Carefully note the position of the rotor when it stops turning. This is the position that the distributor must be in when the distributor is installed.

To install the distributor with the engine undisturbed:

6. Carefully insert the distributor into the block with the rotor positioned as outlined in the previous step. The rotor will turn slightly as the distributor is inserted and return to its original position.

7. Install the retaining clamp and bolt. Install the distributor cap, primary wire, and the vacuum hose(s).

8. Start the engine and check the ignition timing.

To install the distributor with the engine disturbed (engine was turned while the distributor was out) or to install a new distributor:

9. Turn the engine to bring the No. 1 piston to the top of its compression stroke. This may be determined by covering the No. 1 spark plug hole with your thumb and slowly turning the engine. When the timing mark on the crankshaft pulley aligns with the 0 on

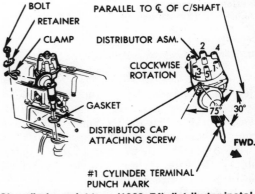

Six cylinder point type (1969–74) distributor installation

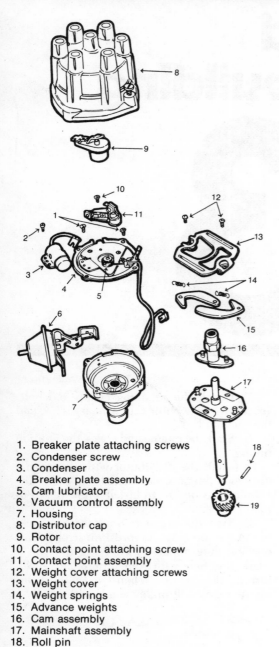

1. Breaker plate attaching screws
2. Condenser screw
3. Condenser
4. Breaker plate assembly
5. Cam lubricator
6. Vacuum control assembly
7. Housing
8. Distributor cap
9. Rotor
10. Contact point attaching screw
11. Contact point assembly
12. Weight cover attaching screws
13. Weight cover
14. Weight springs
15. Advance weights
16. Cam assembly
17. Mainshaft assembly
18. Roll pin
19. Drive gear

Six cylinder point type distributor

1. Condenser
2. Contact point assembly
3. Cam lubricator (through 1972)
4. Retaining ring
5. Breaker plate
6. Felt washer
7. Plastic seal
8. Vacuum advance unit
9. Housing
10. Shim washer
11. Drive gear pin
12. Drive gear
13. Cap
14. Rotor
15. Weight springs
16. Mainshaft
17. Advance weights
18. Cam weight base assembly

V8 point type distributor

the timing scale and your thumb is pushed out by compression, No. 1 piston is at top-dead-center (TDC). If you don't feel compression, you've got No. 6 at TDC.

10. Align the distributor to the engine block so that the vacuum advance unit points in the correct direction.

11. Turn the rotor so that it will point to the No. 1 terminal in the cap. Some distrib-

utors have a punch mark on the gear facing the same way as the rotor tip.

12. Install the distributor into the engine block. It may be necessary to turn the rotor a little in either direction in order to engage the gears.

13. Tap the starter a few times to ensure

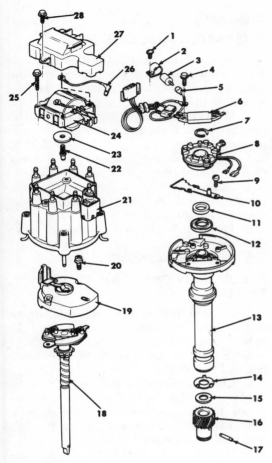

1. Screw
2. Bracket
3. Capacitor
4. Screw
5. Wiring Harness Assy.
6. Module Assembly
7. Thin "C" Washer (Retainer)
8. Pole Piece and Plate Assy. (Pick-Up Coil)
9. Screw
10. Plastic Retainer
11. Felt Washer
12. Plastic Grease Retainer Seal
13. Housing Assembly
14. Thrust Washer (V8 only)
15. Shim (V8 only)
16. Gear
17. Roll Pin
18. Distributor Shaft Assembly
19. Rotor
20. Screw
21. Distributor Cap
22. Resister Brush and Spring
23. Seal
24. Ignition Coil
25. Screw
26. Ground Lead
27. Cover
28. Screw

Exploded view of the HEI distributor

that the oil pump shart is mated to the distributor shaft.

14. Bring the engine to No. 1 TDC again and check to see that the rotor is indeed pointing toward the No. 1 terminal of the cap.

15. After correct positioning is assured, turn the distributor housing so that the points are just opening. Tighten the clamp.

16. Install the cap and primary wire. Check the ignition timing. Install the vacuum hose(s).

1975–82

1. Disconnect the wiring harness connectors at the side of the distributor cap.

2. Remove the distributor cap by turning the latches counterclockwise and lay it aside.

3. Disconnect the vacuum advance line(s).

4. Scribe a mark on the engine in line with the rotor and note the approximate position of the vacuum advance unit in relation to the engine.

5. Remove the distributor hold-down clamp and nut.

6. Slowly lift the distributor. The rotor will turn slightly as this is done. Carefully note the position of the rotor when it stops turning. This is the position it must be in when the distributor is installed.

7. Installation is the same as the point-type distributors.

Firing Order

To avoid confusion, replace the spark plug wires one at a time.

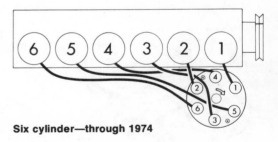

Six cylinder—through 1974

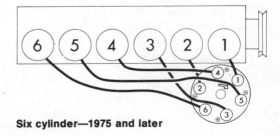

Six cylinder—1975 and later

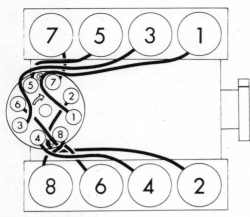

V8 through 1974

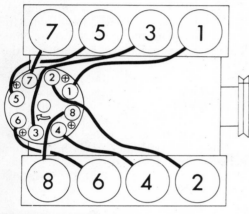

V8—1975 and later

Alternator
ALTERNATOR PRECAUTIONS

1. When installing a battery, ensure that the ground polarity of the battery and the ground polarity of the alternator and the regulator are the same.

2. When connecting a jumper battery, be certain that the correct terminals are connected.

3. When charging, connect the correct charger leads to the battery terminals.

4. Never operate the alternator on an open circuit. Be sure that all connections in the charging circuit are tight.

5. Do not short across or ground any of the terminals on the alternator or regulator.

6. Never polarize an AC system.

PRELIMINARY CHARGING SYSTEM TESTS

1. If you suspect a defect in your charging system, first perform these general checks before going on to more specific tests.

2. Check the condition of the alternator belt and tighten it if necessary.

3. Clean the battery cable connections at the battery. Make sure the connections between the battery wires and the battery clamps are good. Reconnect the negative terminal only and proceed to the next step.

4. With the key off, insert a test light between the positive terminal on the battery and

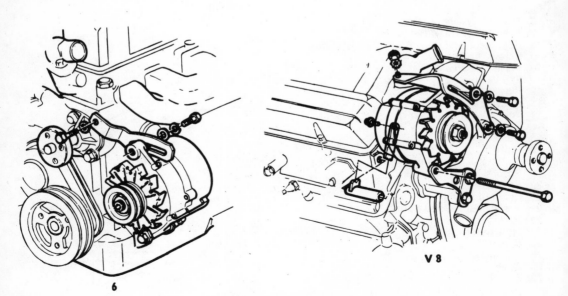

V 8

Typical alternator mounting

the disconnected positive battery terminal clamp. If the test light comes on, there is a short in the electrical system. The short must be repaired before proceeding. If the light does not come on, proceed to the next step.

NOTE: *If the truck is equipped with an electric clock, the clock must be disconnected.*

5. Check the charging system wiring for any obvious breaks or shorts.

6. Check the battery to make sure it is fully charged and in good condition.

CHARGING SYSTEM OPERATIONAL TEST

NOTE: *You will need a current indicator to perform this test. If the current indicator is to give an accurate reading, the battery cables must be the same gauge and length as the original equipment.*

1. With the engine running and all electrical systems turned off, place a current indicator over the positive battery cable.

2. If a charge of roughly five amps is recorded, the charging system is working. If a draw of about five amps is recorded, the system is not working. The needle moves toward the battery when a charge condition is indicated, and away from the battery when a draw condition is indicated.

3. If a draw is indicated, proceed with further testing. If an excessive charge (10–15 amps) is indicated, the regulator may be at fault.

ALTERNATOR OUTPUT TEST— ALTERNATOR WITH EXTERNAL REGULATOR

1. You will need a tachometer and a voltmeter for this test. You will also need a jumper wire.

2. Connect the tachometer to the engine.

3. Disconnect the wiring harness at the voltage regulator. With a jumper wire, connect the "F" wire to the number three wire in the wire harness plug.

4. Connect a voltmeter across the battery terminals, the positive voltmeter lead to the positive battery terminal and the negative lead to the negative terminal. Note the reading.

5. Start the engine and let it idle.

6. Gradually raise the engine speed to 1500–2000 rpm. The reading on the voltmeter should increase one to two volts over the initial reading. If there is no increase in the reading, the alternator is defective and must

be repaired. If the increase is greater than two volts, then the regulator is defective and must be adjusted or replaced. (See voltage adjustment in the regulator section).

OUTPUT TEST—ALTERNATOR WITH INTEGRAL REGULATOR

1. You will need an ammeter for this test.

2. Disconnect the battery ground cable.

3. Disconnect the wire from the battery terminal on the alternator.

4. Connect the ammeter negative lead to the battery terminal wire removed in step three, and connect the ammeter positive lead to the battery terminal on the alternator.

5. Reconnect the battery ground cable and turn on all electrical accessories. If the battery is fully charged, disconnect the coil wire and bump the starter a few times to partially discharge it.

6. Start the engine and run it until you obtain a maximum current reading on the ammeter.

7. If the current is within ten amps of the rated output of the alternator, the alternator is working properly. If the current is not within ten amps, insert a screwdriver in the test hole in the end frame of the alternator and ground the tab in the test hole against the side of the hole.

8. If the current is now within ten amps of the rated output, remove the alternator and have the voltage regulator replaced. If it is still below ten amps of rated output, have the alternator repaired.

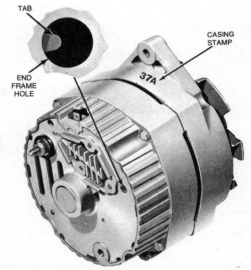

Alternator test hole and power rating location

REMOVAL AND INSTALLATION

1. Disconnect the battery ground cable to prevent diode damage.

2. Disconnect and tag all wiring to the alternator.

3. Remove the alternator brace bolt.

4. Remove the drive belt.

5. Support the alternator and remove the mounting bolt. Remove the alternator.

6. Install the unit on the truck using the reverse procedure of removal. Adjust the belt to have ½ in. deflection under moderate thumb pressure on its longest run.

Regulator

REMOVAL AND INSTALLATION

1969–72

1. Disconnect the ground cable from the battery.

2. Disconnect the wiring harness from the regulator.

3. Remove the mounting screws and remove the regulator.

4. Make sure that the regulator base gasket is in place before instllation.

5. Clean the attaching area for proper grounding.

6. Install the regulator. Do not overtighten the mounting screws, as this will cancel the cushioning effect of the rubber grommets.

1973–82

The regulator on these models is an integral part of the alternator. Alternator disassembly is required to replace it.

VOLTAGE ADJUSTMENT

1969–72

The standard voltage regulator is a conventional double contact unit, although an optional transistorized regulator was available.

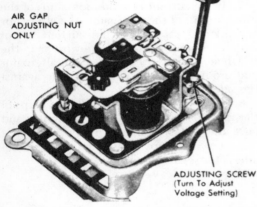

Conventional voltage regulator adjustment

Transistorized voltage regulator adjustment

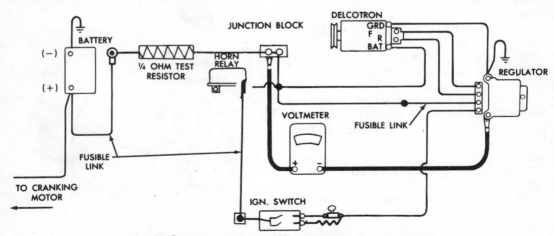

Voltage adjustment hookup for the 1969–72 external regulator

Alternator and Regulator Specifications

Year	Alternator			Regulator						
				Field Relay				Regulator		
	Part No.	Field Current @85°F 12 V (amps)	Output (amps)	Part No.	Air Gap (in.)	Point Gap (in.)	Volts to Close	Air Gap (in.)	Point Gap (in.)	Volts @85°F
'69–'71	1100834, 1100838	2.2–2.6	37	1119515	.015	.030	2.3–3.7	.067	.014	13.8–14.8
	1100839, 1100841, 1100842	2.2–2.6	42	1119515	.015	.030	2.3–3.7	.067	.014	13.8–14.8
	1100843, 1100849	2.2–2.6	61	1119515	.015	.030	2.3–3.7	.067	.014	13.8–14.8
'72	1102452, 1102440, 1102453, 1102456	2.2–2.6	37	1119515	.015	.030	1.5–3.2	.067	.014	13.5–14.4
	1102458, 1102459	2.2–2.6	42	1119515	.015	.030	1.5–3.2	.067	.014	13.5–14.4
	1102455, 1102463	2.2–2.6	61	1119515	.015	.030	1.5–3.2	.067	.014	13.5–14.4
'73–'82	See Casing Stamp			Integral with alternator						

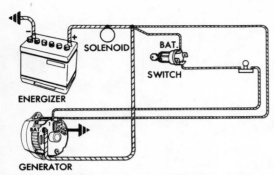

Simplified circuit diagram for the integral regulator alternator

Voltage adjustment procedures are the same for both types except for the point of adjustment. The double contact adjusting screw is located under the cover and the transistorized regulator is adjusted externally after removing an allen screw from the adjustment hole.

1. Insert a ¼ ohm-25 watt fixed resistor into the charging circuit at the relay junction block, between both leads and the terminal Use a ½ ohm-25 watt resistor for 1971–72.

2. Install a voltmeter as shown in the illustration.

3. Warm the engine by running it for several minutes at 1,500 rpm or more.

4. Cycle the voltage regulator by disconnecting and reconnecting the regulator connector.

5. Read the voltage on the voltmeter. If it is between 13.5 and 15.2, the regulator does not need adjustment or replacement. If the voltage is not within these limits, leave the engine running at 1,500 rpm.

6. Disconnect the four-terminal connector and remove the regulator cover (except on transistorized regulators). Reconnect the four-terminal connector and adjust the voltage to between 14.2 and 14.6 volts by turning the adjusting screw while observing the voltmeter.

7. Disconnect the terminal, install the cover, and then reconnect the terminal.

8. Continue running the engine at 1,500 rpm to re-establish the regulator internal temperature.

9. Cycle the regulator by disconnecting/reconnecting the regulator connector. Check the voltage. If the voltage is between 13.5 and 15.2, the regulator is good.

CAUTION: *Always disconnect the regulator before removing or installing the cover*

in order to prevent damage by short-circuiting.

1973–82

There is no voltage adjustment necessary or possible for the integral regulator.

Starter

REMOVAL AND INSTALLATION

1. Disconnect the battery ground cable at the battery.

2. Raise and support the vehicle.

3. Disconnect and tag all wires at the solenoid terminal.

NOTE: *1975–82 starters do not require the "R" terminal. The High Energy Ignition System does not need a cable from solenoid to ignition coil.*

4. Reinstall all nuts as soon as they are removed, since the thread sizes are different.

5. Remove the front bracket from the starter and the two mounting bolts. On engines with a solenoid heat shield, remove the front bracket upper bolt and detach the bracket from the starter.

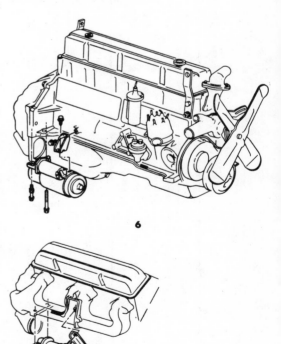

6

V 8

Typical starter installation

6. Remove the front bracket bolt or nut. Lower the starter front end first, and remove it from the truck.

7. Reverse the removal procedures to install the starter. Torque the two mounting bolts to 25–35 ft. lbs.

BRUSH REPLACEMENT

1. Disconnect the field coil connectors from the starter motor solenoid terminal.

2. Remove the through bolts.

3. Remove the end frame and the field frame from the driving housing.

4. Disassemble the brush assembly from the field frame by releasing the spring and removing the supporting pin. Pull the brushes and the brush holders out and disconnect the wiring.

5. Install the new brushes into the holders.

6. Assemble the brush holder using the spring and position the unit on the supporting pin.

7. Install the unit in the starter motor and attach the wiring.

8. Position the field frame over the armature.

9. Install the through bolts.

10. Connect the field coil connectors to the solenoid.

STARTER DRIVE REPLACEMENT

1. Remove the starter motor as previously outlined.

2. Disconnect the field coil connections from the solenoid terminal.

3. Remove the through bolts.

4. Remove the commutator end frame and the field frame assembly from the housing.

5. Remove the armature assembly from the housing. On some models it may be necessary to remove the solenoid and the shift lever assembly from the housing first.

6. Remove the thrust collar from the shaft.

7. Slide a small piece of ½ in. pipe over the end of the shaft so the end of the pipe butts against the edge of the retainer. Carefully tap the end of the pipe with a hammer, driving the retainer towards the armature end of the snap ring.

8. Remove the snap ring from the groove.

9. Slide the retainer and clutch off the shaft.

To assemble the drive mechanism:

1. Slide the drive assembly onto the armature shaft after it has been lubricated with a silicone lubricant.

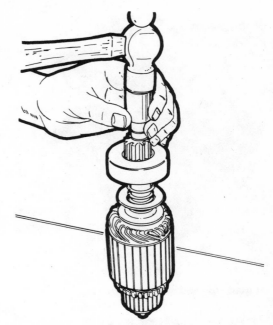

Driving the retainer off the snap ring

2. The retainer is positioned on the shaft with the cupped surface facing away from the pinion.

3. Place the snap-ring over the end of the shaft and slide it into its groove.

4. Place the thrust collar on the shaft with its shoulder next to the snap-ring.

5. Using two pliers, one on either side, force the snap-ring into the retainer.

6. Lubricate the drive housing bushing and slide the armature shaft into the starter housing.

7. Assemble the commutator end of the starter after lubricating the bushing and placing the leather brake washer in position.

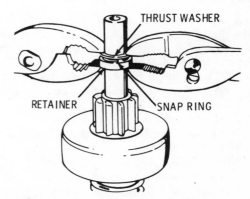

Installing the snap ring on the retainer

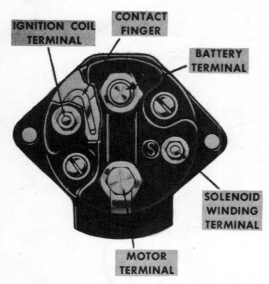

IGNITION COIL TERMINAL

CONTACT FINGER

BATTERY TERMINAL

SOLENOID WINDING TERMINAL

MOTOR TERMINAL

Starter solenoid terminals

SOLENOID REPLACEMENT

1. Remove the screw and washer from the motor connector strap terminal.

2. Remove the two solenoid retaining screws.

3. Twist the housing clockwise to remove the flange key from the keyway in the housing. Then remove the housing.

4. To install the unit, place the return spring on the plunger and place the solenoid body on the drive housing. Turn counterclockwise to engage the flange key. Place the two retaining screws in position and install the screw and washer which secures the strap terminal. Install the unit on the starter.

Battery

Refer to Chapter 1 for details on the battery.

REMOVAL AND INSTALLATION

1. Disconnect the negative (ground) cable and then the positive cable terminal. Special pullers are available to remove clamp-type battery terminals.

NOTE: *To avoid sparks, always disconnect the battery ground cable first, and connect it last.*

2. Remove the hold-down clamp.

3. Remove the battery, being careful not to spill the acid.

NOTE: *Spilled acid can be neutralized with a baking soda/water solution. If you somehow get acid into your eyes, flush with lots of water and visit a doctor.*

4. Clean the cable terminals of any corrosion using a wire brush.

5. Install the battery. Replace the holddown clamp.

6. Connect the positive and then the negative cable terminal. Do not hammer them in place. The terminals should be coated lightly (externally) with grease or petroleum jelly to prevent corrosion.

CAUTION: *Make absolutely sure that the battery is connected properly before you start the engine. Reversed polarity can destroy your alternator and regulator in a matter of seconds.*

ENGINE MECHANICAL

Design

GASOLINE ENGINE

All Blazer and Jimmy engines are water-cooled, overhead valve powerplants, using cast iron cylinder blocks and heads.

The 250 cu in., inline six cylinder engine crankshaft has seven main bearings, with the thrust taken by No. 7. This results in a very rigid crankshaft assembly. The camshaft is low in the block and driven by gears rather than the usual chains and sprockets. Fairly long pushrods actuate the valves through ball-mounted rocker arms. This engine has changed very little over the years, giving a great interchangeability of parts. A major change was introduced in 1975. This is an integral cylinder head and intake manifold casting. The integral design results in better emission control and more power and economy.

The small-block family of V8 engines, 305-307-350-400 cu in., are all derived from the innovative design of the original 1955 265 cu in. Chevrolet V8. This engine introduced the ball-mounted rocker arm design, replacing the once-standard shaft mounted rocker arms. There is extensive interchangeability of components among these engines, extending to the several other small-block displacement sizes available in passenger cars. The 400 cu in. version differs in block design; it does not have cooling passages between the cylinders, as on the smaller V8s.

NOTE: *Don't confuse the Blazer/Jimmy 400 with the big-block engine used in passenger cars, identified variously as 396, 400, or 402 cu in. The small-block engine can quickly be identified by the placement of the distributor at the rear.*

DIESEL ENGINE

The 6.2 liter, 379 cu in. V8, 4 cycle diesel is developed and produced by Chevrolet. It is a totally new engine designed specifically for truck application with heavy duty usage in mind.

The base of the engine (short block) is very similar in design to a V8 gasoline engine; the major difference being the cylinder heads, combustion chamber, fuel distribution system, air intake manifold and the method of ignition. The cylinder block, crankshaft, main bearings, connecting rods and pistons look much the same as their gasoline engine counterparts, although they are of much heavier construction due to the higher compression ratio required to ignite diesel fuel. The intake and exhaust manifolds are of special design and construction.

The cylinder head incorporates a 17 bolt head design which locates 5 bolts around each cylinder. This helps gasket durability. It also includes a high swirl pre-combustion chamber which mixes fuel and air to provide an efficient fuel burn and low emissions. A special cavity in the piston top further assists in mixing the combustion products for complete burning.

Main bearing caps all use 4 bolts instead of the normal 2 to provide rigid support for the crankshaft and minimize stress. The rolled fillet nodular iron crankshaft utilizes a torsional damper, tuned to reduce vibrations.

The engine also uses 3 roller hydraulic lifters running on a forged steel camshaft.

Engine Removal and Installation

Gasoline Engines

1969–76

1. Disconnect the negative battery cable, then the positive battery cable.
2. Drain the cooling system.
3. Remove the air cleaner.
4. Scribe matchmarks on the hood hinges for reassembly and remove the hood.
5. Remove the radiator and fan shroud as outlined later in this chapter.
6. Disconnect and label (to avoid confusion) the wires at the following locations:
   a. starter solenoid
   b. alternator
   c. temperature sending switch
   d. oil pressure sending switch
   e. coil
   f. vacuum advance solenoid and/or the CEC solenoid
   g. TCS solenoid (V8, if so equipped)
7. Disconnect the:
   a. accelerator linkage at the manifold
   b. fuel line from the tank at the fuel pump
   c. heater hoses at the engine block
   d. oil pressure gauge and the vacuum lines at the engine
   e. evaporative emission system lines at the carburetor (on 1978 and later models, the hose at the fuel vapor storage canister)
   f. power steering pump at the mounting bracket (lay the pump aside without disconnecting any of the lines)
   g. ground straps at the engine block
   h. exhaust pipe at the manifold (hang the pipe from the frame with a wire)
   i. TCS switch at the transmission (V8, if so equipped)
   j. vacuum line to the power brake unit at the manifold
8. If equipped with air conditioning, unbolt the compressor at the bracket and lay it aside.

CAUTION: *Do not disconnect any of the refrigerant lines. Evacuation of the air conditioning system should only be performed by someone who has the proper skill and training to do so, as the refrigerant will instantly freeze anything it contacts, including your eyes.*

9. Unbolt the engine fan and remove the fan and pulley.
10. On manual transmission models:
    a. Disconnect the clutch fork return spring at the fork.

Lifting tackle installed on the V8 engine

General Engine Specifications

Year	Engine No. Cyl Displacement (cu in.)	Carburetor Type	Horsepower @ rpm ■	Torque @ rpm (ft. lbs.) ■	Bore x Stroke (in.)	Compression Ratio	Min Oil Pressure @ 2000 rpm
'69–'70	6—250	1 bbl	155 @ 4200	235 @ 1600	3.875 x 3.530	8.5 : 1	40
	8—307	2 bbl	200 @ 4600	300 @ 2400	3.875 x 3.250	9.0 : 1	40
	8—350	4 bbl	255 @ 4600	355 @ 3000	4.000 x 3.480	9.0 : 1	40
'71	6—250	1 bbl	145 @ 4200	235 @ 1600	3.875 x 3.530	8.5 : 1	40
	8—307	2 bbl	200 @ 4600	300 @ 2400	3.875 x 3.250	9.0 : 1	40
	8—350	4 bbl	250 @ 4600	350 @ 3000	4.000 x 3.480	8.5 : 1	40
'72	6—250	1 bbl	110 @ 3800	185 @ 1600	3.875 x 3.530	8.5 : 1	40
	8—307	2 bbl	135 @ 4000	230 @ 2400	3.875 x 3.250	8.5 : 1	40
	8—350	4 bbl	175 @ 4000	290 @ 2400	4.000 x 3.480	8.5 : 1	40
'73	6—250	1 bbl	100 @ 3800	175 @ 2000	3.875 x 3.530	8.25 : 1	40
	8—307	2 bbl	115 @ 3600	205 @ 2000	3.875 x 3.250	8.5 : 1	40
	8—350	4 bbl	155 @ 4000	255 @ 2400	4.000 x 3.480	8.5 : 1	40
'74	6—250	1 bbl	100 @ 3600	175 @ 1800	3.875 x 3.530	8.25 : 1	40
	8—350	2 bbl	145 @ 3800	250 @ 2200	4.000 x 3.480	8.5 : 1	40
	8—350	4 bbl	160 @ 3800	250 @ 2400	4.000 x 3.480	8.5 : 1	40
'75	6—250	1 bbl	105 @ 3800	185 @ 1200	3.875 x 3.530	8.25 : 1	40
	8—350	2 bbl	145 @ 3800	250 @ 2200	4.000 x 3.480	8.5 : 1	40
	8—350	4 bbl	160 @ 3800	250 @ 2400	4.00 x 3.480	8.5 : 1	40
	8—400	4 bbl	175 @ 3600	290 @ 2800	4.125 x 3.750	8.5 : 1	40
'76	6—250	1 bbl	100 @ 3600	175 @ 1800	3.875 x 3.530	8.25 : 1	40
	8—350	4 bbl	165 @ 3800	255 @ 2800	4.000 x 3.480	8.5 : 1	40
	8—400	4 bbl	175 @ 3600	290 @ 2800	4.125 x 3.750	8.5 : 1	40
'77	6—250	1 bbl	100 @ 3600	175 @ 1800	3.875 x 3.530	8.25 : 1	40
	8—305	2 bbl	140 @ 3800	235 @ 2000	3.736 x 3.480	8.5 : 1	40

General Engine Specifications (cont.)

Year	Engine No. Cyl Displacement (cu in.)	Carburetor Type	Horsepower @ rpm ■	Torque @ rpm (ft. lbs.)■	Bore x Stroke (in.)	Compression Ratio	Min Oil Pressure @ 2000 rpm
'77	8—350	4 bbl	165 @ 3800	255 @ 2800	4.000 x 3.480	8.5:1	40
	8—400	4 bbl	175 @ 3600	290 @ 2800	4.125 x 3.750	8.5:1	40
'78	6—250	1 bbl	110 @ 3800	195 @ 1600	3.875 x 3.530	8.3:1	40
	8—305	2 bbl	145 @ 3800	245 @ 2400	3.736 x 3.480	8.5:1	40
	8—350	4 bbl	165 @ 3800	255 @ 2800	4.000 x 3.480	8.5:1	40
	8—400	4 bbl	175 @ 3600	290 @ 2800	4.125 x 3.750	8.5:1	40
'79–'80	6—250	2 bbl	130 @ 3500	210 @ 2400	3.875 x 3.530	8.3:1	40
	8—305	2 bbl	140 @ 4000	240 @ 2000	3.736 x 3.480	8.4:1	45
	8—350	4 bbl	165 @ 3800	270 @ 2000	4.000 x 3.480	8.2:1	45
	8—400	4 bbl	175 @ 3600	290 @ 2800	4.125 x 3.750	8.5:1	40
'81	6—250	2 bbl	130 @ 4000	210 @ 2000	3.870 x 3.530	8.3:1	40–60
	6—250 Calif	2 bbl	130 @ 4000	205 @ 2000	3.870 x 3.530	8.3:1	40–60
	8—305	2 bbl	135 @ 4200	235 @ 2400	3.740 x 3.480	8.5:1	45
	8—305	4 bbl	155 @ 4400	252 @ 2400	3.740 x 3.480	9.2:1	45
	8—350 LD	4 bbl	175 @ 4000	275 @ 2000	4.000 x 3.480	8.2:1	45
	8—350 HD	4 bbl	165 @ 3800	255 @ 2800	4.000 x 3.480	8.3:1	45
'82	6—250	2 bbl	130 @ 4000	210 @ 2000	3.870 x 3.530	8.3:1	40–60
	8—305	4 bbl	140 @ 4200	240 @ 2400	3.740 x 3.480	8.5:1	45
	8—305	4 bbl	155 @ 4400	252 @ 2100	3.740 x 3.480	9.2:1	45
	8—350 LD	4 bbl	175 @ 4000	275 @ 2000	4.000 x 3.480	8.2:1	45
	8—350 HD	4 bbl	165 @ 3800	255 @ 2800	4.000 x 3.480	8.3:1	45
	8—379	Diesel	130 @ 3600	240 @ 2000	3.980 x 3.800	21.5:1	45

■Starting 1972 horsepower and torque are SAE net, rather than gross figures. They are measured at the rear of the transmission with all engine accessories installed and operating. Since the figures vary when a given engine is installed in different models, some are representative rather than exact.

Ring Side Clearance

All measurements are given in inches

Year	Engine No. Cyl Displacement (cu in.)	Top Compression	Bottom Compression	Oil Control
'69–'82	6—250	.0012–.0027	.0012–.0032	.005 max
'69–'73	8—307	.0007–.0027	.0012–.0032	.005 max
'69–'82	8—305, 350, 400	.0012–.0032	.0012–.0032	.002–.007
'82	8—379 Diesel	.0030–.0070	.0015–.0031	.0016–.0038

Valve Specifications

Year	Engine No. Cyl Displacement (cu in.)	Seat Angle (deg)	Face Angle (deg)	Spring Test Pressure (lbs. @ in.)	Spring Installed Height (in.)*	Stem to Guide Clearance (in.)		Stem Diameter (in.)	
						Intake	Exhaust	Intake	Exhaust
'69–'82	6—250	46	45	60 @ 1.66	1²¹/₃₂	.0010–.0027	.0015–.0032	.3414	.3414
'69–'72	8—307, 350	46	45	80 @ 1.70	1²³/₃₂	.0010–.0027	.0010–.0027	.3414	.3414
'73–'82	8—305, 307, 350, 400	46	45	80 @ 1.70①	1²³/₃₂②	.0010–.0027	.0010–.0027③	.3414	.3414
'82	8—379 Diesel	④	⑤	80 @ 1.67	1⁴³/₆₄	.0010–.0027	.0015–.0032	.3429	.3424

*Plus or minus 1/32 in.
① Exhaust—80 @ 1.61 in.
② Exhaust—1¹⁹/₃₂ in. for 1977 and later, 1⅝ earlier.
③ .0012–.0029 for 400.
④ Intake—45°
   Exhaust—31°
⑤ Intake—44°
   Exhaust—30°

b. Disconnect the clutch pedal push rod at the cross shaft lever. Let the push rod hang from the lower lever.

c. At the frame end of the cross shaft, remove the ball stud and retaining nut.

d. Slide the shaft toward the engine, lift it up to clear the bracket and remove the shaft from the engine ball stud.

11. On the six cylinder, remove the rocker arm cover as outlined later in this chapter.

12. Attach a chain or lifting device to the brackets on the engine. If your engine doesn't have lifting eyes, good locations are under the intake manifold bolts on V8s or under the cylinder head bolts at either end on the sixes. You may need to remove the carburetor for clearance. Lift the engine slightly, just enough to take the weight off the motor mounts.

13. On four wheel drive models, support the transmission using a floor jack and disconnect it from the engine. Remove the engine mount bolts.

14. On two wheel drive models:

a. Remove the driveshaft as outlined in Chapter 7.

b. Disconnect the TCS switch at the transmission.

c. Disconnect the speedometer cable at the transmission.

d. Disconnect the shift linkage.

e. On manual transmission models, disconnect the clutch linkage.

Ring Gap

All measurements are given in inches

Year	Engine No. Cyl Displacement (cu in.)	Top Compression	Bottom Compression	Oil Control
'69–'82	6—250	.010–.020	.010–.020	.015–.055
'69–'73	8—307	.010–.020	.010–.020	.015–.055
'69–'76	8—350, 400	.010–.020	.013–.025	.015–.055
'77–'82	8—305, 350, 400	.010–.020	.010–.025	.015–.055
'82	8—379 Diesel	.012–.021	.030–.039	.0098–.020

Piston Clearance

Year	Engine No. Cyl Displacement (cu in.)	Piston to Bore Clearance (in.)
'69	6—250	.0005–.0014
'70–'77	6—250	.0005–.0015
'78–'82	6—250	.0010–.0020
'69–'70	8—307	.0005–.0011
'71–'73	8—307	.0012–.0018
'69	8—350	.0010–.0016
'70	8—350	.0012–.0022
'71–'76	8—350	.0007–.0013
'77–'82	8—305, 350	.0007–.0017
'75–'80	8—400	.0014–.0024
'82	8—379 Diesel	.0040–.0050

f. Remove the engine mount bolts.

g. Remove the transmission cooler lines, if so equipped.

h. Remove the rear mount crossmember.

i. Raise the engine and transmission slightly and check that everything is disconnected and ready for removal.

j. Pull the engine/transmission assembly forward and remove it from the vehicle.

15. On four wheel drive models:

a. Raise the engine slightly and pull it forward until it is disconnected from the transmission.

b. Raise the engine and remove it from the vehicle.

16. Reverse the removal procedure to install.

1977–82

1. Refer to steps 1–8 of the 1969–76 procedure.

2. Raise the vehicle on a hoist and drain the engine oil.

3. Disconnect the exhaust pipe at the manifold.

4. Remove the flywheel splash shield or the converter housing cover, as applicable.

5. Remove the starter motor as outlined earlier in this chapter.

6. On automatic transmission models remove the converter-to-flywheel attaching bolts.

7. Remove the engine mount through bolts.

8. On 1979 and later four wheel drive models, remove the strut rods at the engine mount.

9. Remove the engine-to-bellhousing attaching bolts.

10. Lower the vehicle from the hoist.

11. Using a floor jack, raise the transmission slightly.

12. Attach a lifting device to the engine and raise it slightly, taking the weight off the engine mounts.

13. Remove the engine mount-to-engine brackets.

14. Remove the engine.

15. Reverse the removal procedure to install.

Diesel Engine

1. Disconnect batteries.

2. Raise vehicle.

3. Remove transmission dust cover.

Crankshaft and Connecting Rod Specifications

All measurements are given in inches

Year	Engine No. Cyl Displacement (cu in.)	Crankshaft				Connecting Rod		
		Main Brg Journal Dia	Main Brg Oil Clearance	Shaft End-Play	Thrust on No.	Journal Diameter	Oil Clearance	Side Clearance
'69–'72	6—250	2.2983–2.2993	.0003–.0029	.002–.006	7	1.999–2.000	.0007–.0027	.009–.014
'73–'78	6—250	2.2983–2.2993	.0003–.0029	.002–.006	7	1.999–2.000	.0007–.0027	.006–.017
'79–'82	6—250	2.2979–2.2994	.0010–.0024 ⑦	.002–.006	7	1.999–2.000	.0010–.0030	.006–.017
'69	8—307	2.4484–2.4493 ①	.0008–.0024 ②	.003–.011	5	1.999–2.000	.0007–.0027	.009–.013
'69	8—350	2.4484–2.4493 ①	.0008–.0024 ②	.003–.011	5	2.099–2.100	.0007–.0028	.009–.013
'70	8—307, 350	2.4484–2.4493 ①	.0006–.0018 ③	.002–.006	5	2.199–2.200	.0007–.0028	.008–.014
'71–'76	8—307, 350	2.4484–2.4493 ①	.0011–.0023 ④	.002–.006	5	2.199–2.200	.0013–.0035	.008–.014
'77–'82	8—305, 350	2.4481–2.4490 ⑤	.0011–.0023 ④	.002–.006	5	2.199–2.200	.0013–.0035	.008–.014
'75–'77	8—400	2.6484–2.6493 ⑥	.0011–.0023 ④	.002–.006	5	2.199–2.200	.0013–.0035	.008–.014
'78–'79	8—400	2.6484–2.6493 ⑥	.0011–.0023 ④	.002–.006	5	2.0988–2.0998	.0013–.0035	.008–.014
'82	8—379 Diesel	⑧	⑨	.002–.007	5	2.3981–2.3991	.0018–.0039	.007–.025

① No. 5—2.4479–2.4488
② No. 5—.0017–.0033
③ No. 1—.0003–.0015
   No. 5—.0008–.0023
④ No. 1—.0008–.0020

⑤ No. 1—2.4484–2.4493
⑥ No. 5—2.4479–2.4488
   No. 5—2.6479–2.6488
⑦ No. 7—.0016–.0035

⑧ Nos. 1–4—2.9495–2.9504
   No. 5—2.9492–2.9502
⑨ Nos. 1–4—.0018–.0033
   No. 5—.0022–.0037

Torque Specifications
All readings in ft. lbs.

Year	Engine No. Cyl Displacement (cu in.)	Cylinder Head Bolts	Rod Bearing Bolts	Main Bearing Bolts	Crank-shaft Bolt	Flywheel to Crank-shaft Bolts	Manifold	
							Intake	Exhaust
'69–'71	6—250	95	35	65	—	60	30 ①	25 ②
'72	6—250	95	35	65	—	60	30	25 ②
'73–'74	6—250	95	35	65	—	60	35	30 ②
'75–'82	6—250	95	35	65	—	60	—	30 ③
'69–'73	8—307, 350	65	45	70	—	60	30	20 ④
'74–'82	8—305, 350, 400	65	45	70	60	60	30	20 ④
'82	8—379 Diesel	88–103	44–52	⑤	140–162	60	25–37	18–25

①End bolts—20
②Exhaust to intake
③20 on four end bolts with intake manifold integral with head, see bolt torque sequence illustration for more detail
④Inside bolts on 307 and 350—30
⑤Inner: 105–117
　Outer: 94–105

4. Disconnect torque converter.
5. Disconnect exhaust.
6. Remove starter bolts.
7. Disconnect wires and remove starter.
8. Remove transmission bell housing bolts.
9. Remove left motor mount bolts.
10. Remove right motor mount bolts.
11. Disconnect block heaters.
12. Remove wire harness, trans cooler lines and front battery cable clamp at oil pan.
13. Disconnect fuel return lines at engine.
14. Disconnect oil cooler lines at engine.
15. Remove lower fan shroud bolts.
16. Lower vehicle.
17. Remove hood.
18. Drain cooling system.
19. Remove air cleaner with resonator.
20. Remove primary filter from cowl.
21. Disconnect ground cable at alternator bracket.
22. Disconnect alternator wires and clips.
23. Disconnect TPS. EGR-EPR, fuel cut-off at injection pump.
24. Remove harness from clips at rocker covers. Disconnect the glow plugs.

25. Disconnect EGR-EPR solenoids, glow plugs, controller, temperature sender and move harness aside.
26. Disconnect ground strap, left side.
27. Remove fan.
28. Remove upper radiator hoses at engine.
29. Remove fan shroud.
30. Remove power steering pump and belt.
31. Remove power steering reservoir—lay pump and reservoir aside.
32. Disconnect vacuum at cruise servo and accelerator cable at injection pump.
33. Disconnect heater hose at engine.
34. Disconnect lower radiator hose at engine.
35. Disconnect oil cooler lines at radiator.
36. Disconnect heater hose and overflow at radiator.
37. Disconnect auto trans cooler lines.
38. Remove upper radiator cover.
39. Remove radiator.
40. Remove the detent cable.
41. Remove engine and support transmission.

42. Installation is in the reverse order. If fuel filters were removed, they must be filled with clean diesel fuel to avoid long cranking.

Cylinder Head
REMOVAL AND INSTALLATION
Six Cylinder

1. Drain the cooling system and remove the air cleaner. Disconnect the PCV hose. If equipped, disconnect the air injection hose.

2. Disconnect the accelerator pedal rod at the bellcrank on the manifold, and the fuel and vacuum lines at the carburetor.

3. Disconnect the exhaust pipe at the manifold flange, then remove the manifold bolts and clamps and remove the manifolds and carburetor as an assembly. On 1975 and later engines, remove the carburetor and the exhaust manifold.

4. Remove the fuel and vacuum line retaining clip from the water outlet. Then disconnect the wire harness from the temperature sending unit and coil, leaving the harness clear of clips on the rocker arm cover.

5. Disconnect the radiator hose at the water outlet housing and the battery ground strap at the cylinder head.

6. Disconnect the wires and remove the spark plugs. Disconnect the coil-to-distributor primary wire lead at the coil and remove the coil on models without HEI.

7. Remove the rocker arm cover. Back off the rocker arm nuts, pivot the rocker arms to clear the pushrods and remove the pushrods.

8. Remove the cylinder head bolts, cylinder head and gasket.

To install:

1. Place a new cylinder-head gasket over the dowel pins in the cylinder block with the bead up. Do not use sealer on composition steel/asbestos gaskets.

2. Guide and lower the cylinder head into place over the dowels and gasket.

3. Use sealant on the cylinder head bolts. Install and tighten them down snugly.

4. Tighten the cylinder head bolts a little at a time with a torque wrench in the correct sequence. Final torque should be as specified.

5. Install the valve pushrods down through the cylinder-head openings and seat them in their lifter sockets.

6. Install the rocker arms, balls and nuts and tighten the rocker arm nuts until all pushrod play is taken up.

7. Install the thermostat, the thermostat housing and the water outlet using new gaskets. Then connect the radiator hose.

8. Install the temperature sending switch.

9. Install the spark plugs.

10. Use new plug gaskets (if necessary) and torque to specifications. This is covered in Chapter 2.

11. Install the coil then connect the temperature sending unit and the coil primary wires, and the battery ground cable at the cylinder head.

12. Clean the surfaces and install a new gasket over the manifold studs. Install the manifold. Install the bolts and clamps and torque as specified.

13. Connect the throttle linkage.

14. Connect the PCV fuel and vacuum lines and secure the lines in the clip at the water outlet. Connect the air injection line.

15. Fill the cooling system and check for leaks.

16. Adjust the valves as explained later.

17. Install the rocker arm cover and position the wiring harness in the clips.

18. Clean and install the air cleaner.

V8 (Except Diesel)

1. Remove the intake manifold as described later.

2. Remove the exhaust manifolds as described later and tie out of the way.

3. If the vehicle is equipped with A/C, remove the compressor and the forward mounting bracket and lay the compressor aside. *Do not disconnect any of the refrigerant lines.*

4. Back off the rocker arm nuts and pivot the rocker arms out of the way so that the pushrods can be removed. Identify the pushrods so that they can be installed in their original positions.

5. Remove the cylinder head bolts and remove the heads.

6. Install the cylinder heads using new gaskets. Install the gaskets with the bead up.

NOTE: *Coat a steel gasket on both sides with sealer. If a composition gasket is used, do not use sealer.*

7. Clean the bolts, apply sealer to the threads, and install them hand tight.

8. Tighten the head bolts a little at a time in the sequence shown. Head bolt torque is listed in the "Torque Specifications" chart.

9. Install the intake and exhaust manifolds.

10. Install the A/C compressor.

11. Adjust the valves as explained later.

Diesel Engine

REMOVAL

1. Remove the fuel injection lines. Cap all lines, nozzles and fittings.

2. Remove the intake manifold.

3. Remove the rocker arm covers, after removing any accessory brackets that are in the way.

4. Drain the radiator and remove the dipstick tube.

5. Disconnect the ground wire at the cowl.

6. Raise and support the car, disconnect the exhaust pipe from the manifold and then lower the car.

7. If equipped with AC, remove the compressor and position it out of the way.

8. Remove the alternator.

9. Tag and disconnect the glow plug wires.

10. Remove the rocker arm assemblies and then remove the push rods. Mark the push rods for reinstallation. Keep the rocker arms and push rods in order so they can be installed in the same location.

11. Disconnect the radiator, by-pass and heater hoses.

12. Disconnect the ground strap.

13. Remove the thermostat housing/crossover at the head.

14. Remove the cylinder head bolts (17 on each side). The rear left head bolt may have to remain in the head upon removal.

15. Carefully lift off the cylinder head.

INSPECTION

1. Check for cracks in the exhaust ports, combustion chambers, or external cracks to the coolant chamber.

2. Check the valves for burned heads, cracked faces or damaged stems. Check the deck face for scratches or dents across the gasket fire-ring area. Marks across the coolant seal surfaces can be no deeper than .003 in.

NOTE: *Excessive valve stem to bore clearance will cause excessive oil combustion and may cause valve breakage. Insufficient clearance will result in noisy and sticky functioning of the valve and disturb engine smoothness.*

3. Measure valve stem clearance as follows:

a. Clamp a dial indicator on one side of the cylinder head rocker arm cover gasket rail.

b. Position the indicator so that the movement of the valve stem from side to side (crosswise to the head) will cause a direct movement of the indicator stem. The indicator stem must contact the valve stem just above the valve guide.

c. Drop the valve head about $1/16$ in. off the valve seat.

d. Move the stem from side to side using light pressure to obtain a clearance reading. If the clearance exceeds specifications, it will be necessary to ream the valve guides for oversize valves.

4. Use a spring tester and check the valve spring tension. Springs should be replaced if they are not within 10 lbs. of the specified load (without dampers).

INSTALLATION

1. Clean the cylinder head-to-engine block mating surfaces thoroughly. Install new head gaskets on the engine block. Do NOT coat the gaskets with any kind of sealer. The gaskets come with a special coating that eliminates the need for sealer. The use of any additional sealer will interfere with this coating and lead to leakage.

2. Carefully guide the cylinder head into place on the block. The left rear cylinder head bolt must be installed in the head prior to installation.

3. Coat the threads of the head bolts with sealing compound and then install them finger tight.

4. Tighten each bolt a little at a time (in the sequence illustrated) until the specified torque is achieved.

5. Installation of the remaining components is in the reverse order. Use RTV silicone sealant when installing the rocker arm covers.

CYLINDER HEAD TORQUE SEQUENCES

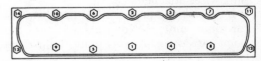

Six cylinder

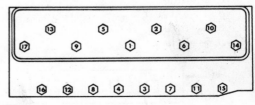

V8

VALVE LASH ADJUSTMENT

Gasoline Engines

All engines described in this book use hydraulic lifters, which require no periodic adjustment. In the event of cylinder head removal or any operation that requires disturbing the rocker arms, the valves will have to be adjusted.

1969–71

Normalize the engine temperature by running it for several minutes. Shut the engine off and remove the valve cover(s). After valve cover removal, torque the cylinder heads to specification. The use of oil stopper clips, readily available on the market is recommended to prevent oil splatter when adjusting valve lash. Restart the engine. Valve lash is set with the engine warm and idling.

Turn the rocker arm nut counterclockwise until the rocker arm begins to clatter. Reverse the direction and turn the rocker arm down slowly until the clatter just stops. This is the zero lash position. Turn the nut down an additional ¼ turn and wait ten seconds until the engine runs smoothly. Continue with additional ¼ turns, waiting ten seconds each time, until the nut has been turned down one full turn from the zero lash position. This one turn, pre-load adjustment must be performed to allow the lifter to adjust itself and prevents possible interference between the valves and pistons. Noisy lifters should be cleaned or replaced.

1972–82

1. Remove the rocker covers and gaskets.
2. Adjust the valves on six cylinder engines as follows:
    a. Mark the distributor housing with a piece of chalk at No. 1 and 6 plug wire positions. Remove the distributor cap with the plug wires attached.
    b. Crank the engine until the distributor rotor points to No. 1 cylinder and the points are open. At this point, adjust the following valves:
- No. 1—Exhaust and Intake
- No. 2—Intake
- No. 3—Exhaust
- No. 4—Intake
- No. 5—Exhaust

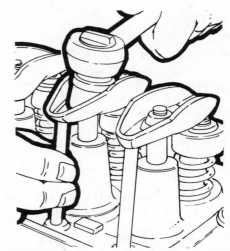

Adjusting the valves, 1972 and later. Six cylinder shown

    c. Back out the adjusting nut until lash is felt at the pushrod, then turn the adjusting nut in until all lash is removed. This can be determined by checking pushrod end-play while turning the adjusting nut. When all play has been removed, turn the adjusting nut in 1 full turn.
    d. Crank the engine until the distributor rotor points to No. 6 cylinder and the points are open. The following valves can be adjusted:
- No. 2—Exhaust
- No. 3—Intake
- No. 4—Exhaust
- No. 5—Intake
- No. 6—Intake and Exhaust
3. Adjust the valves on V8 engines as follows:
    a. Crank the engine until the mark on the damper aligns with the TDC or 0° mark on the timing tab and the engine is in No. 1 firing position. This can be determined by placing the fingers on the No. 1 cylinder valves as the marks align. If the valves do not move, it is in No. 1 firing position. If the valves move, it is in No. 6 firing position and the crankshaft should be rotated one more revolution to the No. 1 firing position.
    b. The adjustment is made in the same manner as 6 cylinder engines.

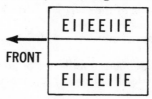

EIIEEIIE

FRONT ←

EIIEEIIE

V8 valve arrangement

FRONT ←   EIIEEIIEEIIE

Six cylinder valve arrangement

c. With the engine in No. 1 firing position, the following valves can be adjusted:

- Exhaust—1,3,4,8
- Intake—1,2,5,7

d. Crank the engine 1 full revolution until the marks are again in alignment. This is No. 6 firing position. The following valves can now be adjusted:

- Exhaust—2,5,6,7
- Intake—3,4,6,8

4. Reinstall the rocker arm covers using new gaskets.

5. Install the distributor cap and wire assembly.

VALVE GUIDE REMOVAL AND INSTALLATION

Valve guides are integral with the cylinder head on all engines. Valve guide bores may be reamed to accommodate oversize valves. If wear permits, valve guides can be knurled to allow the retention of standard valves. Maximum allowable valve stem-to-guide bore clearances are listed under "Valve specifications."

OVERHAUL

See the Engine Rebuilding Section at the end of this chapter.

Rocker Arm Cover
REMOVAL AND INSTALLATION

1. Disconnect the negative battery cable.
2. Remove the air cleaner.
3. Disconnect the crankcase ventilation hose at the rocker arm covers.
4. Disconnect the wiring from the rocker arm clips.
5. Remove the carburetor heat stove pipe, on models so equipped.
6. If the vehicle is equipped with A/C, remove the compressor rear brace. *Do not disconnect any of the refrigerant lines.*
7. Remove the rocker arm attaching bolts and remove the cover. If the cover is difficult to remove, gently tap the front of the cover rearward with your hand or a rubber mallet. If this still does not work, CAREFULLY pry the cover off. Be very careful not to distort the sealing surface or you'll be buying a new cover.
8. On installation, apply a $3/16$ in. bead of sealer to the mating surface after removing all the old loose sealer.
9. Reverse to install.

Rocker Arms
REMOVAL AND INSTALLATION
Gasoline Engines

Rocker arms are removed by removing the adjusting nut. Be sure to adjust the valve lash after replacing the rocker arms. Coat the replacement rocker arm and ball with an engine assembly lubricant before installation.

Rocker arm studs that have damaged threads or are loose in the cylinder heads may be replaced by reaming the bore and installing oversize studs. Oversizes available are 0.003 and 0.013 in. The bores may also be tapped and screw-in studs installed. Several aftermarket companies produce complete rocker arm stud kits with installation tools.

Diesel Engine

1. Remove the rocker arm covers.
2. Remove the rocker arm and shaft.
3. If the rocker arm is to be removed, remove the cotter pin and then remove the rocker arm from the shaft.
4. Lift out the push rods. The push rod upper end must be marked for reinstallation.
5. Install the push rods if removed. Make sure that the marked end is up, failure to do so could cause premature wear or damage.
6. Install the rocker arms and spring onto the shaft in the proper order.
7. Install the rocker arm assembly and tighten the bolts to 35 ft. lbs.
8. Installation of the remaining components is in the reverse order.

Intake Manifold
REMOVAL AND INSTALLATION
1969–74 Six Cylinder

The intake and exhaust manifolds are removed as an assembly.

NOTE: *The 1975–82 engine has an intake manifold intergal with the cylinder head.*

1. Disconnect the negative battery cable.
2. Remove the air cleaner.
3. Disconnect the throttle rods at the bellcrank and remove the throttle return spring.
4. Disconnect the fuel and vacuum lines at the carburetor. Plug the fuel line.
5. Disconnect the crankcase ventilation hose at the rocker arm cover.
6. Disconnect the fuel vapor hose at the canister, if so equipped.

7. Disconnect the exhaust pipe at the manifold flange and discard the packing.

8. Disconnect the EGR valve hose (if equipped).

9. Remove the manifold attaching bolts and clamps and remove the manifold assembly. Discard the gaskets.

10. The manifold assembly can be separated by removing 1 bolt and 2 nuts at the center. Don't tighten these to their final torque until the manifold assembly is installed on the engine.

11. Check the manifold for straightness along the exhaust port faces. If it is distorted more than 0.015 in. it should be replaced. Clean all mounting faces.

12. Installation is the reverse of removal. Use all new gaskets. Bolt torques are given in the Torque Specifications Chart.

V8 (Except Diesel)

1. Disconnect the negative battery cable.
2. Remove the air cleaner.
3. Drain the radiator.
4. Remove the alternator lower mounting bolts and position the unit aside.
5. Disconnect:

    a. Upper radiator and heater hoses at the manifold.

    b. Crankcase ventilation hoses as required.

    c. Fuel line at the carburetor.

    d. Accelerator linkage at the pedal lever.

    e. Vacuum hose at the distributor.

    f. Power brake hose at the carburetor base or manifold.

    g. Ignition coil (without HEI) and temperature sending switch wires.

6. Remove the distributor cap and mark the rotor position relative to the distributor body and the distributor body relative to the block.

7. Remove the distributor.

8. As required, remove the air cleaner bracket, and accelerator bellcrank.

9. Remove the manifold-to-head attaching bolts then remove the manifold and carburetor as an assembly.

10. If the manifold is to be replaced, transfer the carburetor (and mounting studs), water outlet and thermostat (use a new gasket) heater hose adapter, EGR valve (use new gasket) and, if applicable, the choke coil. 1975 and later engines use a carburetor heat choke tube which must be transferred to a new manifold, using a new gasket.

11. Before installing the manifold, thoroughly clean the gasket and seal surfaces of the cylinder heads and manifold.

12. Install the manifold end seals, and the manifold/head gaskets, using a sealing compound around the water passages and where seals butt to gaskets.

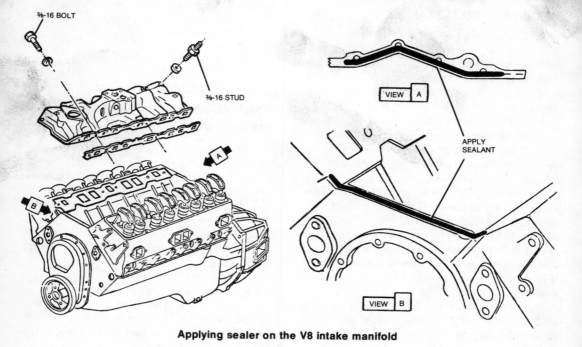

Applying sealer on the V8 intake manifold

Intake Manifold Torque Sequence

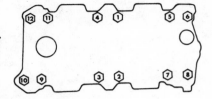

FRONT

V8

NOTE: *1974 and later 350 V8 engines require a new intake manifold side gasket. The new gasket has restricted cross-over ports. The 350 2-bbl uses a restricted cross-over gasket on the right-hand side and an open gasket on the left. The 350 4-bbl uses restricted cross-over gaskets on both sides.*

13. When installing the manifold, care should be taken not to dislocate the end seals. It is helpful to use a pilot in the distributor opening. Tighten the manifold bolts to the specified torque in the sequence illustrated.

14. Install the ignition coil.

15. Install the distributor with the rotor in its original location as indicated by the scribe line. If the engine has been disturbed, refer to "Distributor Removal and Installation."

16. If applicable, install the alternator upper bracket and adjust the belt tension.

17. Connect all components disconnected in Step 5.

18. Filling the cooling system, start the engine, check for leaks and adjust the ignition timing and carburetor idle speed and mixture.

Diesel Engine

Removal

1. Disconnect the batteries and remove the air cleaner.

2. Remove the crankcase ventilator tubes.

3. Disconnect the fuel lines and remove the secondary fuel filter.

4. Loosen the vacuum pump hold-down clamp and then rotate the pump in order to gain access to the manifold bolt.

5. Remove the intake manifold bolts. The injection line clips are retained by the same bolts.

6. Remove the intake manifold.

7. If any further operations are to be performed while the manifold is off, install screened covers or tape over the holes.

Installation

1. Remove the tape or screened cover if installed.

2. Make sure that the gasket surfaces are clean and install a new gasket.

NOTE: *The gasket has an opening for the EGR on light duty applications. On heavy duty applications it has an insert covering the opening.*

3. Install the intake manifold and tighten the bolts in the sequence shown.

4. Install the secondary fuel filter.

5. Install the fuel lines.

6. Installation of the remaining components is in the reverse order.

Exhaust Manifold

REMOVAL AND INSTALLATION

1969-74 Six Cylinder

See the "Intake Manifold Removal and Installation" section.

1975-77 Six Cylinder

1. Disconnect the negative battery cable.

2. Remove the air cleaner.

3. Remove the power steering pump and, if equipped, the AIR pump.

4. Remove the EFE (Early Fuel Evaporation) valve bracket.

5. Disconnect the throttle controls and the throttle return spring.

6. Disconnect the exhaust pipe at the manifold flange.

7. Remove the manifold attaching bolts and remove the manifold. Discard the gasket.

8. Check for cracks in the manifold before it is replaced.

9. Install a new gasket on the exhaust manifold.

Exhaust Manifold Torque Sequence

1975 and later six cylinder with integral cylinder head/intake manifold

10. Clean and oil the bolts and install the bolts, torquing them to specifications.

11. Connect the exhaust pipe, throttle controls, and return spring. Install the air cleaner, start the engine, and check for leaks.

1978 and Later Six Cylinder with Integral Head/Intake Manifold

1. Disconnect the negative battery cable.
2. Remove the air cleaner.
3. Remove the power steering pump and/or the AIR pump brackets, if so equipped.
4. Raise the truck and disconnect the exhaust pipe at the manifold. Disconnect the converter bracket at the transmission mount. If the vehicle is equipped with a manifold converter, disconnect the exhaust pipe from the converter and remove the converter.
5. Lower the truck and remove the rear heat shield and the accelerator cable bracket.
6. Remove the exhaust manifold bolts and remove the manifold.
7. Refer to steps 8–11 of the 1975–77 procedure.

V8 (Except Diesel)

1. If equipped with AIR, remove the air injector assembly. The ¼ in. pipe threads in the manifold are straight cut threads. Do not use a ¼ in. tapered pipe tap to clean the threads.
2. Disconnect the battery.
3. If equipped, remove the carburetor air heater assembly.
4. Remove the spark plug wire heat shields.
5. On the left exhaust manifold, disconnect and remove the alternator.
6. Disconnect the exhaust pipe from the manifold and hang it from the frame out of the way.
7. Bend the locktabs and remove the end bolts, then the center bolts. Remove the manifold.

NOTE: *A 9/16 in. thin wall 6-point socket, sharpened at the leading edge and tapped onto the head of the bolt, simplifies bending the locktabs.*

8. Installation is the reverse of removal. Clean all mating surfaces and use new gaskets. When installing a new right side manifold on 1977 and later models, the carburetor heat stove assembly must be transferred from the old unit. See the illustration. Torque all bolts to specifications from the inside working out.

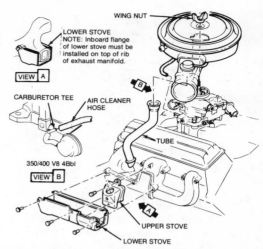

Carburetor heat stove assembly—1977 and later

Diesel Engine

Right Side

1. Disconnect the batteries.
2. Raise the truck and disconnect the exhaust pipe from the manifold. Lower the truck.
3. Tag and disconnect the glow plug wires. Remove the air cleaner duct bracket.
4. Remove the glow plugs, unscrew the manifold bolts and remove the manifold.
5. Installation is in the reverse order.

Left Side

1. Disconnect the batteries.
2. Remove the dipstick tube nut. Remove the dipstick tube.
3. Tag and disconnect the glow plug wires and remove the glow plugs.
4. Remove the manifold bolts. Raise the car and disconnect the exhaust pipe at the manifold.
5. Remove the manifold from the bottom.
6. Start the manifold bolts while the car is still raised, lower the truck and then install the remaining components in the reverse order.

Timing Chain or Gear Cover

NOTE: *The following procedures are for servicing gasoline engines. Diesel engine service may be found at the end of the section.*

REMOVAL AND INSTALLATION—SIX CYLINDER

1. Drain the oil and remove the oil pan on 1969–72 models.
2. Remove the radiator after draining it.
3. Remove the fan, pulley, and belt. Re-

CUT THIS PORTION
FROM NEW SEAL

When the timing gear cover is replaced on 1973 and later six cylinders, the new oil pan front seal must be modified to fit

move any power steering and/or AIR pump drive belts. Remove any braces for the above pumps which will interfere with cover removal and position the pumps out of the way.

4. Remove the crankshaft pulley and damper. Use a puller to remove the damper. Do not attempt to pry or hammer the damper off, for it will be damaged.

5. On 1969–72 models remove the retaining bolts, and remove the cover.

6. Remove the two oil pan-to-front cover attaching screws.

7. Remove the front cover-to-block attaching screws.

8. On 1973 and later models, pull the cover forward slightly and cut the oil pan front seal off flush with the block. Remove the cover. On installation, cut the tabs off a new oil pan front seal and install it to the cover.

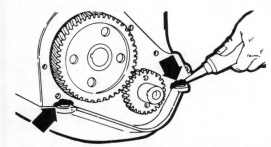

Apply sealer where indicated for the six cylinder

9. On installation, coat the gasket with sealer and use a ⅛ in. bead of silicone sealer at the oil pan to cylinder block joint. Replace the damper before tightening the cover bolts down, so that the cover seal will align. The damper must be drawn into place; it may be broken by hammering.

10. Replace the oil pan if it was removed.

REMOVAL—V8

1. Drain the oil and remove the oil pan. The pan need not be removed on 1975 and later engines.

2. Drain and remove the radiator.

3. Remove the fan, pulley, and belt. Remove any power steering and/or AIR pump drive belts. Remove any braces for these

pumps which will interfere with cover removal and position the pumps out of the way.

4. Remove the water pump.

5. Remove the crankshaft pulley, the damper retaining bolt and damper. Use a puller on the damper. Do not attempt to pry or hammer the damper off.

6. Remove the retaining bolts, and remove the timing cover.

INSTALLATION—1969–74 V8

1. Coat the crankshaft oil seal with engine oil.

2. Coat the new gasket with sealer. Install the cover and gasket. Replace the damper before tightening the cover bolts down, so that the cover seal will align. The damper must be drawn into place; it may be broken by hammering.

3. Replace the oil pan and water pump.

INSTALLATION—1975–82 V8

1. Clean the gasket mating surfaces.

2. Remove any oil pan gasket material that may still be adhering to the oil pan-engine block joint face.

3. Apply a ⅛ in. bead of silicone sealer to the joint formed by the oil pan and cylinder block, as well as to the entire oil pan front lip.

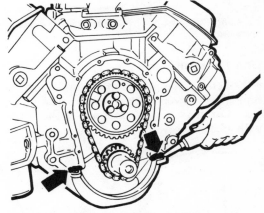

Applying sealer to the V8 oil pan lip

4. Coat the cover gasket with gasket sealer and place it in position on the front cover.

5. Loosely install the front cover on the block. Install the 4 top bolts loosely (about 3 turns). Install two ¼–20 × ½ in. screws in the hole at each side of the front cover and apply a bead of sealant on the bottom of the seal and install it on the cover.

6. Tighten the screws evenly while align-

ing the dowel pins and holes in the front cover.

7. Remove the ¼–20 × ½ in. screws and install the rest of the cover screws.

8. Further installation is the reverse of removal. Refill the engine with oil.

TIMING CHAIN OR GEAR COVER OIL SEAL REPLACEMENT

With Cover Removed

1. After removing the cover, pry the oil seal out of the front of the cover with a large screwdriver.

2. Install a new lip seal with the lip (open side of seal) inside and drive or press the seal into place.

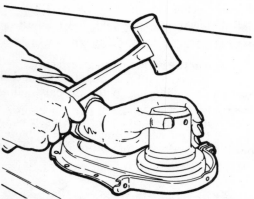

Installing the front cover oil seal with the cover removed

With Cover Installed

1. Refer to the procedure for removing the timing gear cover and remove the damper.

2. Carefully pry the seal out of the cover with a large screwdriver.

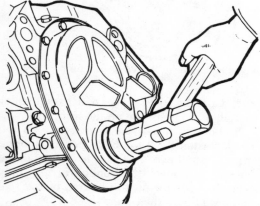

Installing the oil seal with the cover installed

3. Drive the new seal in as illustrated, using a seal driver of the correct diameter between the mallet and the seal.

Timing Chain or Gears
REMOVAL AND INSTALLATION
Six Cylinder

The six cylinder camshaft is gear driven. To remove the camshaft gear, remove the camshaft and press the gear off. The crankshaft gear may be removed with a gear puller while in place in the block.

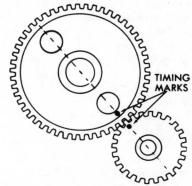

Six cylinder engine timing gear alignment

V8

V8 models are equipped with a timing chain. To replace the chain, remove the radiator core, water pump harmonic balancer, and the crankcase front cover. This will allow access to the timing chain. Crank the engine until the timing marks punched on both sprockets are closest to one another and in line between the shaft centers. Then, take out the three bolts that hold the camshaft sprockets to the camshaft. This is a light press fit on the camshaft and will come off readily. It is located by a dowel.

The chain comes off with the camshaft sprocket.

A gear puller will be required to remove the crankshaft sprocket.

Without disturbing the position of the engine, mount the new crankshaft sprocket on the shaft, then mount the chain over the camshaft sprocket. Arrange the camshaft sprocket in such a way that the timing marks will line up between the shaft centers and the camshaft locating dowel will enter the dowel hole in the cam sprocket.

Place the cam sprocket, with its chain mounted over it, in position on the front of

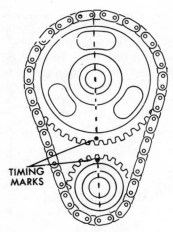

V8 timing sprocket alignment

the camshaft and pull up with the three bolts that hold it to the camshaft.

After the chain and sprocket are in place, turn the engine two full revolutions to make certain that the timing marks are in correct alignment between the shaft centers.

Camshaft

REMOVAL AND INSTALLATION

Six Cylinder Through 1977

1. Remove the grille and radiator. Remove the timing gear cover.

2. Remove the valve cover and gasket, loosen all the valve rocker arm nuts and pivot the arms clear of the pushrods.

3. Remove the distributor and fuel pump.

4. Remove the coil (without HEI), side cover and gasket. Remove the pushrods and valve lifters. Keep them in order for reinstallation.

5. Align the timing gear marks and remove the two camshaft thrust plate retaining screws by working through the holes in the camshaft gear.

6. Remove the camshaft and gear assembly by pulling it out through the front of the block. Be careful not to dislodge the camshaft bearings.

NOTE: *If replacing either the camshaft or camshaft gear, the gear must be pressed off the camshaft. The replacement parts must be assembled in the same manner (under pressure). In placing the gear on the camshaft, press the gear onto the shaft until it bottoms against the gear spacer ring. The end clearance of the thrust plate should be .001 to .005 in.*

7. Install the camshaft assembly in the engine.

NOTE: *Pre-lube the cam lobes with an engine assembly lubricant. Do not dislodge the cam bearings when inserting the camshaft.*

8. Turn the crankshaft and camshaft to align and bring the timing marks together. Push the camshaft into this aligned position.

9. Runout on the camshaft gear should not exceed .004 in. Crankshaft gear runout should not exceed .003 in.

10. Backlash between the two gears should be between .004 and .006 in.

11. Install the timing gear cover and gasket.

12. Install the oil pan and gaskets, if removed.

13. Install the harmonic balancer.

14. Line up the keyway in the balancer with the key on the crankshaft and press the balancer onto the shaft until it bottoms against the crankshaft gear.

15. Install the valve lifters and pushrods. Install the side cover with a new gasket. Attach the coil wires; install the fuel pump.

16. Install the distributor and set the timing as described under the distributor "Removal and Installation" section at the beginning of the chapter.

17. Pivot the rocker arms over the pushrods and adjust the valves.

18. Add oil to the engine. Install and adjust the fan belt.

19. Install the radiator or shroud.

20. Install the grille assembly.

21. Fill the cooling system, start the engine and check for leaks.

22. Check and adjust the ignition timing.

1978 and Later Six Cylinder

When removing the camshaft on all 1978 and later models, the radiator support will, in all probability, be in the way. To remove it requires extensive disassembly of the front end, including the battery tray, fan shroud, grille and headlight assemblies, fenders and fender skirts. In the long run, it's probably easier to take out the engine.

1. Remove the engine as previously outlined.

2. Remove the rocker arm cover.

3. Loosen the rocker arms enough to allow removal of the push rods. Organize the rods in a safe place as they must be installed in their original positions.

4. Mark the distributor housing at the no.

1 and no. 6 spark plug tower position. Disconnect the spark plug wires at the plugs and remove the distributor cap.

5. Slowly turn the engine over until the distributor rotor points to the no. 1 position.

6. Disconnect the distributor lead at the coil, remove the distributor hold down bolts and remove the distributor.

7. Remove the push rod covers.

8. Remove the valve lifters and organize them in a safe place as they must be installed in their original positions.

9. Remove the front cover as previously outlined.

10. Remove the fuel pump.

11. Refer to step 5–17 of the "Six Cylinder Through 1977" procedure.

12. Install the engine as previously outlined.

V8

1. Remove the intake manifold and timing chain cover as previously described. Remove the rocker arm covers and gaskets, loosen all the rocker arm nuts and pivot the arms clear of the pushrods. Remove the pushrods and valve lifters, keeping them in order for reinstallation.

2. Remove the grille and radiator.

3. Remove the fuel pump and pump pushrod.

4. Remove the camshaft sprocket bolts, sprocket and timing chain. A light blow to the lower edge of a tight sprocket should free it (use a plastic mallet).

5. Install two $5/_{18}$–18 × 4 in. bolts in the camshaft bolt holes and pull it from the block.

6. To install, reverse the removal procedure aligning the timing marks.

NOTE: *Pre-lube the cam lobes with engine assembly lubricant. Do not dislodge the cam bearings when installing the camshaft.*

Front Cover

NOTE: *The following procedures are for the diesel engine.*

REMOVAL

1. Drain the cooling system and remove the water pump.

2. Rotate the engine until the marks on the pump gear and the camshaft gear align.

3. Scribe a mark aligning the injection pump flange and the front cover.

4. Remove the crankshaft pulley and the torsional damper.

5. Remove the 4 front cover-to-oil pan bolts.

6. Remove the fuel return line clips.

7. Remove the injection pump driven gear and then remove the injection pump retaining bolts from the front cover.

8. Remove the baffle. Remove the remaining front cover bolts and remove the front cover.

INSTALLATION

1. Clean all sealing surfaces and place a $1/_{18}$ in. bead of sealant as shown in the illustration. Apply RTV sealer to the bottom portion of the front cover where it attaches to the oil pan.

2. Install the front cover and then install the baffle.

3. Install the injection pump making sure the scribe marks on the pump and the front cover align.

4. Install the injection pump driven gear making sure that the marks on the pump gear and the cam gear align.

5. Installation of the remaining components is in the reverse order.

Timing Chain and Sprockets

REMOVAL AND INSTALLATION

1. Remove the front cover.

2. Remove the bolt and washer attaching the camshaft gear to the camshaft sprocket.

3. Remove the injection pump gear.

4. Slide the cam sprocket and timing chain off the shaft and then remove the crankshaft sprocket.

5. Install the crank sprocket, the cam sprocket and the timing chain together. Make sure the timing marks on the sprockets are aligned.

6. Rotate the crankshaft 360° so that the camshaft gear and the injection pump gear are aligned.

7. Install the front cover. Anytime the timing chain, gear or sprockets are removed it will be necessary to retime the engine.

Camshaft

REMOVAL

1. Disconnect the batteries, raise the car and drain the cooling system.

2. Disconnect the exhaust pipe at the manifolds.

3. Remove the fan shroud, the fan and the radiator. Lower the car.

4. Remove the vacuum pump and the intake manifold.

5. Remove the injection lines. Cap all lines, nozzles and fittings.

6. Remove the water pump and then remove the injection pump gear.

7. Scribe a mark on the front cover aligning the pump flange and the cover.

8. Remove the injection pump, the power steering pump and the alternator.

9. If equipped with AC, remove the compressor and position it out of the way.

10. Remove the rocker arm covers, the rocker arm shaft assembly and the push rods. Place parts in a rack so they may be installed in the original location.

11. Remove the thermostat housing/crossover from the cylinder heads.

12. Remove the cylinder head with the exhaust manifolds attached.

13. Remove the valve lifter clamps, guide plates and valve lifters. Keep parts in order so they may be installed in the original location.

14. Remove the front cover.

15. Remove the timing chain.

16. Remove the fuel pump and the cam retainer plate.

17. If equipped with AC, remove the condenser mounting bolts and lift out the condenser. This may require some assistance.

18. Remove the camshaft.

INSTALLATION

Whenever a new camshaft is installed, it is a good idea to replace the valve lifters, oil and filter to insure durability of the cam lobes and lifters. Coat the cam lobes with "Molycote".

1. Lubricate the cam journals with engine oil and install the camshaft.

2. Install the retainer plate, fuel pump and timing chain.

3. Install the front cover, valve lifters, guide plates and clamps.

4. Install the cylinder head, push rods and rocker arm shaft assemblies.

5. Install the rocker arm covers.

6. Install the injection pump to the front cover making sure the marks are in alignment.

7. Install the injection pump driven gear making sure the marks are aligned.

8. Install the water pump and fuel injection lines.

9. Install the alternator, the power steering and the AC.

10. Install the crankshaft pulley and the

fan. Install and adjust all drive belts as necessary.

11. Install the fan shroud and the radiator. Fill the system with coolant.

12. Connect all necessary wires and hoses.

13. Raise the car, connect the exhaust pipes to the manifolds and then lower the car.

14. Install the vacuum pump and intake manifold.

15. Start the engine and check for leaks.

Pistons and Connecting Rods
GASOLINE ENGINE

Piston and connecting rod removal, installation and piston ring removal/installation are detailed in the "Engine Rebuilding" Section at the end of this chapter. Removal and installation are outlined with the engine out of the vehicle, but the same procedures may be used with block in the chassis. Remove the cylinder heads and oil pan for piston and connecting rod removal. Piston and connecting rod positioning is illustrated in the accompanying illustrations.

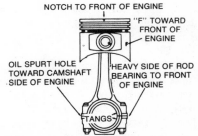

Six cylinder engine piston-to-connecting rod relationship

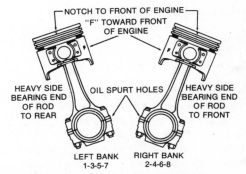

V8 piston-to-connecting rod relationship

DIESEL ENGINE
REMOVAL

1. Remove the intake manifold and cylinder head(s).

2. Remove the oil pan and oil pump assembly.

3. Stamp the cylinder number on the machined surfaces of the bolt bosses of the connecting rod and cap to aid in installation.

4. Examine the cylinder bore. If a ridge exists, remove it with a ridge reamer before attempting to remove the piston and rod assembly.

5. Remove the connecting rod bearing cap and bearing. Use a short piece of ⅜ in. hose to cover the bolt threads. This will prevent damage to the threads themselves and to the bearing journal.

6. Remove the rod and piston assembly through the top of the cylinder bore. Repeat this procedure on the other cylinders.

INSTALLATION

1. Make sure that the thread covers are still on all of the rod bolts.

2. Coat the rings and piston with clean engine oil and then install a ring compressing tool onto the piston.

3. Install each rod and piston into its respective cylinder bore so that the curved edge of the valve depression in top of the piston is toward the inner side of the engine (THE ACTUAL DEPRESSION ITSELF WILL BE ON THE OUTER SIDE).

4. Lubricate the crankpin with clean engine oil and install the connecting rod bearing and cap, with the bearing index tang in the rod and cap on the same side.

5. When all pistons have been correctly installed in their cylinders, tighten the connecting rod bolt nuts to 45 ft. lbs.

ENGINE LUBRICATION

Oil Pan

REMOVAL AND INSTALLATION

Six Cylinder

1. Disconnect the battery ground cable.

2. Raise and support the vehicle. Disconnect the starter leaving the wires attached and swing it out of the way. Leave the starter in place on 1976 automatic transmission models.

3. Remove the flywheel or converter cover.

4. Drain the engine oil.

5. On models through 1975, there may be enough clearance to remove the oil pan without raising the engine. If there isn't, remove the bolts securing the engine mounts to the

crossmember and raise the engine high enough to insert a 2 in. × 4 in. piece of wood between the engine mounts and the crossmember brackets.

6. On 1976 and later models:

   a. Remove the front engine mount through bolts.

   b. Using a floor jack, raise the engine about three inches.

   c. Install the through bolts and tighten them just enough to hold them in place.

   d. Lower the engine so it rests on the engine mounts in a slightly raised position. This should provide enough clearance.

7. Remove the oil pan attaching screws.

8. Remove the oil pan.

9. Clean all gasket surfaces and install a new seal in the rear main bearing groove and a new seal in the crankcase front cover. Installation is the reverse of removal. Install new side gaskets on the block, but do not use sealer. Fill the engine with oil and run the engine, checking for leaks.

V8

1. Drain the engine oil.

2. On models through 1978, remove the oil dipstick and tube.

3. If necessary, remove the exhaust pipe crossover.

4. If equipped with automatic transmission, remove the converter housing pan.

5. On models through 1978, remove the starter brace and bolt and swing the starter aside.

6. On 1979 and later four wheel drive models equipped with automatic transmission, remove the strut rods at the engine mounts.

7. Remove the oil pan and discard the gaskets.

8. Installation is the reverse of removal. Clean all gasket surfaces and use new gaskets to assemble. Use gasket sealer to retain the side gaskets to the cylinder block. Install a new oil pan rear seal in the rear main bearing cap slot with the ends butting the side gaskets. Install a new front seal in the crankcase front cover with the ends butting the side gaskets. Reassemble, fill the engine with oil and check for leaks.

Diesel Engine

1. Disconnect the batteries, raise the car and drain the oil.

2. Remove the transmission dust cover.

3. Remove the oil pan bolts.

4. Remove the left side engine mount thru-bolt.

5. Raise the engine and remove the oil pan.

6. Clean the entire sealing surface and apply a $^3/_{32}$ in. bead of sealer. The sealer must be wet to the touch when the pan bolts are tightened down.

7. Install the oil pan and tighten the bolts to 15 ft. lbs.

8. Lower the engine and install the engine mount thru-bolt.

9. Install the transmission dust cover and lower the car.

10. Refill with oil and connect the batteries.

Oil Pump

REMOVAL AND INSTALLATION

NOTE: *When installing an oil pump, fill it with clean oil.*

Six Cylinder

1. Drain the oil and remove the oil pan.

2. Remove the 2 flange mounting bolts and remove the pickup pipe bolt.

3. Remove the pump and screen as an assembly.

4. To install, align the oil pump driveshaft with the distributor tang and install the oil pump. Position the flange over the distributor lower bushing, using no gasket. The oil pump should slide easily into place. If not, remove it and reposition the slot to align with the distributor tang.

5. Reinstall the oil pan and fill the engine with oil.

V8

1. Drain the oil and remove the oil pan.

2. Remove the bolt holding the pump to the rear main bearing cap. Remove the pump and extension shaft.

3. To install, assemble the pump and extension shaft to the rear main bearing cap aligning the slot on the top of the extension shaft with the drive tang on the distributor driveshaft. The installed position of the oil pump screen is with the bottom edge parallel to the oil pan rails. Further installation is the reverse of removal.

Diesel Engine

REMOVAL

1. Remove oil pan.

2. Remove pump-to-rear main bearing cap bolt and remove pump and extension shaft.

DISASSEMBLY

1. Remove the pump cover attaching screws and the pump cover.

2. Mark the gear teeth so they may be reassembled with the same teeth indexing. Remove the idler gear and drive gear and shaft from the pump body.

3. Remove the pressure regulator valve retaining pin, the pressure regulator valve and all related parts.

CLEANING AND INSPECTION

1. Wash all parts in cleaning solvent and dry with compressed air.

2. Inspect the pump body and cover for cracks or excessive wear.

3. Inspect pump gears for damage or excessive wear.

The pump gears and body are not serviced separately. If the pump gears or body are damaged or worn, replacement of the entire oil pump assembly is necessary.

4. Check the drive gear shaft for looseness in the pump body.

5. Inspect inside the pump cover for wear that would permit oil to leak past the ends of the gears.

6. Inspect the pickup screen and pipe assembly for damage to the screen, pipe or relief grommet.

7. Check the pressure regulator valve for fit.

ASSEMBLY

1. Install the pressure regulator valve and related parts.

2. Install the drive gear and shaft in the pump body.

3. Install the idler gear in the pump body with the smooth side of gear towards pump cover opening.

4. Install the pump cover and torque attaching screws to specifications.

5. Turn driveshaft by hand to check for smooth operation.

INSTALLATION

1. Assemble pump and extension shaft to rear main bearing cap, aligning hex on top end of extension shaft with drive hex on lower end of vacuum pump drive shaft.

2. Install pump to rear bearing cap bolt and torque to specifications.

3. Install oil pan.

Rear Main Bearing Oil Seal Replacement

GASOLINE ENGINE

Both halves of the rear main oil seal can be replaced without removing the crankshaft. Always replace the upper and lower seal together. The lip should face the front of the engine. Be very careful that you do not break the sealing bead in the channel on the outside portion of the seal while installing it. An installation tool can be fabricated to protect the seal bead.

1. Remove the oil pan and rear main bearing cap.

2. Remove the oil seal from the bearing cap by prying it out with a small screwdriver.

3. Remove the upper half of the seal with

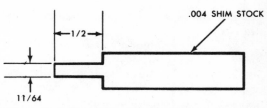

Dimensions for fabricating an oil seal installation tool

a small punch. Drive it around far enough to be gripped with pliers.

4. Clean the crankshaft and bearing cap.

5. Coat the lips and bead of the seal with light engine oil, keeping oil from the ends of the seal.

6. Position the fabricated tool between the crankshaft and seal seat.

7. Position the seal between the crankshaft and tip of the tool so that the seal bead contacts the tip of the tool. The oil seal lip should face forward.

8. Roll the seal around the crankshaft using the tool to protect the seal bead from the sharp corners of the crankcase.

9. The installation tool should be left installed until the seal is properly positioned with both ends flush with the block.

10. Remove the tool.

11. Install the other half of the seal in the bearing cap using the tool in the same manner as before. Light thumb pressure should install the seal.

12. Install the bearing cap with sealant applied to the mating areas of the cap and block. Keep sealant from the ends of the seal.

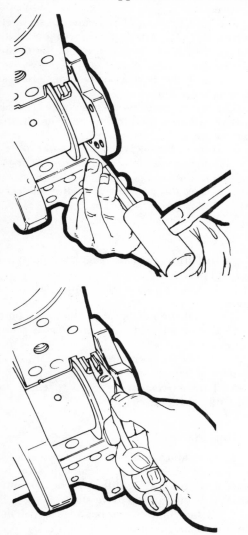

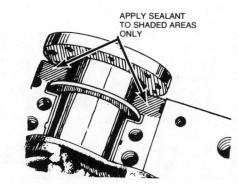

Sealing the bearing cap

13. Torque the rear main bearing cap to specifications.

14. Further installation is the reverse of removal.

Removing the upper half of the bearing seal

DIESEL ENGINE

Upper Oil Seal

REPAIR

Tools have been released to provide a means of correcting upper seal leaks without the necessity of removing the crankshaft. The procedure of seal leak correction is detailed below.

1. Drain the oil, remove the oil pan and then remove the rear main bearing cap.

2. Insert a packing tool against one end of the upper seal and drive the old seal gently into the groove until it is packed tight. This usually varies between ¼–¾ of an inch. Repeat the procedure on the other side.

3. Measure the amount the seal was driven up on one side and add $1/16$ min. Cut this amount from the old seal removed from the main bearing cap. Repeat procedure for other side.

4. Place a drop of sealer on each end of the seal and cap.

5. Using two screwdrivers, work these two pieces of seal into the cylinder block. Use the packing tool and pack each piece up into the block.

6. Replace the lower seal and replace the cap.

7. Installation of the remaining components is in the reverse order.

DIESEL ENGINE

Lower Oil Seal

REMOVAL

1. Drain the oil and remove the oil pan and pump.

2. Remove the rear main bearing cap.

3. Remove the rear main bearing insert and oil seal.

4. Clean the bearing cap and seal grooves. Check for cracks.

INSTALLATION

1. Apply Loctite® 496 or the equivalent and install the seal into the cap by hand.

2. Use a seal installer and hammer the seal into the groove. To check if the seal is fully seated in the cap, slide the tool away from the seal. With the tool fully seated in the cap, slide the tool against the seal. If the tool butts against the seal, it must be driven further into the groove. If the undercut area of the tool slides over the seal, it's fully seated.

3. With the tool slightly rotated, cut the seal flush with the mating surface of the cap.

Use a small screwdriver and pack the seal end fibers toward the center, away from the edges.

4. Clean and install the bearing insert.

5. Apply a thin film of anarobic sealant to the cap. Keep the sealant off the seal and bearing.

6. Just prior to assembly apply a light coating of oil to the crankshaft surface that will contact the seal.

7. Install the bearing cap and tighten to specifications.

8. Installation of the remaining components is in the reverse order.

ENGINE COOLING

Refer to Chapter 1 for the coolant level checking procedure. The coolant should periodically be drained and the system flushed with clean water, at the intervals specified in Chapter 1. Service stations have reverse flushing equipment available; there are also permanently-installed do-it-yourself reverse flushing attachments available.

There is a coolant drain cock at the bottom of most radiators. Six-cylinder engines have a coolant drain plug on the left side of the engine block; V8s have one on each side.

The coolant should always be maintained at a minimum of −20°F freezing protection, regardless of the prevailing temperature. This concentration assures rust protection and the highest possible boiling point. It also prevents the heater core from freezing on air-conditioned models.

Some simple modifications can be made to the cooling system for improved performance under severe conditions. The fan can be replaced with either a high-output unit, a clutch

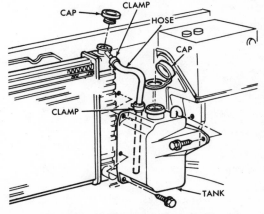

Factory installed coolant recovery tank

type designed for air conditioned models, or a flex-type. The flex unit flattens out at high rpm, moving less air and reducing the horsepower required to drive it. The clutch type is regulated to a set maximum speed, varying with temperature. An overflow tank maintains the proper coolant level in the radiator by storing water which escapes out the radiator overflow tube for return to the engine as it cools. It also keeps the system free of air, a major cause of rust.

RADIATOR

REMOVAL AND INSTALLATION

1969-72

1. Drain the radiator and remove the hoses.

2. Disconnect and plug the automatic transmission cooler lines.

3. On six cylinder engines, remove the finger guard.

4. Remove the upper retainers with the fan shroud attached (V8 models) and rest the fan shroud over the engine.

5. Lift the radiator out of the lower retainers.

6. Installation is the reverse of removal. Fill the cooling system, check the automatic transmission fluid level and run the engine, checking for leaks.

1973-82

1. Drain the radiator. On some 1973 models, you will have to detach the lower radiator hose. Most models are equipped with a drain cock.

2. Disconnect the hoses and automatic transmission cooler line. Plug the cooler lines.

3. Disconnect the coolant recovery system hose.

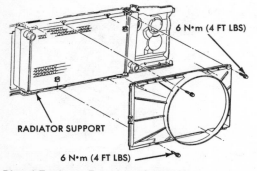

RADIATOR SUPPORT

6 N•m (4 FT LBS)

6 N•m (4 FT LBS)

Diesel Engine—Fan shroud mounting

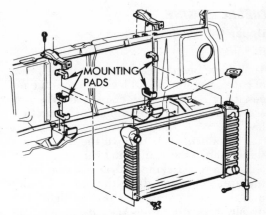

MOUNTING PADS

Typical radiator mounting

4. If the vehicle has a fan shroud, detach the shroud and hang it over the fan to provide clearance.

5. Remove the mounting panel from the radiator support and remove the upper mounting pads.

6. Lift the radiator up and out of the truck. Lift the shroud out if necessary.

7. Installation is the reverse of removal. Fill the cooling system and check the automatic transmission fluid level, and run the engine, checking for leaks.

COOLANT DRAINING, FLUSHING, AND REFILLING

NOTE: *Never add cold water to a hot engine. A cracked engine block or head could result.*

1. With the engine cold and the heater on, open the petcock at the bottom rear of the radiator. If your radiator doesn't have one, detach the lower hose. Remove the radiator cap. Let the coolant drain into a container.

CAUTION: *Don't let antifreeze mixture run onto the ground; it is deadly to grass, flowers, and any creature that drinks it.*

2. Remove the single engine block drain plug on the left side of a six cylinder engine. Remove the block drain plugs from both sides of a V8 engine.

3. Fill the radiator with water and let it run out the radiator and engine drains until it comes out clean.

4. Close the petcock and replace the block drains.

5. Pour in the required amount of antifreeze. Fill the radiator with water.

6. Leave the radiator cap off, turn the heater on, and start the engine. Run it until the thermostat opens, adding water as nec-

essary. Without a coolant recovery system, the level should be 1¼ in. below the filler neck hot and 3 in. below cold. With a coolant recovery system, the radiator should be full and the level in the catch tank should be between FULL COLD and FULL HOT.

7. Replace the radiator cap.

Water Pump

REMOVAL AND INSTALLATION

Gasoline Engine

1. Drain the radiator and loosen the fan pulley bolts.

2. Disconnect the heater hose and radiator. Disconnect the lower radiator hose at the water pump.

3. Loosen the alternator swivel bolt and remove the fan belt. Remove the fan bolts, fan and pulley.

4. Remove the water pump attaching bolts and remove the pump and gasket from the engine. On six cylinder engines, remove the water pump straight out of the block to avoid damaging the impeller.

NOTE: *Do not store viscous drive fan clutches in any other position than the normal installed position. They should be supported so that the clutch disc remains vertical; otherwise, silicone fluid may leak out.*

5. Installation is the reverse of removal. Clean gasket surfaces and install new gaskets. Coat the gasket with sealer. A ⁵/₁₆ in. x 24 x 1 in. guide stud installed in one hole of the fan will make installing the fan onto the hub easier. It can be removed after the other 3 bolts are started. Fill the cooling system and adjust the fan belt tension.

Diesel Engine

REMOVAL

1. Disconnect the batteries.

2. Remove the fan and the fan shroud.

3. Drain the radiator. If equipped with A/C, remove the A/C hose bracket nuts.

4. Remove the oil filler tube.

5. Remove the alternator pivot bolt and then remove the drive belt. Remove the lower bracket.

6. Remove the power steering belt. Remove the power steering pump and position it out of the way.

7. Remove the AC belt if so equipped.

8. Disconnect the by-pass hose and the lower radiator hose.

9. Unscrew the water pump mounting

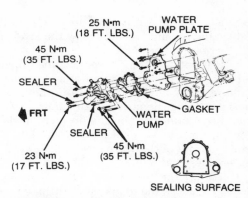

Diesel engine water pump mounting

bolts. Remove the water pump plate and the water pump.

10. If the water pump gasket is to be repaired, remove the plate attaching bolts to the water pump and replace the gasket.

INSTALLATION

1. All flanges must be free of oil. Apply anarobic sealer as shown in the illustration. The sealer must still be wet to the touch when the bolts are torqued.

2. Attach the water pump and plate assembly.

3. Connect the by-pass hose and the lower radiator hose.

4. Install the power steering pump and the alternator. Adjust all drive belts.

5. Install the oil filler tube.

6. Install the fan shroud and the fan.

7. Fill system with coolant, connect batteries start the engine and check for leaks.

Thermostat

The factory installed thermostat is a 195°F unit.

NOTE: *Poor heater output and slow warming is often caused by a thermostat stuck in the open position; occasionally one sticks shut causing immediate overheating. Do not attempt to correct a chronic overheating condition by permanently removing the thermostat. Thermostat flow restriction is designed into the system; without it, localized overheating due to turbulence may occur.*

REMOVAL AND INSTALLATION

Gasoline Engine

1. Drain approximately ⅓ of the coolant into a clean container. The coolant can be

used again, unless it is very dirty. This will reduce the coolant level to below the level of the thermostat housing.

2. It is not necessary to remove the upper radiator hose from the thermostat housing. Remove the 2 retaining bolts from the thermostat housing. Remove the 2 retaining bolts from the thermostat housing (located on the front top of the V8 intake manifold and directly in front of the valve cover on six cylinder engines) and remove the thermostat.

3. To test the thermostat, place it in hot water, 25° above the temperature stamped on the valve. Submerge the valve and agitate the water. The valve should open fully. Remove the thermostat and place it in water 10° below the temperature stamped on the valve. The valve should close completely.

4. Installation is the reverse of removal. Use a new gasket and sealer. Refill the cooling system and run the engine, checking for leaks.

Diesel Engine

REMOVAL

The thermostat is located in the coolant crossover pipe at the front of the engine.

1. Disconnect the battery cables.
2. Drain the cooling system until the coolant level is below that of the thermostat.
3. Remove the water outlet attaching bolts and remove the outlet.
4. Remove the thermostat.

INSTALLATION

1. Make sure the sealing surfaces are clean and then place a $1/8$ in. bead of RTV sealant around the coolant outlet sealing surface on the thermostat housing.
2. Place the thermostat in the housing and install the coolant outlet while the RTV sealant is still wet.
3. Connect the batteries and refill the cooling system.

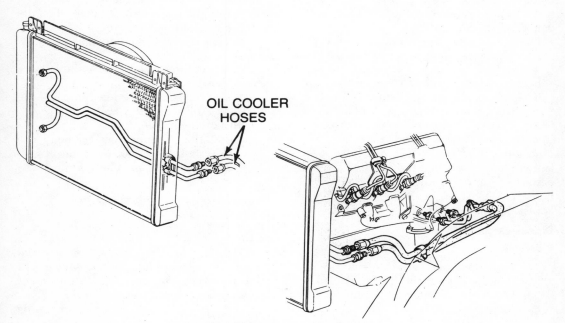

OIL COOLER HOSES

Diesel engine oil cooler lines

ENGINE REBUILDING

Most procedures involved in rebuilding an engine are fairly standard, regardless of the type of engine involved. This section is a guide accepted rebuilding procedures. Examples of standard rebuilding practices are illustrated and should be used along with specific details concerning your particular engine, found earlier in this chapter.

The procedures given here are those used by any competent rebuilder. Obviously some of the procedures cannot be performed by the do-it-yourself mechanic, but are provided so that you will be familiar with the services that should be offered by rebuilding or machine shops. As an example, in most instances, it is more profitable for the home mechanic to remove the cylinder heads, buy the necessary parts (new valves, seals, keepers, keys, etc.) and deliver these to a machine shop for the necessary work. In this way you will save the money to remove and install the cylinder head and the mark-up on parts.

On the other hand, most of the work involved in rebuilding the lower end is well within the scope of the do-it-yourself mechanic. Only work such as hot-tanking, actually boring the block or Magnafluxing (invisible crack detection) need be sent to a machine shop.

Tools

The tools required for basic engine rebuilding should, with a few exceptions, be those included in a mechanic's tool kit. An accurate torque wrench, and a dial indicator (reading in thousandths) mounted on a universal base should be available. Special tools, where required, are available from the major tool suppliers. The services of a competent automotive machine shop must also be readily available.

Precautions

Aluminum has become increasingly popular for use in engines, due to its low weight and excellent heat transfer characteristics. The following precautions must be observed when handling aluminum (or any other) engine parts:

—Never hot-tank aluminum parts.
—Remove all aluminum parts (identification tags, etc.) from engine parts before hot-tanking (otherwise they will be removed during the process).

—Always coat threads lightly with engine oil or anti-seize compounds before installation, to prevent seizure.
—Never over-torque bolts or spark plugs in aluminum threads. Should stripping occur, threads can be restored using any of a number of thread repair kits available (see next section).

Inspection Techniques

Magnaflux and Zyglo are inspection techniques used to locate material flaws, such as stress cracks. Magnaflux is a magnetic process, applicable only to ferrous materials. The Zyglo process coats the matrial with a fluorescent dye penetrant, and any material may be tested using Zyglo. Specific checks of suspected surface cracks may be made at lower cost and more readily using spot check dye. The dye is sprayed onto the suspected area, wiped off, and the area is then sprayed with a developer. Cracks then will show up brightly.

Overhaul

The section is divided into two parts. The first, Cylinder Head Reconditioning, assumes that the cylinder head is removed from the engine, all manifolds are removed, and the cylinder head is on a workbench. The camshaft should be removed from overhead cam cylinder heads. The second section, Cylinder Block Reconditioning, covers the block, pistons, connecting rods and crankshaft. It is assumed that the engine is mounted on a work stand, and the cylinder head and all accessories are removed.

Procedures are identified as follows:
Unmarked—Basic procedures that must be performed in order to successfully complete the rebuilding process.
Starred (*)—Procedures that should be performed to ensure maximum performance and engine life.
Double starred (**)—Procedures that may be performed to increase engine performance and reliability.

When assembling the engine, any parts that will be in frictional contact must be pre-lubricated, to provide protection on initial start-up. Any product specifically formulated for this purpose may be used. NOTE: *Do not use engine oil.* Where semi-permanent (locked but removable) installation of bolts or nuts is desired, threads should be cleaned and located with Loctite® or a similar product (non-hardening).

Repairing Damaged Threads

Several methods of repairing damaged threads are available. Heli-Coil® (shown here), Keenserts® and Microdot® are among the most widely used. All involve basically the same principle—drilling out stripped threads, tapping the hole and installing a pre-wound insert—making welding, plugging and oversize fasteners unnecessary.

Two types of thread repair inserts are usually supplied—a standard type for most Inch Coarse, Inch Fine, Metric Coarse and Metric Fine thread sizes and a spark plug type to fit most spark plug port sizes. Consult the individual manufacturer's catalog to determine exact applications. Typical thread repair kits will contain a selection of pre-wound threaded inserts, a tap (corresponding to the outside diameter threads of the insert) and an installation tool. Spark plug inserts usually differ because they require a tap equipped with pilot threads and a combined reamer/tap section. Most manufacturers also supply blister-packed thread repair inserts separately in addition to a master kit containing a variety of taps and inserts plus installation tools.

Before effecting a repair to a threaded hole, remove any snapped, broken or damaged bolts or studs. Penetrating oil can be used to free frozen threads; the offending item can be removed with locking pliers or with a screw or stud extractor. After the hole is clear, the thread can be repaired, as follows:

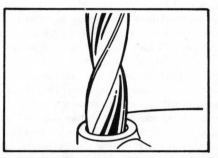

Drill out the damaged threads with specified drill. Drill completely through the hole or to the bottom of a blind hole

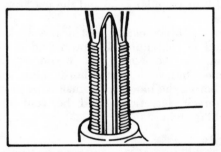

With the tap supplied, tap the hole to receive the thread insert. Keep the tap well oiled and back it out frequently to avoid clogging the threads

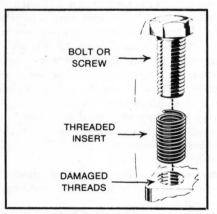

Damaged bolt holes can be repaired with thread repair inserts

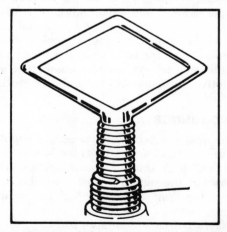

Screw the threaded insert onto the installation tool until the tang engages the slot. Screw the insert into the tapped hole until it is ¼–½ turn below the top surface. After installation break off the tang with a hammer and punch

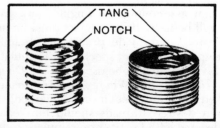

Standard thread repair insert (left) and spark plug thread insert (right)

Standard Torque Specifications and Fastener Markings

The Newton-metre has been designated the world standard for measuring torque and will gradually replace the foot-pound and kilogram-meter. In the absence of specific torques, the following chart can be used as a guide to the maximum safe torque of a particular size/grade of fastener.

- There is no torque difference for fine or coarse threads.
- Torque values are based on clean, dry threads. Reduce the value by 10% if threads are oiled prior to assembly.
- The torque required for aluminum components or fasteners is considerably less.

U. S. BOLTS

SAE Grade Number	1 or 2			5			6 or 7		

Bolt Markings

Manufacturer's marks may vary—number of lines always 2 less than the grade number.

Usage	Frequent			Frequent			Infrequent		
Bolt Size (inches)—(Thread)	Maximum Torque			Maximum Torque			Maximum Torque		
	Ft-Lb	kgm	Nm	Ft-Lb	kgm	Nm	Ft-Lb	kgm	Nm
¼—20	5	0.7	6.8	8	1.1	10.8	10	1.4	13.5
—28	6	0.8	8.1	10	1.4	13.6			
⁵⁄₁₆—18	11	1.5	14.9	17	2.3	23.0	19	2.6	25.8
—24	13	1.8	17.6	19	2.6	25.7			
⅜—16	18	2.5	24.4	31	4.3	42.0	34	4.7	46.0
—24	20	2.75	27.1	35	4.8	47.5			
⁷⁄₁₆—14	28	3.8	37.0	49	6.8	66.4	55	7.6	74.5
—20	30	4.2	40.7	55	7.6	74.5			
½—13	39	5.4	52.8	75	10.4	101.7	85	11.75	115.2
—20	41	5.7	55.6	85	11.7	115.2			
⁹⁄₁₆—12	51	7.0	69.2	110	15.2	149.1	120	16.6	162.7
—18	55	7.6	74.5	120	16.6	162.7			
⅝—11	83	11.5	112.5	150	20.7	203.3	167	23.0	226.5
—18	95	13.1	128.8	170	23.5	230.5			
¾—10	105	14.5	142.3	270	37.3	366.0	280	38.7	379.6
—16	115	15.9	155.9	295	40.8	400.0			
⅞— 9	160	22.1	216.9	395	54.6	535.5	440	60.9	596.5
—14	175	24.2	237.2	435	60.1	589.7			
1— 8	236	32.5	318.6	590	81.6	799.9	660	91.3	894.8
—14	250	34.6	338.9	660	91.3	849.8			

METRIC BOLTS

NOTE: *Metric bolts are marked with a number indicating the relative strength of the bolt. These numbers have nothing to do with size.*

Description	Torque ft-lbs (Nm)			
Thread size x pitch (mm)	Head mark—4		Head mark—7	
6 x 1.0	2.2–2.9	(3.0–3.9)	3.6–5.8	(4.9–7.8)
8 x 1.25	5.8–8.7	(7.9–12)	9.4–14	(13–19)
10 x 1.25	12–17	(16–23)	20–29	(27–39)
12 x 1.25	21–32	(29–43)	35–53	(47–72)
14 x 1.5	35–52	(48–70)	57–85	(77–110)
16 x 1.5	51–77	(67–100)	90–120	(130–160)
18 x 1.5	74–110	(100–150)	130–170	(180–230)
20 x 1.5	110–140	(150–190)	190–240	(160–320)
22 x 1.5	150–190	(200–260)	250–320	(340–430)
24 x 1.5	190–240	(260–320)	310–410	(420–550)

NOTE: *This engine rebuilding section is a guide to accepted rebuilding procedures. Typical examples of standard rebuilding procedures are illustrated. Use these procedures along with the detailed instructions earlier in this chapter, concerning your particular engine.*

Cylinder Head Reconditioning

Procedure	Method
Remove the cylinder head:	See the engine service procedures earlier in this chapter for details concerning specific engines.
Identify the valves:	Invert the cylinder head, and number the valve faces front to rear, using a permanent felt-tip marker.
Remove the rocker arms:	Remove the rocker arms with shaft(s) or balls and nuts. Wire the sets of rockers, balls and nuts together, and identify according to the corresponding valve.
Remove the valves and springs:	Using an appropriate valve spring compressor (depending on the configuration of the cylinder head), compress the valve springs. Lift out the keepers with needlenose pliers, release the compressor, and remove the valve, spring, and spring retainer. See the engine service procedures earlier in this chapter for details concerning specific engines.
Check the valve stem-to-guide clearance: 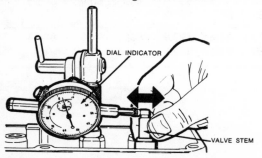 **Check the valve stem-to-guide clearance**	Clean the valve stem with lacquer thinner or a similar solvent to remove all gum and varnish. Clean the valve guides using solvent and an expanding wire-type valve guide cleaner. Mount a dial indicator so that the stem is at 90° to the valve stem, as close to the valve guide as possible. Move the valve off its seat, and measure the valve guide-to-stem clearance by rocking the stem back and forth to actuate the dial indicator. Measure the valve stems using a micrometer, and compare to specifications, to determine whether stem or guide wear is responsible for excessive clearance. NOTE: *Consult the Specifications tables earlier in this chapter.*

DIAL INDICATOR

VALVE STEM

Cylinder Head Reconditioning

Procedure	Method
De-carbon the cylinder head and valves: 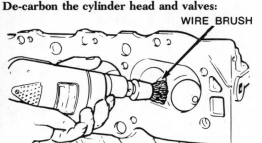 WIRE BRUSH **Remove the carbon from the cylinder head with a wire brush and electric drill**	Chip carbon away from the valve heads, combustion chambers, and ports, using a chisel made of hardwood. Remove the remaining deposits with a stiff wire brush. **NOTE:** *Be sure that the deposits are actually removed, rather than burnished.*
Hot-tank the cylinder head (cast iron heads only): **CAUTION:** *Do not hot-tank aluminum parts.*	Have the cylinder head hot-tanked to remove grease, corrosion, and scale from the water passages. **NOTE:** *In the case of overhead cam cylinder heads, consult the operator to determine whether the camshaft bearings will be damaged by the caustic solution.*
Degrease the remaining cylinder head parts:	Clean the remaining cylinder head parts in an engine cleaning solvent. Do not remove the protective coating from the springs.
Check the cylinder head for warpage: 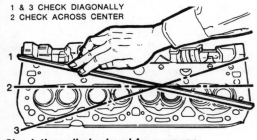 1 & 3 CHECK DIAGONALLY 2 CHECK ACROSS CENTER **Check the cylinder head for warpage**	Place a straight-edge across the gasket surface of the cylinder head. Using feeler gauges, determine the clearance at the center of the straight-edge. If warpage exceeds .003″ in a 6″ span, or .006″ over the total length, the cylinder head must be resurfaced. **NOTE:** *If warpage exceeds the manufacturer's maximum tolerance for material removal, the cylinder head must be replaced.* When milling the cylinder heads of V-type engines, the intake manifold mounting position is altered, and must be corrected by milling the manifold flange a proportionate amount.
*Knurl the valve guides: 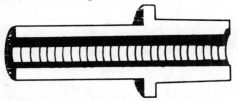 **Cut-away view of a knurled valve guide**	*Valve guides which are not excessively worn or distorted may, in some cases, be knurled rather than replaced. Knurling is a process in which metal is displaced and raised, thereby reducing clearance. Knurling also provides excellent oil control. The possibility of knurling rather than replacing valve guides should be discussed with a machinist.
Replace the valve guides: **NOTE:** *Valve guides should only be replaced if damaged or if an oversize valve stem is not available.*	See the engine service procedures earlier in this chapter for details concerning specific engines. Depending on the type of cylinder head, valve guides may be pressed, hammered, or shrunk in. In cases where the guides are shrunk into the head, replacement should be left to an equipped machine shop. In other

Cylinder Head Reconditioning

Procedure	Method

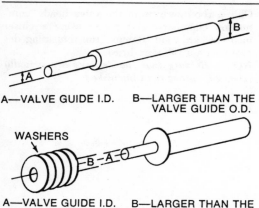

A—VALVE GUIDE I.D.   B—LARGER THAN THE VALVE GUIDE O.D.

WASHERS

A—VALVE GUIDE I.D.   B—LARGER THAN THE VALVE GUIDE O.D.

Valve guide installation tool using washers for installation

cases, the guides are replaced using a stepped drift (see illustration). Determine the height above the boss that the guide must extend, and obtain a stack of washers, their I.D. similar to the guide's O.D., of that height. Place the stack of washers on the guide, and insert the guide into the boss.
NOTE: *Valve guides are often tapered or beveled for installation.* Using the stepped installation tool (see illustration), press or tap the guides into position. Ream the guides according to the size of the valve stem.

Replace valve seat inserts:

Replacement of valve seat inserts which are worn beyond resurfacing or broken, if feasible, must be done by a machine shop.

Resurface (grind) the valve face:

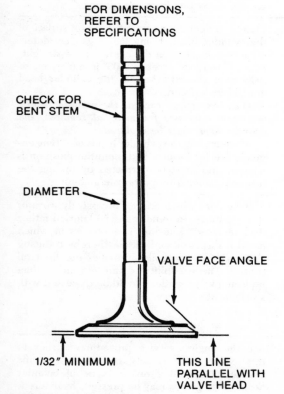

FOR DIMENSIONS, REFER TO SPECIFICATIONS

CHECK FOR BENT STEM

DIAMETER

VALVE FACE ANGLE

1/32" MINIMUM   THIS LINE PARALLEL WITH VALVE HEAD

Critical valve dimensions

Using a valve grinder, resurface the valves according to specifications given earlier in this chapter.
CAUTION: *Valve face angle is not always identical to valve seat angle.* A minimum margin of 1/32" should remain after grinding the valve. The valve stem top should also be squared and resurfaced, by placing the stem in the V-block of the grinder, and turning it while pressing lightly against the grinding wheel.
NOTE: *Do not grind sodium filled exhaust valves on a machine. These should be hand lapped.*

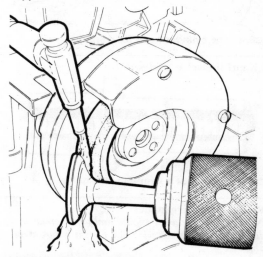

Valve grinding by machine

Cylinder Head Reconditioning

Procedure	Method
Resurface the valve seats using reamers of grinder: 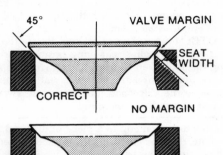  **Valve seat width and centering**  **Reaming the valve seat with a hand reamer**	Select a reamer of the correct seat angle, slightly larger than the diameter of the valve seat, and assemble it with a pilot of the correct size. Install the pilot into the valve guide, and using steady pressure, turn the reamer clockwise. **CAUTION:** *Do not turn the reamer counterclockwise.* Remove only as much material as necessary to clean the seat. Check the concentricity of the seat (following). If the dye method is not used, coat the valve face with Prussian blue dye, install and rotate it on the valve seat. Using the dye marked area as a centering guide, center and narrow the valve seat to specifications with correction cutters. **NOTE:** *When no specifications are available, minimum seat width for exhaust valves should be 5/64″, intake valves 1/16″.* After making correction cuts, check the position of the valve seat on the valve face using Prussian blue dye.
	To resurface the seat with a power grinder, select a pilot of the correct size and coarse stone of the proper angle. Lubricate the pilot and move the stone on and off the valve seat at 2 cycles per second, until all flaws are gone. Finish the seat with a fine stone. If necessary the seat can be corrected or narrowed using correction stones.
Check the valve seat concentricity:  **Check the valve seat concentricity with a dial gauge**	Coat the valve face with Prussian blue dye, install the valve, and rotate it on the valve seat. If the entire seat becomes coated, and the valve is known to be concentric, the seat is concentric. *Install the dial gauge pilot into the guide, and rest of the arm on the valve seat. Zero the gauge, and rotate the arm around the seat. Run-out should not exceed .002″.

In the first illustration: "45°", "VALVE MARGIN", "SEAT WIDTH", "CORRECT", "NO MARGIN", "INCORRECT"

Cylinder Head Reconditioning

Procedure	Method
*Lap the valves: NOTE: *Valve lapping is done to ensure efficient sealing of resurfaced valves and seats.*	Invert the cylinder head, lightly lubricate the valve stems, and install the valves in the head as numbered. Coat valve seats with fine grinding compound, and attach the lapping tool suction cup to a valve head. NOTE: *Moisten the suction cup.* Rotate the tool between the palms, changing position and lifting the tool often to prevent grooving. Lap the valve until a smooth, polished seat is evident. Remove the valve and tool, and rinse away all traces of grinding compound.

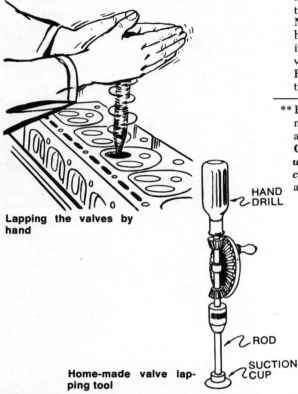

Lapping the valves by hand

HAND DRILL

ROD

SUCTION CUP

Home-made valve lapping tool

** Fasten a suction cup to a piece of drill rod, and mount the rod in a hand drill. Proceed as above, using the hand drill as a lapping tool.
CAUTION: *Due to the higher speeds involved when using the hand drill, care must be exercised to avoid grooving the seat.* Lift the tool and change direction of rotation often.

Check the valve springs:	Place the spring on a flat surface next to a square. Measure the height of the spring, and rotate it against the edge of the square to measure distortion. If spring height varies (by comparison) by more than $1/16''$ or if distortion exceeds $1/16''$, replace the spring.

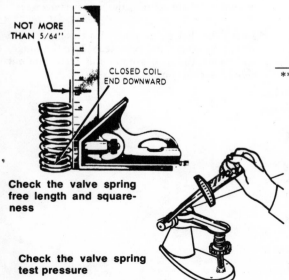

NOT MORE THAN 5/64''

CLOSED COIL END DOWNWARD

Check the valve spring free length and squareness

Check the valve spring test pressure

** In addition to evaluating the spring as above, test the spring pressure at the installed and compressed (installed height minus valve lift) height using a valve spring tester. Springs used on small displacement engines (up to 3 liters) should be ∓ 1 lb of all other springs in either position. A tolerance of ∓ 5 lbs is permissible on larger engines.

Cylinder Head Reconditioning

Procedure	Method
*Install valve stem seals: 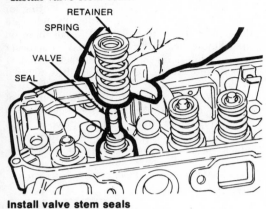 **Install valve stem seals**	*Due to the pressure differential that exists at the ends of the intake valve guides (atmospheric pressure above, manifold vacuum below), oil is drawn through the valve guides into the intake port. This has been alleviated somewhat since the addition of positive crankcase ventilation, which lowers the pressure above the guides. Several types of valve stem seals are available to reduce blow-by. Certain seals simply slip over the stem and guide boss, while others require that the boss be machined. Recently, Teflon guide seals have become popular. Consult a parts supplier or machinist concerning availability and suggested usages. **NOTE:** *When installing seals, ensure that a small amount of oil is able to pass the seal to lubricate the valve guides; otherwise, excessive wear may result.*
Install the valves:	See the engine service procedures earlier in this chapter for details concerning specific engines. Lubricate the valve stems, and install the valves in the cylinder head as numbered. Lubricate and position the seals (if used) and the valve springs. Install the spring retainers, compress the springs, and insert the keys using needlenose pliers or a tool designed for this purpose. **NOTE:** *Retain the keys with wheel bearing grease during installation.*
Check valve spring installed height: 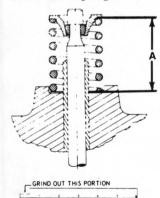 **Valve spring installed height (A)**  **Measure the valve spring installed height (A) with a modified steel rule**	Measure the distance between the spring pad the lower edge of the spring retainer, and compare to specifications. If the installed height is incorrect, add shim washers between the spring pad and the spring. **CAUTION:** *Use only washers designed for this purpose.*

Cylinder Head Reconditioning

Procedure	Method
Inspect the rocker arms, balls, studs, and nuts: 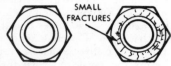 **Stress cracks in the rocker nuts**	Visually inspect the rocker arms, balls, studs, and nuts for cracks, galling, burning, scoring, or wear. If all parts are intact, liberally lubricate the rocker arms and balls, and install them on the cylinder head. If wear is noted on a rocker arm at the point of valve contact, grind it smooth and square, removing as little material as possible. Replace the rocker arm if excessively worn. If a rocker stud shows signs of wear, it must be replaced (see below). If a rocker nut shows stress cracks, replace it. If an exhaust ball is galled or burned, substitute the intake ball from the same cylinder (if it is intact), and install a new intake ball. **NOTE:** *Avoid using new rocker balls on exhaust valves.*
Replace rocker studs: 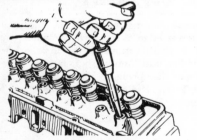 **Extracting a pressed-in rocker stud** 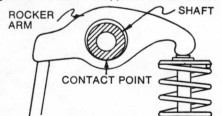 **Ream the stud bore for oversize rocker studs**	In order to remove a threaded stud, lock two nuts on the stud, and unscrew the stud using the lower nut. Coat the lower threads of the new stud with Loctite, and install. Two alternative methods are available for replacing pressed in studs. Remove the damaged stud using a stack of washers and a nut (see ilustration). In the first, the boss is reamed .005–.006″ oversize, and an oversize stud pressed in. Control the stud extension over the boss using washers, in the same manner as valve guides. Before installing the stud, coat it with white lead and grease. To retain the stud more positively drill a hole through the stud and boss, and install a roll pin. In the second method, the boss is tapped, and a threaded stud installed.
Inspect the rocker shaft(s) and rocker arms: **Check the rocker arm-to-rocker shaft contact area**	Remove the rocker arms, springs and washers from rocker shaft. **NOTE:** *Lay out parts in the order as they are removed.* Inspect rocker arms for pitting or wear on the valve contact point, or excessive bushing wear. Bushings need only be replaced if wear is excessive, because the rocker arm normally contacts the shaft at one point only. Grind the valve contact point of rocker arm smooth if necessary, removing as little material as possible. If excessive material must be removed to smooth and square the arm, it should be replaced. Clean out all oil holes and passages in rocker shaft. If shaft is grooved or worn, replace it. Lubricate and assemble the rocker shaft.

Cylinder Head Reconditioning

Procedure	Method
Inspect the pushrods:	Remove the pushrods, and, if hollow, clean out the oil passages using fine wire. Roll each pushrod over a piece of clean glass. If a distinct clicking sound is heard as the pushrod rolls, the rod is bent, and must be replaced.
	*The length of all pushrods must be equal. Measure the length of the pushrods, compare to specifications, and replace as necessary.
*Inspect the valve lifters: 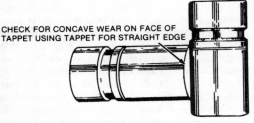 CHECK FOR CONCAVE WEAR ON FACE OF TAPPET USING TAPPET FOR STRAIGHT EDGE **Check the lifter face for squareness**	Remove lifters from their bores, and remove gum and varnish, using solvent. Clean walls of lifter bores. Check lifters for concave wear as illustrated. If face is worn concave, replace lifter, and carefully inspect the camshaft. Lightly lubricate lifter and insert it into its bore. If play is excessive, an oversize lifter must be installed (where possible). Consult a machinist concerning feasibility. If play is satisfactory, remove, lubricate, and reinstall the lifter.
*Testing hydraulic lifter leak down:	Submerge lifter in a container of kerosene. Chuck a used pushrod or its equivalent into a drill press. Position container of kerosene so pushrod acts on the lifter plunger. Pump lifter with the drill press, until resistance increases. Pump several more times to bleed any air out of lifter. Apply very firm, constant pressure to the lifter, and observe rate at which fluid bleeds out of lifter. If the fluid bleeds very quickly (less than 15 seconds), lifter is defective. If the time exceeds 60 seconds, lifter is sticking. In either case, recondition or replace lifter. If lifter is operating properly (leak down time 15–60 seconds), lubricate and install it.

Cylinder Block Reconditioning

Procedure	Method
Checking the main bearing clearance: 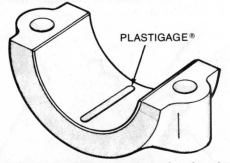 PLASTIGAGE® **Plastigage® installed on the lower bearing shell**	Invert engine, and remove cap from the bearing to be checked. Using a clean, dry rag, thoroughly clean all oil from crankshaft journal and bearing insert. NOTE: *Plastigage® is soluble in oil; therefore, oil on the journal or bearing could result in erroneous readings.* Place a piece of Plastigage along the full length of journal, reinstall cap, and torque to specifications. NOTE: **Specifications are given in the engine specifications earlier in this chapter.** Remove bearing cap, and determine bearing clearance by comparing width of Plastigage to the scale on Plastigage envelope. Journal taper is determined by comparing width of the Plas-

Cylinder Block Reconditioning

Procedure	Method

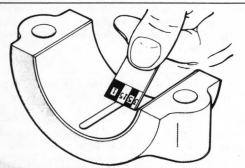

Measure Plastigage® to determine main bearing clearance

tigage strip near its ends. Rotate crankshaft 90° and retest, to determine journal eccentricity. **NOTE:** *Do not rotate crankshaft with Plastigage installed.* If bearing insert and journal appear intact, and are within tolerances, no further main bearing service is required. If bearing or journal appear defective, cause of failure should be determined before replacement.

*Remove crankshaft from block (see below). Measure the main bearing journals at each end twice (90° apart) using a micrometer, to determine diameter, journal taper and eccentricity. If journals are within tolerances, reinstall bearing caps at their specified torque. Using a telescope gauge and micrometer, measure bearing I.D. parallel to piston axis and at 30° on each side of piston axis. Subtract journal O.D. for bearing I.D. to determine oil clearance. If crankshaft journals appear defective, or do not meet tolerances, there is no need to measure bearings; for the crankshaft will require grinding and/or undersize bearings will be required. If bearing appears defective, cause for failure should be determined prior to replacement.

Check the connecting rod bearing clearance:

Connecting rod bearing clearance is checked in the same manner as main bearing clearance, using Plastigage. Before removing the crankshaft, connecting rod side clearance also should be measured and recorded.

*Checking connecting rod bearing clearance, using a micrometer, is identical to checking main bearing clearance. If no other service is required, the piston and rod assemblies need not be removed.

Remove the crankshaft:

Using a punch, mark the corresponding main bearing caps and saddles according to position (i.e., one punch on the front main cap and saddle, two on the second, three on the third, etc.). Using number stamps, identify the corresponding connecting rods and caps, according to cylinder (if no numbers are present). Remove the main and connecting rod caps, and place

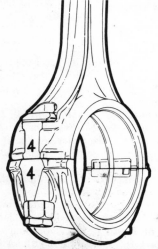

Match the connecting rod to the cylinder with a number stamp

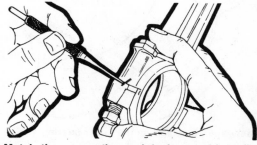

Match the connecting rod and cap with scribe marks

Cylinder Block Reconditioning

Procedure	Method
	sleeves of plastic tubing or vacuum hose over the connecting rod bolts, to protect the journals as the crankshaft is removed. Lift the crankshaft out of the block.
Remove the ridge from the top of the cylinder: RIDGE CAUSED BY CYLINDER WEAR CYLINDER WALL TOP OF PISTON **Cylinder bore ridge**	In order to facilitate removal of the piston and connecting rod, the ridge at the top of the cylinder (unworn area; see illustration) must be removed. Place the piston at the bottom of the bore, and cover it with a rag. Cut the ridge away using a ridge reamer, exercising extreme care to avoid cutting too deeply. Remove the rag, and remove cuttings that remain on the piston. **CAUTION:** *If the ridge is not removed, and new rings are installed, damage to rings will result.*
Remove the piston and connecting rod: **Push the piston out with a hammer handle**	Invert the engine, and push the pistons and connecting rods out of the cylinders. If necessary, tap the connecting rod boss with a wooden hammer handle, to force the piston out. **CAUTION:** *Do not attempt to force the piston past the cylinder ridge* (see above).
Service the crankshaft:	Ensure that all oil holes and passages in the crankshaft are open and free of sludge. If necessary, have the crankshaft ground to the largest possible undersize.
	** Have the crankshaft Magnafluxed, to locate stress cracks. Consult a machinist concerning additional service procedures, such as surface hardening (e.g., nitriding, Tuftriding) to improve wear characteristics, cross drilling and chamfering the oil holes to improve lubrication, and balancing.
Removing freeze plugs:	Drill a small hole in the middle of the freeze plugs. Thread a large sheet metal screw into the hole and remove the plug with a slide hammer.
Remove the oil gallery plugs:	Threaded plugs should be removed using an appropriate (usually square) wrench. To remove soft, pressed in plugs, drill a hole in the plug, and thread in a sheet metal screw. Pull the plug out by the screw using pliers.

Cylinder Block Reconditioning

Procedure	Method
Hot-tank the block: NOTE: *Do not hot-tank aluminum parts.*	Have the block hot-tanked to remove grease, corrosion, and scale from the water jackets. **NOTE:** *Consult the operator to determine whether the camshaft bearings will be damaged during the hot-tank process.*

Check the block for cracks:	Visually inspect the block for cracks or chips. The most common locations are as follows:
	    Adjacent to freeze plugs.
	    Between the cylinders and water jackets.
	    Adjacent to the main bearing saddles.
	    At the extreme bottom of the cylinders.
	Check only suspected cracks using spot check dye (see introduction). If a crack is located, consult a machinist concerning possible repairs.

	** Magnaflux the block to locate hidden cracks. If cracks are located, consult a machinist about feasibility of repair.
Install the oil gallery plugs and freeze plugs:	Coat freeze plugs with sealer and tap into position using a piece of pipe, slightly smaller than the plug, as a driver. To ensure retention, stake the edges of the plugs. Coat threaded oil gallery plugs with sealer and install. Drive replacement soft plugs into block using a large drift as a driver.
	* Rather than reinstalling lead plugs, drill and tap the holes, and install threaded plugs.
Check the bore diameter and surface: 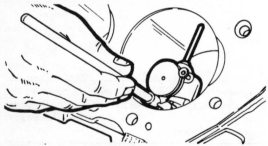 **Measure the cylinder bore with a dial gauge**	Visually inspect the cylinder bores for roughness, scoring, or scuffing. If evident, the cylinder bore must be bored or honed oversize to eliminate imperfections, and the smallest possible oversize piston used. The new pistons should be given to the machinist with the block, so that the cylinders can be bored or honed exactly to the piston size (plus clearance). If no flaws are evident, measure the bore diameter using a telescope gauge and micrometer, or dial gauge, parallel and perpendicular to the engine centerline, at the top (below the ridge) and bottom of the bore. Subtract the bottom measurements from the top to determine taper, and the parallel to

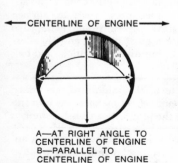

Cylinder bore measuring points

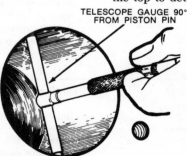

Measure the cylinder bore with a telescope gauge

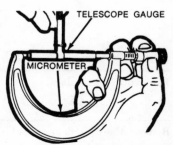

Measure the telescope gauge with a micrometer to determine the cylinder bore

Cylinder Block Reconditioning

Procedure	Method
	the centerline measurements from the perpendicular measurements to determine eccentricity. If the measurements are not within specifications, the cylinder must be bored or honed, and an oversize piston installed. If the measurements are within specifications the cylinder may be used as is, with only finish honing (see below). **NOTE:** *Prior to submitting the block for boring, perform the following operation(s).*
Check the cylinder block bearing alignment:  **Check the main bearing saddle alignment**	Remove the upper bearing inserts. Place a straightedge in the bearing saddles along the centerline of the crankshaft. If clearance exists between the straightedge and the center saddle, the block must be alignbored.
*Check the deck height:	The deck height is the distance from the crankshaft centerline to the block deck. To measure, invert the engine, and install the crankshaft, retaining it with the center main cap. Measure the distance from the crankshaft journal to the block deck, parallel to the cylinder centerline. Measure the diameter of the end (front and rear) main journals, parallel to the centerline of the cylinders, divide the diameter in half, and subtract it from the previous measurement. The results of the front and rear measurements should be identical. If the difference exceeds .005″, the deck height should be corrected. **NOTE:** *Block deck height and warpage should be corrected at the same time.*
Check the block deck for warpage:	Using a straightedge and feeler gauges, check the block deck for warpage in the same manner that the cylinder head is checked (see Cylinder Head Reconditioning). If warpage exceeds specifications, have the deck resurfaced. **NOTE:** *In certain cases a specification for total material removal (cylinder head and block deck) is provided. This specification must not be exceeded.*
Clean and inspect the pistons and connecting rods: 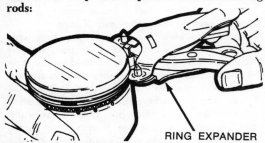 RING EXPANDER **Remove the piston rings**	Using a ring expander, remove the rings from the piston. Remove the retaining rings (if so equipped) and remove piston pin. **NOTE:** *If the piston pin must be pressed out, determine the proper method and use the proper tools; otherwise the piston will distort.* Clean the ring grooves using an appropriate tool, exercising care to avoid cutting too deeply. Thoroughly clean all carbon and varnish from the piston with solvent. **CAUTION:** *Do not use a wire brush or caustic solvent on pistons.* Inspect the pistons for scuffing, scoring, cracks, pitting, or excessive ring

Cylinder Block Reconditioning

| **Procedure** | **Method** |

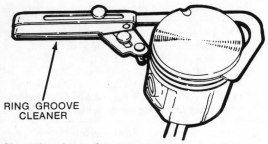

RING GROOVE
CLEANER

Clean the piston ring grooves

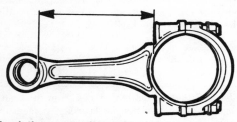

Check the connecting rod length (arrow)

groove wear. If wear is evident, the piston must be replaced. Check the connecting rod length by measuring the rod from the inside of the large end to the inside of the small end using calipers (see illustration). All connecting rods should be equal length. Replace any rod that differs from the others in the engine.

* Have the connecting rod alignment checked in an alignment fixture by a machinist. Replace any twisted or bent rods.

* Magnaflux the connecting rods to locate stress cracks. If cracks are found, replace the connecting rod.

Fit the pistons to the cylinders:

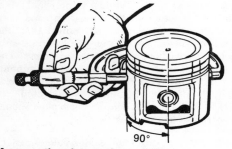

90°

Measure the piston prior to fitting

Using a telescope gauge and micrometer, or a dial gauge, measure the cylinder bore diameter perpendicular to the piston pin, 2½″ below the deck. Measure the piston perpendicular to its pin on the skirt. The difference between the two measurements is the piston clearance. If the clearance is within specifications or slightly below (after boring or honing), finish honing is all that is required. If the clearance is excessive, try to obtain a slightly larger piston to bring clearance within specifications. Where this is not possible, obtain the first oversize piston, and hone (or if necessary, bore) the cylinder to size.

Assemble the pistons and connecting rods:

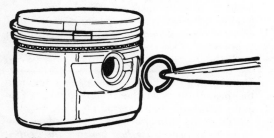

Install the piston pin lock-rings (if used)

Inspect piston pin, connecting rod small end bushing, and piston bore for galling, scoring, or excessive wear. If evident, replace defective part(s). Measure the I.D. of the piston boss and connecting rod small end, and the O.D. of the piston pin. If within specifications, assemble piston pin and rod.
CAUTION: *If piston pin must be pressed in, determine the proper method and use the proper tools; otherwise the piston will distort.*
    Install the lock rings; ensure that they seat properly. If the parts are not within specifications, determine the service method for the type of engine. In some cases, piston and pin are serviced as an assembly when either is defective. Others specify reaming the piston and connecting rods for an oversize pin. If the connecting rod bushing is worn, it may in many cases be replaced. Reaming the piston and replacing the rod bushing are machine shop operations.

Cylinder Block Reconditioning

Procedure	Method

Clean and inspect the camshaft:

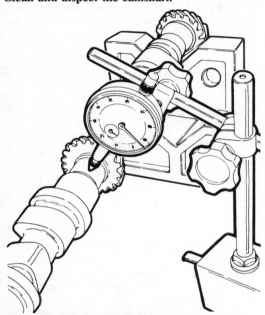

Check the camshaft for straightness

Degrease the camshaft, using solvent, and clean out all oil holes. Visually inspect cam lobes and bearing journals for excessive wear. If a lobe is questionable, check all lobes as indicated below. If a journal or lobe is worn, the camshaft must be reground or replaced.

NOTE: *If a journal is worn, there is a good chance that the bushings are worn.* If lobes and journals appear intact, place the front and rear journals in V-blocks, and rest a dial indicator on the center journal. Rotate the camshaft to check straightness. If deviation exceeds .001", replace the camshaft.

*Check the camshaft lobes with a micrometer, by measuring the lobes from the nose to base and again at 90° (see illustration). The lift is determined by subtracting the second measurement from the first. If all exhaust lobes and all intake lobes are not identical, the camshaft must be reground or replaced.

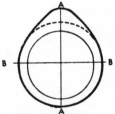

Camshaft lobe measurement

Replace the camshaft bearings:

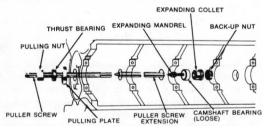

Camshaft bearing removal and installation tool (OHV engines only)

If excessive wear is indicated, or if the engine is being completely rebuilt, camshaft bearings should be replaced as follows: Drive the camshaft rear plug from the block. Assemble the removal puller with its shoulder on the bearing to be removed. Gradually tighten the puller nut until bearing is removed. Remove remaining bearings, leaving the front and rear for last. To remove front and rear bearings, reverse position of the tool, so as to pull the bearings in toward the center of the block. Leave the tool in this position, pilot the new front and rear bearings on the installer, and pull them into position: Return the tool to its original position and pull remaining bearings into position.

NOTE: *Ensure that oil holes align when installing bearings.* Replace camshaft rear plug, and stake it into position to aid retention.

Finish hone the cylinders:

Chuck a flexible drive hone into a power drill, and insert it into the cylinder. Start the hone, and remove it up and down in the cylinder at a rate which will produce approximately a 60° cross-hatch pattern.

NOTE: *Do not extend the hone below the cylinder bore.* After developing the pattern, remove

Cylinder Block Reconditioning

Procedure	Method

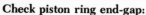
CROSS HATCH PATTERN

50°-60°

Cylinder bore after honing

the hone and recheck piston fit. Wash the cylinders with a detergent and water solution to remove abrasive dust, dry, and wipe several times with a rag soaked in engine oil.

Check piston ring end-gap:

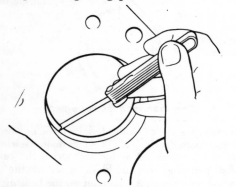

Check the piston ring end gap

Compress the piston rings to be used in a cylinder, one at a time, into that cylinder, and press them approximately 1″ below the deck with an inverted piston. Using feeler gauges, measure the ring end-gap, and compare to specifications. Pull the ring out of the cylinder and file the ends with a fine file to obtain proper clearance.

CAUTION: *If inadequate ring end-gap is utilized, ring breakage will result.*

Install the piston rings:

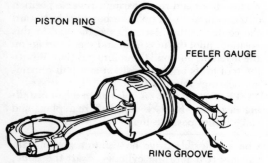
PISTON RING

FEELER GAUGE

RING GROOVE

Check the piston ring side clearance

Inspect the ring grooves in the piston for excessive wear or taper. If necessary, recut the groove(s) for use with an overwidth ring or a standard ring and spacer. If the groove is worn uniformly, overwidth rings, or standard rings and spacers may be installed without recutting. Roll the outside of the ring around the groove to check for burrs or deposits. If any are found, remove with a fine file. Hold the ring in the groove, and measure side clearance. If necessary, correct as indicated above.

NOTE: *Always install any additional spacers above the piston ring.*

The ring groove must be deep enough to allow the ring to seat below the lands (see illustration). In many cases, a "go-no-go" depth gauge will be provided with the piston rings. Shallow grooves may be corrected by recutting, while deep grooves require some type of filler or expander

Cylinder Block Reconditioning

Procedure	Method
	behind the piston. Consult the piston ring supplier concerning the suggested method. Install the rings on the piston, lowest ring first, using a ring expander. **NOTE:** *Position the rings as specified by the manufacturer.* Consult the engine service procedures earlier in this chapter for details concerning specific engines.
Install the camshaft:	Liberally lubricate the camshaft lobes and journals, and install the camshaft. **CAUTION:** *Exercise extreme care to avoid damaging the bearings when inserting the camshaft.* Install and tighten the camshaft thrust plate retaining bolts.
	See the engine service procedures earlier in this chapter for details concerning specific engines.
Check camshaft end-play (OHV engines only): **Check the camshaft end-play with a feeler gauge**	Using feeler gauges, determine whether the clearance between the camshaft boss (or gear) and backing plate is within specifications. Install shims behind the thrust plate, or reposition the camshaft gear and retest endplay. In some cases, adjustment is by replacing the thrust plate. See the engine service procedures earlier in this chapter for details concerning specific engines.
DIAL INDICATOR CAMSHAFT **Check the camshaft end-play with a dial indicator**	* Mount a dial indicator stand so that the stem of the dial indicator rests on the nose of the camshaft, parallel to the camshaft axis. Push the camshaft as far in as possible and zero the gauge. Move the camshaft outward to determine the amount of camshaft endplay. If the endplay is not within tolerance, install shims behind the thrust plate, or reposition the camshaft gear and retest. See the engine service procedures earlier in this chapter for details concerning specific engines.
Install the rear main seal:	See the engine service procedures earlier in this chapter for details concerning specific engines.
Install the crankshaft:  INSTALLING BEARING SHELL REMOVING BEARING SHELL **Remove or install the upper bearing insert using a roll-out pin**	Thoroughly clean the main bearing saddles and caps. Place the upper halves of the bearing inserts on the saddles and press into position. **NOTE:** *Ensure that the oil holes align.* Press the corresponding bearing inserts into the main bearing caps. Lubricate the upper main bearings, and lay the crankshaft in position. Place a strip of Plastigage on each of the crankshaft journals, install the main caps, and torque to specifications. Remove the main caps, and compare the Plastigage to the scale on the Plastigage envelope. If clearances are within tolerances, remove the Plastigage, turn the crankshaft 90°, wipe off all oil and retest. If all clearances are correct,

Cylinder Block Reconditioning

Procedure	Method

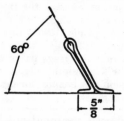

Home-made bearing roll-out pin

remove all Plastigage, thoroughly lubricate the main caps and bearing journals, and install the main caps. If clearances are not within tolerance, the upper bearing inserts may be removed, without removing the crankshaft, using a bearing roll out pin (see illustration). Roll in a bearing that will provide proper clearance, and retest. Torque all main caps, excluding the thrust bearing cap, to specifications. Tighten the thrust bearing cap finger tight. To properly align the thrust bearing, pry the crankshaft the extent of its axial travel several times, the last movement held toward the front of the engine, and torque the thrust bearing cap to specifications. Determine the crankshaft end-play (see below), and bring within tolerance with thrust washers.

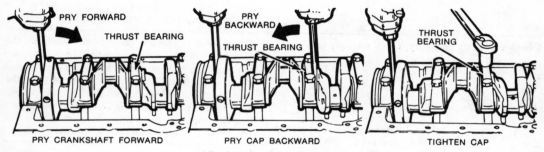

Aligning the thrust bearing

Measure crankshaft end-play:

Mount a dial indicator stand on the front of the block, with the dial indicator stem resting on the nose of the crankshaft, parallel to the crankshaft axis. Pry the crankshaft the extent of its travel rearward, and zero the indicator. Pry the crankshaft forward and record crankshaft end-play. **NOTE:** *Crankshaft end-play also may be measured at the thrust bearing, using feeler gauges (see illustration).*

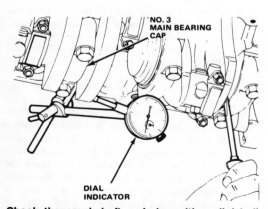

Check the crankshaft end-play with a dial indicator

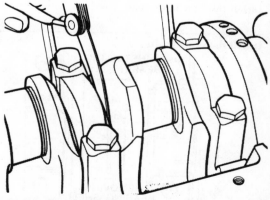

Check the crankshaft end-play with a feeler gauge

Cylinder Block Reconditioning

Procedure	Method
Install the pistons:	Press the upper connecting rod bearing halves into the connecting rods, and the lower halves into the connecting rod caps. Position the piston ring gaps according to specifications (see car section), and lubricate the pistons. Install a ring compresser on a piston, and press two long (8") pieces of plastic tubing over the rod bolts. Using the tubes as a guide, press the pistons into the bores and onto the crankshaft with a wooden hammer handle. After seating the rod on the crankshaft journal, remove the tubes and install the cap finger tight. Install the remaining pistons in the same manner. Invert the engine and check the bearing clearance at two points (90° apart) on each journal with Plastigage.

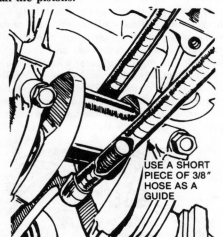

USE A SHORT PIECE OF 3/8" HOSE AS A GUIDE

Use lengths of vacuum hose or rubber tubing to protect the crankshaft journals and cylinder walls during piston installation

RING COMPRESSOR

Install the piston using a ring compressor

NOTE: *Do not turn the crankshaft with Plastigage installed.* If clearance is within tolerances, remove *all* Plastigage, thoroughly lubricate the journals, and torque the rod caps to specifications. If clearance is not within specifications, install different thickness bearing inserts and recheck.

CAUTION: *Never shim or file the connecting rods or caps.* Always install plastic tube sleeves over the rod bolts when the caps are not installed, to protect the crankshaft journals.

Procedure	Method
Check connecting rod side clearance:	Determine the clearance between the sides of the connecting rods and the crankshaft using feeler gauges. If clearance is below the minimum tolerance, the rod may be machined to provide adequate clearance. If clearance is excessive, substitute an unworn rod, and recheck. If clearance is still outside specifications, the crankshaft must be welded and reground, or replaced.

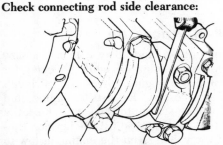

Check the connecting rod side clearance with a feeler gauge

Procedure	Method
Inspect the timing chain (or belt):	Visually inspect the timing chain for broken or loose links, and replace the chain if any are found. If the chain will flex sideways, it must be replaced. Install the timing chain as specified. Be sure the timing belt is not stretched, frayed or broken. **NOTE:** *If the original timing chain is to be reused, install it in its original position.*

Cylinder Block Reconditioning

Procedure	Method
Check timing gear backlash and runout (OHV engines):	Mount a dial indicator with its stem resting on a tooth of the camshaft gear (as illustrated). Rotate the gear until all slack is removed, and zero the indicator. Rotate the gear in the opposite direction until slack is removed, and record gear backlash. Mount the indicator with its stem resting on the edge of the camshaft gear, parallel to the axis of the camshaft. Zero the indicator, and turn the camshaft gear one full turn, recording the runout. If either backlash or runout exceed specifications, replace the worn gear(s).

Check the camshaft gear backlash

Check the camshaft gear run-out

Completing the Rebuilding Process

Follow the above procedures, complete the rebuilding process as follows:

Fill the oil pump with oil, to prevent cavitating (sucking air) on initial engine start up. Install the oil pump and the pickup tube on the engine. Coat the oil pan gasket as necessary, and install the gasket and the oil pan. Mount the flywheel and the crankshaft vibration damper or pulley on the crankshaft. NOTE: *Always use new bolts when installing the flywheel.* Inspect the clutch shaft pilot bushing in the crankshaft. If the bushing is excessively worn, remove it with an expanding puller and a slide hammer, and tap a new bushing into place.

Position the engine, cylinder head side up. Lubricate the lifters, and install them into their bores. Install the cylinder head, and torque it as specified. Insert the pushrods and install the rocker shaft(s) or position the rocker arms on the pushrods. Adjust the valves.

Install the intake and exhaust manifolds, the carburetor(s), the distributor and spark plugs. Adjust the point gap and the static ignition timing. Mount all accessories and install the engine in the car. Fill the radiator with coolant, and the crankcase with high quality engine oil.

Break-in Procedure

Start the engine, and allow it to run at low speed for a few minutes, while checking for leaks. Stop the engine, check the oil level, and fill as necessary. Restart the engine, and fill the cooling system to capacity. Check the point dwell angle and adjust the ignition timing and the valves. Run the engine at low to medium speed (800–2500 rpm) for approximately ½ hour, and retorque the cylinder head bolts. Road test the car, and check again for leaks.

Follow the manufacturer's recommended engine break-in procedure and maintenance schedule for new engines.

Emission Controls and Fuel System

EMISSION CONTROLS

The emission control devices required on a Blazer or Jimmy are determined by the weight classification. Light duty models use the same emission controls as passenger cars; these are all 1969–74 models, 1975 two wheel drive models and all 1979–82 models. Heavy duty models operate under less stringent rules and use a few less emission control devices; these are 1975 four wheel drive models and all 1976–78 models.

PCV (Positive Crankcase Ventilation) was the earliest form of automotive emission control, dating back to 1955 on General Motors vehicles. Still in use today, it routes cylinder fumes from the crankcase through a PCV valve and back into the combustion chamber for reburning.

In 1966, the AIR (Air Injector Reactor) system was introduced on General Motors vehicles to satisfy California emission requirements. This system pumps oxygen to the exhaust gases as they exit from the cylinder, where they are ignited and burned more completely to further reduce hydrocarbon and carbon monoxide exhaust emissions.

General Motors introduced the CCS (Controlled Combustion System) in 1968, which uses various components and design calibrations to further reduce pollutants.

CEC (Combined Emission Control) and TCS (Transmission Controlled Spark) have been used since 1970 and basically do not allow distributor vacuum advance in Low gear.

In 1973, the EGR (Exhaust Gas Recirculation) system was developed in response to more stringent Federal exhaust emission standards regarding NO_x (oxides of nitrogen). Oxides of nitrogen are formed at higher combustion chamber temperatures and increase with higher temperatures. The EGR system is designed to reduce combustion temperature thereby reducing the formation of NO_x.

The ECS (Evaporative Control System) and the EFE (Early Fuel Evaporation System) are designed to control fuel vapors that escape from the fuel tank and carburetor through evaporation. These systems seal the fuel tank to retain vapors in a charcoal canister. The canister is purged and the vapors burned during engine operation.

The PAIR (Pulse Air Injection Reactor) system was introduced in 1979 on the six cylinder. Through the use of exhaust gas backpressure, air is injected into the exhaust system to further the exhaust gas burning process.

Certain late model engines are equipped with ESC (Electronic Spark Control). The ESC controls engine detonation by adjusting spark timing.

The following sections are devoted to the description and service of each separate system.

Positive Crankcase Ventilation

PCV is the earliest form of emission control. Prior to its use, crankcase vapors were vented into the atmosphere through a road draft tube or crankcase breather. The PCV system first appeared on General Motors vehicles in 1955. Beginning 1961, the PCV system was used on all California models and in 1963 the system became standard on all models.

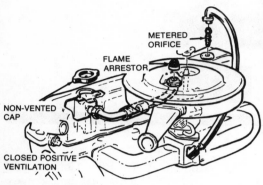

Typical PCV system

This system draws crankcase vapors that are formed through normal combustion into the intake manifold and subsequently into the combustion chambers to be burned. Fresh air is introduced to the crankcase by way of a hose connected to the carburetor air cleaner or a vented oil filler cap on older models. Manifold vacuum is used to draw the vapors from the crankcase through a PCV valve and into the intake manifold. Vented and nonvented filler caps were used on various models until 1968, after which only nonvented caps were used.

SERVICE

Other than checking and replacing the PCV valve and associated hoses, there is no other service required. Engine operating conditions that would direct suspicion to the PCV system are rough idle, oil present in the air cleaner, oil leaks and excessive oil sludging or dilution. If any of the above conditions exist, remove the PCV valve and shake it. A clicking sound indicates that the valve is free. If no clicking sound is heard, replace the valve. Inspect the PCV breather in the air cleaner. Replace the breather if it is so dirty

that it will not allow gases to pass through. Check all the PCV hoses for condition and tight connections. Replace any hoses that have deteriorated.

Air Injector Reactor (Air Pump)

This system was first introduced on California vehicles in 1966. The AIR system injects compressed air into the exhaust system, near enough to the exhaust valves to continue the burning of the normally unburned segment of the exhaust gases. To do this it employs an air injection pump and a system of hoses, valves, tubes, etc., necessary to carry the compressed air from the pump to the exhaust manifolds.

A diverter valve is used to prevent backfiring. The valve senses sudden increases in manifold vacuum and ceases the injection of air during fuel-rich periods. During coasting, this valve diverts the entire air flow through a muffler and during high engine speeds, expels it through a relief valve. Check valves in the system prevent exhaust gases from entering the pump.

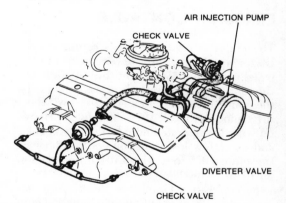

Typical AIR system components

TESTING

Check Valve

To test the check valve, disconnect the hose at the diverter valve. Blow into the hose and suck on it. Air should flow only into the engine.

Diverter Valve

Pull off the vacuum line to the top of the valve with the engine running. There should be vacuum in the line. Replace the line. No air should be escaping with the engine running at a steady idle. Open and quickly close the throttle. A blast of air should come out of the valve muffler for at least one second.

Air Injection System Diagnosis Chart

Problem	Cause	Cure
1. Noisy drive belt	1a Loose belt 1b Seized pump	1a Tighten belt 1b Replace
2. Noisy pump	2a Leaking hose 2b Loose hose 2c Hose contacting other parts 2d Diverter or check valve failure 2e Pump mounting loose 2g Defective pump	2a Trace and fix leak 2b Tighten hose clamp 2c Reposition hose 2d Replace 2e Tighten securing bolts 2g Replace
3. No air supply	3a Loose belt 3b Leak in hose or at fitting 3c Defective anti-backfire valve 3d Defective check valve 3e Defective pump	3a Tighten belt 3b Trace and fix leak 3c Replace 3d Replace 3e Replace
4. Exhaust backfire	4a Vacuum or air leaks 4b Defective anti-backfire valve 4c Sticking choke 4d Choke setting rich	4a Trace and fix leak 4b Replace 4c Service choke 4d Adjust choke

Air Pump

Disconnect the hose from the diverter valve. Start the engine and accelerate it to about 1,500 rpm. The airflow should increase as the engine is accelerated. If no airflow is noted or it remains constant, check the following:

1. Drive belt tension.

2. Listen for a leaking pressure relief valve. If it is defective, replace the whole relief/diverter valve.

3. Foreign matter in pump filter openings. If the pump is defective or excessively noisy, it must be replaced.

SERVICE

All hoses and fittings should be inspected for condition and tightness of connections. Check the drive belt for wear and tension periodically.

NOTE: *The AIR system is not completely silent under normal conditions. Noises will rise in pitch as engine speed increases. If the noise is excessive, eliminate the air pump itself by disconnecting the drive belt. If the noise disappears, the air pump is not at fault.*

AIR PUMP REMOVAL AND INSTALLATION

1. Disconnect the output hose.

2. Hold the pump from turning by squeezing the drive belt.

3. Loosen the pulley bolts.

4. Loosen the alternator so the belt can be removed.

5. Remove the pulley.

6. Remove the pump mounting bolts and the pump.

7. Install the pump with the mounting bolts loose.

8. Install the pulley and tighten the bolts finger-tight.

9. Install and adjust the drive belt.

10. Squeeze the drive belt to prevent the pump from turning.

11. Torque the pulley bolts to 25 ft. lbs. Tighten the pump mountings.

12. Check and adjust the belt tension again, if necessary.

13. Connect the hose.

14. If any hose leaks are suspected, pour soapy water over the suspected area with the engine running. Bubbles will form wherever air is escaping.

FILTER REPLACEMENT

1. Disconnect the air and vacuum hoses from the diverter valve.

2. Loosen the pump pivot and adjusting bolts and remove the drive belt.

3. Remove the pivot and adjusting bolts from the pump. Remove the pump and the diverter valve as an assembly.

CAUTION: *Do not clamp the pump in a*

vise or use a hammer or pry bar on the pump housing.

4. To change the filter, break the plastic fan from the hub. It is seldom possible to remove the fan without breaking it.

5. Remove the remaining portion of the fan filter from the pump hub. Be careful that filter fragments do not enter the air intake hole.

6. Position the new centrifugal fan filter on the pump hub. Place the pump pulley against the fan filter and install the securing screws. Torque the screws alternately to 95 in. lbs. and the fan filter will be pressed onto the pump hub.

7. Install the pump on the engine and adjust its drive belt.

NOTE: *A slight amount of interference between the fan filter and the pump housing bore is normal. After a new fan filter has been installed, it may squeal upon initial operation or until its outside diameter sealing lip is worn in. This may require a short period of pump operation at various engine speeds.*

Controlled Combustion System

The CCS system is a combination of systems and calibrations. Many of these are not visible or serviceable, but are designed into the engine. Originally, in 1968–69, the system was comprised of special carburetion and distributor settings, higher engine operating temperatures and a thermostatically-controlled air cleaner. In later years, the thermostatically-controlled air cleaner (CHA) was used independently of the other settings on some engines. Likewise, some engines used the special settings without CHA. In 1970, the TCS system was incorporated; the system was renamed CEC in 1971. The name reverted to TCS in 1972. In 1973, EGR was also added to the system.

The various systems, CHA, TCS, CEC and EGR are all part of the Controlled Combustion System.

Service

Refer to the CHA, TCS, CEC or EGR Sections for maintenance and service (if applicable).

CARBURETOR HEATED AIR

The use of carburetor heated air dates back to 1960 when it was first used on heavy trucks.

This system is designed to warm the air entering the carburetor when underhood tem-peratures are low. This allows more precise calibration of the carburetor.

The thermostatically-controlled air cleaner is composed of the air cleaner body, a filter, sensor unit, vacuum diaphragm, damper door and associated hoses and connections. Heat radiating from the exhaust manifold is trapped by a heat stove and is ducted to the air cleaner to supply heated air to the carburetor. A movable door in the air cleaner snorkel allows air to be drawn in from the heat stove (cold operation) or from the underhood air (warm operation). Periods of extended idling, climbing a grade or high-speed operation are followed by a considerable increase in engine compartment temperature. Excessive fuel vapors enter the intake manifold causing an over-rich mixture, resulting in a rough idle. To overcome this, some engines may be equipped with a hot idle compensator.

Service

1. Either start with a cold engine or remove the air cleaner from the engine for at least half an hour. While cooling the air cleaner, leave the engine compartment hood open.

2. Tape a thermometer, of known accuracy, to the inside of the air cleaner so that it is near the temperature sensor unit. Install the air cleaner on the engine but do not fasten its securing nut.

3. Start the engine. With the engine cold and the outside temperature less than 90°F., the door should be in the "heat on" position (closed to outside air).

NOTE: *Due to the position of the air cleaner on some trucks, a mirror may be necessary when observing the position of the air door.*

4. Operate the throttle lever rapidly to ½–

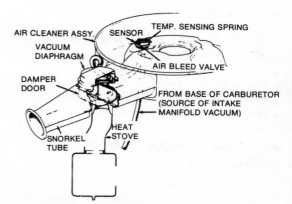

Typical carburetor heated air system

¾ of its opening and release it. The air door should open to allow outside air to enter and then close again.

5. Allow the engine to warm up to normal temperature. Watch the door. When it opens to the outside air, remove the cover from the air cleaner. The temperature should be over 90°F and no more than 130°F; 115°F is about normal. If the door does not work within these temperature ranges, or fails to work at all, check for linkage or door bindings.

If binding is not present and the air door is not working, proceed with the vacuum tests, given below. If these indicate no faults in the vacuum motor and the door is not working, the temperature sensor is defective and must be replaced.

Vacuum Motor Test

NOTE: *Be sure that the vacuum hose which runs between the temperature switch and the vacuum motor is not pinched by the retaining clip under the air cleaner. This could prevent the air door from closing.*

1. Check all of the vacuum lines and fittings for leaks. Correct any leaks. If none are found, proceed with the test.

2. Remove the hose which runs from the sensor to the vacuum motor. Run a hose directly from the manifold vacuum source to the vacuum motor.

3. If the motor closes the air door, it is functioning properly and the temperature sensor is defective.

4. If the motor does *not* close the door and no binding is present in its operation, the vacuum motor is defective and must be replaced.

NOTE: *If an alternate vacuum source is applied to the motor, insert a vacuum gauge in the line by using a T-fitting. Apply at least 9 in. Hg of vacuum in order to operate the motor.*

TRANSMISSION CONTROLLED SPARK

Introduced in 1970, this system controls exhaust emissions by eliminating vacuum advance in the lower forward gears.

The 1970 system consists of a transmission switch, solenoid vacuum switch, time delay relay, and a thermostatic water temperature switch. The solenoid vacuum switch is de-energized in the lower gears via the transmission switch and closes off distributor vacuum. The two-way transmission switch is activated by the shifter shaft on manual transmissions, and by fluid pressure on automatic transmis-

sions. The switch energizes the solenoid in High gear, the plunger extends and uncovers the vacuum port, and the distributor receives full vacuum. The temperature switch overrides the system until the engine temperature reaches 82°F. This allows vacuum advance in all gears, thereby preventing stalling after starting. A time delay relay opens fifteen seconds after the ignition is switched on. Full vacuum advance during this delay eliminates the possibility of stalling.

The 1971 system is similar, except that the vacuum solenoid (called a Combination Emissions Control solenoid) serves two functions. One function is to control distributor vacuum; the added function is to act as a deceleration throttle stop in High gear. This cuts down on emissions when the vehicle is coming to a stop in High gear. Two throttle settings are necessary; one for curb idle and one for emission control on coast.

The 1972 six cylinder system is similar to that used in 1971, except that an idle stop solenoid was added to the system and the name was changed back to TCS. In the energized position, the solenoid maintains engine speed at a predetermined fast idle. When de-energized the solenoid allows the throttle plates to close beyond the normal idle position; thus cutting off the air supply and preventing engine run-on. The six cylinder is the only 1972 engine with a CEC valve, which serves the same deceleration function as in 1971. The time delay relay delays full vacuum twenty seconds after the transmission is shifted into High gear. 1972 V8 engines use a vacuum advance solenoid similar to that used in 1970. The solenoid controls distributor vacuum advance and performs no throttle positioning function. The idle stop solenoid used on V8s operates in the same manner as the one on six cylinder engines. Air conditioned trucks have an additional anti-diesel (run-on) solenoid which engages the compressor clutch for three seconds after the ignition is switched off.

The 1973 TCS system on the six cylinder engine is identical to that on the 1972 six, except for recalibration of the temperature switch. The system used on 1973 V8 engines changed slightly from 1972. In place of the CEC solenoid on the six, the V8 continues to use a vacuum advance solenoid. The other differences are: the upshift delay relay, previously located under the instrument panel had been done away with; a 20 second time delay relay identical to the one on six cylinder engines is used; V8s use manifold vacuum with TCS and ported (above the throttle plates) vacuum without TCS.

The six cylinder TCS system was revised for 1974–75 by replacing the CEC solenoid with a vacuum advance solenoid. Otherwise the system remains the same as 1973.

Testing

If there is a TCS system malfunction, first connect a vacuum gauge in the hose between the solenoid valve and the distributor vacuum unit. Drive the vehicle or raise it on a frame lift and observe the vacuum gauge. If full vacuum is available in all gears, check for the following:

1. Blown fuse.
2. Disconnected wire at solenoid-operated vacuum valve.
3. Disconnected wire at transmission switch.
4. Temperature override switch energized due to low engine temperature.
5. Solenoid failure.

If no vacuum is available in any gear, check the following:

1. Solenoid valve vacuum lines switched.
2. Clogged solenoid vacuum valve.
3. Distributor or manifold vacuum lines leaking or disconnected.
4. Transmission switch or wire grounded.

Tests for individual components are as follows:

IDLE STOP SOLENOID

This unit may be checked simply by observing it while an assistant switches the ignition on and off. It should extend further with the current switched on. The unit is not repairable.

SOLENOID VACUUM VALVE

Check that proper manifold vacuum is available. Connect the vacuum gauge in the line between the solenoid valve and the distributor. Apply 12 volts to the solenoid. If vacuum is still not available, the valve is defective, either mechanically or electrically. The unit is not repairable. If the valve is satisfactory, check the relay next.

RELAY

1. With the engine at normal operating temperature and the ignition on, ground the solenoid vacuum valve terminal with the black lead. The solenoid should energize (no vacuum) if the relay is satisfactory.

2. With the solenoid energized as in Step 1, connect a jumper from the relay terminal with the green/white stripe lead to ground. The solenoid should de-energize (vacuum available) if the relay is satisfactory.

3. If the relay worked properly in Steps 1 and 2, check the temperature switch. The relay unit is not repairable.

TEMPERATURE SWITCH

The vacuum valve solenoid should be de-energized (vacuum availale) with the engine cold. If it is not, ground the green/white stripe wire from the switch. If the solenoid now de-energizes, replace the switch. If the switch was satisfactory, check the transmission switch.

TRANSMISSION SWITCH

With the engine at normal operating temperature and the transmission in one of the no-vacuum gears, the vacuum valve solenoid should be energized (no vacuum). If not, remove and ground the switch electrical lead. If the solenoid energizes, replace the switch.

EXHAUST GAS RECIRCULATION

The EGR system and valve were introduced in 1973. Its purpose is to control oxides of nitrogen which are formed during the peak combustion temperatures. The end products of combustion are relatively inert gases derived from the exhaust gases which are directed into the EGR valve to help lower peak combustion temperatures.

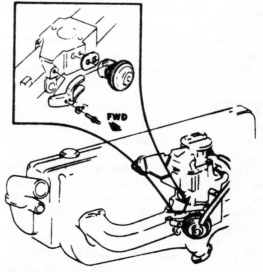

Six cylinder EGR valve

The EGR valve contains a vacuum diaphragm operated by manifold vacuum. The vacuum signal port is located in the carburetor body and is exposed to engine vacuum in the off-idle and part-throttle operation. In 1974, a thermo-delay switch was added to delay operation of the valve during engine warm-up, when NO_x levels are already at a minimum.

On six cylinder engines, the EGR valve is on the intake manifold adjacent to the carburetor. On V8 engines, the valve is on the right rear side of the intake manifold adjacent to the rocker arm cover.

Service

The EGR valve is not serviceable, except for replacement. To check the valve, proceed as follows:

1. Connect a tachometer to the engine.
2. With the engine running at normal operating temperature, with the choke valve fully open, set the engine rpm at 2,000. The transmission should be in Park (automatic) or Neutral (manual) with the parking brake On and the wheels blocked.
3. Disconnect the vacuum hose at the valve. Make sure that vacuum is available at the valve and look at the tachometer to see if the engine speed increass. If it does, a malfunction of the valve is indicated.
4. If necessary, replace the valve.

Evaporation Control System

Introduced on California vehicles in 1970, and nationwide in 1971, this system reduces the amount of escaping gasoline vapors. Float bowl emissions are controlled by internal carburetor modifications. Redesigned bowl vents, reduced bowl capacity, heat shields, and improved intake manifold-to-carburetor insulation serve to reduce vapor loss into the atmosphere. The venting of fuel tank vapors into the air has been stopped. Fuel vapors are directed through lines to a canister containing an activated charcoal filter. Unburned vapors are trapped here until the engine is started. When the engine is running, the canister is purged by air drawn in by manifold vacuum. The air and fuel vapors are directed into the engine to be burned.

SERVICE

Replace the filter in the engine compartment canister at the intervals shown in the "Maintenance Intervals Chart" in Chapter 1. If the fuel tank cap requires replacement, ensure that the new cap is the correct part for your truck.

Early Fuel Evaporation System

This system is used on various models from 1975. The six cylinder system consists of an EFE valve mounted at the flange of the exhaust manifold, an actuator, a thermal vacuum switch (TVS), and a vacuum solenoid. The TVS is on the right side of the engine forward of the oil pressure switch. The TVS is normally closed and sensitive to oil temperature.

The V8 EFE system consists of an EFE valve at the flange of the exhaust manifold, an actuator, and a thermal vacuum switch. The TVS is located in the coolant outlet housing and directly controls vacuum.

In both systems, manifold vacuum is applied to the actuator, which in turn, closes the EFE valve. This routes hot exhaust gases to the base of the carburetor. When coolant (V8) or oil (six cylinder) temperatures reach a set limit, vacuum is denied to the actuator allowing an internal spring to return the actuator to its normal position, opening the EFE valve.

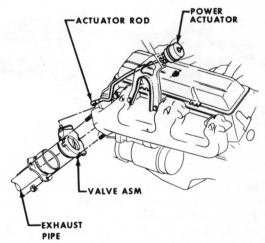

V8 EFE, or vacuum operated heat riser system

Throttle Return Control System

A throttle return control system (TRC) is used on some truck engines. When the truck is coasting against the engine, the control valve is open to allow vacuum to operate the throttle lever actuator. The throttle lever actuator then pushes the throttle lever slightly open reducing the HC (hydrocarbon) emission level

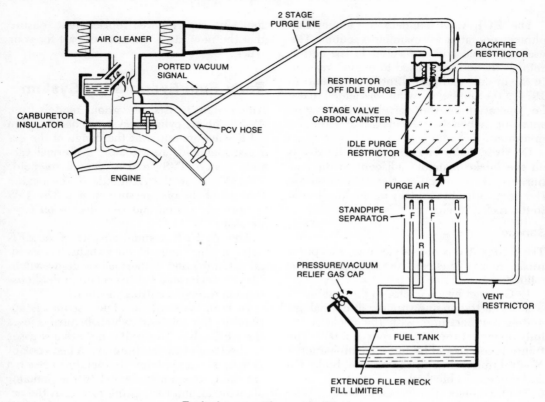

Typical evaporation control system

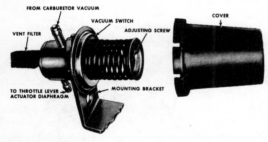

Throttle return control valve

during coasting. When manifold vacuum drops below a predetermined level, the control valve closes, the throttle lever retracts, and the throttle lever closes to the idle position.

SERVICE

Control Valve Check and Adjustment

1. Disconnected the valve-to-carburetor hose and connect it to an external vacuum source with a vacuum gauge.

2. Disconnect the valve-to-actuator hose at the connector and connect it to a vacuum gauge.

3. Place a finger firmly over the end of the bleed fitting.

4. Apply a minimum of 23 in. Hg vacuum to the control valve and seal off the vacuum source. The gauge on the actuator side should read the same as the gauge on the source side. If not, the valve needs adjustment. If vacuum drops off on either side (with the finger still on the bleed fitting), the valve is defective and should be replaced.

5. With a minimum of 23 in. Hg vacuum in the valve, remove the finger from the bleed fitting. The vacuum level in the actuator side will drop to zero and the reading on the source side will drop to a value that will be the valve set point of 21.5 in. Hg. If the valve is not within ½ in. Hg vacuum of the specified valve set point, adjust the valve.

6. Gently pry off the conical plastic cover.

7. Turn the adjusting screw in (clockwise) to raise the set point or out (counterclockwise) to lower the set point.

8. Recheck the valve set point.

9. If necessary, repeat the adjustment.

Throttle Valve Check and Adjustment

1. Disconnect the valve-to-actuator hose at the valve and connect it to an external vacuum source.

2. Apply 20 in. Hg vacuum to the actuator and seal the vacuum source. If the vacuum gauge reading drops, the valve is leaking and should be replaced.

3. Check the throttle lever, shaft, and linkage for freedom of operation.

4. Start the engine and warm it to operating temperature.

5. Note the idle rpm.

6. Apply 20 in. Hg vacuum to the actuator and manually operate the throttle. Allow it to close against the extended actuator plunger. Note the engine rpm.

7. Release and reapply 20 in. Hg vacuum to the actuator and note the rpm at which the engine speed increases (do not assist the actuator).

8. If the engine speed obtained in Step 7 is not within 150 rpm of that obtained in Step 6, then the actuator may be binding. If the binding cannot be corrected, replace the actuator.

9. Release the vacuum from the actuator and the engine speed should return to within 50 rpm of the speed noted in Steps 4 and 5.

To adjust the actuator:

10. Turn the screw on the actuator plunger until the specified TRC speed range (1475–1525 rpm) is obtained.

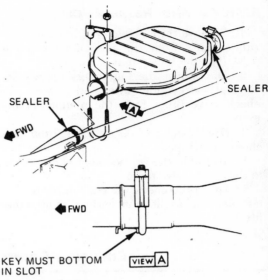

KEY MUST BOTTOM IN SLOT

VIEW A

Catalytic converter installation

6. Install the exhaust pipe and tailpipe into the converter with sealer.

7. Loosely install the support of the transmission.

8. Install new U-bolts and clamps, check all clearances and tighten the clamps.

9. Lower the truck.

Catalytic Converter

An underfloor catalytic converter is used to control exhaust emissions. Control is accomplished by placing a catalyst in the exhaust system in such a way as to enable all exhaust gas flow from the engine to pass through it and undergo a chemical reaction before passing into the atmosphere.

REMOVAL AND INSTALLATION

WARNING: *Catalytic converter operating temperatures are extremely high. Outside converter temperatures can go well over 1,000°F. Use extreme care when working on the catalytic converter or when working anywhere around it.*

1. Raise and support the truck.

2. Remove the clamps at the front and rear of the converter.

3. Cut the converter pipes at the front and rear of the converter and remove it.

4. Remove the support from the transmission.

5. Remove the converter pipe-to-exhaust pie and the converter pipe-to-tailpipe.

To install the converter:

Pulse Air Injection Reactor System

This system consists of four air valves which inject fresh air into the exhaust system in order to further the combustion process of the exhaust gases. The firing of the engine creates a pulsating flow of exhaust gases, which are either positive or negative pressure. A negative pressure at the pulse air valve will result in air being injected into the exhaust system. A positive pressure will force the check valve closed and no exhaust gases will flow into the fresh air supply.

Regularly inspect the pulse air valves, pipes, grommets and hose for cracks and leaks. Replace the necessary part if any defects are found. If a check valve fails, exhaust gases will get into the carburetor through the air cleaner and cause the engine to surge and perform poorly.

If exhaust gases pass through a pulse air valve, the paint will be burned off the rocker arm cover plenum as a result of the excessive heat. The rubber grommets and hose will also deteriorate. Failure of the pulse air valve can also be indicated by a hissing sound.

REMOVAL AND INSTALLATION

1. Remove the air cleaner. Disconnect the rubber hose from the plenum connecting pipe. (See the illustration.)

2. Disconnect the four check valuve fittings at the cylinder head and remove the check valve pipes from the plenum grommets.

3. Disconnect the check valve from the check valve pipe.

4. Assemble the replacement check valve to the check valve pipe.

5. Attach the check valve assembly to the cylinder head as illustrated. Hand tighten the fittings.

6. Using a 1 inch open end wrench as a lever, align the check valve on pipe "A" with the plenum grommet. Using the palm of your left hand, press the check valve into the grommet. Using a silicone lubricant on the grommet will make things a little easier. Repeat this procedure for pipe "B" using your left hand for the tool and your right hand for installing the valve in the grommet.

Deceleration Valve

A deceleration valve is used on most 6 cylinder engines and most automatic transmission equipped V8's to prevent backfiring in the

Emission Control System Checks

System	Condition	Checks(s)
Positive Crankcase Ventilation	Oil leaks, Rough idle	Plugged system Improper hose routing
Air Injector Reactor	Noise	Loose belt or hose Worn pump Diverter valve stuck open Misaligned pump Improper hose mounting
	"Pop" on deceleration	Diverter valve stuck closed
Controlled Combustion System	Rough idle, stumble or stall	Vacuum hose leak Air cleaner damper stuck: Defective thermostat Defective vacuum diaphragm General tune-up
Transmission Controlled Spark/ Combined Emission Control	Rough idle, stumble or stall Dieseling Poor fuel economy No vacuum advance	Vacuum leak Idle stop solenoid stuck ① Vacuum solenoid stuck ① Relay, transmission and temperature switch operation ①
Carburetor Heated Air	Rough idle, stumble or stall	Vacuum hose leak Air cleaner damper stuck: Defective thermostat Defective vacuum diaphragm
Exhaust Gas Recirculated	Rough idle, stumble or stall	Corroded valve shaft Defective valve diaphragm
Evaporative Emission Control	Fuel odor Bulged or collapsed fuel tank	Leak in the fuel system Missing, plugged or incorrect gap cap Incorrect hose routing Plugged line or separator

① Use a test wire from the battery to the solenoid or switch to check for mechanical movement exhaust system during decleration. When deceleration causes a sudden increase of vacuum in the signal line the valve opens allowing air to bleed into the intake manifold.

Electronic Spark Control (ESC)

The Electronic Spark Control (ESC) system is a closed loop system that controls engine detonation by adjusting the spark timing. There are two basic components in this system, the controller and the sensor.

The controller processes the sensor signal and remodifies the EST signal to the distributor to adjust the spark timing. The process is continuous so that the presence of detonation is monitored and controlled. The controller is not capable of memory storage.

The sensor is a magnetorestrictive device, mounted in the engine block that detects the presence, or absence, and intensity of detonation according to the vibration characteristics of the engine. The output is an electrical signal which is sent to the controller.

NOTE: *Service on vehicles ESC system is complex and should be maintained by a qualified mechanic.*

FUEL SYSTEM

NOTE: *Servicing the Diesel Engine fuel system is covered at the end of the carburetor section.*

Fuel Pump

The fuel pump is a single action diaphragm type. All fuel pumps are serviced by replacement only. No adjustments or repairs are possible.

The pump is operated by an eccentric on the camshaft. On six cylinder engines, the eccentric acts directly on the pump rocker arm. On V8 engines, a pushrod between the camshaft eccentric and the fuel pump operates the pump rocker arm.

TESTING

Fuel pumps should always be tested on the vehicle. The larger line between the pump and tank is the suction side of the system and the smaller line, between the pump and carburetor is the pressure side. A leak in the pressure side would be apparent because of dripping fuel. A leak in the suction side is usually only apparent because of a reduced volume of fuel delivered to the pressure side.

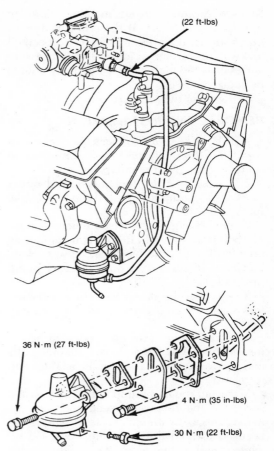

(22 ft-lbs)

36 N·m (27 ft-lbs)

4 N·m (35 in-lbs)

30 N·m (22 ft-lbs)

V8 fuel pump location and installation details

1. Tighten any loose line connections and look for any kinks or restrictions.

2. Disconnect the fuel line at the carburetor. Disconnect the distributor-to-coil primary wire. Place a container at the end of the fuel line and crank the engine a few revolutions. If little or no gasoline flows from the line, either the fuel pump is inoperative or the line is plugged. Disconnect the line at the pump and at the tank; blow through the line with compressed air and try the test again. Reconnect the line. If the problem is traced to the tank, the tank and the gauge unit must be removed to check the condition of the inlet filter screen. See Chapter 10 for tank removal.

3. If fuel flows in good volume, check the fuel pump pressure to be sure.

4. Attach a pressure gauge to the pressure side of the fuel line.

5. Run the engine (on the gas in the carburetor) and note the reading on the gauge. Stop the engine and compare the reading with

the specifications listed in the "Tune-Up Specifications" chart. If the pump is operating properly, the pressure will be as specified and will be constant at idle speed. If pressure varies or is too high or low, the pump should be replaced.

6. Remove the pressure gauge.

REMOVAL AND INSTALLATION

NOTE: *When you connect the fuel pump outlet fitting, always use 2 wrenches to avoid damaging the pump.*

1. Disconnect the fuel intake and outlet lines at the pump and plug the pump intake line.

2. On V8 engines, you can remove the upper bolt from the right front engine mounting boss (on front of the block) and insert a long bolt ($\frac{3}{8} - 16 \times 2$ in.) to hold the fuel pump pushrod.

3. Remove the pump mounting bolts and lockwashers; remove the pump and its gasket.

4. If the rocker arm pushrod is to be removed from V8s, remove the adapter bolts and lockwashers and remove the adapter and its gasket.

5. Install the fuel pump with a new gasket reversing the removal procedure. Coat the mating surfaces with sealer. Heavy grease can be used to hold the fuel pump pushrod up while installing the pump, if you didn't install the long bolt in step 2.

6. Connect the fuel lines and check for leaks.

Carburetor

REMOVAL AND INSTALLATION

1. Remove the air cleaner and mounting gasket.

2. Disconnect the fuel and vacuum lines from the carburetor.

3. Disconnect the choke coil rod or heated air line tube.

4. Disconnect the throttle linkage.

5. On automatic transmission models, disconnect the throttle valve linkage.

6. Remove all vacuum hoses and electrical connectors.

7. Remove the idle stop electrical wiring from the idle stop solenoid, if so equipped.

8. Remove the carburetor attaching nuts and/or bolts, gasket or insulator, and remove the carburetor.

9. Install the carburetor using a reverse of the removal procedure. Use a new gasket and tighten the mounting bolts evenly.

OVERHAUL

Efficient carburetion depends greatly on careful cleaning and inspection during overhaul, since dirt, gum, water, or varnish in or on the carburetor parts are often responsible for poor performance.

Overhaul your carburetor in a clean, dust-free area. Carefully disassemble the carburetor, referring often to the exploded views and directions packaged with the rebuilding kit. Keep all similar and look-alike parts segregated during disassembly and cleaning to avoid accidental interchange during assembly. Make a note of all jet sizes.

When the carburetor is disassembled, wash all parts (except diaphragms, electric choke units, pump plunger, and any other plastic, leather, fiber, or rubber parts) in clean carburetor solvent. Do not leave parts in the solvent any longer than is necessary to sufficiently loosen the deposits. Excessive cleaning may remove the special finish from the float bowl and choke valve bodies, leaving these parts unfit for service. Rinse all parts in clean solvent and blow them dry with compressed air or allow them to air dry. Wipe clean all cork, plastic, leather, and fiber parts with a clean, lint-free cloth.

Blow out all passages and jets with compressed air and be sure that there are no restrictions or blockages. Never use wire or similar tools to clean jets, fuel passages, or air bleeds. Clean all jets and valves separately to avoid accidental interchange.

Check all parts for wear or damage. If wear or damage is found, replace the defective parts. Especially check the following:

1. Check the float needle and seat for wear. If wear is found, replace the complete assembly.

2. Check the float hinge pin for wear and the float(s) for dents or distortion. Replace the float if fuel has leaked into it.

3. Check the throttle and choke shaft bores for wear or an out-of-round condition. Damage or wear to the throttle arm, shaft, or shaft bore will often require replacement of the throttle body. These parts require a close tolerance of fit; wear may allow air leakage, which could affect starting and idling.

NOTE: *Throttle shafts and busings are not included in overhaul kits. They can be purchased separately.*

4. Inspect the idle mixture adjusting

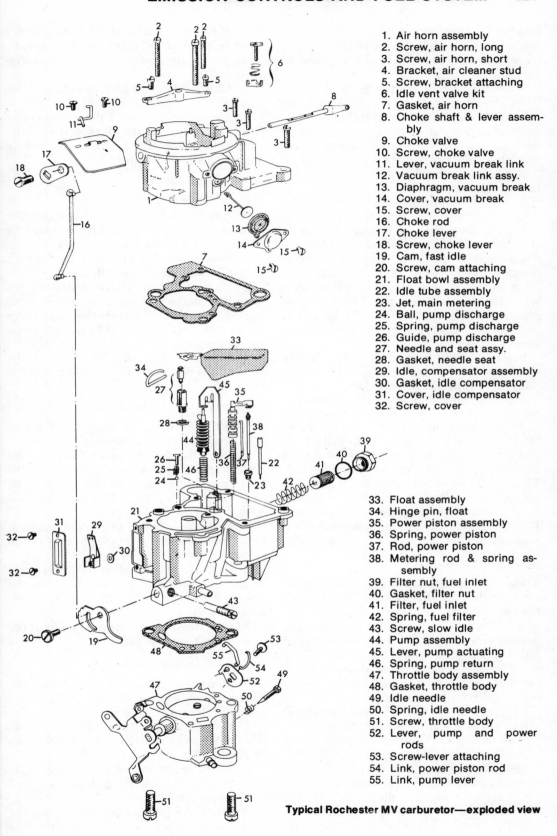

1. Air horn assembly
2. Screw, air horn, long
3. Screw, air horn, short
4. Bracket, air cleaner stud
5. Screw, bracket attaching
6. Idle vent valve kit
7. Gasket, air horn
8. Choke shaft & lever assembly
9. Choke valve
10. Screw, choke valve
11. Lever, vacuum break link
12. Vacuum break link assy.
13. Diaphragm, vacuum break
14. Cover, vacuum break
15. Screw, cover
16. Choke rod
17. Choke lever
18. Screw, choke lever
19. Cam, fast idle
20. Screw, cam attaching
21. Float bowl assembly
22. Idle tube assembly
23. Jet, main metering
24. Ball, pump discharge
25. Spring, pump discharge
26. Guide, pump discharge
27. Needle and seat assy.
28. Gasket, needle seat
29. Idle, compensator assembly
30. Gasket, idle compensator
31. Cover, idle compensator
32. Screw, cover

33. Float assembly
34. Hinge pin, float
35. Power piston assembly
36. Spring, power piston
37. Rod, power piston
38. Metering rod & spring assembly
39. Filter nut, fuel inlet
40. Gasket, filter nut
41. Filter, fuel inlet
42. Spring, fuel filter
43. Screw, slow idle
44. Pump assembly
45. Lever, pump actuating
46. Spring, pump return
47. Throttle body assembly
48. Gasket, throttle body
49. Idle needle
50. Spring, idle needle
51. Screw, throttle body
52. Lever, pump and power rods
53. Screw-lever attaching
54. Link, power piston rod
55. Link, pump lever

Typical Rochester MV carburetor—exploded view

needles for burrs or grooves. Any such condition requires replacement of the needle, since you will not be able to obtain a satisfactory idle.

5. Test the accelerator pump check valves. They should pass air one way but not the other. Test for proper seating by blowing and sucking on the valve. Replace the valve as necessary. If the valve is satisfactory, wash the valve again to remove breath moisture.

6. Check the bowl cover for warped surfaces with a straightedge.

7. Closely inspect the valves and seats for wear and damage, replacing as necessary.

8. After the carburetor is assembled, check the choke valve for freedom of operation.

Carburetor overhaul kits are recommended for each overhaul. These kits contain all gaskets and new parts to replace those which deteriorate most rapidly. Failure to replace all parts supplied with the kit (especially gaskets) can result in poor performance later.

Some carburetor manufacturers supply overhaul kits of three basic types: minor repair; major repair; and gasket kits.

After cleaning and checking all components, reassemble the carburetor, using new parts and referring to the exploded view. When reassembling, make sure that all screws and jets are tight in their seats, but do not overtighten as the tips will be distorted. Tighten all screws gradually, in rotation. Do not tighten needle valves into their seats; uneven jetting will result. Always use new gaskets. Be sure to adjust the float level when reassembling.

ADJUSTMENTS

These adjustments are arranged by carburetor model. All Blazers and Jimmys use General Motors Rochester carburetors. The first number of the carburetor model number indicates the number of barrels, while the last letter indicates the type of choke used. These are V for the manifold mounted choke coil, C for the choke coil mounted on the carburetor, and E for electric choke.

NOTE: *Most of these adjustments require that measurements be made to thousandths of an inch, using some sort of gauge. Drill bits are ideal for this purpose.*

The following should be tended to before attempting any running adjustments.

1. Throughly warm up the engine. Be sure that it is at normal operating temperature.

2. Check all carburetor mounting nuts.

Also check the intake manifold-to-cylinder head bolts. If air is leaking at these points, attempts at adjustment will lead to frustration.

3. Check the manifold heat control valve (if used) to be sure that it is free.

4. Make sure that the choke is fully open.

5. Make sure that the idle speed and mixture (Chapter 2) are correct. The engine should be idling smoothly.

Model MV (1969-74)

FAST IDLE SPEED

NOTE: *The fast idle speed adjustment must be made with the manual transmission in Neutral and the automatic in Park.*

1. Position the fast idle lever on the high step or position of the fast idle cam.

2. Be sure that the choke is properly adjusted and in the wide open position with the engine warm. Disconnect the distributor vacuum advance hose on 1974 manual transmission models.

3. Bend the fast idle lever, using the screwdriver slot, until the specified speed is obtained.

CHOKE ROD (FAST IDLE CAM)

NOTE: *Adjust the fast idle speed before making choke rod adjustments.*

1. Place the fast idle cam follower on the second step of the fast idle cam and hold it firmly against the rise to the high step. If the cam has no steps, align the cam index line with the tang contact point.

2. Rotate the choke valve in the direction of a closed choke by applying force to the choke coil lever.

3. Bend the choke rod, at the lower angle to give the specified opening between the lower edge of the choke valve and the inside air horn wall.

NOTE: *Measurement must be made at the center of the choke valve.*

CHOKE VACUUM BREAK

The adjustment of the vacuum break diaphragm unit insures correct choke valve opening after engine starting.

1. Remove the air cleaner on vehicles with Therm/AC air cleaner; plug the sensor's vacuum take off port.

2. Using an external vacuum source, apply vacuum to the vacuum break diaphragm until the plunger is fully seated.

3. When the plunger is seated, push the choke valve toward the closed position. The

Carburetor Application

Year	Engine	Carburetor
'69 – '74	6 — 250	MV
'75 – '76	6 — 250	1MV
'77 – '78	6 — 250	1ME
'79 – '82	6 — 250	2SE
'77 – '78	8 — 305	2GC
'79 – '82	8 — 305	M2ME/MC
'69 – '73	8 — 307	2GV
'74	8 — 350 2 bbl	2GV
'75	8 — 350 2 bbl	2GC
'69 – '74	8 — 350 4 bbl	4MV
'75	8 — 350, 2WD	M4MC
'75	8 — 350, 4WD	4MV
'76 – '78	8 — 350	4MV
'79 – '82	8 — 350	M4ME/MC
'75 – '76	8 — 400	4MV
'77 – '79	8 — 400	M4MC

vacuum break rod should be in the end of the slot.

4. Holding the choke valve in this position, place the specified gauge between the lower edge of the choke valve and the air horn wall.

5. If the measurement is not correct, bend the vacuum break rod at the angle.

CHOKE UNLOADER

1. Apply pressure to the choke valve and hold it in the closed position. The rod should be in the end of the slot.

2. Open the throttle valve to the wide open position.

3. Check the dimension between the lower edge of the choke plate and the air horn wall; if adjustment is needed, bend the unloader

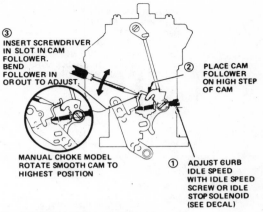

Model MV fast idle adjustment

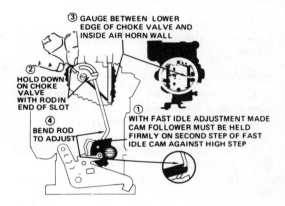

NOTE: MANUAL CHOKE MODELS WITH SMOOTH CONTOUR CAM.

USE THE SAME PROCEDURE AS ABOVE EXCEPT FOR STEP (1). AS THERE ARE NO STEPS ON MANUAL CHOKE CAM, THE INDEX LINE ON SIDE OF CAM SHOULD BE LINED UP WITH CONTACT POINT OF THE FAST IDLE CAM FOLLOWER TANG.

Model MV fast idle cam (choke rod) adjustment

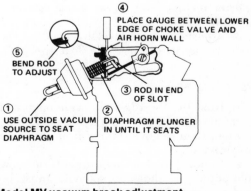

Model MV vacuum break adjustment

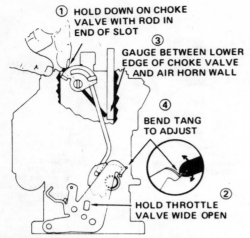

① HOLD DOWN ON CHOKE VALVE WITH ROD IN END OF SLOT

③ GAUGE BETWEEN LOWER EDGE OF CHOKE VALVE AND AIR HORN WALL

④ BEND TANG TO ADJUST

② HOLD THROTTLE VALVE WIDE OPEN

Model MV choke unloader adjustment

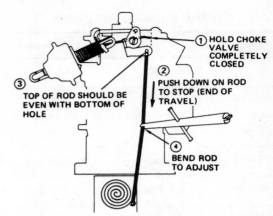

① HOLD CHOKE VALVE COMPLETELY CLOSED

② PUSH DOWN ON ROD TO STOP (END OF TRAVEL)

③ TOP OF ROD SHOULD BE EVEN WITH BOTTOM OF HOLE

④ BEND ROD TO ADJUST

Model MV automatic choke coil rod adjustment

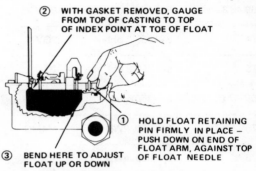

② WITH GASKET REMOVED, GAUGE FROM TOP OF CASTING TO TOP OF INDEX POINT AT TOE OF FLOAT

① HOLD FLOAT RETAINING PIN FIRMLY IN PLACE – PUSH DOWN ON END OF FLOAT ARM, AGAINST TOP OF FLOAT NEEDLE

③ BEND HERE TO ADJUST FLOAT UP OR DOWN

Model MV float level adjustment

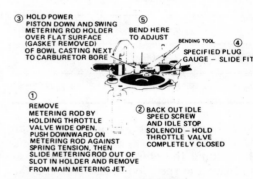

③ HOLD POWER PISTON DOWN AND SWING METERING ROD HOLDER OVER FLAT SURFACE (GASKET REMOVED) OF BOWL CASTING NEXT TO CARBURETOR BORE

⑤ BEND HERE TO ADJUST

④ BENDING TOOL

SPECIFIED PLUG GAUGE – SLIDE FIT

① REMOVE METERING ROD BY HOLDING THROTTLE VALVE WIDE OPEN. PUSH DOWNWARD ON METERING ROD AGAINST SPRING TENSION, THEN SLIDE METERING ROD OUT OF SLOT IN HOLDER AND REMOVE FROM MAIN METERING JET.

② BACK OUT IDLE SPEED SCREW AND IDLE STOP SOLENOID – HOLD THROTTLE VALVE COMPLETELY CLOSED

Model MV metering rod adjustment

tang on the throttle lever to adjust to specification.

AUTOMATIC CHOKE COIL ROD

1. Disconnect the coil rod from the upper choke lever and hold the choke valve closed.
2. Push down on the coil rod to the end of its travel.
3. The top of the rod should be even with the bottom of the hole in the choke lever.
4. To make adjustments, bend the rod at the center.

FLOAT LEVEL

1. Remove the top of the carburetor. Hold the float retainer pin in place and the float arm against the top of the float needle by pushing down on the float arm at the outer end toward the float bowl casting.
2. Using an adjustable T scale, measure the distance from the toe of the float to the float bowl gasket surface.

NOTE: *The float bowl gasket should be removed and the gauge held on the index point on the float for accurate measurement.*

3. Adjust the float level by bending the float arm up or down at the float arm junction.

METERING ROD

1. Hold the throttle valve wide-open and push down on the metering rod against spring tension, then remove the rod from the main metering jet.
2. In order to check adjustment, the slow idle screw or idle stop solenoid must be backed out and the fast idle cam rotated so

that the fast idle cam follower does not contact the steps on the cam.

3. With the throttle valve closed, push down on the power piston until it contacts its stop.
4. With the power piston depressed, swing the metering rod holder over the flat surface of the bowl casting next to the carburetor bore.
5. Insert a specified size gauge between the bowl casting sealing bead and the lower surface of the metering rod holder. The drill should slide smoothly between both surfaces.

6. If adjustment is needed, carefully bend the metering rod holder up or down at the inner end. After adjustment, reinstall the metering rod.

IDLE VENT (1969)

1. The engine idle must be set at the specified rpm and the choke valve held wideopen so that the fast idle cam follower is not contacting the cam.

NOTE: *If the carburetor is off the engine, a preliminary idle setting can be made by turning the idle speed screw in 1½ turns from the closed throttle valve position.*

2. With the throttle stop screw held against the idle stop screw, the idle vent valve should be open .050 in. To check, a drill bit may be inserted between the top of the air horn casting and the bottom surface of the valve.

3. If adjustment is necessary, turn the slotted vent valve head with a screwdriver. Turning the head clockwise *increases* the clearance.

NOTE: *On models equipped with an idle stop solenoid, the solenoid must be activated when checking and adjusting the valve.*

C.E.C. SOLENOID (1971–73)

NOTE: *Do not use the C.E.C. valve to set idle rpm.*

1. With the engine running, and transmission in Neutral (manual) or Drive (Automatic), air conditioner OFF, distributor vacuum hose removed and plugged, and fuel tank vapor hose disconnected, manually extend the C.E.C. valve plunger to contact the throttle lever.

2. Adjust the plunger length to obtain the C.E.C. valve rpm.

3. Reconnect the vapor hose and vacuum hose.

Model 1MV, 1ME (1975–78)

NOTE: *Any adjustments not illustrated for the 1MV or 1ME are similar to those for the MV. Be sure to check the text against the illustration, since some gauge points will change.*

FAST IDLE SPEED

1. Check and adjust the idle speed.
2. With the engine at normal operating temperature, air cleaner ON, EGR valve signal line disconnected and plugged and the air conditioning OFF, connect a tachometer.

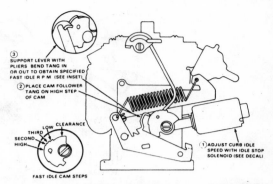

Models 1MV and 1ME fast idle speed adjustment

3. Disconnect the vacuum advance hose at the distributor and plug the line.

4. With the transmission in Neutral (Park on automatic), start the engine and set the fast idle cam follower on the high step of the cam.

5. Bend the tang in or out to obtain the fast idle speed.

FAST IDLE CAM (CHOKE ROD)

1. Check and adjust the fast idle speed.
2. Set the fast idle cxam follower on the second step of the cam.
3. Apply force to the choke coil rod to hold the choke valve toward the closed position.
4. Measure the clearance between the upper edge (lower-1975 and 1978) of the choke valve and the inside of the air horn wall.
5. Bend the rod at the lower angle to adjust.

CHOKE UNLOADER

1. Hold the choke valve down by applying light force to the choke coil lever.
2. Open the throttle valve to wide open.

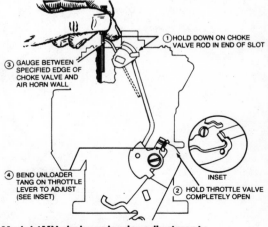

Model 1MV choke unloader adjustment

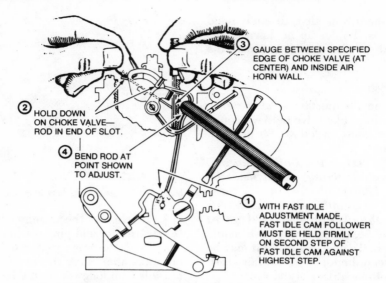

GAUGE BETWEEN SPECIFIED
EDGE OF CHOKE VALVE (AT
CENTER) AND INSIDE AIR
HORN WALL.

② HOLD DOWN
ON CHOKE VALVE—
ROD IN END OF SLOT.

④ BEND ROD AT
POINT SHOWN
TO ADJUST.

① WITH FAST IDLE
ADJUSTMENT MADE,
FAST IDLE CAM FOLLOWER
MUST BE HELD FIRMLY
ON SECOND STEP OF
FAST IDLE CAM AGAINST
HIGHEST STEP.

Fast idle cam (choke rod) adjustment for the 1MV and 1ME

3. Measure the clearance between the upper edge (lower for 1978) of the choke valve and the air horn wall.

4. If adjustment is necessary, bend the tang on the throttle lever.

FLOAT LEVEL

This adjustment is the same as for the Model MV, shown earlier.

AUTOMATIC CHOKE COIL ROD (1975)

1. Detach the top of the rod. Pull the rod up to the end of its travel. Completely close the choke valve.

2. The bottom of the rod should be even with the top of the lever.

3. If adjustment is necessary, bend the rod.

AUTOMATIC CHOKE COIL ROD (1976)

1. Detach the top of the rod. Completely close the choke valve. Push the rod down to the end of its travel.

2. The top of the rod should be even with the bottom of the hole in the choke lever.

3. Bend the rod to adjust.

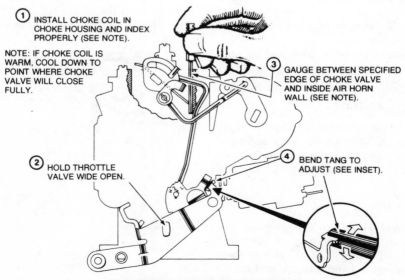

① INSTALL CHOKE COIL IN
CHOKE HOUSING AND INDEX
PROPERLY (SEE NOTE).

NOTE: IF CHOKE COIL IS
WARM, COOL DOWN TO
POINT WHERE CHOKE
VALVE WILL CLOSE
FULLY.

③ GAUGE BETWEEN SPECIFIED
EDGE OF CHOKE VALVE
AND INSIDE AIR HORN
WALL (SEE NOTE).

② HOLD THROTTLE
VALVE WIDE OPEN.

④ BEND TANG TO
ADJUST (SEE INSET).

Model 1ME choke unloader adjustment

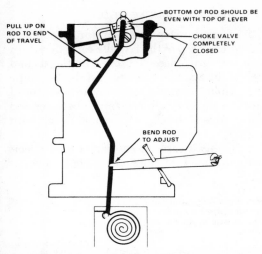

1975 Model 1MV automatic choke coil rod adjustment

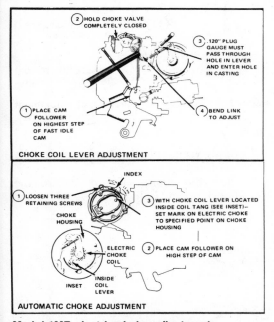

CHOKE COIL LEVER ADJUSTMENT

AUTOMATIC CHOKE ADJUSTMENT

Model 1ME electric choke adjustments

AUTOMATIC CHOKE ADJUSTMENT (1977–78 1ME)

1. Loosen the three choke housing retaining screws.
2. Place the cam follower on the high step of the cam.
3. Set the mark on the electric choke to the center mark on the index.
4. Tighten the housing screws.

PRIMARY VACUUM BREAK (1975)

1. With an outside vacuum source, apply vacuum to the primary vacuum break dia-

phragm until the plunger is fully seated. The primary diaphragm is the one on the opposite side from the idle speed solenoid.
2. Measure the clearance between the lower edge of the choke valve and the air horn wall.
3. Bend the vacuum break rod to adjust the clearance. Be sure there is no binding or interference.

AUXILIARY VACUUM BREAK (1975)

1. With an outside vacuum source, apply vacuum to the auxiliary vacuum break diaphragm (on the same side of the carburetor as the idle speed solenoid) until the plunger seats.
2. Place the cam follower on the high step of the fast idle cam.
3. Measure the clearance between the upper edge of the choke valve and the air horn wall. Bend the link between the vacuum break and the choke valve to adjust.

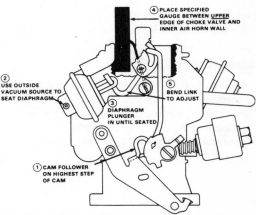

1975 Model 1MV auxiliary vacuum break adjustment

VACUUM BREAK (1976–77)

1. Place the cam follower on the highest step of the fast idle cam.
2. Tape over the diaphragm housing bleed hole.
3. Apply vacuum until the plunger seats.
4. Push up on the choke coil lever rod in the end of the slot.
5. Measure between the upper end of the choke valve and the air horn. Bend the rod to adjust.

VACUUM BREAK (1978)

1. Place the cam follower on the high step of the cam.

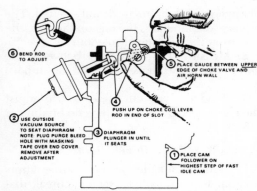

1976–77 Models 1MV and 1ME primary vacuum break adjustment

2. Apply vacuum in order to seat the diaphragm.

3. Push down on the choke valve. Compress the plunger spring and seat the plunger stem, if so equipped.

4. Measure the distance between the lower edge of the choke valve and the inside air horn wall.

5. Bend the link to adjust to specification.

Model 2GV (1969–74)

NOTE: *Severe high gear lean surge can be corrected in 307 V8 engines using this carburetor by adding an internal baffle to the air cleaner housing. Details are given in the September 1971 GMC Service News Letter.*

FAST IDLE CAM (CHOKE ROD)

1. Turn the stop screw in until it contacts the bottom step of the fast idle cam, then turn it in one turn. Place the screw on the second step of the fast idle cam, against the top step.

2. Hold the choke valve toward the closed position and check the clearance between the upper edge of the choke valve and the air horn wall.

3. If this measurement varies from specifications, bend the tang on the choke lever.

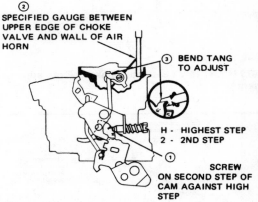

Model 2GV fast idle cam (choke rod) adjustment

CHOKE VACUUM BREAK

1. Apply vacuum to the diaphragm to fully seat the plunger.

2. Push the choke valve in toward the closed position and hold it there.

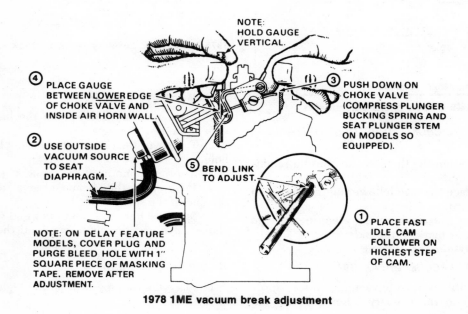

1978 1ME vacuum break adjustment

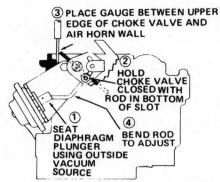

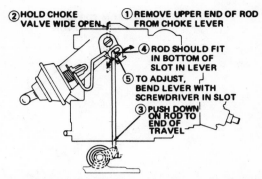

Model 2GV choke vacuum break adjustment

Model 2GV automatic choke coil rod adjustment

3. Check the distance between the upper edge of the choke valve and the air horn wall.

4. If this dimension is not within specifications, bend the vacuum break rod to adjust.

CHOKE UNLOADER

1. Hold the throttle valves wide-open and use a rubber band to hold the choke valve toward the closed position.

2. Measure the distance between the upper edge of the choke valve and the air horn wall.

3. If this measurement is not within specifications, bend the unloader tang on the throttle lever to correct it.

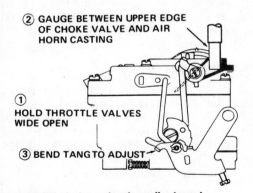

Model 2GV choke unloader adjustment

AUTOMATIC CHOKE COIL ROD

1. Hold the choke valve completely open.

2. With the choke coil rod disconnected from the upper lever, push downward on the end the rod to the end of its travel.

3. With the rod pushed fully downward, the bottom of the rod should be even with the bottom of the slotted hole in the lever.

4. To adjust the lever, bend it by using a screwdriver in the smaller slot.

Accelerator Pump Rod

1. Back the idle stop screw out and close the throttle valves in their bores.

2. Measure the distance from the top of the air horn ring to the top of the pump rod.

3. Bend the pump rod at a lower angle to correct this dimension.

Float Level

Invert the air horn, and with the gasket in place and the needle seated, measure the level as follows:

On plastic floats, measure from the air horn gasket to the lip on the toe of the float.

On brass floats, measure from the air horn gasket to the lower edge of the float seam.

Bend the float tang to adjust the level.

Float Drop

Holding the air horn right side up, measure float drop as follows:

On plastic floats, measure from the air horn gasket to the lip at the toe of the float.

On brass floats, measure from the air horn gasket surface to the bottom of the float.

Bend the float tang to adjust either type float.

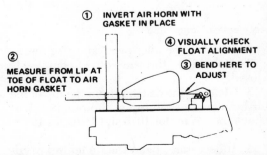

2GV and 2GC float level adjustment (plastic float)

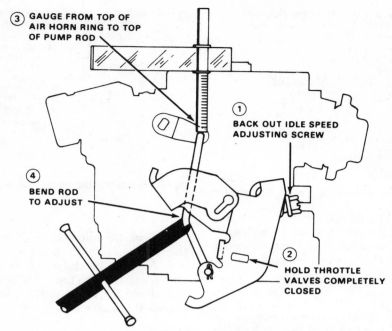

③ GAUGE FROM TOP OF
AIR HORN RING TO TOP
OF PUMP ROD

① BACK OUT IDLE SPEED
ADJUSTING SCREW

④ BEND ROD
TO ADJUST

② HOLD THROTTLE
VALVES COMPLETELY
CLOSED

2GV and 2GC accelerator pump rod adjustment

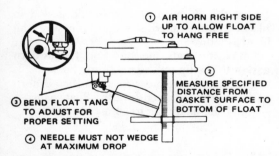

① AIR HORN RIGHT SIDE
UP TO ALLOW FLOAT
TO HANG FREE

② MEASURE SPECIFIED
DISTANCE FROM
GASKET SURFACE TO
BOTTOM OF FLOAT

③ BEND FLOAT TANG
TO ADJUST FOR
PROPER SETTING

④ NEEDLE MUST NOT WEDGE
AT MAXIMUM DROP

2GV and 2GC float drop adjustment (brass float)

Model 2GC (1975, 1977–78)

NOTE: *Any adjustments not illustrated for the 2GC are similar to those for the 2GV. Be sure to check the text against the illustration, since some gauge points will change.*

Accelerator Pump Rod

1. Back out the idle speed adjusting screw.
2. Hold the throttle valve completely closed.
3. Measure the distance from the top of the air horn ring to the top of the pump rod. It should be 1⅝ in. for 1975 and $1^{21}/_{32}$ for 1977–78.
4. If necessary, bend the pump rod to adjust.

Fast Idle Cam

1. Place the idle speed screw on the second step of the fast idle cam against the highest step.
2. Measure the clearance between the upper edge of the choke valve and the air horn wall. It should be .400 in. for 1975 and .260 for 1977–78.
3. Bend the choke lever tang to adjust.

Choke Unloader

1. With the throttle valves wide open, place the choke valve in the closed position.
2. Measure the clearance between the upper edge of the choke valve and the air horn casting. It should be .350 in. for 1975 and .325 for 1977–78.
3. Bend the throttle lever tang to adjust.

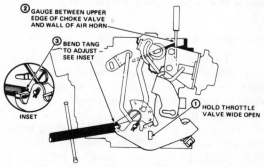

② GAUGE BETWEEN UPPER
EDGE OF CHOKE VALVE
AND WALL OF AIR HORN

③ BEND TANG
TO ADJUST –
SEE INSET

INSET

① HOLD THROTTLE
VALVE WIDE OPEN

1977–78 2GC choke unloader adjustment

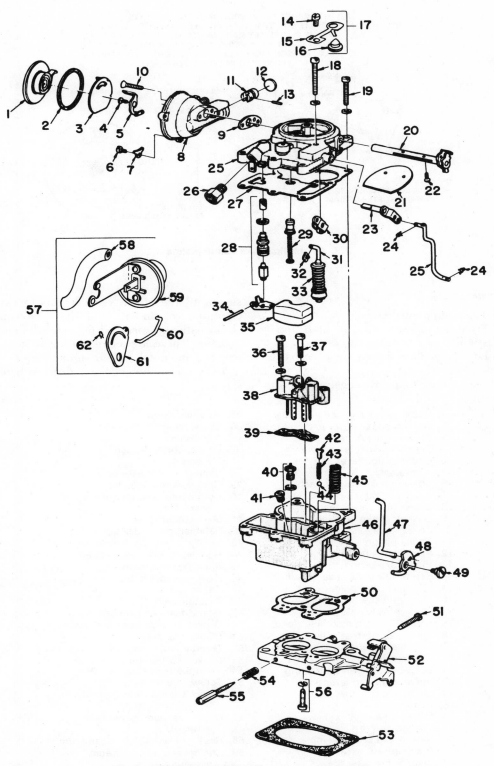

Typical Rochester 2GC carburetor—exploded view

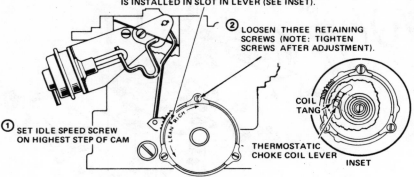

③ WITH CHOKE VALVE WIDE OPEN (ENGINE COLD)
ROTATE COVER AGAINST COIL TENSION UNTIL CHOKE
VALVE CLOSES. SET MARK ON COVER TO SPECIFIED
POINT ON CHOKE HOUSING. NOTE: ON MODELS WITH
SLOTTED COIL PICK-UP LEVER, MAKE SURE COIL TANG
IS INSTALLED IN SLOT IN LEVER (SEE INSET).

② LOOSEN THREE RETAINING
SCREWS (NOTE: TIGHTEN
SCREWS AFTER ADJUSTMENT).

① SET IDLE SPEED SCREW
ON HIGHEST STEP OF CAM

COIL
TANG

THERMOSTATIC
CHOKE COIL LEVER

INSET

2GC automatic choke coil adjustment

Automatic Choke Coil

1. The engine must be cold.

2. Place the idle screw on the high step of the fast idle cam.

3. Loosen the thermostatic choke coil cover retaining screws.

4. Rotate the choke cover against coil tension until the choke valve begins to close. Continue rotating it until the index mark aligns with the specified point on the choke housing. These are: centered for 1975 manual, and one notch rich for automatic.

5. Tighten the choke cover retaining screws.

1. Choke cover and coil assembly
2. Gasket, choke cover and coil
3. Choke baffle plate
4. Screw, choke piston lever
5. Choke piston lever and link assembly
6. Screw, choke cover attaching
7. Retainers, choke cover
8. Choke housing assembly
9. Gasket, choke housing
10. Screw, choke housing attaching
11. Choke piston
12. Plug, choke housing
13. Pin, choke piston
14. Screw, idle vent valve attaching
15. Idle vent valve holder
16. Idle vent valve
17. Idle vent valve assembly
18. Screw, air horn attaching (long)
19. Screw, air horn attaching (short)
20. Choke shaft and lever assembly
21. Choke valve
22. Screw, choke valve attaching
23. Pump shaft and lever assy.
24. Clips, pump rod attaching
25. Pump rod
26. Fitting, fuel inlet
27. Gasket, air horn
28. Needle and seat assembly
29. Power piston assembly
30. Inner pump lever
31. Pump plunger assembly
32. Clip, pump plunger
33. Spring, pump duration
34. Float hinge pin
35. Float assembly
36. Screw, cluster attaching (outside)
37. Screw, cluster attaching (center)
38. Venturi cluster assembly
39. Gasket, venturi cluster
40. Power valve and gasket assembly
41. Main metering jet
42. Retainer, pump discharge spring
43. Spring, pump discharge
44. Ball, pump discharge (steel)
45. Spring, pump return
46. Float bowl assembly
47. Choke rod
48. Fast idle cam
49. Screw, fast idle cam attaching
50. Gasket, throttle body to bowl
51. Screw, idle speed
52. Throttle body assembly
53. Gasket, carburetor to manifold
54. Spring, idle mixture needle
55. Screw, idle mixture
56. Screw & lockwasher, throttle body attaching
57. Choke, vacuum diaphragm assembly
58. Hose, choke vacuum diaphragm
59. Choke vacuum diaphragm assembly
60. Link, vacuum diaphragm to choke lever
61. Lever, choke shaft lever
62. Clip, vacuum diaphragm link

Choke Vacuum Break

1. Disconnect the vacuum house. Using an outside vacuum source, seat the vacuum diaphragm.

2. Cover the vacuum break bleed hole with a small piece of tape so that the diaphragm will be held inward.

3. Place the idle speed screw on the high step of the fast idle cam.

4. Hold the choke oil lever inside the choke housing toward the closed choke position.

5. Measure the clearance between the upper edge of the choke valve and the air horn wall. It should be .130 in. when the vehicle is new, .160 after 22,500 miles.

6. Bend the vacuum break rod to adjust.

7. After adjustment remove the piece of tape and reconnect the vacuum hose.

Float Level, Float Drop

These procedures are the same as for the model 2GV, covered earlier. Float level is $^{21}/_{32}$ in. for 1975 and $^{19}/_{32}$ in. for 1977–78. Float drop is $^{31}/_{32}$ in. for 1975 and $1^9/_{32}$ in. for 1977–78.

Rochester 2SE (1979–82)

Float Adjustment

1. Hold the float retainer in place with your hand and push the float down against the needle.

2. Place a ⅛ in. gauge for '79, $^3/_{16}$ in. from '80 at the toe of the float.

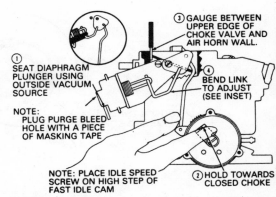

Model 2GC choke vacuum break adjustments

3. Remove the float and bend the arm as necessary to adjust the level.

Fast Idle Adjustment

1. Refer to the underhood emissions sticker. Disconnect and plug any hoses indicated on the sticker.

2. Adjust the curb idle speed as outlined in Chapter Two.

3. Place the fast idle screw on the high step of the fast idle cam.

4. Turn the screw in or out to adjust the fast idle speed.

Electric Choke Setting

1. Loosen the three choke coil retaining screws.

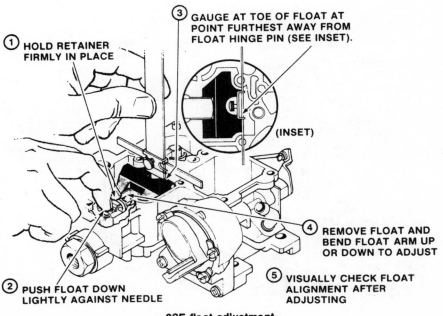

2SE float adjustment

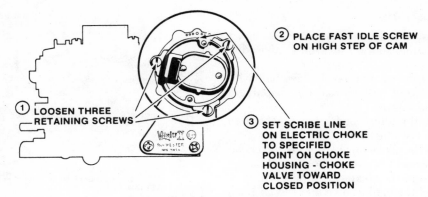

① LOOSEN THREE RETAINING SCREWS

② PLACE FAST IDLE SCREW ON HIGH STEP OF CAM

③ SET SCRIBE LINE ON ELECTRIC CHOKE TO SPECIFIED POINT ON CHOKE HOUSING - CHOKE VALVE TOWARD CLOSED POSITION

2SE electric choke adjustment

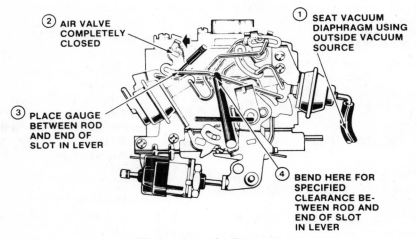

② AIR VALVE COMPLETELY CLOSED

① SEAT VACUUM DIAPHRAGM USING OUTSIDE VACUUM SOURCE

③ PLACE GAUGE BETWEEN ROD AND END OF SLOT IN LEVER

④ BEND HERE FOR SPECIFIED CLEARANCE BE-TWEEN ROD AND END OF SLOT IN LEVER

2SE air valve rod adjustment

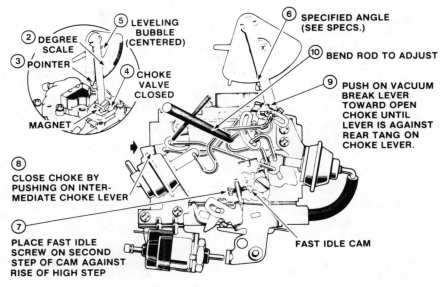

② DEGREE SCALE

⑤ LEVELING BUBBLE (CENTERED)

③ POINTER

④ CHOKE VALVE CLOSED

MAGNET

⑥ SPECIFIED ANGLE (SEE SPECS.)

⑩ BEND ROD TO ADJUST

⑨ PUSH ON VACUUM BREAK LEVER TOWARD OPEN CHOKE UNTIL LEVER IS AGAINST REAR TANG ON CHOKE LEVER.

⑧ CLOSE CHOKE BY PUSHING ON INTER-MEDIATE CHOKE LEVER

⑦ PLACE FAST IDLE SCREW ON SECOND STEP OF CAM AGAINST RISE OF HIGH STEP

FAST IDLE CAM

2SE fast idle cam adjustment

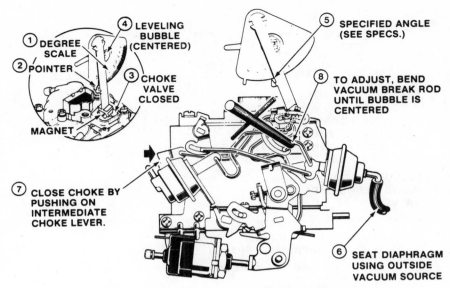

① DEGREE SCALE
② POINTER
④ LEVELING BUBBLE (CENTERED)
③ CHOKE VALVE CLOSED
⑤ SPECIFIED ANGLE (SEE SPECS.)
⑧ TO ADJUST, BEND VACUUM BREAK ROD UNTIL BUBBLE IS CENTERED
MAGNET
⑦ CLOSE CHOKE BY PUSHING ON INTERMEDIATE CHOKE LEVER.
⑥ SEAT DIAPHRAGM USING OUTSIDE VACUUM SOURCE

2SE primary side vacuum break adjustment

2. Place the fast idle screw on the high step of the fast idle adjusting cam.

3. Set the line on the choke 1 notch counterclockwise from the center mark.

Air Valve Rod Adjustment

1. Fully seat the diaphragm using an outside vacuum source.

2. Be sure the air valve is completely closed.

3. Place a .040 in. gauge between the rod and the end of the slot in the lever.

4. Bend the rod to obtain .040 in. clearance.

Fast Idle Cam Choke Rod Adjustment

1. The choke coil lever and the fast idle adjustments must be correct before performing this adjustment.

2. Install a special choke valve measuring gauge (no. J-26701) on the carburetor.

3. Rotate the degree scale until the zero mark is opposite the pointer.

4. With the choke valve completely closed, place the magnet directly on top of the choke valve.

5. Rotate the bubble until it is centered.

6. Rotate the scale to place the specified degree mark opposite the pointer.

7. Place the fast idle screw on the second highest step of the fast idle cam.

8. Close the choke by pushing on the intermediate choke lever.

9. Push on the vacuum break lever toward the open choke lever until the lever is against the rear tang on the choke lever.

10. Bend the fast idle cam rod until the bubble on the gauge is centered. Remove the gauge.

Primary Side Vacuum Break Adjustment

1. Refer to steps 1–5 of the Fast Idle Cam Choke Rod Adjustment.

2. Rotate the scale to place the specified degree opposite the pointer. Refer to the "Carburetor Specifications Chart."

3. Fully seat the choke vacuum diaphragm using an outside vacuum source.

4. Hold the choke valve toward the closed position by pushing on the intermediate choke lever.

5. Bend the vacuum break rod until the bubble is centered and remove the gauge.

Rochester M2MC/ME (1979–82)

All adjustments for this carburetor are the same as the Rochester M4MC with the following exceptions:

Fast Idle Speed Adjustment

1. Place the transmission in Park or Neutral.

2. Refer to the vehicle emission label and position the cam follower on the cam as per label.

3. Disconnect and plug the vacuum hose at the EGR valve.

4. Turn the fast idle speed screw to obtain

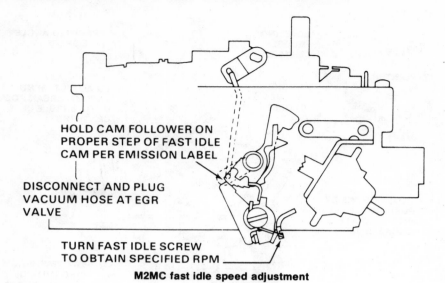

HOLD CAM FOLLOWER ON
PROPER STEP OF FAST IDLE
CAM PER EMISSION LABEL

DISCONNECT AND PLUG
VACUUM HOSE AT EGR
VALVE

TURN FAST IDLE SCREW
TO OBTAIN SPECIFIED RPM

M2MC fast idle speed adjustment

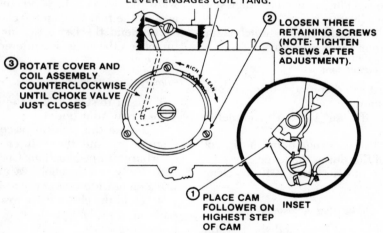

④ ALIGN MARK ON COVER WITH SPECIFIED POINT ON
HOUSING.
NOTE: MAKE SURE SLOT IN
LEVER ENGAGES COIL TANG.

② LOOSEN THREE
RETAINING SCREWS
(NOTE: TIGHTEN
SCREWS AFTER
ADJUSTMENT).

③ ROTATE COVER AND
COIL ASSEMBLY
COUNTERCLOCKWISE
UNTIL CHOKE VALVE
JUST CLOSES

RICH   LEAN

① PLACE CAM   INSET
FOLLOWER ON
HIGHEST STEP
OF CAM

M2MC automatic choke coil adjustment

the fast idle speed listed on the emission sticker.

5. Connect the vacuum hose.

Automatic Choke Coil

1. Install the thermostatic coil and cover with a gasket between the choke cover and the choke housing. The thermostatic coil must be installed in the slot in the inside of the choke coil lever pick-up arm.

2. Place the fast idle cam follower on the high step of the fast idle cam.

3. Rotate the cover and coil assembly counterclockwise until the choke valve just opens.

4. Align the index point on the cover with the specified mark on the choke housing.

5. Tighten the retaining screws or replace the rivets (Use cover kit).

NOTE: *There is no adjustment for Air Valve Spring or Rear Vacuum Break on the M2MC.*

Model 4MV (Quadrajet)
FAST IDLE SPEED

1. Position the fast idle lever on the high step of the fast idle cam.

2. Be sure that the choke is wide-open and the engine warm. On 1973–1974 models with

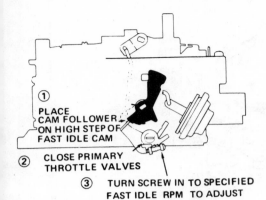

① PLACE CAM FOLLOWER ON HIGH STEP OF FAST IDLE CAM

② CLOSE PRIMARY THROTTLE VALVES

③ TURN SCREW IN TO SPECIFIED FAST IDLE RPM TO ADJUST

Model 4MV fast idle speed adjustment

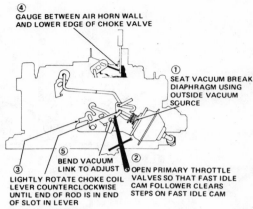

④ GAUGE BETWEEN AIR HORN WALL AND LOWER EDGE OF CHOKE VALVE

① SEAT VACUUM BREAK DIAPHRAGM USING OUTSIDE VACUUM SOURCE

⑤ BEND VACUUM LINK TO ADJUST

③ LIGHTLY ROTATE CHOKE COIL LEVER COUNTERCLOCKWISE UNTIL END OF ROD IS IN END OF SLOT IN LEVER

② OPEN PRIMARY THROTTLE VALVES SO THAT FAST IDLE CAM FOLLOWER CLEARS STEPS ON FAST IDLE CAM

Model 4MV choke vacuum break adjustment

manual transmission, disconnect the distributor vacuum advance hose.

3. Turn the fast idle screw to gain the proper fast idle rpm.

CHOKE ROD (FAST IDLE CAM)

1. Place the cam follower on the second step of the fast idle cam against the high step.

2. Close the choke valve by exerting counterclockwise pressure on the external choke lever.

3. Insert a gauge of the proper size between the lower (upper starting 1975) edge of the choke valve and the inside air horn wall.

4. To adjust, bend the choke rod.

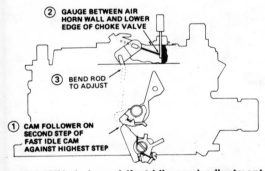

② GAUGE BETWEEN AIR HORN WALL AND LOWER EDGE OF CHOKE VALVE

③ BEND ROD TO ADJUST

① CAM FOLLOWER ON SECOND STEP OF FAST IDLE CAM AGAINST HIGHEST STEP

Model 4MV choke rod (fast idle cam) adjustment

VACUUM BREAK

1. Fully seat the vacuum break diaphragm using an outside vacuum source.

2. Open the throttle valve enough to allow the fast idle cam follower to clear the fast idle cam.

3. Turn the vacuum break lever counterclockwise toward the closed choke position. The end of the vacuum break rod should be at the outer end of the slot in the vacuum break diaphragm plunger.

4. The specified clearance should register

from the lower end of the choke valve to the inside air horn wall.

5. If the clearance is not correct, bend the vacuum break link.

CHOKE UNLOADER

1. Push upon the vacuum break lever to close the choke and fully open the throttle valves.

2. Measure the distance from the lower (upper starting 1975) edge of the choke valve to the air horn wall.

3. To adjust, bend the tang on the fast idle lever.

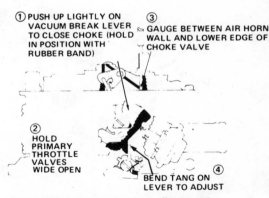

① PUSH UP LIGHTLY ON VACUUM BREAK LEVER TO CLOSE CHOKE (HOLD IN POSITION WITH RUBBER BAND)

③ GAUGE BETWEEN AIR HORN WALL AND LOWER EDGE OF CHOKE VALVE

② HOLD PRIMARY THROTTLE VALVES WIDE OPEN

④ BEND TANG ON LEVER TO ADJUST

Model 4MV choke unloader adjustment

AUTOMATIC CHOKE COIL ROD

1. Close the choke valve by rotating the choke coil lever counterclockwise.

2. Disconnect the thermostatic coil rod from the upper lever.

3. Push down on the rod until it contacts the bracket of the coil.

4. The rod must fit in the notch of the upper level.

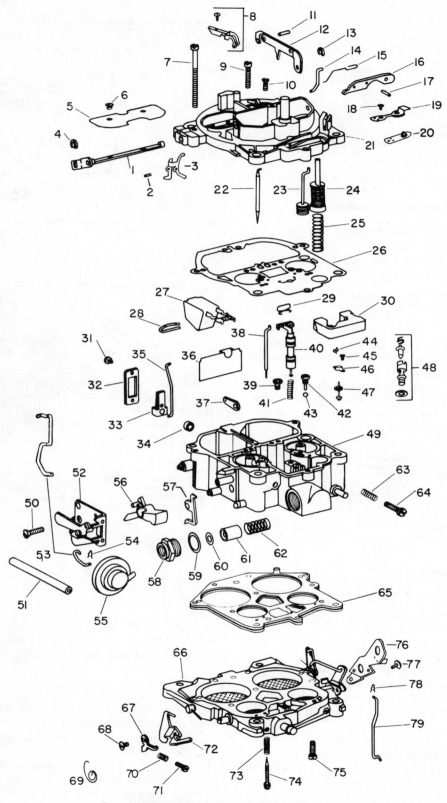

Typical Rochester 4MV carburetor—exploded view

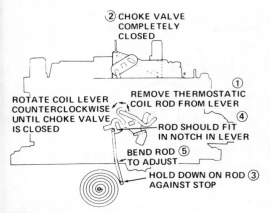

Model 4MV automatic choke coil rod

5. If it does not, it must be bent on the curved portion just below the upper lever.

NOTE: *1976 models that hesitate or stall on acceleration during warmup may be cured by installation of a new choke coil no. 460110.*

SECONDARY CLOSING

This adjustment assures proper closing of the secondary throttle plates.

1. Set the slow idle as per instructions in Chapter 2. Make sure that the fast idle cam follower is not resting on the fast idle cam.

2. There should be .020 in. clearance between the secondary throttle actuating rod and the front of the slot on the secondary throttle lever with the closing tang on the throttle lever resting against the actuating lever.

3. Bend the tang on the primary throttle actuating rod to adjust.

SECONDARY OPENING

1. Open the primary throttle valves until the actuating link contacts the upper tang on the secondary lever.

2. With two point linkage, the bottom of the link should be in the center of the secondary lever slot.

3. With the 1969 three point linkage, there should be .070 in. clearance between the link and the middle tang.

4. Bend the upper tang on the secondary lever to adjust as necessary.

FLOAT LEVEL

With the air horn assembly removed, measure the distance from the air horn gasket

1. Choke shaft and lever assembly
2. Roll pin, air valve lockout lever
3. Lever, air valve lockout
4. Clip, choke rod (upper)
5. Choke valve
6. Screw, choke valve (2)
7. Screw, air horn (long)
8. Secondary metering rod holder and screw
9. Screw, air horn (short)
10. Screw, air horn (countersunk) (2)
11. Roll pin, dash pot lever
12. Dash pot actuating
13. Clip, air valve rod
14. Rod, air valve
15. Lever, idle vent valve
16. Lever, pump actuating
17. Roll pin, pump lever
18. Screw, idle vent valve
19. Idle vent valve
20. Idle vent valve (thermostatic type
21. Air horn assembly
22. Metering rod, secondary (2)
23. Dashpot assembly (early)
24. Pump assembly
25. Spring, pump return
26. Gasket, air horn
27. Float assembly
28. Hinge pin, float assembly
29. Spring, primary metering rod retainer
30. Insert, float bowl
31. Screw, idle compensator cover (2)
32. Cover, idle compensator
33. Idle compensator assembly
34. Seal, idle compensator
35. Choke rod
36. Baffle, secondary bores
37. Lever, choke rod (lower end)
38. Primary metering rod (2)
39. Main metering jet, primary (2)
40. Power piston assembly
41. Spring, power piston
42. Retainer, pump discharge ball
43. Ball, pump discharge
44. Pull clip float needle (early)
45. Screw, float needle diaphragm retainer (early)
46. Retainer, float needle assembly (early)
47. Float needle and diaphragm assy. (early)
48. Needle and seat assembly (standard)
49. Float bowl assembly
50. Screw, vacuum break control
51. Hose, vacuum control
52. Vacuum break control assembly
53. Rod, vacuum break control
54. Clip, vacuum break rod
55. Vacuum diaphragm assembly
56. Fast idle cam
57. Lever, secondary lockout
58. Filter nut, fuel inlet
59. Gasket, filter nut
60. Gasket, fuel filter
61. Filter, fuel inlet
62. Spring, filter relief
63. Spring, idle adjusting screw
64. Screw, idle adjusting
65. Gasket, throttle body to bowl
66. Throttle body assembly
67. Fast idle lever
68. Screw, cam and fast idle lever attaching
69. Spring, cam and fast idle lever
70. Spring, fast idle screw
71. Screw, fast idle adjusting
72. Fast idle cam follower lever
73. Spring, idle mixture needle (2)
74. Idle mixture needle (2)
75. Screw, throttle body to bowl attaching
76. Throttle lever, primary
77. Screw, throttle lever attaching
78. Clip, pump rod
79. Pump rod

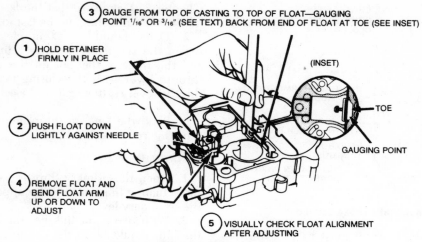

4MV and M4MC float level adjustment

surface (gasket removed) to the top of the float at the toe. Measure at a point $^3/_{16}$ in. back from the toe for all models except for 1973–76, which should be measured at a point $^1/_{16}$ in. back.

NOTE: *Make sure that the retaining pin is firmly held in place and that the tang of the float is firmly against the needle and seat assembly.*

ACCELERATOR PUMP

1. Close the primary throttle valves by backing out the slow idle screw and making sure that the fast idle cam follower is off the steps of the fast idle cam.
2. Bend the secondary throttle closing tang away from the primary throttle lever, if necessary.
3. With the pump in the inner hole (unless specified otherwise in the carburetor chart) in the pump lever, measure from the top of the choke valve wall to the top of the pump stem.
4. To adjust, bend the pump lever.
5. After adjusting, readjust the secondary throttle tang and the slow idle screw.

AIR VALVE SPRING

To adjust the air valve spring windup, loosen the allen head lockscrew and turn the adjusting screw counterclockwise to remove all spring tension. With the air valve closed, turn the adjusting screw clockwise the specified number of turns after the torsion spring contacts the pin on the shaft. Hold the adjusting screw in this position and tighten the lockscrew.

Model M4MC/ME (1975, 1977–82)

NOTE: *Any adjustments not illustrated for the M4MC are similar to those for the 4MV. Be sure to check the text against the illustration, since some gauge points will change.*

PUMP ROD

1. Take the fast idle cam follower off the fast idle cam steps.
2. Back out the ide speed screw until the throttle valves are completely closed.
3. Be sure that the secondary actuating rod is not preventing the throttle from closing completely. If the primary throttle valves do not close completely, bend the secondary closing tang out of position, then readjust later.
4. Place the pump rod in the inner hole in the lever unless specified otherwise in the "Carburetor Specifications Chart."

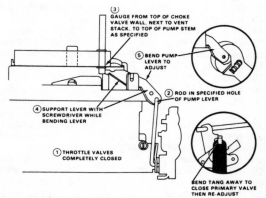

Model M4MC pump rod adjustment

5. Measure the clearance from the top of the choke valve wall, next to the vent stack, and the top of the pump stem.

6. To adjust the dimension, support the pump lever and bend the pump lever.

7. Adjust the idle speed.

8. If necessary, readjust the secondary actuating rod.

FAST IDLE SPEED

1. Hold the cam follower on the high step of the fast idle cam.

2. Turn the fast idle screw out until the primary throttle valves are closed.

3. Turn the fast idle screw in to contact the lever, then turn the screw in three turns.

4. Check the fast idle speed, adjust by turning the screw.

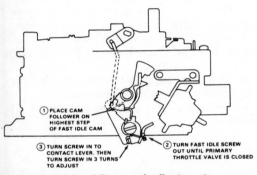

Model M4MC fast idle speed adjustment

CHOKE COIL LEVER

1. Loosen the three retaining screws or remove the rivets and remove the cover and coil assembly from the choke housing.

2. Place the cam follower on the high step of the fast idle cam.

3. Push up on the thermostatic coil tang (counterclockwise) until the choke valve closes.

4. Insert a .120 in. drill bit into the hole (at about the 4 o'clock position) in the choke housing.

5. The lower edge of the choke coil lever should just contact the side of the bit.

6. Bend the choke rod to adjust.

NOTE: *A "stat" cover retainer kit is necessary when reinstalling a riveted cover.*

CHOKE ROD (FAST IDLE CAM)

1. Adjust the fast idle.

2. Place the cam follower on the second step of the fast idle cam firmly against the rise of the high step.

3. Close the choke valve by pushing up on the choke coil lever inside the choke housing.

4. Measure the clearance between the up-

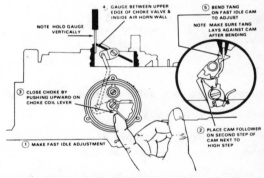

Model M4MC choke rod (fast idle cam) adjustment

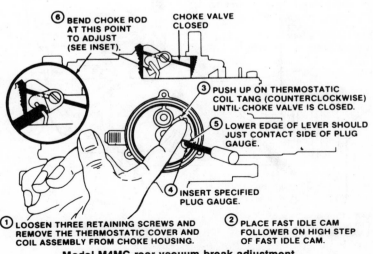

Model M4MC rear vacuum break adjustment

per edge of the choke valve and the inside of the air horn wall.

5. Bend the tang on the fast idle cam to adjust the clearance. Be sure that the tang lies against the cam after bending it.

6. Recheck the fast idle speed.

AIR VALVE DASHPOT

1. Seat the front vacuum diaphagm using an outside vacuum source.

2. The air valves must be completely closed.

3. Measure the clearance between the air valve dashpot and the end of the slot in the air valve lever. It should be .015 in.

4. Bend the air valve dashpot rod to adjust the clearance.

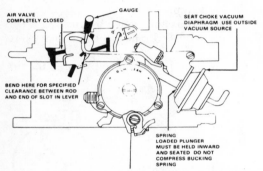

Model M4MC air valve dashpot adjustment

FRONT VACUUM BREAK

1. Remove the thermostatic cover and coil assembly from the choke housing.

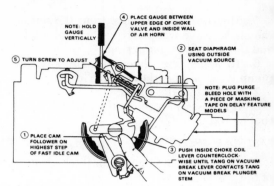

Model M4MC front vacuum break adjustment

2. Place the cam follower on the high step of the fast idle cam.

3. Seat the front vacuum diaphragm using an outside vacuum source.

4. Push up on the inside choke coil lever until the tang on the vacuum break lever contacts the tang on the vacuum break plunger.

5. Measure the clearance between the upper edge of the choke valve and the air horn wall.

6. Turn the adjusting screw on the vacuum break plunger lever to adjust.

7. Reconnect the vacuum hose after adjustment.

REAR VACUUM BREAK

1. Remove the thermostatic cover and coil assembly from the choke housing.

2. Place the cam follower on the high step of the fast idle cam.

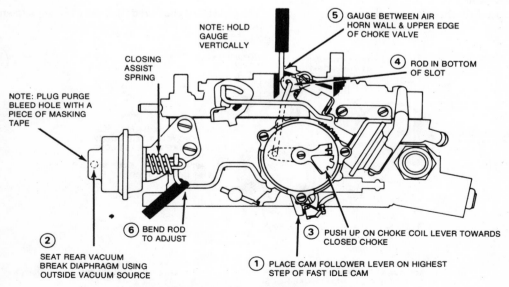

Model M4MC rear vacuum break adjustment

3. Plug the bleed hose in the vacuum break unit cover with tape.

4. Seat the rear vacuum diaphragm using an outside vacuum source.

5. Push up the choke coil lever inside the choke housing toward the closed position.

6. With the choke rod in the bottom slot of the choke lever, measure the clearance between the upper edge of the choke valve and air horn wall.

7. Bend the vacuum break rod if necessary to adjust.

8. After adjustment, remove the tape and install the vacuum hose.

CHOKE UNLOADER

1. Install the thermostaic coil and cover with a gasket between the choke cover and the choke housing. The thermostatic coil must be installed in the slot in the inside of the choke coil lever pick-up arm.

2. Hold the throttle valves wide open with the choke valve completely closed. On a warm engine, close the choke valve by pushing up on the tang of the intermediate choke lever which contacts the fast idle cam. A rubber band will hold it in position.

3. Measure the distance between the upper edge of the choke valve and the air horn wall.

4. Bend the tang on the fast idle lever to adjust the clearance. Check to be sure that the tang on the fast idle cam lever is contacting the center of the fast idle cam after adjustment.

AIR VALVE SPRING

1. Remove the front vacuum break diaphragm and the air valve dashpot rod.

2. Loosen the lockscrew.

3. Turn the tension adjusting screw counterclockwise until the air valve opens partway.

4. Turn the tension adjusting screw clockwise while tapping lightly on the casting with the handle of a screwdriver.

5. When the air valve just closes, turn the tension adjusting screw clockwise the specified number of turns after the spring contacts the pin.

6. Tighten the lockscrew and reinstall the diaphragm and dashpot rod.

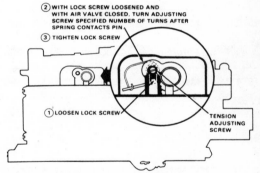

Model M4MC air valve spring adjustment (© Chevrolet Motor Division)

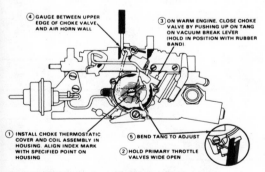

Model M4MC choke unloader adjustment

FLOAT LEVEL

Use the procedure given earlier for the model 4MV, measuring at a point $3/16$ in. from the toe of the float.

Rochester Model MV, 1MV, 1ME Carburetor Specifications

Year	Model	Fast Idle Speed (rpm)	Choke Rod (Fast Idle Cam) (in.)	Choke Vacuum Break (in.)	Auxiliary Vacuum Break (in.)	Choke Unloader (in.)	Float Level (in.)	Metering Rod (in.)	CEC Solenoid (rpm)
1969	All	2400	.180	.260	—	.350	¼	.070	—
1970	All	2400	.190	.230	—	.350	¼	.070	—
1971	Manual	2400	.180	.230	—	.350	¼	.080	1000
	Automatic	2400	.180	.230	—	.350	¼	.080	750
1972	Manual	2400	.150	.225	—	.500	¼	.078	1000
	Manual, Calif.	2400	.150	.225	—	.500	¼	.076	1000
	Automatic	2400	.125	.190	—	.500	¼	.079	650
	Automatic, Calif.	2400	.125	.190	—	.500	¼	.078	650
1973	Manual	2400	.275	.350	—	.500	¼	.080	1000
	Automatic	2400	.245	.300	—	.500	¼	.080	650
1974	Manual	1800	.275	.350	—	.500	.295	.080	—
	Automatic	1800	.245	.300	—	.500	.295	.080	—
	Manual, Calif.	1800	.300	.375	—	.500	.295	.080	—
1975	Automatic	1800	.260	.300	.290	.325	$11/_{32}$	.080	—
	Manual	1800	.275	.300	.290	.325	$11/_{32}$	.080	—
	Automatic, Calif.	1800	.245	.300	.150	.275	$11/_{32}$	.080	—
	Manual, Calif.	1800	.275	.350	.170	.275	$11/_{32}$	.080	—
1976	17056004	2400	.130	.165	—	.335	$11/_{32}$	.080	—
	17056006	2400	.130	.165	—	.270	¼	.080	—
	17056007	2400	.130	.165	—	.275	¼	.070	—
1977	17057006	2400	.150	.180	—	.275	$5/_{16}$	.070	—
	17057007	2400	.150	.180	—	.275	$5/_{16}$	.070	—

Rochester Model MV, 1MV, 1ME Carburetor Specifications (cont.)

Year	Model	Fast Idle Speed (rpm)	Choke Rod (Fast Idle Cam) (in.)	Choke Vacuum Break (in.)	Auxiliary Vacuum Break (in.)	Choke Unloader (in.)	Float Level (in.)	Metering Rod (in.)	CEC Solenoid (rpm)
1978	17058006	2400	.275	.275	—	.520	5/16	.070	—
	17058007	2400	.275	.275	—	.520	5/16	.070	—

Rochester Model M2MC/ME Carburetor Specifications

Year	Model	Float Level (in.)	Accelerator Pump	Fast Idle Speed (rpm)	Fast Idle Cam (Choke Rod)	Choke Unloader	Front Vacuum Break
1979	17059100, 17059102, 17059142, 17059144	15/32	13/32	1600	.243	.243	.171
	17059101, 17059103, 17059143, 17059145	15/32	13/32	1300	.243	.243	.171
1980	17080100, 17080102, 17080142, 17080143, 17080144, 17080145	7/16	9/32	①	38°	38°	29°
1981	17081101, 17081103, 17081142, 17081143, 17081144, 17081145	13/32	5/16	①	38°	38°	25°

① See the underhood emissions sticker

Rochester Model 2GV Carburetor Specifications*

Year	Model	Choke Rod (Fast Idle Cam) (in.)	Choke Vacuum Break (in.)	Choke Unloader (in.)	Accelerator Pump Rod (in.)	Float Level (in.)	Float Drop (in.)
1969	All	.095	.130	.215	1.125	$^{27}/_{32}$	1.750
1970	All	.060	.140	.215	1.375	$^{23}/_{32}$	1.750
1971	All	.040	.080	.215	1.047	$^{21}/_{32}$	1.750
1972	Automatic	.040	.080	.210	1.313	$^{21}/_{32}$	1.281
	Automatic, Calif.	.040	.080	.210	1.313	$^{21}/_{32}$	1.281
	Manual	.075	.110	.210	1.313	$^{21}/_{32}$	1.281
	Manual, Calif.	.075	.110	.210	1.313	$^{21}/_{32}$	1.281
1973	All	.150	.080	.215	1.313	$^{21}/_{32}$	1.281
1974	Manual	.200	.140	.250	1.281	$^{19}/_{32}$	1.281
	Automatic	.245	.130	.325	1.188	$^{19}/_{32}$	1.281

*Model 2GC specifications are given in the text.

Rochester Model 2SE Carburetor Specifications

Year	Model	Float Level (in.)	Fast Idle Speed (rpm)	Air Valve Rod	Fast Idle Cam (Choke rod) (deg)	Vacuum Break (deg)
1979	17059640	1/8	2000	.040	17	20
	17059641, 17059643	1/8	1800	.040	17	23.5
	17059642	1/8	①	.040	17	①
	17059764	1/8	2100	.040	17	20
	17059765	1/8	2100	.040	17	23.5
1980	17080621	1/8	①	2°	17°	22°
	17080622	1/8	①	2°	17°	22°
	17080623	1/8	①	2°	17°	22°

Rochester Model 2SE Carburetor Specifications (cont.)

Year	Model	Float Level (in.)	Fast Idle Speed (rpm)	Air Valve Rod	Fast Idle Cam (Choke rod) (deg)	Vacuum Break (deg)
1980	17080626	1/8	①	2°	17°	22°
	17080720	1/8	①	2°	17°	20°
	17080721	1/8	①	2°	17°	23.5°
	17080722	1/8	①	2°	17°	20°
	17080723	1/8	①	2°	17°	23.5°
1981	17081621	3/16	①	1°	15°	26°
	17081622	3/16	①	1°	15°	26°
	17081623	3/16	①	1°	15°	26°
	17081624	3/16	①	1°	15°	26°
	17081625	3/16	①	1°	15°	26°
	17081626	3/16	①	1°	15°	26°
	17081627	3/16	①	1°	15°	26°
	17081629	3/16	①	1°	15°	24°
	17081630	3/16	①	1°	15°	26°
	17081633	3/16	①	1°	15°	26°
	17081720	3/16	①	1°	15°	30°
	17081725	3/16	①	1°	15°	30°
	17081726	3/16	①	1°	15°	30°
	17081727	3/16	①	1°	15°	30°
1982	17082334	3/16	①	1°	15°	26°
	17082335	3/16	①	1°	15°	26°
	17082336	3/16	①	1°	15°	26°
	17082337	3/16	①	1°	15°	26°
	17082338	3/16	①	1°	15°	26°

Rochester Model 2SE Carburetor Specifications (cont.)

Year	Model	Float Level (in.)	Fast Idle Speed (rpm)	Air Valve Rod	Fast Idle Cam (Choke rod) (deg)	Vacuum Break (deg)
1982	17082339	3/16	①	1°	15°	26°
	17082341	3/16	①	1°	15°	30°
	17082342	3/16	①	1°	15°	30°
	17082344	3/16	①	1°	15°	30°
	17082345	3/16	①	1°	15°	30°
	17082431	3/16	①	1°	15°	24°
	17082433	3/16	①	1°	15°	24°
	17082480	3/16	①	1°	15°	26°
	17082481	3/16	①	1°	15°	26°
	17082482	3/16	①	1°	15°	23°
	17082483	3/16	①	1°	15°	26°
	17082484	3/16	①	1°	15°	26°
	17082485	3/16	①	1°	15°	26°
	17082486	3/16	①	1°	15°	28°
	17082487	3/16	①	1°	15°	28°
	17082488	3/16	①	1°	15°	28°
	17082489	3/16	①	1°	15°	28°

① See the underhood emission sticker

Rochester Model 4MV Carburetor Specifications

Year	Model	Fast Idle Speed (rpm)	Choke Rod (Fast Idle Cam) (in.)	Vacuum Break (in.)	Choke Unloader (in.)	Float Level (in.)	Accelerator Pump Rod (in.)	Air Valve Spring (turns)
1969	All	2400	.100	.245	.450	$7/32$	$5/16$	$7/16$
1970	Manual	2400	.100	.275	.450	$1/4$	$5/16$	$7/16$
	Automatic	2400	.100	.245	.450	$1/4$	$5/16$	$7/16$
1971	All	2400	.100	.260	.450	$1/4$	$5/16$	$7/16$
1972	Automatic	1500	.100	.215	.450	$3/16$	$3/8$	$1/2$
	Manual	1350	.100	.215	.450	$3/16$	$3/8$	$1/2$
1973	Manual	1300	.430	.215	.450	$7/32$	$13/32$	$1/2$
	Automatic	1600	.430	.215	.450	$7/32$	$13/32$	$1/2$
1974	Manual	1300	.430	.230	.450	$1/4$	$13/32$	$7/8$
	Automatic	1600	.430	.230	.450	$1/4$	$13/32$	$7/8$
1975	All 350	1600	.430	.210	.450	$11/32$	.275	$7/8$
	400, Automatic	1600	.430	.200	.450	$15/32$	.275	$3/4$
	All 350, Calif.	1600	.430	.230	.450	$11/32$	.275	$7/8$
	400, Automatic, Calif.	1600	.430	.230	.450	$11/32$	.275	$3/4$
1976	350—49 State	1600	.290	.145	.295	$11/32$	$9/32$	$7/8$
	350—Calif.	1600	.290	.155	.295	$11/32$	$9/32$	$7/8$
	400—49 State	1600	.290	.138	.295	$11/32$	$9/32$	$3/4$
	400—Calif.	1600	.290	.155	.295	$11/32$	$9/32$	$3/4$
1977	Automatic—All	1600	.220	.110	.295	$11/32$	$9/32$	$7/8$
	Manual—49 State	1600	.220	.115	.295	$11/32$	$9/32$	$7/8$
	Manual—Calif.	1600	.290	.120	.295	$11/32$	$9/32$	$7/8$
1978	All	1700	.277	.123	.260	$15/32$	$9/32$	$7/8$

Rochester Model M4MC/ME Carburetor Specifications

Year	Model	Float Level (in.)	Accelerator Pump (in.)	Fast Idle Speed (rpm)	Fast Idle Cam (Choke Rod)	Choke Unloader	Air Valve Spring (turns)	Front Vacuum Break	Rear Vacuum Break
1975	350—Automatic	15/32	9/32	1600	.300	.325	7/8	.180	.170
	350—Manual	15/32	9/32	1600	.300	.325	7/8	.180	.170
1977	400—Automatic 49 State	11/32	9/32	1600	.220	.280	7/8	—	—
	400—Automatic Calif.	11/32	9/32	1600	.220	.280	7/8	—	—
1978	400—Automatic 49 State	15/32	9/32	1700	.314	.277	7/8	—	—
	400—Automatic Calif.	15/32	9/32	1600	.314	.277	7/8	—	—
1979	350—Manual 49 State	15/32	13/32	1300	.314	.277	7/8	—	.129
	350—Manual Calif.	15/32	13/32	1600	.314	.277	7/8	—	.149
	350—Automatic 49 State	15/32	13/32	1600	.314	.277	7/8	—	.129
	350—Automatic Calif.	15/32	13/32	1600	.314	.277	7/8	—	.149
	400—Automatic 49 State	15/32	13/32	1600	.314	.277	7/8	—	.129
	400—Automatic Calif.	15/32	9/32 ①	1600	.314	.277	7/8	—	.149
1980	17080201	15/32	9/32	②	46°	42°	7/8	—	23°
	17080205	15/32	9/32	②	46°	42°	7/8	—	23°
	17080206	15/32	9/32	②	46°	42°	7/8	—	23°
	17080213	3/8	9/32	②	37°	40°	1	23°	30°
	17080215	3/8	9/32	②	37°	40°	1	23°	30°
	17080224	15/32	9/32	②	46°	42°	7/8	—	23°
	17080225	15/32	9/32	②	46°	42°	7/8	—	23°
	17080226	15/32	9/32	②	46°	42°	7/8	—	23°

CHILTON'S
FUEL ECONOMY
& TUNE-UP TIPS

Tune-Up • Spark Plug Diagnosis • Emission Controls

Fuel System • Cooling System • Tires and Wheels

General Maintenance

CHILTON'S FUEL ECONOMY & TUNE-UP TIPS

Fuel economy is important to everyone, no matter what kind of vehicle you drive. The maintenance-minded motorist can save both money and fuel using these tips and the periodic maintenance and tune-up procedures in this Repair and Tune-Up Guide.

There are more than 130,000,000 cars and trucks registered for private use in the United States. Each travels an average of 10-12,000 miles per year, and, in total they consume close to 70 billion gallons of fuel each year. This represents nearly ⅔ of the oil imported by the United States each year. The Federal government's goal is to reduce consumption 10% by 1985. A variety of methods are either already in use or under serious consideration, and they all affect your driving and the cars you will drive. In addition to "down-sizing", the auto industry is using or investigating the use of electronic fuel delivery, electronic engine controls and alternative engines for use in smaller and lighter vehicles, among other alternatives to meet the federally mandated Corporate Average Fuel Economy (CAFE) of 27.5 mpg by 1985. The government, for its part, is considering rationing, mandatory driving curtailments and tax increases on motor vehicle fuel in an effort to reduce consumption. The government's goal of a 10% reduction could be realized — and further government regulation avoided — if every private vehicle could use just 1 less gallon of fuel per week.

How Much Can You Save?

Tests have proven that almost anyone can make at least a 10% reduction in fuel consumption through regular maintenance and tune-ups. When a major manufacturer of spark plugs sur-

TUNE-UP

1. Check the cylinder compression to be sure the engine will really benefit from a tune-up and that it is capable of producing good fuel economy. A tune-up will be wasted on an engine in poor mechanical condition.

2. Replace spark plugs regularly. New spark plugs alone can increase fuel economy 3%.

3. Be sure the spark plugs are the correct type (heat range) for your vehicle. See the Tune-Up Specifications.

Heat range refers to the spark plug's ability to conduct heat away from the firing end. It must conduct the heat away in an even pattern to avoid becoming a source of pre-ignition, yet it must also operate hot enough to burn off conductive deposits that could cause misfiring.

The heat range is usually indicated by a number on the spark plug, part of the manufacturer's designation for each individual spark plug. The numbers in bold-face indicate the heat range in each manufacturer's identification system.

Periodically, check the spark plugs to be sure they are firing efficiently. They are excellent indicators of the internal condition of your engine.

Manufacturer	Typical Designation
AC	R **45** TS
Bosch (old)	WA **145** T30
Bosch (new)	HR **8** Y
Champion	RBL **15** Y
Fram/Autolite	**415**
Mopar	P-**62** PR
Motorcraft	BRF-**42**
NGK	BP **5** ES-15
Nippondenso	W **16** EP
Prestolite	14GR **5** 2A

On AC, Bosch (new), Champion, Fram/Autolite, Mopar, Motorcraft and Prestolite, a higher number indicates a hotter plug. On Bosch (old), NGK and Nippondenso, a higher number indicates a colder plug.

4. Make sure the spark plugs are properly gapped. See the Tune-Up Specifications in this book.

5. Be sure the spark plugs are firing efficiently. The illustrations on the next 2 pages show you how to "read" the firing end of the spark plug.

6. Check the ignition timing and set it to specifications. Tests show that almost all cars

veyed over 6,000 cars nationwide, they found that a tune-up, on cars that needed one, increased fuel economy over 11%. Replacing worn plugs alone, accounted for a 3% increase. The same test also revealed that 8 out of every 10 vehicles will have some maintenance deficiency that will directly affect fuel economy, emissions or performance. Most of this mileage-robbing neglect could be prevented with regular maintenance.

Modern engines require that all of the functioning systems operate properly for maximum efficiency. A malfunction anywhere wastes fuel. You can keep your vehicle running as efficiently and economically as possible, by being aware of your vehicles operating and performance characteristics. If your vehicle suddenly develops performance or fuel economy problems it could be due to one or more of the following:

PROBLEM	POSSIBLE CAUSE
Engine Idles Rough	Ignition timing, idle mixture, vacuum leak or something amiss in the emission control system.
Hesitates on Acceleration	Dirty carburetor or fuel filter, improper accelerator pump setting, ignition timing or fouled spark plugs.
Starts Hard or Fails to Start	Worn spark plugs, improperly set automatic choke, ice (or water) in fuel system.
Stalls Frequently	Automatic choke improperly adjusted and possible dirty air filter or fuel filter.
Performs Sluggishly	Worn spark plugs, dirty fuel or air filter, ignition timing or automatic choke out of adjustment.

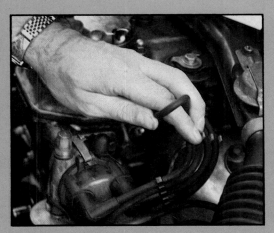

Check spark plug wires on conventional point type ignition for cracks by bending them in a loop around your finger.

Be sure that spark plug wires leading to adjacent cylinders do not run too close together. (Photo courtesy Champion Spark Plug Co.)

have incorrect ignition timing by more than 2°.

7. If your vehicle does not have electronic ignition, check the points, rotor and cap as specified.

8. Check the spark plug wires (used with conventional point-type ignitions) for cracks and burned or broken insulation by bending them in a loop around your finger. Cracked wires decrease fuel efficiency by failing to deliver full voltage to the spark plugs. One misfiring spark plug can cost you as much as 2 mpg.

9. Check the routing of the plug wires. Misfiring can be the result of spark plug leads to adjacent cylinders running parallel to each other and too close together. One wire tends to pick up voltage from the other causing it to fire "out of time".

10. Check all electrical and ignition circuits for voltage drop and resistance.

11. Check the distributor mechanical and/or vacuum advance mechanisms for proper functioning. The vacuum advance can be checked by twisting the distributor plate in the opposite direction of rotation. It should spring back when released.

12. Check and adjust the valve clearance on engines with mechanical lifters. The clearance should be slightly loose rather than too tight.

SPARK PLUG DIAGNOSIS

Normal

APPEARANCE: This plug is typical of one operating normally. The insulator nose varies from a light tan to grayish color with slight electrode wear. The presence of slight deposits is normal on used plugs and will have no adverse effect on engine performance. The spark plug heat range is correct for the engine and the engine is running normally.

CAUSE: Properly running engine.

RECOMMENDATION: Before reinstalling this plug, the electrodes should be cleaned and filed square. Set the gap to specifications. If the plug has been in service for more than 10-12,000 miles, the entire set should probably be replaced with a fresh set of the same heat range.

Oil Deposits

APPEARANCE: The firing end of the plug is covered with a wet, oily coating.

CAUSE: The problem is poor oil control. On high mileage engines, oil is leaking past the rings or valve guides into the combustion chamber. A common cause is also a plugged PCV valve, and a ruptured fuel pump diaphragm can also cause this condition. Oil fouled plugs such as these are often found in new or recently overhauled engines, before normal oil control is achieved, and can be cleaned and reinstalled.

RECOMMENDATION: A hotter spark plug may temporarily relieve the problem, but the engine is probably in need of work.

Incorrect Heat Range

APPEARANCE: The effects of high temperature on a spark plug are indicated by clean white, often blistered insulator. This can also be accompanied by excessive wear of the electrode, and the absence of deposits.

CAUSE: Check for the correct spark plug heat range. A plug which is too hot for the engine can result in overheating. A car operated mostly at high speeds can require a colder plug. Also check ignition timing, cooling system level, fuel mixture and leaking intake manifold.

RECOMMENDATION: If all ignition and engine adjustments are known to be correct, and no other malfunction exists, install spark plugs one heat range colder.

Photos Courtesy Champion Spark Plug Co.

Carbon Deposits

APPEARANCE: Carbon fouling is easily identified by the presence of dry, soft, black, sooty deposits.

CAUSE: Changing the heat range can often lead to carbon fouling, as can prolonged slow, stop-and-start driving. If the heat range is correct, carbon fouling can be attributed to a rich fuel mixture, sticking choke, clogged air cleaner, worn breaker points, retarded timing or low compression. If only one or two plugs are carbon fouled, check for corroded or cracked wires on the affected plugs. Also look for cracks in the distributor cap between the towers of affected cylinders.

RECOMMENDATION: After the problem is corrected, these plugs can be cleaned and reinstalled if not worn severely.

MMT Fouled

APPEARANCE: Spark plugs fouled by MMT (Methycyclopentadienyl Maganese Tricarbonyl) have reddish, rusty appearance on the insulator and side electrode.

CAUSE: MMT is an anti-knock additive in gasoline used to replace lead. During the combustion process, the MMT leaves a reddish deposit on the insulator and side electrode.

RECOMMENDATION: No engine malfunction is indicated and the deposits will not affect plug performance any more than lead deposits (see Ash Deposits). MMT fouled plugs can be cleaned, regapped and reinstalled.

High Speed Glazing

APPEARANCE: Glazing appears as shiny coating on the plug, either yellow or tan in color.

CAUSE: During hard, fast acceleration, plug temperatures rise suddenly. Deposits from normal combustion have no chance to fluff-off; instead, they melt on the insulator forming an electrically conductive coating which causes misfiring.

RECOMMENDATION: Glazed plugs are not easily cleaned. They should be replaced with a fresh set of plugs of the correct heat range. If the condition recurs, using plugs with a heat range one step colder may cure the problem.

Ash (Lead) Deposits

APPEARANCE: Ash deposits are characterized by light brown or white colored deposits crusted on the side or center electrodes. In some cases it may give the plug a rusty appearance.

CAUSE: Ash deposits are normally derived from oil or fuel additives burned during normal combustion. Normally they are harmless, though excessive amounts can cause misfiring. If deposits are excessive in short mileage, the valve guides may be worn.

RECOMMENDATION: Ash-fouled plugs can be cleaned, gapped and reinstalled.

Detonation

APPEARANCE: Detonation is usually characterized by a broken plug insulator.

CAUSE: A portion of the fuel charge will begin to burn spontaneously, from the increased heat following ignition. The explosion that results applies extreme pressure to engine components, frequently damaging spark plugs and pistons.

Detonation can result by over-advanced ignition timing, inferior gasoline (low octane) lean air/fuel mixture, poor carburetion, engine lugging or an increase in compression ratio due to combustion chamber deposits or engine modification.

RECOMMENDATION: Replace the plugs after correcting the problem.

Photos Courtesy Fram Corporation

EMISSION CONTROLS

13. Be aware of the general condition of the emission control system. It contributes to reduced pollution and should be serviced regularly to maintain efficient engine operation.

14. Check all vacuum lines for dried, cracked or brittle conditions. Something as simple as a leaking vacuum hose can cause poor performance and loss of economy.

15. Avoid tampering with the emission control system. Attempting to improve fuel econ-

FUEL SYSTEM

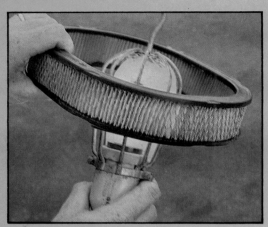

Check the air filter with a light behind it. If you can see light through the filter it can be reused.

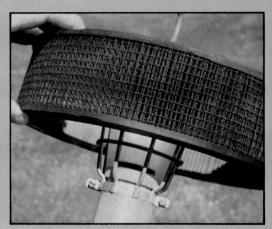

Extremely clogged filters should be discarded and replaced with a new one.

18. Replace the air filter regularly. A dirty air filter richens the air/fuel mixture and can increase fuel consumption as much as 10%. Tests show that ⅓ of all vehicles have air filters in need of replacement.

19. Replace the fuel filter at least as often as recommended.

20. Set the idle speed and carburetor mixture to specifications.

21. Check the automatic choke. A sticking or malfunctioning choke wastes gas.

22. During the summer months, adjust the automatic choke for a leaner mixture which will produce faster engine warm-ups.

COOLING SYSTEM

29. Be sure all accessory drive belts are in good condition. Check for cracks or wear.

30. Adjust all accessory drive belts to proper tension.

31. Check all hoses for swollen areas, worn spots, or loose clamps.

32. Check coolant level in the radiator or expansion tank.

33. Be sure the thermostat is operating properly. A stuck thermostat delays engine warm-up and a cold engine uses nearly twice as much fuel as a warm engine.

34. Drain and replace the engine coolant at least as often as recommended. Rust and scale

TIRES & WHEELS

38. Check the tire pressure often with a pencil type gauge. Tests by a major tire manufacturer show that 90% of all vehicles have at least 1 tire improperly inflated. Better mileage can be achieved by over-inflating tires, but never exceed the maximum inflation pressure on the side of the tire.

39. If possible, install radial tires. Radial tires deliver as much as ½ mpg more than bias belted tires.

40. Avoid installing super-wide tires. They only create extra rolling resistance and decrease fuel mileage. Stick to the manufacturer's recommendations.

41. Have the wheels properly balanced.

omy by tampering with emission controls is more likely to worsen fuel economy than improve it. Emission control changes on modern engines are not readily reversible.

16. Clean (or replace) the EGR valve and lines as recommended.

17. Be sure that all vacuum lines and hoses are reconnected properly after working under the hood. An unconnected or misrouted vacuum line can wreak havoc with engine performance.

---

23. Check for fuel leaks at the carburetor, fuel pump, fuel lines and fuel tank. Be sure all lines and connections are tight.

24. Periodically check the tightness of the carburetor and intake manifold attaching nuts and bolts. These are a common place for vacuum leaks to occur.

25. Clean the carburetor periodically and lubricate the linkage.

26. The condition of the tailpipe can be an excellent indicator of proper engine combustion. After a long drive at highway speeds, the inside of the tailpipe should be a light grey in color. Black or soot on the insides indicates an overly rich mixture.

27. Check the fuel pump pressure. The fuel pump may be supplying more fuel than the engine needs.

28. Use the proper grade of gasoline for your engine. Don't try to compensate for knocking or "pinging" by advancing the ignition timing. This practice will only increase plug temperature and the chances of detonation or pre-ignition with relatively little performance gain.

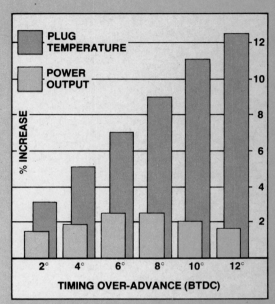

Increasing ignition timing past the specified setting results in a drastic increase in spark plug temperature with increased chance of detonation or preignition. Performance increase is considerably less. (Photo courtesy Champion Spark Plug Co.)

---

that form in the engine should be flushed out to allow the engine to operate at peak efficiency.

35. Clean the radiator of debris that can decrease cooling efficiency.

36. Install a flex-type or electric cooling fan, if you don't have a clutch type fan. Flex fans use curved plastic blades to push more air at low speeds when more cooling is needed; at high speeds the blades flatten out for less resistance. Electric fans only run when the engine temperature reaches a predetermined level.

37. Check the radiator cap for a worn or cracked gasket. If the cap does not seal properly, the cooling system will not function properly.

---

42. Be sure the front end is correctly aligned. A misaligned front end actually has wheels going in different directions. The increased drag can reduce fuel economy by .3 mpg.

43. Correctly adjust the wheel bearings. Wheel bearings that are adjusted too tight increase rolling resistance.

Check tire pressures regularly with a reliable pocket type gauge. Be sure to check the pressure on a cold tire.

GENERAL MAINTENANCE

Check the fluid levels (particularly engine oil) on a regular basis. Be sure to check the oil for grit, water or other contamination.

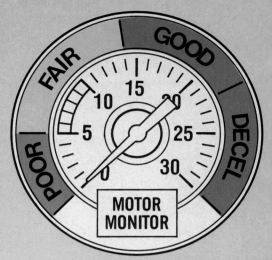

A vacuum gauge is another excellent indicator of internal engine condition and can also be installed in the dash as a mileage indicator.

44. Periodically check the fluid levels in the engine, power steering pump, master cylinder, automatic transmission and drive axle.

45. Change the oil at the recommended interval and change the filter at every oil change. Dirty oil is thick and causes extra friction between moving parts, cutting efficiency and increasing wear. A worn engine requires more frequent tune-ups and gets progressively worse fuel economy. In general, use the lightest viscosity oil for the driving conditions you will encounter.

46. Use the recommended viscosity fluids in the transmission and axle.

47. Be sure the battery is fully charged for fast starts. A slow starting engine wastes fuel.

48. Be sure battery terminals are clean and tight.

49. Check the battery electrolyte level and add distilled water if necessary.

50. Check the exhaust system for crushed pipes, blockages and leaks.

51. Adjust the brakes. Dragging brakes or brakes that are not releasing create increased drag on the engine.

52. Install a vacuum gauge or miles-per-gallon gauge. These gauges visually indicate engine vacuum in the intake manifold. High vacuum = good mileage and low vacuum = poorer mileage. The gauge can also be an excellent indicator of internal engine conditions.

53. Be sure the clutch is properly adjusted. A slipping clutch wastes fuel.

54. Check and periodically lubricate the heat control valve in the exhaust manifold. A sticking or inoperative valve prevents engine warm-up and wastes gas.

55. Keep accurate records to check fuel economy over a period of time. A sudden drop in fuel economy may signal a need for tune-up or other maintenance.

Rochester Model M4MC/ME Carburetor Specifications (cont.)

Year	Model	Float Level (in.)	Accelerator Pump (in.)	Fast Idle Speed (rpm)	Fast Idle Cam (Choke Rod)	Choke Unloader	Air Valve Spring (turns)	Front Vacuum Break	Rear Vacuum Break
1980	17080227	15/32	9/32	②	46°	42°	7/8	—	23°
	17080229	3/8	9/32	②	37°	40°	1	23°	30°
	17080290	15/32	9/32	②	46°	42°	7/8	—	26°
	17080291	15/32	9/32	②	46°	42°	7/8	—	26°
	17080292	15/32	9/32	②	46°	42°	7/8	—	26°
	17080295	15/32	9/32	②	46°	42°	7/8	—	23°
	17080297	15/32	9/32	②	46°	42°	7/8	—	23°
	17080503	15/32	9/32	②	46°	42°	7/8	—	26°
	17080506	15/32	9/32	②	46°	42°	7/8	—	26°
	17080508	15/32	9/32	②	46°	42°	7/8	—	26°
	17080513	3/8	9/32	②	37°	40°	1	23°	30°
	17080515	3/8	9/32	②	37°	40°	1	23°	30°
	17080523	15/32	9/32	②	46°	42°	7/8	—	23°
	17080524	15/32	9/32	②	46°	42°	7/8	—	23°
	17080525	15/32	9/32	②	46°	42°	7/8	—	23°
	17080526	15/32	9/32	②	46°	42°	7/8	—	23°
	17080527	15/32	9/32	②	46°	42°	7/8	—	23°
	17080528	15/32	9/32	②	46°	42°	7/8	—	23°
	17080529	3/8	9/32	②	37°	40°	1	23°	30°
1981	17080212	3/8	9/32	②	46°	40°	3/4	24°	30°
	17080213	3/8	9/32	②	37°	40°	1	23°	30°
	17080215	3/8	9/32	②	37°	40°	1	23°	30°
	17080298	3/8	9/32	②	37°	40°	1	23°	30°
	17080507	3/8	9/32	②	37°	40°	3/4	23°	30°

Rochester Model M4MC/ME Carburetor Specifications (cont.)

Year	Model	Float Level (in.)	Accelerator Pump (in.)	Fast Idle Speed (rpm)	Fast Idle Cam (Choke Rod)	Choke Unloader	Air Valve Spring (turns)	Front Vacuum Break	Rear Vacuum Break
1981	17080512	3/8	9/32	②	46°	40°	¾	24°	30°
	17080513	3/8	9/32	②	37°	40°	7/8	23°	30°
	17081200	15/32	9/32	②	46°	42°	7/8	24°	23°
	17081201	15/32	9/32	②	46°	42°	7/8	23°	23°
	17081205	15/32	9/32	②	46°	42°	7/8	23°	23°
	17081206	15/32	9/32	②	46°	42°	7/8	23°	23°
	17081220	15/32	9/32	②	46°	42°	7/8	23°	23°
	17081226	15/32	9/32	②	46°	42°	7/8	24°	23°
	17081227	15/32	9/32	②	46°	42°	7/8	24°	23°
	17081290	13/32	9/32	②	46°	42°	7/8	23°	24°
	17081291	13/32	9/32	②	46°	42°	7/8	23°	24°
	17081292	13/32	9/32	②	46°	42°	7/8	23°	24°
	17081506	13/32	9/32	②	46°	42°	7/8	23°	36°
	17081508	13/32	9/32	②	46°	36°	7/8	23°	36°
	17081524	13/32	5/16 ①	②	46°	38°	7/8	25°	36°
	17081526	13/32	5/16 ①	②	46°	38°	7/8	25°	36°
1982	17080212	3/8	9/32	②	40°	40°	¾	24°	30°
	17080213	3/8	9/32	②	37°	40°	1	23°	30°
	17080215	3/8	9/32	②	37°	40°	1	23°	30°
	17080298	3/8	9/32	②	37°	40°	1	23°	30°
	17080507	3/8	9/32	②	37°	40°	1	23°	30°
	17080512	3/8	9/32	②	46°	40°	¾	24°	30°
	17080513	3/8	9/32	②	37°	40°	¾	23°	30°
	17082213	3/8	9/32	②	37°	40°	1	23°	30°

Rochester Model M4MC/ME Carburetor Specifications (cont.)

Year	Model	Float Level (in.)	Accelerator Pump (in.)	Fast Idle Speed (rpm)	Fast Idle Cam (Choke Rod)	Choke Unloader	Air Valve Spring (turns)	Front Vacuum Break	Rear Vacuum Break
1982	17082220	$^{13}/_{32}$	$^9/_{32}$	②	46°	39°	$^7/_8$	24°	34°
	17082221	$^{13}/_{32}$	$^9/_{32}$	②	46°	39°	$^7/_8$	24°	34°
	17082222	$^{13}/_{32}$	$^9/_{32}$	②	46°	39°	$^7/_8$	24°	34°
	17082223	$^{13}/_{32}$	$^9/_{32}$	②	46°	39°	$^7/_8$	24°	34°
	17082224	$^{13}/_{32}$	$^9/_{32}$	②	46°	39°	$^7/_8$	24°	34°
	17082225	$^{13}/_{32}$	$^9/_{32}$	②	46°	39°	$^7/_8$	24°	34°
	17082226	$^{13}/_{32}$	$^9/_{32}$	②	46°	39°	$^7/_8$	24°	34°
	17082227	$^{13}/_{32}$	$^9/_{32}$	②	46°	39°	$^7/_8$	24°	34°
	17082230	$^{13}/_{32}$	$^9/_{32}$	②	46°	39°	$^7/_8$	26°	36°
	17082231	$^{13}/_{32}$	$^9/_{32}$	②	46°	39°	$^7/_8$	26°	36°
	17082234	$^{13}/_{32}$	$^9/_{32}$	②	46°	39°	$^7/_8$	26°	36°
	17082235	$^{13}/_{32}$	$^9/_{32}$	②	46°	39°	$^7/_8$	26°	36°
	17082290	$^{13}/_{32}$	$^9/_{32}$	②	46°	39°	$^7/_8$	24°	34°
	17082291	$^{13}/_{32}$	$^9/_{32}$	②	46°	39°	$^7/_8$	24°	34°
	17082292	$^{13}/_{32}$	$^9/_{32}$	②	46°	39°	$^7/_8$	24°	34°
	17082293	$^{13}/_{32}$	$^9/_{32}$	②	46°	39°	$^7/_8$	24°	34°
	17082506	$^{13}/_{32}$	$^9/_{32}$	②	46°	39°	$^7/_8$	23°	36°
	17082508	$^{13}/_{32}$	$^9/_{32}$	②	46°	39°	$^7/_8$	23°	36°
	17082513	$^3/_8$	$^9/_{32}$	②	37°	40°	$^3/_4$	23°	30°
	17082524	$^{13}/_{32}$	$^5/_{16}$ ①	②	46°	39°	$^7/_8$	25°	36°
	17082526	$^{13}/_{32}$	$^5/_{16}$ ①	②	46°	39°	$^7/_8$	25°	36°

① Outer hole
② See the underhood emission sticker

DIESEL FUEL SYSTEM

Fuel Line Heater
REMOVAL AND INSTALLATION

1. Disconnect the batteries and remove the air cleaner.
2. Remove the crankcase ventilator bracket from the intake manifold and position it out of the way.
3. Disconnect the fuel lines to the secondary fuel filter and then remove the filter.
4. Loosen the vacuum pump hold-down clamp and rotate the pump to gain access to the manifold bolts.
5. Remove the intake manifold. Install screened covers or tape over the openings.
6. Remove all but #5 and #7 fuel injection lines. Cap all lines, nozzles and fittings.
7. Disconnect the fuel line at the fuel supply pump.
8. Disconnect the fuel line clip and the wire connector.
9. Remove the fuel line heater and the fuel line to the primary filter.
10. Installation is in the reverse order.

Fuel Supply Pump

These engines use a small mechanical fuel pump (much like the ones on gasoline engines) to deliver fuel from the tank and lines to the injection pump.

REMOVAL AND INSTALLATION

1. Disconnect and plug the two fuel lines.
2. Remove the two mounting bolts.
3. Remove the pump and gasket.
4. Install the pump and gasket. Tighten the mounting bolts to 27 ft. lbs.
5. Install both fuel lines.
6. Start the engine and check for leaks.

Injection Pump
REMOVAL

1. Disconnect the batteries.
2. Remove the fan and the fan shroud.
3. Remove the intake manifold.
4. Remove all fuel lines. Cap all lines, nozzles and fittings.
5. Disconnect the accelerator cables at the injection pump. Disconnect the detent cable if applicable.
6. Tag and disconnect all necessary wires and hoses at the injection pump.

7. Disconnect the fuel return line and the line at the pump.
8. If equipped with AC, remove the AC hose retainer bracket.
9. Remove the oil filler tube complete with PCV vent hose assembly.
10. Scribe or paint a mark on the front cover and align, alignment mark on pump and front cover.
11. It will be necessary to rotate the engine in order to gain access to the injection pump retaining bolts through the oil filler neck hole.
12. Remove the pump-to-front cover nuts, remove the pump and cap all lines and fittings.

TESTING

1. Drain all fuel from the pump.
2. Connect an air line to the pump inlet connection. Make sure that the air supply is clean and dry.
3. Seal off the return line fitting and completely immerse the pump in a bath of clean test oil.
4. Raise the air pressure in the pump to 20 psi. Leave the pump immersed in the oil for 10 min. to allow any trapped air to escape.
5. Watch for leaks after the 10 min. period. If the pump is not leaking, reduce the pressure to 2 psi for 30 sec. If there is still no leak, increase the pressure to 20 psi again. If still no leaks are seen, the pump is OK.

INSTALLATION

1. Replace the gasket.
2. Align the locating pin on the pump hub with the slot in the injection pump gear. At the same time, align the timing marks.
3. Attach the pump to the front cover and tighten the mounting nuts to 30 ft. lbs.

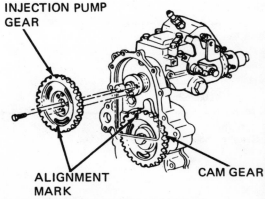

INJECTION PUMP GEAR

ALIGNMENT MARK

CAM GEAR

Diesel injection pump alignment marks

4. Attach pump-to-drive gear and tighten the bolts to 20 ft. lbs.

5. Install the oil filler tube along with the PCV vent hose assembly.

6. Install the AC hose retainer bracket if removed.

7. Install the fuel line at the pump and tighten to 20 ft. lbs. Install the fuel return line.

8. Connect all wires and hoses. Connect the accelerator cable.

9. Connect the intake manifold.

10. Install the intake manifold.

11. Install the fan shroud, the fan and connect the batteries.

Injection Timing

ADJUSTMENT

For the engine to be properly timed, the marks on top of the engine front cover and the injection pump flange must be aligned. This is done with the engine turned off.

1. Loosen the three pump retaining nuts.

2. Use the proper tool and rotate the pump until the two timing marks are in alignment.

3. Tighten the retaining nuts to 30 ft. lbs. and then adjust the throttle rod.

ESTABLISHING A NEW TIMING MARK

When a new front cover has been installed, a new timing mark will also be required.

1. Remove the injection pump and then position the No. 1 cylinder at TDC of the compression stroke.

2. Install a special timing tool into the injection pump. Do not use a gasket.

3. The slot on the injection pump gear should be in the vertical 6 o'clock position and the timing marks on the gears will be aligned. If not, remove the tool and rotate the engine 360°.

4. Fasten the gear to the fixture and tighten.

5. Install a 10mm nut to the upper housing stud to hold the fixture flange nut finger tight.

6. Torque the large bolt (18mm) counterclockwise (toward left bank) to 50 ft. lbs. Tighten the 10mm nut.

7. Make sure that the crankshaft has not rotated and the fixture did not bind on the 10mm nut.

8. Strike a scriber with a mallet to mark the TDC position on the front cover.

9. Remove the tool, install the injection pump and attach the gear to the pump hub.

10. Adjust injection timing.

Throttle Position Switch Adjustment

1. Loosen assemble throttle position switch to the injection pump with the throttle lever in the closed position.

2. Attach an ohmmeter across the IGN (pink) and EGR (yellow) terminals or wires.

3. Insert the proper "switch-closed" gage block between the gage boss on the injection pump and the wide open stop screw on the throttle shaft.

4. Rotate and hold the throttle lever against the gage block.

5. Rotate the throttle switch clockwise (facing throttle switch) until continuity just occurs (high meter reading) across the IGN and EGR terminals or wires. Hold the switch body in this position and tighten the mounting screws.

NOTE: *The switch point must only be set while rotating the switch body in the clockwise direction.*

6. Release the throttle lever and allow it to return to the idle position. Remove the "switch-closed" gage bar and insert a "switch-open" gage bar.

7. Rotate the throttle lever against the "switch-open" gage bar. There should be no continuity across the IGN and EGR terminals or wires.

8. If no continuity exists, the switch is set properly. If there is continuity, the switch must be reset by repeating the entire procedure again.

9. Remove the gage bar and the ohmmeter.

Transmission Vacuum Regulator Valve Adjustment

1. Attach the vacuum regulator valve snugly, but loosely, to the injection pump. The switch body must be free to rotate on the pump.

2. Apply approximately 9–10 psi of vacuum to the inboard nipple. Attach a vacuum gauge to the outboard nipple.

3. Insert a vacuum regulator valve gage bar between the gage boss on the injection pump and the wide open stop screw on the throttle lever.

4. Rotate and hold the throttle shaft against the gage bar.

5. Slowly rotate the vacuum regulator valve

body clockwise (facing the valve) until the vacuum gauge reads 5.6 psi. Hold the valve at this position and tighten the mounting screws.

NOTE: *The valve must only be set while rotating in the clockwise direction.*

6. Check by releasing the throttle shaft and allowing it to return to the idle stop position. Rotate the throttle shaft back against the gage bar and check that the vacuum gauge still reads 5.6 psi. If not, the valve must be reset again.

Throttle Shaft Seal Replacement

NOTE: *A special tool is required; Tool J-29601.*

1. Disconnect the batteries.

2. Remove the air cleaner and the intake manifold. Cover the holes with screened covers or tape.

3. Disconnect the injection pump fuel solenoid, the housing pressure cold advance wires and the fuel return pipe.

4. Remove the T.P.S. switch or vacuum regulator valve, the throttle rod and return springs. Loosen and move aside the fast idle solenoid.

5. Remove the throttle cable bracket.

6. Install tool J-29601 over the throttle shaft with slots of tool engaging pin. Put the spring clip over the throttle shaft advance cam and tighten the wing nut. Without loosening the wingnut, pull the tool off the shaft. (This provides the proper alignment on reassembly).

7. Drive the pin from the throttle shaft and remove the throttle shaft advance cam and fiber washer. Remove any burrs from the shaft that may have resulted from pin removal.

8. Clean the injection pump cover, upper portion of the pump, the throttle shaft and the guide stud area. Place several rags in the engine valley to catch fuel.

9. Remove injection pump cover and remove screws from the cover.

NOTE: *Extreme care must be exercised to keep foreign material out of the pump when the cover is off.*

If any objects are dropped into the pump, they must be removed before the engine is started or injection pump damage or engine damage could occur.

10. Observe position at metering valve spring over the top of the guide stud. This position must be exactly duplicated during reassembly.

11. Remove the guide stud and washer. Note location of parts prior to removal.

12. Rotate the min-max governor assembly up to provide clearance and remove from the throttle shaft. If idle governor spring becomes disengaged from throttle block, it must be reinstalled with tightly wound coils toward throttle block.

13. Remove the throttle shaft assembly and examine the shaft for unusual wear or damage, replace if required.

14. Examine the throttle shaft bushings in the pump housing for any evidence of damage or unusual wear and leaks. Remove the pump and send to the local Roosa Master dealer if bushing replacement is necessary.

15. Remove the throttle shaft seals. Do not attempt to cut the seals to remove, as any nicks in the seal seat will cause leakage.

16. Install new shaft seals using care not to cut the seals on the sharp edges of the shaft. Apply a light coating of clean chassis grease on the seals.

17. Carefully slide the throttle shaft back into the pump to the point where the min-max governor assembly will slide back onto the throttle shaft.

18. Rotate the min-max governor assembly downward, hold in position and slide the throttle shaft and governor into position.

19. Install a new mylar washer, the throttle shaft advance cam, (do not tighten cam screw at this time), and a new throttle shaft drive pin.

20. Align the throttle shaft advance cam so tool J-29601 can be reinstalled over the throttle shaft, pin in the slots and the spring clip over the advance cam.

21. Put a .005″ feeler gage between the cam and the mylar washer. Tighten the cam screw and remove tool J-29601.

22. Reinstall the guide stud with a new washer, making certain that the upper extension of the metering valve spring rides on top of the guide stud. Torque the guide stud to 85 in. lbs. Overtorquing the guide stud may strip the aluminum threads in the housing.

23. Hold the throttle in the idle position.

24. Install new pump cover seal. Make sure the screws are not in the cover and position the cover about ¼ inch forward (toward shaft end) and about ⅛ inch above the pump.

25. Move the cover rearward and downward into position, being careful not to cut the seal. Reinstall the cover screws. Be care-

ful not to drop and lose the flat washer and internal lock washer with each screw. Flat washer must be against pump cover. Torque to 33 in. lbs. Install vacuum regulator valve or T.P.S. switch as outlined.

26. Reconnect the negative cables to both batteries.

27. Turn the ignition switch to the run position and touch the pink solenoid wire to the solenoid. A clicking noise should be heard as the wire is connected and disconnected. If this clicking is not observed, the linkage may be jammed in a wide open throttle position and the engine *MUST NOT* be started. If clicking is observed, connect the pump solenoid and housing pressure cold advance wires, then proceed to Step 30.

28. Remove the cover. Ground the solenoid lead (opposite the hot lead) and connect the pink wire. With the ignition switch in the run position, the solenoid in the cover should move the linkage. If not, the solenoid must be replaced. Minimum voltage across the solenoid terminals must be 12.0.

29. Reinstall the cover and repeat Step 27.

30. Reinstall throttle cable bracket, detent cable and fast idle solenoid.

31. Reinstall the throttle cable and return springs. Make sure the timing mark on the pump and housing are aligned and make sure the nuts attaching the pump to the housing are tight. Install fuel return pipe.

32. Start the engine and check for leaks.

33. Idle roughness may be observed due to the air in the pump, give it plenty of time to purge by allowing the engine to idle. It may be necessary to shut the engine down for several minutes to allow air bubbles to rise to the top of the pump where they will be purged.

34. Adjust vacuum regulator valve.

35. Remove the screened covers on tape, then reinstall the intake and air cleaner.

Injection Nozzle

Removal

1. Disconnect the batteries.

2. Disconnect the fuel line clip and remove the fuel return hose.

3. Remove the fuel injection line.

4. Remove the injection nozzle using the special tool if possible. If not, use a 30mm open end wrench. Be sure to remove the nozzle using the large 30mm hex nut. Failure to do this will result in damage to the injection nozzle. Always cap the nozzle and lines to prevent damage and contamination.

Testing

If all of the following tests are satisfied, the nozzle holder can be installed in the engine without any changes. If any one of the tests is not satisfied, the complete nozzle holder assembly must be replaced.

PREPARATION

1. Connect the nozzle holder assembly to the test line.

2. Close the shutoff valve to the pressure gauge.

3. Fill and flush the nozzle holder assembly with test oil by activating the lever repeatedly and briskly. This will apply test oil to all functionally important areas of the nozzle and purge it of air.

OBTAINING PRESSURE CHECK

1. Open shutoff valve at pressure gauge ¼ turn.

2. Depress lever of tester slowly. Note at what pressure the needle of the pressure gauge stopped, indicating an increase in pressure (nozzle does not chatter) or at which pressure the pressure dropped substantially (nozzle chatters). The maximum observed pressure is the opening pressure.

3. The opening pressure should not fall below the lower limit of 1600 psi.

4. Replace nozzles which fall below the lower limit.

LEAKAGE TEST

1. Further open shutoff valve at pressure gauge (½ to 1-½ turns).

2. Blow-dry nozzle tip.

3. Install two clear plastic lines (approximately 1–1½″) over leak-off connections.

4. Depress lever of manual test stand slowly until gauge reads a pressure of 1380 psi. Observe tip of nozzle. A drop may form but not drop off within a period of 10 seconds.

5. Replace the nozzle holder assembly if a droplet drops off the nozzle bottom within the 10 seconds.

CHATTER TEST

1. Close shutoff lever at pressure gauge.

2. Depress lever of manual test stand slowly noting whether chatter noises can be heard.

3. If no chatter is heard, increase the speed

of lever movement until it reaches a point where the nozzle chatters.

4. The chatter indicates that the nozzle needle moves freely and that the nozzle seat, guide, as well as the pintle, have no mechanical defects.

5. Replace nozzles which do not chatter.

SPRAY PATTERN

1. Close shutoff valve at pressure gauge.

2. Depress lever of manual test stand downward abruptly and quickly. The spray should have a tight, evenly shaped conical pattern which is well atomized. This pattern should be concentric to the nozzle axis. Streamlike injections indicate a defect.

INSTALLATION

1. Remove protective caps from the nozzle.

2. Install nozzle and torque to 50 ft. lbs.

3. Connect fuel injection line, torque nut to 20 ft. lbs.

4. Install fuel return hose.

5. Install fuel line clip.

6. Connect battery.

Injection Pump Fuel Lines

REMOVAL

1. Disconnect the batteries.

2. Disconnect the air cleaner bracket at the valve cover.

3. Remove the crankcase ventilator bracket and position it out of the way.

4. Disconnect the fuel lines and remove the secondary fuel filter.

5. Loosen the vacuum pump hold-down clamp and then rotate the pump to gain access to the mainfold bolt.

6. Remove the intake manifold bolts. The injection line clips are retained by the same bolts.

7. Remove the intake manifold and cover the holes with screened covers or tape.

8. Remove the injection line clips at the loom brackets.

9. Remove the injection lines at the nozzles and cover the nozzles with protective caps.

10. Tag and disconnect injection lines at the injection pump.

11. Remove fuel line from injection pump.

INSTALLATION

1. Install the injection lines.

2. Remove the covers or tape and install the intake manifold.

3. Install the secondary fuel filter and lines.

4. Tighten the vacuum pump hold-down clamp and then install the crankcase ventilator.

5. Connect the air cleaner and the batteries.

Chassis Electrical

HEATER

Blower Motor

REMOVAL AND INSTALLATION

1. Disconnect the negative battery cable.

2. On 1969–72 models, scribe the hood and fender location of the right hood hinge. Remove the hinge.

3. Mark the position of the blower motor in relation to its case. Remove the electrical connections at the motor. Disconnect the rubber motor cooling tube on air conditioned models.

4. Remove the blower attaching screws and remove the assembly. Pry gently on the flange if the sealer sticks.

5. The blower wheel can be removed from the motor shaft by removing the nut at the center.

To assemble the unit:

6. Assemble the blower wheel to the motor with the open end of the wheel away from the motor and install the unit into the blower case. Connect the ground strap and the electrical connection.

7. On models through 1972, position the hood hinge using the scribe marks and attach the hinge. Check the hood alignment.

8. Connect the battery.

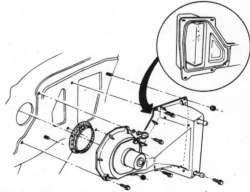

1969–72 heater blower motor assembly

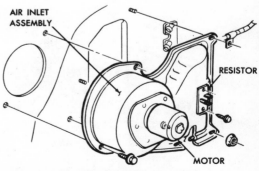

1973–80 heater blower motor assembly

Core

REMOVAL AND INSTALLATION

1969–72 Without Air Conditioning

1. Drain the cooling system and disconnect the battery.

2. Remove the electrical connection at the blower.

3. Remove the heater hoses at the core tubes.

4. Loosen and move the right front fender skirt. Remove enough screws so that the skirt can be moved outward.

5. Working from under the dash, remove the seal on the temperature door cable and disconnect the cable from the temperature door.

6. Pull the case away from the mounting

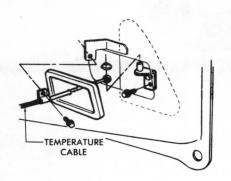

TEMPERATURE
CABLE

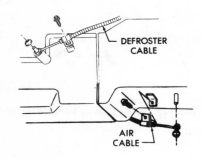

DEFROSTER
CABLE

AIR
CABLE

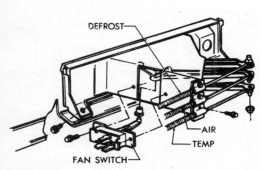

DEFROST

AIR

TEMP

FAN SWITCH

1969–72 heater controls

studs after removing the retaining bolts and nuts.

7. Remove the core retainers and remove the core.

The installation procedure is the reverse of removal.

1969–72 With Factory Installed Air Conditioning

NOTE: *Models with dealer installed air conditioning use the same procedure as those without air conditioning.*

1. Drain the coolant. Disconnect the battery ground cable.

2. Detach the heater hoses from the core tubes at the firewall.

3. Remove the stud nuts on the engine side of the firewall.

4. Remove the glove box.

5. Unplug the relay connector and remove the right ball outlet hose.

6. Remove the screw holding the panel outlet air distributor to the heater case. Remove the heater case retaining screws.

7. Pull the heater case away from the firewall; reach in and disconnect the resistor connector. Remove the resistor harness grommet and remove the harness.

8. Remove the heater case. Remove the core mounting straps. Reverse the procedure for installation.

1973–82 Without Air Conditioning

1. Disconnect the battery ground cable.

2. Disconnect the heater hoses at the core tubes and drain the coolant into a clean container. The coolant may be used again if it is still clean. Plug the core tubes to prevent any excess spillage.

3. Remove the nuts from the distributor duct studs in the engine compartment.

4. Remove the glove compartment and door.

5. Disconnect the "Air-Defrost" and "Temperature" door cables.

6. Remove the floor outlet and remove the defroster duct-to-heater distributor screw.

7. Remove the heater distributor-to-dash panel screws. Pull the assembly rearward to gain access to the wiring harness and disconnect the wires attached to the unit.

8. Remove the heater unit from the truck.

9. Remove the heater core retaining straps and remove the core from the truck.

10. Installation is the reverse of removal. Be sure that the core-to-case and case-to-dash

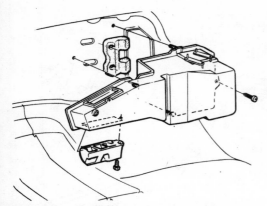

1973–80 heater distribution duct—without air conditioning

panel sealer is intact. Fill the cooling system and check for leaks.

1973–82 With Air Conditioning

1. Disconnect the battery ground cable.
2. Drain the coolant.
3. Remove the heater hoses from the core tubes. Plug the tubes to prevent spillage.
4. Remove the glove box and door.
5. Remove the screws holding the center duct to the selector duct and to the instrument panel. Remove the center upper and lower ducts.
6. Disconnect the control cable at the temperature door.

7. Remove the three stud nuts from the firewall. Remove the selector duct to firewall screw inside the truck.
8. Pull the selector duct assembly back until the core tubes clear the firewall, then lower it to disconnect the vacuum and electrical connections.
9. Disconnect the vacuum and electrical harness.
10. Remove the selector duct assembly and remove the core mounting straps.
11. Remove the heater core.
12. Reverse the procedure for installation.

RADIO

REMOVAL AND INSTALLATION
1969–72

1. Disconnect the negative battery cable and remove the flex hoses from the heater distributor duct under the dashboard.
2. Remove the air conditioning heater control head by removing the attaching screws and pushing the unit back and down.
3. Remove the ash tray and the ash tray retainer.
4. Remove the electrical connections from the rear of the radio and also the front attaching knobs and nuts.
5. Remove the mounting screw on the side

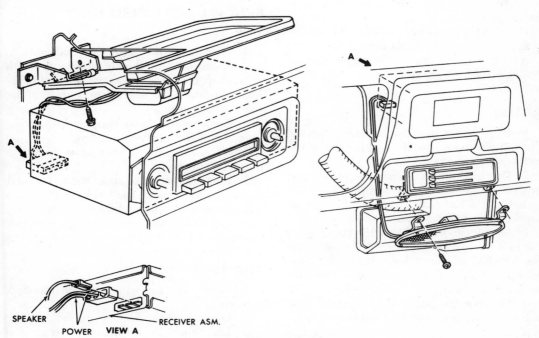

1969–72 radio installation

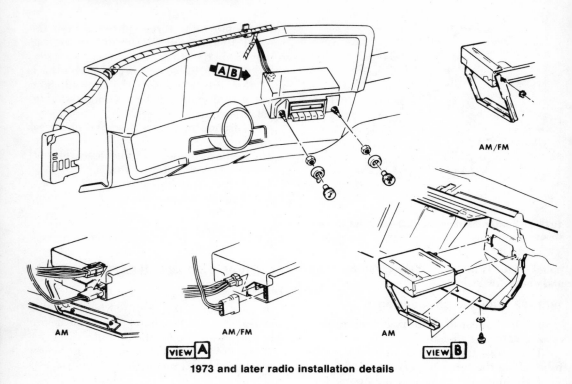

1973 and later radio installation details

of the radio chassis. Push the radio back and up before slipping it down and out of the instrument panel.

6. To install the radio, reverse the removal procedure.

CAUTION: *Make certain that the speaker is attached to the radio before the unit is turned ON. If it is not, the output transistors will be damaged.*

1973-82

1. Remove the negative battery cable and the control knobs, bezels, and nuts from the radio control shafts.

2. On AM radios, remove the support bracket stud nut and its lockwasher.

3. On AM/FM radios, remove the support bracket-to-instrument panel screws.

4. Lifting the rear edge of the radio, push the radio forward until the control shafts clear the instrument panel. Then lower the radio far enough so that the electrical connections can be disconnected.

5. Remove the power lead, speaker, and antenna wires and then pull out the unit.

6. To install the radio, reverse the procedure.

WINDSHIELD WIPERS

Motor

REMOVAL AND INSTALLATION

1969-72

1. Disconnect the battery ground cable.

2. Reach through the air intake grille with an L-shaped wire and remove the spring retainer to detach the wiper drive rods from the motor crank arm.

3. Remove the radio speaker for access. Disconnect the left defroster hose.

4. Disconnect the washer hoses from the pump on the motor.

5. Remove the motor attaching screws and the motor from inside the truck.

6. Reverse the procedure for installation, making sure that the motor is in the park position.

1973-82

1. Make sure the wipers are in the park position.

2. Disconnect the battery ground cable.

3. Disconnect the wiring and hoses at the windshield washer pump.

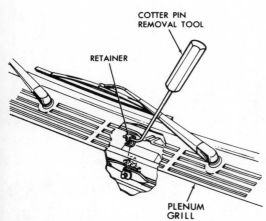

Removing the 1969–72 wiper drive rod spring retainer

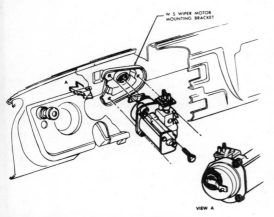

1969–72 wiper motor installation

1973 and later wiper motor mounting details

4. Remove the plastic air intake cover screen and reach in to loosen the wiper drive rod attaching screws. There is a small access hole provided. Remove the drive rod from the motor crank arm.

5. Unbolt and remove the motor.

6. Reverse the procedure for installation, making sure to lubricate the motor crank arm pivot.

NOTE: *Failure of the washers to operate or to shut off is often caused by grease or dirt on the electromagnetic contacts. Simply unplug the wire and pull off the plastic cover for access. Likewise, failure of the wipers to park is often caused by grease or dirt on the park switch contacts. The park switch is under the cover behind the pump.*

INSTRUMENT CLUSTER

REMOVAL AND INSTALLATION

1969–72

1. Disconnect the negative battery terminal. If equipped, remove the throttle knob.

2. Remove the windshield wiper knob and nut, the light switch rod (depress the shaft retaining button behind the panel) and bezel. If equipped, disconnect and plug the oil pressure line to the gauge.

3. Disconnect the speedometer cable and the chassis wiring harness which is located at the rear of the instrument panel. Protect the column jacket with a rag or other covering so that it doesn't become scratched.

4. Remove the cluster retaining screws and remove the cluster.

5. To install the cluster, reverse the removal procedure.

1973–76

1. Remove the negative battery cable.

2. Remove the steering column cover and the cluster bezel (face panel).

3. Remove the knob from the clock (if equipped).

4. Remove the lens retaining screws and the lens.

5. Remove the transmission gear indicator (PRNDL) and the cluster retainer.

6. Disconnect the speedometer cable by depressing the spring clip and pulling the cable out of the speedometer head. Disconnect and plug the oil pressure line, if so equipped.

7. Disconnect the cluster wiring harness and remove the cluster retaining screws and pull out the cluster.

8. To install the cluster, reverse the removal procedure.

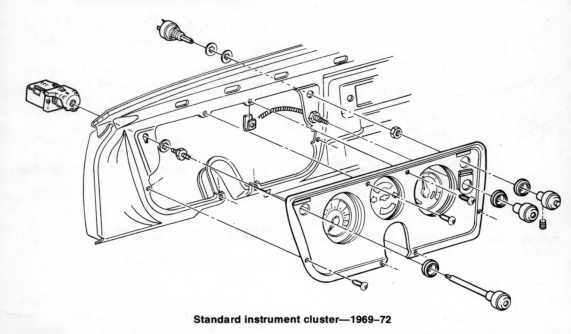

Standard instrument cluster—1969–72

1977 and Later

1. Disconnect the negative battery cable.
2. Remove the knob from the headlight switch and the radio knobs.

3. Remove the eight attaching screws from the instrument bezel.
4. Reach up under the instrument panel and disconnect the speedometer cable by depressing the tab on the rear of the speedom-

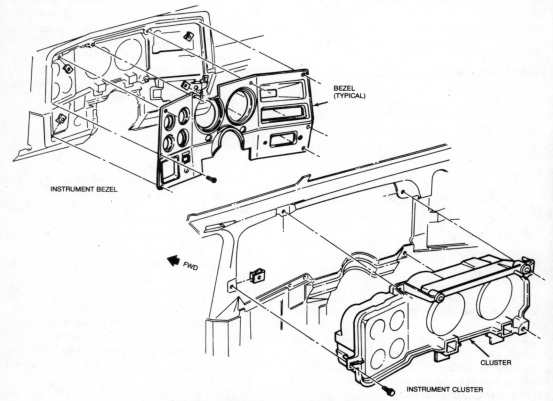

1973 and later instrument cluster—typical

eter head and pulling the cable free while holding the tab down.

5. Disconnect the oil pressure gauge line at the fitting in the engine compartment.

6. Pull the instrument cluster out slightly and disconnect the line from the oil pressure gauge.

7. Remove the instrument cluster.

8. Reverse the above to install.

Speedometer Cable
REPLACEMENT

1. Disconnect the speedometer cable from the rear of the speedometer head. Unscrew through 1972, unclip from 1973.

2. Remove the old cable by pulling it out from the speedometer end of the cable housing. If the old cable is broken, the speedometer cable will have to be disconnected from the transmission and the cable removed from the other end.

3. Lubricate the entire length of the new cable with speedometer cable lubricant and feed the cable into the cable housing.

4. Connect the speedometer cable to the speedometer head and to the transmission if disconnected there.

Ignition Switch
REMOVAL AND INSTALLATION
1969-72

1. Disconnect the battery ground cable.

2. Remove the lock cylinder by positioning the switch in "ACC" position and inserting a thin piece of wire in the small hole in the cylinder face. Push in on the wire and turn the key counterclockwise until the lock cylinder can be removed.

3. Remove the metal ignition switch nut.

4. Remove the ignition switch from under the dash and remove the wiring connector.

5. To remove the "theft-resistant" connector, the switch must be removed from under the dash. Use a small screwdriver, unsnap the locking tangs on the connector, and unplug the connector.

To install the switch:

6. Snap the connector into place on a new switch.

7. Install the switch in the dash and install the metal ignition switch nut.

8. Install the lock cylinder.

9. Connect the battery cable.

10. Test the operation of the switch.

1973-82

See Chapter 8 for the column mounted ignition switch removal and installation.

LIGHTING

Headlight
REMOVAL AND INSTALLATION

1. Remove the headlight bezel by releasing the attaching screws.

2. Remove the spring from the retaining ring and turn the unit to disengage it from the headlamp adjusting screws.

3. Disconnect the wiring harness connector.

NOTE: *Do not disturb the adjusting screws.*

4. Remove the retaining ring and the headlamp from the mounting ring.

5. Position the new sealed beam unit in the mounting ring and install the retaining ring.

NOTE: *The number which is moulded into the lens must be at the top.*

6. Attach the wiring connector.

7. Install the headlamp assembly, twisting it slightly to engage the adjusting screws.

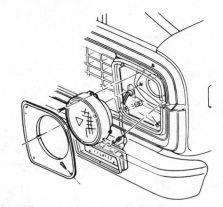

1969-72 Blazer headlight details

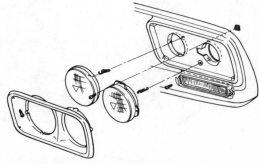

1970-72 Jimmy headlight details

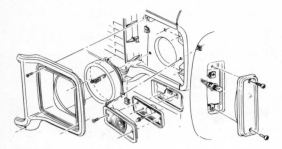

1973–78 front lighting

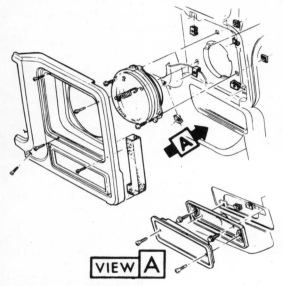

1979–80 front lighting

8. Install the retaining ring spring and check the operation of the unit. Install the bezel.

FUSIBLE LINKS

Fusible links are sections of wire, with special insulation, designed to melt under electrical overload. Replacements are simply spliced into the wire in most cases. Circuits protected by fusible links, 1969–74, are: engine wiring, battery charging, alternator, and headlights. For 1975–76, the circuits are: high beam indicator, horn, ignition, and starter solenoid. For 1977–80 the circuits protected by fusible links are the ignition, horn, headlight high beam and the air conditioner blower (high position).

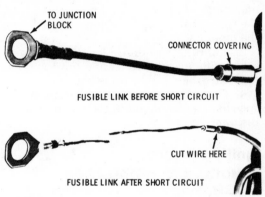

Fusible link

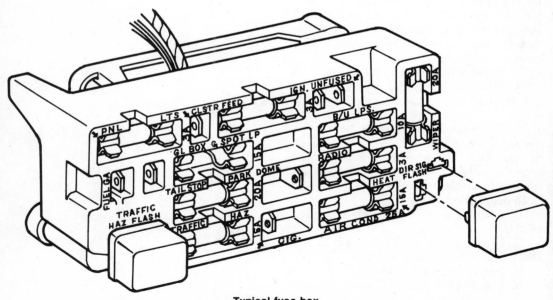

Typical fuse box

CIRCUIT BREAKERS

A circuit breaker is an electrical switch which breaks the circuit in case of an overload. All models have a circuit breaker in the headlight switch to protect the headlight and parking light systems. An overload may cause the lights to flash on and off. 1974–82 wiper motors are protected by a circuit breaker at the motor. If the motor overheats, which sometimes happens with heavy snow blocking the wiper arm, the circuit breaker will switch it off until it cools.

FUSES AND FLASHERS

The fuse block is mounted to the firewall, inside the truck, to the left of the steering column. The turn signal flasher and the hazard warning flasher plug into the fuse block. Each fuse receptacle is marked as to the circuits it protects and the correct amperage. In-line fuses are also used to protect some circuits. These are: 1969–75 ammeter, and 1975–82 underhood light and air conditioning system.

NOTE: *A special heavy duty turn signal flasher is required to properly operate the turn signals when a trailer's lights are connected to the system.*

WIRING DIAGRAMS

Wiring diagrams have been left out of this book. As trucks have become more complex, and available with longer and longer option lists, wiring diagrams have grown in size and complexity also. It has become virtually impossible to provide a readable reproduction in a reasonable number of pages. Information on ordering wiring diagrams from the vehicle manufacturer can be found in the owner's manual.

Clutch and Transmission

MANUAL TRANSMISSION

COLUMN SHIFT LINKAGE ADJUSTMENT

1. Place the column lever in the neutral position.

2. Under the truck, loosen the shift rod clamps. These are at the bottom of the column on 1969–72 models, and at the transmission end for 1973–82.

3. Make sure that the two levers on the transmission are in their center, neutral, positions.

4. Install a 3/16 to 7/32 in. pin or drill bit through the alignment holes in the levers at the bottom of the steering column. This holds these levers in the neutral position.

5. Tighten the shift rod clamps.

6. Remove the pin and check the shifting operation.

REMOVAL AND INSTALLATION

Two Wheel Drive

1. Raise the vehicle and support it on jack stands.

2. Drain the transmission.

3. Disconnect the speedometer cable, TCS switch and backup light wire at the transmission.

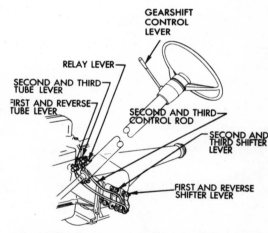

1969–72 manual transmission column shift linkage

4. Disconnect the shift control rods from the three speed transmission. On four speeds, pull up the boot and remove the gearshift lever. This can be done by pressing down firmly on the slotted collar plate with a pair of channel lock pliers and turning counterclockwise to release the lever. Plug the opening to keep out dirt.

5. Remove the power take-off unit, if any.

6. Remove the driveshaft after marking the alignment of the shaft to the flange.

7. Position a jack under the transmission to support the weight of the transmission.

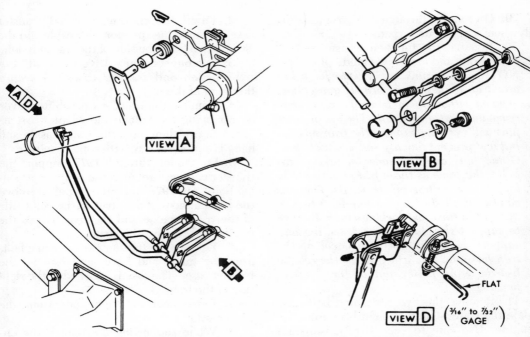

1973 and later four wheel drive manual transmission column shift linkage

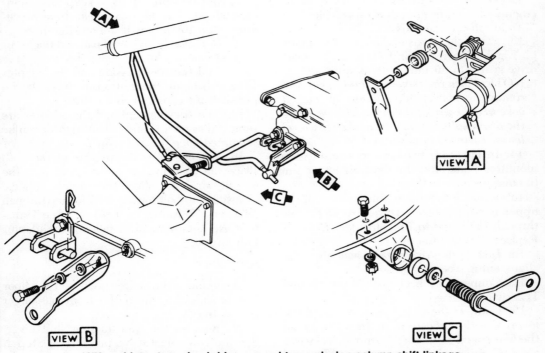

1973 and later two wheel drive manual transmission column shift linkage

8. Remove the crossmember. Visually inspect to see if other equipment, brackets or lines, must be removed to permit removal of the transmission.

NOTE: *Mark the position of the crossmember when removing to prevent incorrect installation. The tapered surface should face the rear.*

9. On models through 1977, remove the flywheel housing underpan.

10. Remove the top two transmission to housing bolts and insert two guide pins.

NOTE: *Guide pins are nice to have but aren't absolutely necessary. If you choose to go on without them, be very careful when removing the transmission. The use of guide pins will not only support the transmission but will prevent damage to the clutch disc. Guide pins can be made by taking two bolts, the same as those just removed only longer, and cutting off the heads. The pins can be installed with your hands. If they're difficult to turn, use locking pliers. Be sure to support the clutch release bearing and support assembly during removal of the transmission. This will prevent the release bearing from falling out of the flywheel housing.*

11. Remove the two remaining bolts and slide the transmission straight back from the engine. Use care to keep the transmission drive gear straight in line with the clutch disc hub.

12. When the transmission is free from the engine, move it from under the vehicle.

To install the transmission:

13. Place the transmission on the guide pins and slide it forward starting the main drive gear into the clutch disc's splines.

NOTE: *Place the transmission in gear and rotate the transmission flange or output yoke to aid entry of the main drive gear into the disc's splines. Make sure the clutch release bearing is in position.*

14. Install the two lower transmission mounting bolts, and the flywheel lower pan (if equipped).

15. Remove the guide pins and install the upper mounting bolts. Torque to 55 ft. lbs. through 1972, and to 75 ft. lbs. for 1973–82. Replace the crossmember.

16. Install the driveshaft, watching the alignment marks.

17. Connect the backup light switch and TCS switch (if used).

18. Connect the shift levers, or install the lever. Use the procedure in Step 4 to install the four speed shift lever, turning clockwise.

19. Connect the speedometer cable and refill the transmission.

20. Lower the vehicle.

Four Wheel Drive

THREE SPEED

1. Jack up the vehicle and support it safely on stands. Remove the skid plate, if any.

2. Drain the transmission and transfer case. Remove the speedometer cable and the TCS switch from the side of the transmission.

3. Disconnect the driveshafts at the transmission and transfer case and secure them out of the way.

4. Remove the transfer case shifter lever by removing the bolt to the adapter assembly. You can then push the shifter aside and hang it out of the way with rope or wire.

5. On models through 1977, support the transfer case and remove the adapter attaching bolts. On 1978 and later models, remove the bolts attaching the strut to the right side of the transfer case and the rear part of the engine and remove the strut.

6. Remove the transfer case securing bolts from the frame and lower and remove the transfer case. (The case is attached at the right side of the frame.)

7. Disconnect the shift rods from the transmission.

8. While supporting the rear of the engine, remove the adapter mounting bolts.

9. Remove the upper transmission bolts and insert two guide pins to keep the assembly aligned. See the two wheel drive procedure (Step 10) for details on making these.

10. Remove the flywheel pan and the lower transmission-to-clutch housing bolts.

11. Pull the transmission and the adapter straight back on the guide pins until the input shaft is free of the clutch disc.

12. The transmission and the adapter are removed as on assembly. The adapter can be separated once the assembly is out.

13. Installation is the reverse of removal. Place the transmission in gear and turn the output shaft to align the clutch splines. Transmission bolt torque is 55 ft. lbs. through 1972, and 75 ft. lbs. for 1973–82. See Transfer Case Removal and Installation for adapter bolt torques.

FOUR SPEED

1. Remove the shifter boots and the floor mat or carpeting from the front passenger compartment.

2. Remove the transmission shift lever. See the two wheel drive procedure, Step 4, for details on removing the lever. Remove the console box and the center floor heater outlet.

3. Remove the transmission floor cover after releasing the attaching screws. It will be necessary to rotate the cover 90° to clear the transfer case shift lever.

4. Remove the skid plate, if any. Discon-

nect the transfer case shift lever link assembly and the lever from the adapter.

5. Remove the back-up light wire, the TCS switch, and the speedometer cable from the side of the transmission.

6. Raise and support the truck. Support the engine. Drain the transmission and transfer case. Detach both drive shafts and secure them out of the way.

7. Remove the transmission mount-to-frame bolts. To do this, it will be necessary to open the locking tabs. Remove the transfer case-to-frame bracket bolts.

8. While supporting the transmission and transfer case, remove the crossmember bolts and the crossmember. It will be necessary to rotate the crossmember to remove it from the frame.

9. Remove the lower flywheel housing cover.

NOTE: *On V8 engines it is necessary to remove the exhaust crossover pipe.*

10. Remove the transmission-to-bellhousing bolts. Remove the upper bolts first and install guide pins. See the two wheel drive procedure, Step 10, for details on making these.

11. Slide the transmission back until the main drive gear clears the clutch assembly and then lower the unit.

12. Install the transfer case on the transmission as an assembly. Attach the assembly to the bellhousing. Put the transmission in gear and turn the output shaft to align the clutch splines.

13. Install the bellhousing cover and, on V8 models, the exhaust crossover pipe.

14. Install the frame crossmember, the retaining adapter, and the transfer case.

15. Install the front and rear driveshafts.

16. Connect the speedometer cable, backup lights, and TCS switches.

17. Fill the transmission and the transfer case to the proper level with the specified lubricant (given in Chapter 1).

18. Position the transfer case shift lever and the shift lever link on the shift rail bar.

19. Install the transmission floor cover and the center heating duct.

20. Install the console box.

21. Install the transmission shift lever. See the three speed procedure. Step 13, for bolt torques.

CLUTCH

LINKAGE ADJUSTMENT

This adjustment is for the amount of clutch pedal free travel before the throwout bearing contacts the clutch release fingers. It is required periodically to compensate for clutch lining wear. Incorrect adjustment will cause gear grinding and clutch slippage or wear.

NOTE: *If you have a problem with grinding when shifting into gear, shorten the pedal stop bumper to ⅜ in. and readjust the linkage.*

1969–72

1. Disconnect the clutch fork return spring at the fork on the clutch housing.

2. Loosen the outer adjusting nut (A) and

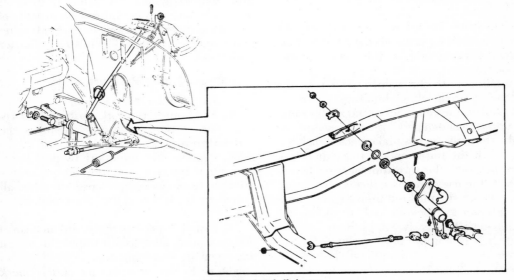

1969–72 clutch linkage

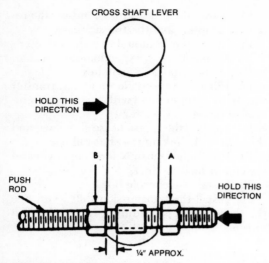

1969–72 clutch linkage adjustment

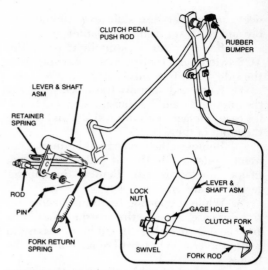

1973 and later clutch linkage adjustment

back it off approximately ½ in. from the swivel.

3. Hold the clutch fork pushrod against the fork to move the throwout bearing against the clutch fingers. The pushrod will slide through the swivel at the cross-shaft.

4. Rotate the lever until the clutch pedal contacts the bumper mounted on the parking brake support.

5. Adjust the inner adjusting nut (B) to obtain ³/₁₆–¼ in. clearance between nut (B) and the swivel.

6. Release the pushrod, connect the return spring and tighten the outer nut (A) to lock the swivel against the inner nut (B).

7. Check the free travel at the pedal and readjust as necessary. It should be ¾ to 1 in.

1973–82

Models from 1974 have a switch on the pedal linkage to prevent the starter from being operated unless the pedal is depressed.

1. Disconnect the return spring at the clutch fork on the clutch housing.

2. Rotate the clutch lever and shaft assembly until the clutch pedal is firmly against the rubber bumper on the brake pedal bracket.

3. Push the outer end of the clutch fork rearward until the throwout bearing lightly contacts the pressure plate levers.

4. Detach the pushrod from the clutch lever. Loosen the locknut and adjust the rod length so that the swivel slips freely into the gauge hole (the upper hole on the lever). Increase the rod length until all lash is removed.

5. Remove the swivel from the gauge hole. Insert the swivel in the lower, original, hole in the lever. Install two washers and the cotter pin. Tighten the locknut, being careful not to change the rod length. Reinstall the spring and check pedal free travel. It should be 1⅜–1⅝ in.

NOTE: *If you have a problem with drive-line chatter in reverse on an early 1973 four wheel drive model, this can be corrected with a service kit (no. 340607) containing a new clutch cross shaft and relocated clutch fork springs. The kit components were installed in later models.*

REMOVAL AND INSTALLATION

There are two types of clutch pressure plates used, diaphragm and coil spring. In general, the larger heavy duty clutches are usually of the coil spring pressure plate type. Most removal and installation details are similar for both types.

Diaphragm Spring Pressure Plate

1. Remove the transmission.

2. Disconnect the fork pushrod and remove the flywheel housing. Remove the clutch throwout bearing from the fork.

3. Remove the clutch fork by pressing it away from the ball mounting with a screwdriver until the fork snaps loose from the ball or remove the ball stud from the clutch housing.

4. Install a pilot tool (an old mainshaft makes a good pilot tool) to hold the clutch while you are removing it.

NOTE: *Before removing the clutch, mark*

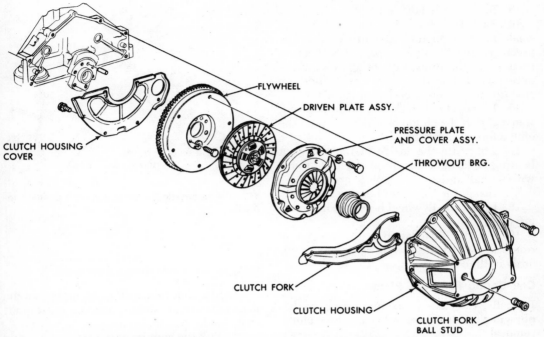

Assembly details of a typical clutch with a diaphragm spring pressure plate

the flywheel, clutch cover and one of the pressure plate lug nuts so the assembly can be installed in its original position, as it is a balanced unit.

5. Loosen the clutch attaching bolts one turn at a time to prevent distortion of the clutch cover until the tension is released.

6. Remove the clutch pilot tool and the clutch from the vehicle.

Inspect the clutch disc for wear, scoring, or signs of overheating. Replace it as necessary. If the clutch disc is oil-soaked, examine the engine and transmission seals. Inspect the flywheel and pressure plate for scoring, overheating, or excessive wear. The flywheel can be refaced, if necessary, although heavy scoring or overheating warrant replacement. Worn pressure plates must be replaced.

To install:

7. Install the pressure plate in the cover assembly, aligning the notch in the pressure plate with the notch in the cover flange.

8. Install the pressure plate retracting springs, the lockwashers and the drive strap to the pressure plate bolts. Tighten them to 11 ft. lbs.

9. Turn the flywheel until the X mark is at the bottom.

10. Install the clutch disc, pressure plate and cover, using an old mainshaft as an aligning tool.

11. Turn the clutch until the X mark on the clutch cover aligns with the X mark on the flywheel.

12. Install the attaching bolts and tighten them a little at a time in a crisscross pattern until the spring pressure is taken up.

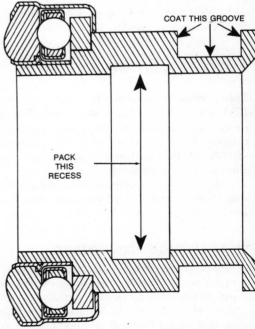

Clutch throwout bearing lubrication points

13. Remove the aligning tool.

14. Pack the clutch ball fork seat with a small amount of high temperature grease. Too much grease will cause slippage. Install a new retainer in the groove of the clutch fork, if necessary. Install the retainer with the high side up and the open end on the horizontal.

15. If the clutch fork ball was removed, reinstall it in the clutch housing and snap the clutch fork onto the ball.

16. Lubricate the inside of the throwout bearing collar and the throwout fork groove with a small amount of graphite grease.

17. Install the throwout bearing.

18. Install the flywheel housing and transmission.

19. Further installation is the reverse of removal. Adjust the clutch linkage as previously outlined.

Coil Spring Pressure Plate

Basically, the same procedures apply to diaphragm clutch removal as to coil spring clutch removal.

1. ·Before removing the clutch, punch-mark the flywheel, clutch cover and one pressure plate lug so that the components can be reassembled in their original locations.

2. Loosen the attaching screws one turn at a time to prevent distortion.

3. Place ⅜ in. spacers between the clutch levers and the cover to hold the levers down as the screws are removed.

4. Adjust the clutch after installation.

AUTOMATIC TRANSMISSION

The automatic transmission used through 1981 is the Turbo Hydra-Matic 350. Pan removal, fluid and filter change are covered in Chapter 1. No band adjustments are necessary or possible on this transmission; it uses clutches instead of bands.

A 4 speed automatic overdrive transmission, the Model 700R4 was introduced in 1982.

SHIFT LINKAGE ADJUSTMENT

NOTE: *Incorrect linkage adjustment may result in premature transmission failure, due to the controls not being fully engaged with the detent. Partial engagement of clutches and other internal parts will result in early transmission failure.*

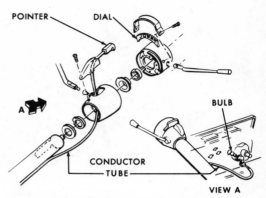

1969–72 automatic transmission shift position indicator

1969–72

1. The shift tube and levers located in the mast jacket of the steering column must move freely and must not bind.

2. Pull the shift lever toward the steering wheel and allow the lever to be positioned in Drive by the transmission detent. The pointer may be out of adjustment, so don't use it as a reference for positioning the lever.

3. Release the selector lever. The lever should not go into Low unless the lever is lifted.

4. Lift the lever toward the steering wheel and permit the lever to be placed in Neutral by the transmission detent.

5. Release the lever; it should not go into Reverse unless the lever is lifted.

6. If the linkage is adjusted correctly, the shift lever will not move past the Neutral detent and the Drive detent unless the lever is lifted so it can pass over the mechanical stop in the steering column.

7. If adjustment is necessary, place the lever in the Drive position. If the indicator pointer is out of alignment, you must rely upon the detent position to determine what gear you are in (see Steps 2 and 3).

8. Loosen the adjustment swivel or clamp at the bottom of the column and move the shift lever so that it contacts the Drive stop in the column.

9. Tighten the swivel and recheck the adjustment (see Steps 2 and 6).

10. If the indicator pointer fails to line up properly with the gear symbol, adjust the position of the pointer and scale.

11. If necessary, readjust the neutral safety switch.

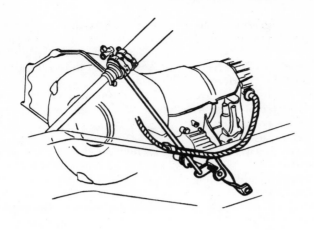

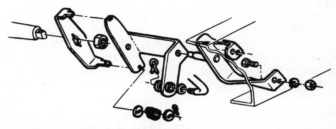

1969–72 automatic transmission shift linkage

1973–82

1. The shift tube and lever assembly must be free in the mast jacket.

2. Lift the selector lever toward the steering wheel and allow the selector lever to be positioned in Drive by the detent. Do not use the selector lever pointer as a reference.

3. Release the selector lever. The lever

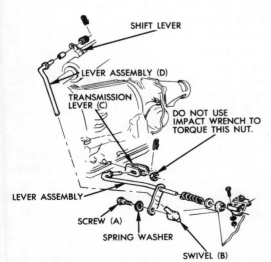

1973 and later automatic transmission shift linkage adjustment points

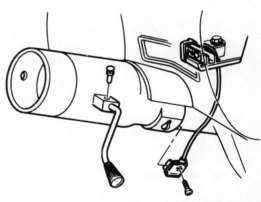

The adjustment point for the 1973 and later automatic transmission shift position indicator is accessible after removing the lower column cover

should not be able to go into Low unless the lever is lifted.

4. Lift the selector lever toward the steering wheel and allow the lever to be positioned in Neutral by the transmission detent.

5. Release the selector lever. The lever should not be able to engage reverse unless the lever is lifted. A properly adjusted linkage will prevent the lever from moving beyond both the Neutral and Drive detents unless the lever is lifted.

6. If adjustment is required, remove the screw (A) and spring washer from the swivel clamp (B).

7. Set the transmission lever (C) in Neutral by moving it to L₁ and then three detents clockwise.

8. Put the transmission selector lever in Neutral as determined by the mechanical stop in the steering column. Do not use the indicator pointer as a reference. The pointer is the last thing to be adjusted.

9. Assemble the swivel spring and washer to the lever (D) and tighten.

10. Readjust the Neutral safety switch if necessary.

11. To adjust the shift position indicator, remove the column cover at the bottom of the instrument panel and loosen the screw to move the pointer.

12. Check the operation. With the switch in RUN, and the transmission in Reverse, be sure that the key cannot be removed and that the steering wheel is locked.

With the key in LOCK and the shift lever in PARK, be sure that the key can be removed, the steering wheel is locked, and that the transmission remains in PARK when the steering column is locked.

DOWNSHIFT CABLE ADJUSTMENT

This cable runs from the carburetor linkage to the transmission. It regulates the throttle position at which a downshift occurs.

1969–71

1. Remove the air cleaner.
2. Loosen the detent cable screw.
3. With the choke off and the accelerator linkage adjusted, position the carburetor lever in the wide open position.

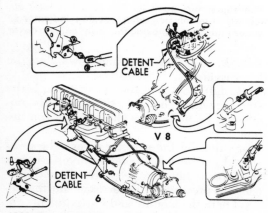

1969–71 downshift cable details

4. Pull the detent cable rearward until the wide open throttle stop in the transmission is felt. The cable must be pulled through the detent position to reach the wide open throttle stop.

5. Tighten the detent cable screw and check the linkage for proper operation.

1972

1. Remove the air cleaner.
2. Pry up on each side of the snap-lock with a screwdriver to release the lock.
3. Compress the locking tabs and disconnect the locking tabs from the bracket.
4. Pull the carburetor to the wide open throttle position against the stop on the carburetor.
5. With the carburetor held in this position, pull the cable housing rearward (through the detent) until the wide open throttle stop in the transmission is felt.
6. Push the snap-lock on the cable downward until it is flush with the cable.
7. Do not lubricate the cable. Install the air cleaner.

1973–82

With the snap-lock disengaged from the bracket, position the carburetor at the wide open throttle position. Push the snap-lock downward until the top is flush with the rest of the cable.

NOTE: *The 700R4 transmission uses a downshift switch that adjusts itself, after installation, when gas pedal is floored.*

NEUTRAL SAFETY/BACKUP LIGHT SWITCH REPLACEMENT AND ADJUSTMENT

This switch is on top of the steering column, behind the instrument panel or on the left side of the transmission. It prevents the starting circuit from being completed unless the shift lever is in Neutral or Park. The same switch causes the backup lights to go on in Reverse.

NOTE: *The three speed manual transmission backup light switch is on the column. On the four speed, it is on the transmission, near the top cover.*

1969–72

1. Disconnect the negative battery cable.
2. Disconnect the wiring plug. Remove the screws and the switch.
3. Place the shift lever in Drive. Locate

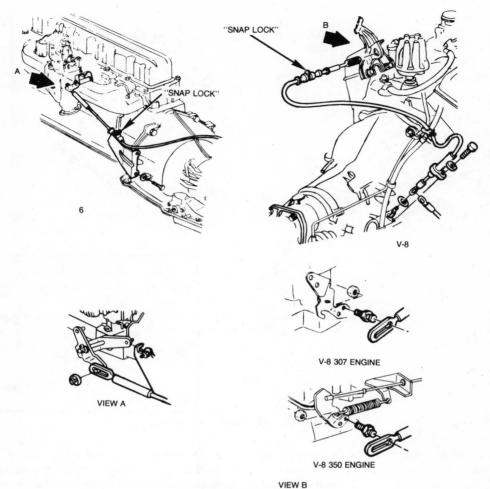

1972–74 downshift cable details

the lever tang against the transmission selector plate.

4. Align the slot in the contact support with

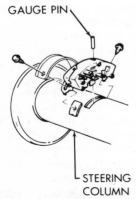

Neutral safety/backup light switch

the hole in the switch and insert a ⅜/₃₂ in. drill bit to hold the support in place.

5. Place the contact support drive slot over the shifter tube drive tang and tighten the screws. Remove the bit.

6. Connect the wiring plug and the battery cable and check that the engine will start only in Neutral and Park (foot on the brake!) and that the backup lights work only in Reverse. Loosen the screws and move the switch to correct.

1973–82

1. Disconnect the negative battery cable.

2. Disconnect the switch wiring plug. Remove the screws and the switch.

3. Place the shift lever in Neutral.

4. Insert a ⅜/₃₂ in. (.096 in.) drill bit, ⅜ in. into the switch hole on a used switch. A

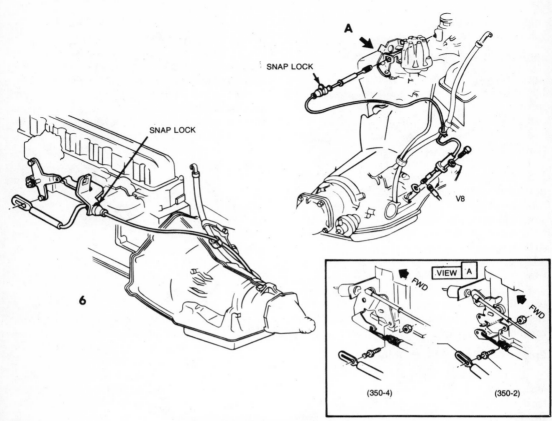

1975 and later downshift cable details

new switch is held in the Neutral position by a plastic shear pin, so the bit isn't needed.

5. Insert the switch tang into the column slot and install the screws.

6. Remove the locating bit. With a new switch, shift out of Neutral to shear the plastic pin.

7. Connect the wiring plug and the battery cable and check that the engine will start only in Neutral and Park (foot on the brake!) and that the backup lights work only in Reverse. Loosen the screws and move the switch to correct.

TRANSMISSION REMOVAL AND INSTALLATION

NOTE: *It would be best to drain the transmission before starting.*

Two Wheel Drive

1. Disconnect the battery ground cable. Disconnect the detent cable at the carburetor.

2. Raise and support the truck.

3. Remove the driveshaft, after matchmarking its flanges.

4. Disconnect the speedometer cable, downshift cable, vacuum modulator line, shift linkage, and fluid cooler lines at the transmission. Remove the filler tube.

5. Support the transmission and unbolt the rear mount from the crossmember. Remove the crossmember.

6. Remove the converter underpan, matchmark the flywheel and converter, and remove the converter bolts.

7. Support the engine and lower the transmission slightly for access to the upper transmission to engine bolts.

8. Remove the transmission to engine bolts and pull the transmission back. Rig up a strap or keep the front of the transmission up so the converter doesn't fall out.

9. Reverse the procedure for installation. Bolt the transmission to the engine first (28 ft. lbs. for 1969, 35 ft. lbs. for 1970 and later), then the converter to the flywheel (35 ft. lbs.). Make sure that the converter attaching lugs are flush and that the converter can turn freely before installing the bolts.

NOTE: *Lubricate the internal yoke splines at the transmission end of the driveshaft with lithium base grease. The grease should seep out through the vent hole.*

1969–72 Four Wheel Drive

1. Disconnect the battery ground cable. Disconnect the detent cable at the carburetor.

2. Raise and support the truck.

3. Remove the driveshafts, after matchmarking their flanges.

4. Remove the transfer case shift lever.

5. Disconnect the speedometer cable, downshift cable, vacuum modulator line, shift linkage, and fluid cooler lines at the transmission. Remove the filler tube.

6. Support the transmission and transfer case separately. Remove the transmission to adapter case bolts. Unbolt the transfer case from the frame bracket and remove it.

7. Proceed with Steps 5 through 9 of the two wheel drive procedure. See Transfer Case Removal and Installation for adapter bolt torques.

From 1973 Four Wheel Drive

1. Disconnect the battery ground cable and remove the transmission dipstick. Detach the downshift cable at the carburetor. Remove the transfer case shift lever knob and boot.

2. Raise and support the truck.

3. Remove the skid plate, if any. Remove the flywheel cover.

4. Matchmark the flywheel and torque converter, remove the bolts, and secure the converter so it doesn't fall out of the transmission.

5. Detach the shift linkage, speedometer cable, vacuum modulator line, downshift cable and cooler lines at the transmission. Remove the filler tube.

6. Remove the exhaust crossover pipe to manifold bolts.

7. Unbolt the transfer case adapter from the crossmember. Disconnect the engine-to-transmission strut rod at the transmission.

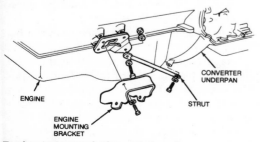

Engine-to-transmission strut rod

Support the transmission and transfer case. Remove the crossmember.

8. Move the exhaust system aside. Detach the driveshafts after matchmarking their flanges. Disconnect the parking brake cable.

9. Unbolt the transfer case from the frame bracket. Support the engine. Unbolt the transmission from the engine, pull the assembly back, and remove.

10. Reverse the procedure for installation. Bolt the transmission to the engine first (30 ft. lbs.), then the converter to the flywheel (35 ft. lbs.). Make sure that the converter attaching lugs are flush and that the converter can turn freely before installing the bolts. See Transfer Case Removal and Installation for adapter bolt torques.

TRANSFER CASE

There are four transfer cases used. The Dana 20 is used, 1969–74, mainly in three speed manual transmission applications with the smaller engines. It can be identified by the two plunger shift control rods at the right front. The New Process 205 is a conventional transfer case, used mainly with the larger engines, 1969–74, and as the only conventional transfer case, 1975–80. It has a large New Process emblem on the back of the case. The New Process 203 is the full time four wheel drive unit, used on all 1973–74 V8s and all 1975–79 automatic transmission models. It was installed with all engines and transmissions for a short time at the beginning of the 1975 model year. It can be identified by the H LOC and L LOC positions on the shifter. The full-time four wheel drive was discontinued in 1980. The New Process 208 aluminum part-time transfer case was introduced in 1981.

NOTE: *Models with the New Process 203 full time four wheel drive transfer case, especially with manual transmission, may give a front wheel "chatter" or vibration on sharp turns. This is a normal characteristic of this drivetrain combination. If it occurs shortly after shifting out of a LOC position, the transfer case is probably still locked up. This should correct itself after about a mile of driving, or can be alleviated by backing up for a short distance.*

CAUTION: *Owners of full time four wheel drive models (New Process 203 transfer case) often consider either removing the front driveshaft or installing locking front hubs*

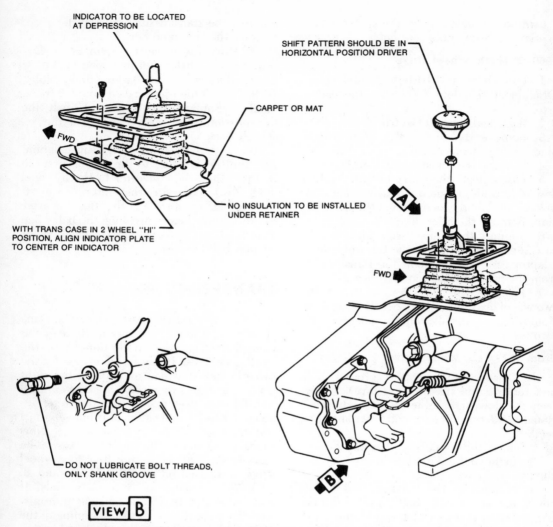

INDICATOR TO BE LOCATED
AT DEPRESSION

SHIFT PATTERN SHOULD BE IN
HORIZONTAL POSITION DRIVER

CARPET OR MAT

FWD

NO INSULATION TO BE INSTALLED
UNDER RETAINER

WITH TRANS CASE IN 2 WHEEL "HI"
POSITION, ALIGN INDICATOR PLATE
TO CENTER OF INDICATOR

A

FWD

B

DO NOT LUBRICATE BOLT THREADS,
ONLY SHANK GROOVE

VIEW B

Dana 20 (1969–74) transfer case shift linkage—not all models have the pointer shown

and operating in a LOC position, as a means of improving gas mileage. This practice will submit the transfer case to stresses beyond its design limits and will void all warranties. Use of any lubricant additive in the transfer case is also not recommended.

New Process 203

SHIFT LINKAGE ADJUSTMENT

The full time four wheel drive transfer case is the only one on which linkage adjustment is necessary or possible.

1. Place the selector lever in the cab in the Neutral position.

2. Detach the adjustable rod ends from the transfer case levers.

3. Align the gauge holes in levers A and B with the gauge hole in the shifter assembly and insert a $^{11}/_{64}$ (.172) in. drill bit. This will position levers A and B in Neutral.

4. Position arms F and G in the straight down (six o'clock) position.

5. Loosely assemble the swivel (E), the lock nuts (D) and the rod (C), and rotate the swivel until the ends of rod (C) will simultaneously enter lever B and arm F.

6. Lock the assembly in place with the retainers (K).

7. Tighten the lock nuts (D) against the swivel (E). Be careful not to change the position of the arm (F) while you are tightening the nuts.

8. Repeat Steps 5, 6 and 7 for rod H to lever A and arm G.

9. Remove the drill bit.

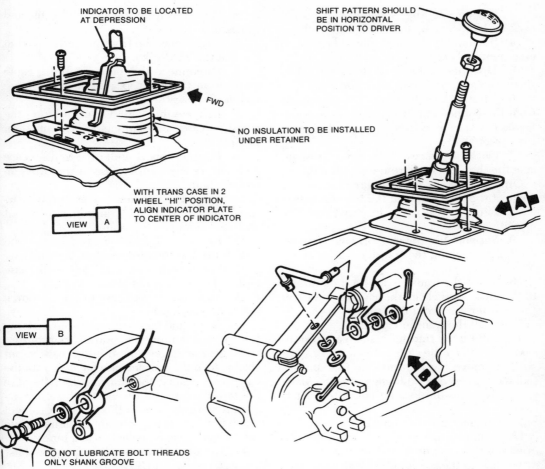

INDICATOR TO BE LOCATED AT DEPRESSION

SHIFT PATTERN SHOULD BE IN HORIZONTAL POSITION TO DRIVER

FWD

NO INSULATION TO BE INSTALLED UNDER RETAINER

WITH TRANS CASE IN 2 WHEEL "HI" POSITION, ALIGN INDICATOR PLATE TO CENTER OF INDICATOR

VIEW A

VIEW B

DO NOT LUBRICATE BOLT THREADS ONLY SHANK GROOVE

A

New Process 205 transfer case shift linkage—not all models have the pointer shown

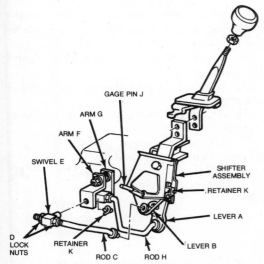

GAGE PIN J

ARM G

ARM F

SWIVEL E

SHIFTER ASSEMBLY

RETAINER K

LEVER A

LEVER B

D LOCK NUTS

RETAINER K

ROD C   ROD H

New Process 203 (1973–79) full time four wheel drive transfer case shift linkage

New Process 208

SHIFT LINKAGE ADJUSTMENT

1. Put transfer case lever in 4HI detent.
2. Push lower shifter lever forward to 4HI stop.
3. Install rod swivel in shift lever hole.
4. Hang .200 thick gauge cover rod behind swivel.
5. Run rear rod nut against gauge with shifter against 4HI stop.
6. Remove gauge and push swivel rearward against nut.
7. Run front rod nut against swivel and tighten.

TRANSFER CASE REMOVAL AND INSTALLATION—EXCEPT NP208.

1. Raise and support the truck.
2. Drain the transfer case.

3. Disconnect the speedometer cable, back-up light switch, and the TCS switch.

4. If necessary, remove the skid plate and crossmember supports.

5. Disconnect the front and rear drive-shafts and support them out of the way.

6. On the Dana 20, remove the clevis pin from the connecting link between the transfer case and control adaptor and disconnect the shifter shafts.

7. On New Process 205 models, disconnect the shift lever rod from the shift rail link.

On New Process 203 full time models, disconnect the shift levers at the transfer case.

8. Remove the transfer case-to-frame mounting bolts.

9. Support the transfer case and remove the bolts attaching the transfer case to transmission adapter.

10. Move the transfer case to the rear until the input shaft clears the adapter and lower the transfer case from the truck.

To install the transfer case:

11. Lifting the transfer case on a transmission jack, attach the case to the adapter.

12. Remove the transmission jack and install the transfer case-to-frame rail bolts. Make certain to bend the locking tabs after installation.

13. Connect the shift linkage.

14. Connect the front driveshaft to the front transfer case output shaft and the rear drive shaft to the rear output shaft.

15. Install the crossmember and skid plate, if equipped.

16. Connect the speedometer cable, backup light and TCS switches.

17. Fill the transfer case to the proper level with lubricant (specified in Chapter 1).

18. Lower the vehicle.

NP 208

1. Place the transfer case in 4H.

2. Raise the vehicle.

3. Drain the lubricant from the transfer case.

4. Remove the cotter pin from the shift lever swivel.

5. Mark the transfer case front and rear output shaft yokes and propeller shafts for assembly alignment reference.

6. Disconnect the speedometer cable and indicator switch wires.

7. Disconnect the front propeller shaft at the transfer case yoke.

8. Disconnect the parking brake cable guide from the pivot located on right frame rail, if necessary.

9. Remove the engine strut rod from the transfer case on automatic transmission models.

10. Place a support under the transfer case and remove the transfer case-to-transmission adapter bolts.

11. Move the transfer case assembly rearward until free of the transmission output shaft and remove the assembly.

12. Remove all gasket material from the rear of the transmission adapter housing.

13. Install the transmission-to-transfer case gasket on the transmission.

14. Shift the transfer case to 4H position if not done previously.

15. Rotate the transfer case output shaft (by turning yoke) until the transmission output shaft gear engages the transfer case input shaft. Move the transfer case forward until the case seats against the transmission. Be sure the transfer case is flush against the transmission. Severe damage to the transfer case will result if the attaching bolts are tightened while the transfer case is cocked or in a bind.

16. Install the transfer case attaching bolts. Tighten the bolts to 30 ft. lbs.

17. Connect the speedometer driven gear to the transfer case.

18. Connect the front and rear propeller shafts to the transfer case. Be sure to align the shafts-to-yokes using the reference marks made during removal. Tighten the shaft-to-yoke clamp strap nuts to 15 ft. lbs.

19. Remove the support stand from under the transfer case.

20. Connect the parking brake cable if disconnected.

21. Attach the cotter pin to the shift lever swivel.

22. Connect the engine strut to the transfer case on automatic models.

23. Fill the transfer case with Dexron® II.

24. Lower the vehicle.

Adapter To Transfer Case Torque

Model	Year	Torque (ft. lbs.)
Dana 20	'69–'74	45
NP 205	'69–'72	35
NP 205	'73–'80	25
NP 203	'73–'79	38
NP 208	from 1981	30

Adapter To Frame Torque

Model	Torque (ft. lbs.)
Dana 20	45
NP 205	130
NP 203 (bracket to frame)	50 upper, 65 lower

Adapter To Transmission Torque

Model	Torque (ft. lbs.)
Dana 20	45
NP 205	22 manual, 35 automatic
NP 203	40
NP 208	30

Drive Train

DRIVELINE

Front Driveshaft
REMOVAL AND INSTALLATION

1. Raise and safely support the front of the truck as necessary.

2. Matchmark the driveshaft and flanges on the front axle and transfer case so that the shaft can be replaced in its original position.

3. Remove the U-bolts or straps at the axle end of the shaft. Compress the shaft slightly and tape the bearings into place to avoid losing them.

4. Remove the U-bolts or straps at the transfer case end of the shaft. Tape the bearings into place.

5. Remove the driveshaft.

6. Reverse the procedure for installation, making sure that the constant velocity joint (the big double one) is at the transfer case end.

7. See Chassis Greasing in Chapter 1 for details on front driveshaft lubrication.

Rear Driveshaft
REMOVAL AND INSTALLATION

1. Raise and safely support the rear of the truck as necessary. There is less chance of lubricant leakage from the rear of the transmission on two wheel drive models if the rear is raised.

2. Matchmark the driveshaft and flanges on the rear axle and transfer case or transmission.

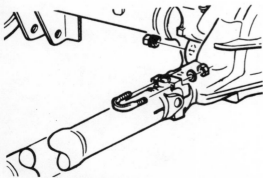

Driveshaft U-bolt retainers

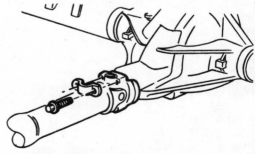

Driveshaft strap retainers

3. Remove the U-bolts or straps at the axle end of the shaft. Tape the bearings into place to avoid losing them.

4. If there are U-bolts or straps at the front end of the shaft, remove them. Tape the bearings into place. Compress the shaft slightly and remove it. All four wheel drive models are of this type.

5. If there are no fasteners at the front end of the shaft, slide the shaft forward slightly to disengage the axle flange, then pull it back out of the transmission. Most two wheel drive models are of this type.

6. Reverse the procedure for installation. On two wheel drive automatic transmission models, lubricate the internal yoke splines at the transmission end of the shaft with lithium base grease. The grease should seep out through the vent hole. On most 1975–80 four wheel drive models, the driveshaft can be installed either way, since both U-joints are the same size.

NOTE: *A thump in the rear driveshaft sometimes occurs when releasing the brakes after braking to a stop, especially on a downgrade. This is most common with automatic transmission. It is often caused by the driveshaft splines binding and can be cured by removing the driveshaft, inspecting the splines for rough spots or sharp edges, and carefully lubricating. A similar thump may be caused by the clutch plates in Positraction (1969–73) limited slip rear axles binding. If this isn't caused by wear, it can be cured by draining and refilling the rear axle with the special lubricant and adding Positraction additive, both of which are available from dealers.*

U-JOINT OVERHAUL

U-Joint is mechanic's jargon for universal joint. U-joints should not be confused with U-bolts, which are U-shaped bolts used to hold U-joints in place to the axle or transfer case.

There are three types of U-joints used in these trucks. The first is held together by wire snap rings in the yokes. The second type, first used 1975, is held together with injection molded plastic retainer rings. This type cannot be reassembled, once disassembled. Repair kits are available, however. The third type is the large constant velocity joint (looks like a double U-joint) at the transfer case end of the front driveshaft.

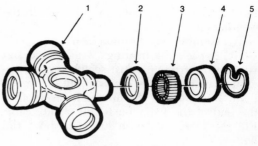

1. Trunnion 4. Cap
2. Seal 5. Snap ring
3. Bearings

Snap ring type U-joint

Snap Ring Type

These U-joints may be found on all models.

1. Remove the driveshaft(s) from the truck.

2. Remove the snap ring from the yoke and remove the lubrication fitting.

3. Support the yoke in a bench vise. Never clamp the driveshaft tube.

4. Use a socket to press against one trunnion bearing to press the opposite bearing from the yoke.

NOTE: *The bearing cap cannot be pressed out.*

5. Grasp the cap and work it out.

6. Support the other side of the yoke and press the other bearing cap from the yoke and remove as in Steps 4 and 5.

7. Remove the trunnion from the driveshaft yoke.

8. If equipped with a sliding sleeve, remove the trunnion bearings from the sleeve yoke in the same manner as above. Remove the seal retainer from the end of the sleeve and pull the seal and washer from the retainer.

9. Disassemble the other U-joint. Clean and check the condition of all parts. You can

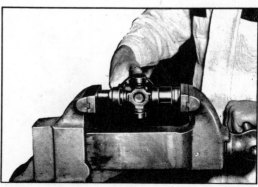

Using a socket to press out the snap ring

buy U-joint repair kits to replace all the wearing parts.

To assemble the trunnion bearings:

10. Repack the bearings with grease and replace the trunnion dust seals after any operation that requires disassembly of the U-joint. Be sure that the lubricant reservoir at the end of the trunnion is full of lubricant. Fill the reservoirs with lubricant from the bottom.

11. Install the trunnion into the driveshaft yoke and press the bearings into the yoke over the trunnion hubs as far as it will go.

12. Install the lockrings.

13. Hold the trunnion in one hand and tap the yoke slightly to seat the bearings against the lockrings.

14. Replace the driveshaft.

Molded Retainer Type, 1975–82

This type is found only on some 1975 and later models. It is held together with injection molded plastic rings.

NOTE: *Don't disassemble these joints unless you have a repair kit. The factory installed joints cannot be reassembled.*

1. Remove the driveshaft.

2. Support the driveshaft in a horizontal position. Place the U-joint so that the lower ear of the shaft yoke is supported by a 1⅛ in. socket. Press the lower bearing cup out of the yoke ear. This will shear the plastic retaining the lower bearing cup.

NOTE: *Never clamp the driveshaft tubing in a vise.*

3. If the bearing cup is not completely removed, lift the cross, insert a spacer and press the cup completely out.

4. Rotate the driveshaft, shear the opposite plastic retainer, and press the other bearing cup out in the same manner.

5. Remove the cross from the yoke. Production U-joints cannot be reassembled.

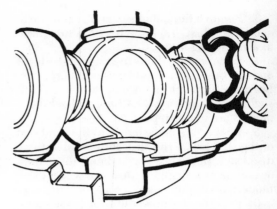

Installing the repair kit snap ring on the molded retainer type U-joint

There are no bearing retainer grooves in the cups. Discard all parts that were removed and substitute those in the overhaul kit.

6. Remove the sheared plastic bearing retainer from the yoke. Drive a small pin or punch through the injection holes to aid in removal.

7. If the other U-joint is to be serviced, remove the bearing cups from the slip yoke in the manner previously described.

8. Be sure that the seals are installed on the service bearing cups to hold the needle bearings in place for handling. Grease the bearings if they aren't pregreased.

9. Install one bearing cup partway into one side of the yoke and turn this ear to the bottom.

10. Insert the cross into the yoke so that the trunnion seats freely in the bearing cup.

11. Install the opposite bearing cup partway. Be sure that both trunnions are started straight into the bearing cups.

Strike the molded retainer type U-joint yoke as shown to seat the snap rings

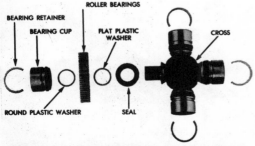

Components of the molded retainer type U-joint repair kit

12. Press against opposite bearing cups, working the cross constantly to be sure that it is free in the cups. If binding occurs, check the needle rollers to be sure that one needle has not become lodged under an end of the trunnion.

13. As soon as one bearing retainer groove is exposed, stop pressing and install the bearing retainer snap-ring.

14. Continue to press until the opposite bearing retainer can be installed. If difficulty installing the snap-rings is encountered, rap the yoke with a hammer to spring the yoke ears slightly.

15. Assemble the other half of the U-joint in the same manner.

16. Check that the cross is free in the cups. If it is too tight, rap the yoke ears again to help seat the bearing retainers.

17. Replace the driveshaft.

Constant Velocity Joint

This is the big joint at the transfer case end of the front driveshaft.

1. Remove the front driveshaft from the truck.

2. Remove the rear trunnion snapring from the center yoke.

3. Remove the grease fitting.

4. Place the joint in a vise.

5. Drive one rear trunnion baring cap from the center yoke until it protrudes approximately ⅜ in.

6. Release the vise and grasp the protruding portion of the cup in a vise and strike the center yoke until the cup is removed. Remove the cup seal with a thin screwdriver.

7. Repeat Steps 4, 5, and 6 for the remaining bearing cup.

8. When the center yoke cups have been removed, remove the rear yoke half bearing cups.

9. Remove the rear trunnion.

10. Remove the rear yoke half from the driveshaft by gently pulling it off. Remove all loose needle bearings and the spring seal.

11. Remove the front trunnion from the center yoke and the front yoke in the manner previously described. Remove all four bearing cups before the trunnions are removed.

12. Clean and inspect all needle bearings, cups, seals, trunnions, fittings, and yokes.

13. Assemble the needle bearings in the cups (27 per cap). Assemble the needle bearings in the front yoke (28 total). Use heavy grease to retain the bearing rollers. Install the seals in the bearing cups.

14. Install the front trunnion in the driveshaft, and install the center yoke in the front trunnion.

15. Install one bearing cup and seal assembly in the front yoke. Drive it into position so that the snap-ring can be installed. Install the snap-ring and the remaining cup and seal in the front yoke. Install the other snap-ring.

16. Install the front trunnion bearing cups in the center yoke in the same manner.

17. With the front trunnion completely installed, install the seal on the driveshaft with the large face first. Gently slip the rear yoke half on the driveshaft using care not to disturb the rollers. Insert the rear trunnion into the center yoke.

18. Install the rear yoke half bearing caps on the rear trunnion. Install one rear trunnion bearing cap in the center yoke and press it into the yoke until the snap-ring can be installed. Install the remaining cap and snapring.

19. Grease the joint as explained under Chassis Greasing in Chapter 1.

20. Install the driveshaft with the constant velocity joint at the transfer case end.

FRONT DRIVE AXLE

The front axle is the Dana (Spicer) model 44. It has open steering knuckles that pivot on ball joints. See Chapter 1 for Front Wheel Bearing Lubrication and Adjustment.

Locking Hub

REMOVAL AND INSTALLATION

Locking hubs were optional through 1974 with conventional four wheel drive, and standard equipment for 1975 and later.

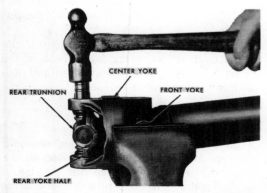

CENTER YOKE

FRONT YOKE

REAR TRUNNION

REAR YOKE HALF

Driving out the constant velocity joint bearing cups

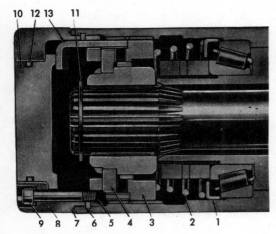

1. Spring retainer plate
2. Pressure spring
3. Inner clutch ring and bushing
4. Axle shaft sleeve and clutch ring assembly
5. Outer clutch retaining ring
6. Internal snap-ring
7. O-ring
8. Retaining plate
9. Retaining plate bolts and seals
10. Actuator knob
11. Axle shaft snap-ring
12. O-ring
13. Actuating cam body

Details of the locking front hub assembly

NOTE: *Locking hubs may not be used with full time four wheel drive. See Chapter 6, under Transfer Case, for details. Locking hubs should be run in the lock position for at least 10 miles each month to assure proper differential lubrication.*

This procedure requires snap ring pliers and a special hub nut wrench. It isn't very easy without them. You will have to modify this procedure if you have non-factory installed hubs.

1. Set the hub in the Lock position.

2. Remove the outer retaining plate allen head bolts and take off the plate, O-ring, and knob.

3. Take out the large snap ring inside the hub and remove the outer clutch retaining ring and actuating cam body.

4. Relieve pressure on the axle shaft snap ring and remove it.

5. Take out the axle shaft sleeve and clutch ring assembly and the inner clutch ring and bushing assembly. Remove the spring and retainer plate.

6. Clean all the hub components in a safe solvent and dry them. Lubricate everything with a high temperature grease.

7. Install the spring retainer plate with the flange side to the bearing and seat it against the outer bearing cup.

8. Install the spring with the large end against the retainer plate.

NOTE: *When the spring is properly installed and seated it will extend past the spindle nuts about ⅞ in.*

9. Place the inner clutch ring and bushing assembly into the axle shaft sleeve and clutch ring assembly. Install these components, push in, and install the axle shaft snap ring. If there are two axle shaft snap ring grooves, use the inner one.

NOTE: *You can install a ⅞ 16 in. bolt in the axle and pull out to aid in seating the snap ring.*

10. Install the actuating cam body with the cams out. Replace the outer clutch retaining ring and then the internal snap ring.

11. Install a new O-ring, then install the actuating knob and retaining plate in the lock position. The grooves in the knob must fit into the actuator cam body. Install the cover bolts and seals.

Axle Shaft
REMOVAL AND INSTALLATION

NOTE: *The front spindles and universal joints were changed during the 1972 model year. You have to know which one you have to order the correct parts. The early design is stamped 603351 or 603352 on the front of the left axle tube; the later design is 603333 or 603334. The only interchangeable part is the inner hub seal.*

1. Follow Steps 1–6 of the Front Wheel Bearing Lubrication and Adjustment procedure in Chapter 1.

2. Pull out the axle shaft and universal joint assembly.

3. When installing the axle shaft, turn the shaft slowly to align the splines with the differential.

4. Reassemble everything and adjust the wheel bearings following Steps 7–15 of the Front Wheel Bearing Lubrication and Adjustment procedure in Chapter 1.

U-JOINT OVERHAUL

1. Remove the axle shaft.

2. Squeeze the ends of the trunnion bearings in a vise to relieve the load on the snap rings. Remove the snap rings.

3. Support the yoke in a vise and drive on one end of the trunnion bearing with a

brass drift enough to drive the opposite bearing from the yoke.

4. Support the other side of the yoke and drive the other bearing out.

5. Remove the trunnion.

6. Clean and check all parts. You can buy U-joint repair kits to replace all the wearing parts.

7. Lubricate the bearings with wheel bearing grease.

8. Replace the trunnion and press the bearings into the yoke and over the trunnion hubs far enough to install the lock rings.

9. Hold the trunnion in one hand and tap the yoke lightly to seat the bearings against the lock rings.

10. The axle slingers can be pressed off the shafts.

NOTE: *Always replace the slingers if the spindle seals are replaced.*

You can use the spindle to start the slinger on the shaft.

11. Replace the shaft.

BALL JOINT REPLACEMENT

The steering knuckle pivot ball joints may need replacement when there is excessive steering play, hard steering, irregular tire wear (especially on the inner edge), or persistent tie rod loosening.

This procedure requires a shop press. Your best bet would be to remove the steering knuckle and take it to the machine shop with the new parts.

1. Remove the hub assembly as previously outlined.

2. Remove the spindle attaching bolts.

3. Tap on the end of the spindle lightly with a wooden mallet (not a metal hammer) to break it loose from the steering knuckle.

4. Remove the spindle and the bronze

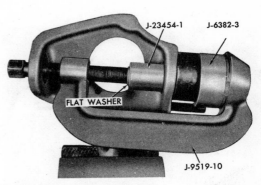

Removing the upper ball joint

washer. Replace the washer if it was distorted during removal or if it appears worn.

5. Remove the cotter pin from the tie rod nut.

6. Loosen the tie rod nut and tap on the nut with a wooden mallet in order to break the studs loose from the knuckle arm.

7. Remove the nuts and disconnect the tie rod.

8. Remove the steering arm attaching nuts. Use new, self-locking nuts on installation.

9. Remove the cotter pin from the upper ball joint socket nut.

10. Remove the retaining nuts from the upper and lower ball joint sockets.

11. Remove the knuckle by forcing a wedge between the lower ball stud and the yoke, then between the upper ball stud and the yoke.

NOTE: *If you have to loosen the upper ball stud adjusting sleeve to remove the knuckle, don't loosen it more than two turns. The soft threads on the yoke are easily damaged.*

12. Remove the lower ball joint snap ring.

13. Remove the lower ball joint as illustrated using special tool no. J-9519-10 (or a similar C-clamp), J-23454-1 (a solid metal punch), and J-6382-3 (or a piece of 2½ in. outer diameter steel pipe with a 3/16 in. wall thickness cut to a length of 2½ ins.). The lower ball joint must be removed before the upper ball joint can be serviced.

14. Remove the upper ball joint, using the same tools, as illustrated.

15. Press the new lower ball joint into the knuckle and install the snap ring. The lower joint doesn't have a cotter pin hole.

16. Press the upper ball joint into the knuckle.

17. Position the knuckle to the yoke. Install new stud nuts finger tight.

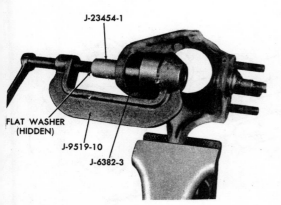

Removing the lower ball joint

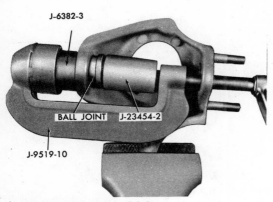

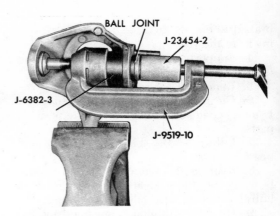

Installing the lower ball joint

Installing the upper ball joint

18. Push up on the knuckle and tighten the lower nut to 70 ft. lbs.

19. Using a spanner wrench, install and torque the upper ball stud adjusting sleeve to 50 ft. lbs. Torque the upper stud nut to 100 ft. lbs. and install the cotter pin. Don't loosen the nut, but make it tighter to line up the cotter pin hole.

20. Replace the steering arm, using new nuts and torquing to 90 ft. lbs.

21. Attach the tie rod to the steering arm. Tighten the nuts to 45 ft. lbs.

22. Check the knuckle turning torque with a spring scale hooked to the tie rod hole in the steering arm. With the knuckle straight ahead, measure the right angle pull to keep the knuckle turning after initial breakaway, in both directions. The pull should be 25 lbs or less for axles assembled after Feb. 10, 1976, and 33 lbs for earlier models.

23. Replace the axle shaft and other components. Tighten the steering linkage nuts to 45 ft. lbs.

REAR AXLE

Some models are equipped with a locking differential rear axle. If you're not sure which one is in your truck, block the front wheels and jack up the rear of the truck. With the transmission in Neutral, spin one of the rear wheels in a forward motion with your hands. If the other wheel travels in the same direction, it is a locking differential.

Axle Shaft, Bearing, And Seal
REMOVAL AND INSTALLATION
All Axles Except 1974–82 Locking Differential

This procedure applies to all standard rear axles and to those (1969–73) with the optional Positraction limited slip differential.

1. Support the axle on jackstands.
2. Remove the wheels and brake drums.
3. Clean off the differential cover area,

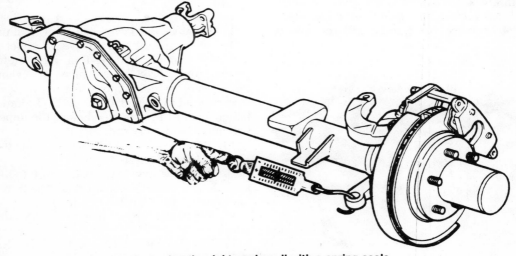

Measuring the right angle pull with a spring scale

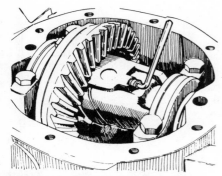

Removing the pinion shaft lockscrew

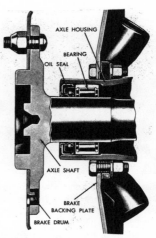

Rear axle bearing and oil seal details

loosen the cover to drain the lubricant, and remove the cover.

4. Turn the differential until you can reach the differential pinion shaft lockscrew. Remove the lockscrew and the pinion shaft.

5. Push in on the axle end. Remove the C-lock from the inner (button) end of the shaft.

6. Remove the shaft, being careful of the oil seal.

7. You can pry the oil seal out of the housing by placing the inner end of the axle shaft behind the steel case of the seal, then prying it out carefully.

8. A puller or a slide hammer is required to remove the bearing from the housing.

9. Pack the new or reused bearing with wheel bearing grease and lubricate the cavity between the seal lips with the same grease.

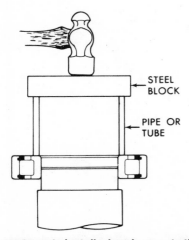

The correct way to install a bearing—note that the one illustrated is being driven over a shaft. When installing the axle tube bearing, you would drive on the outer bearing race to prevent damaging the bearing rollers. The pipe exerts even pressure all around so that the bearing goes on straight without distortion

10. The bearing has to be driven into the housing. Don't use a drift, you might cock the bearing in its bore. Use a piece of pipe or a large socket instead. Drive only on the outer bearing race. In a similar manner, drive the seal in flush with the end of the tube.

11. Slide the shaft into place, turning it slowly until the splines are engaged with the differential. Be careful of the oil seal.

12. Install the C-lock on the inner axle end. Pull the shaft out so that the C-lock seats in the counterbore of the differential side gear.

13. Position the differential pinion shaft through the case and the pinion gears, aligning the lockscrew hole. Install the lockscrew.

14. Install the cover with a new gasket and tighten the bolts evenly in a criss-cross pattern.

15. Fill the axle with lubricant as specified in Chapter 1.

16. Replace the brake drums and wheels.

1974–82 Locking Differential Axles

This axle uses a thrust block on the differential pinion shaft.

1. Follow Steps 1–3 of the preceding procedure.

2. Rotate the differential case so that you can remove the lockscrew and support the pinion shaft so it can't fall into the housing. Remove the differential pinion shaft lockscrew.

3. Carefully pull the pinion shaft partway out and rotate the differential case until the shaft touches the housing at the top.

4. Use a screwdriver to position the C-lock with its open end directly inward. You can't push in the axle shaft till you do this. Do not force the axle shaft in.

When you remove the axle shaft C-lock on 1974 and later locking differentials, pull the differential pinion shaft partway out and rest it against the case

5. Push the axle shaft in and remove the C-lock. Remove the axle shaft and repeat steps 4 and 5 for the other shaft.

6. Follow Steps 7–11 of the preceding procedure.

7. Keep the pinion shaft partway out of the differential case while installing the C-lock on the axle shaft. Put the C-lock on the axle shaft and carefully pull out on the axle shaft until the C-lock is clear of the thrust block.

8. Follow Steps 13–16 of the previous procedure.

DETERMINING AXLE RATIO

Axle ratios available in these trucks are 2.76:1, 3.07:1, 3.4:1, 3.73:1, and 4.11:1. The 4.11:1 ratio was not available with four wheel drive until 1973; the 3.40:1 ratio was available only on 1973–75 two wheel drive models.

NOTE: *The ratios given here are for rear axles; front axle ratios are the same or nearly*

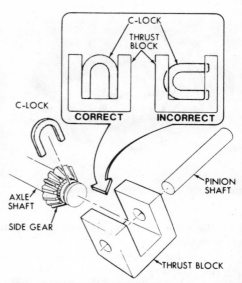

Position the axle shaft C-lock as shown for removal on the 1974 and later locking differential

so. (The 4.11:1 front axle ratio is actually 4.09:1.)

The axle ratio is obtained by dividing the number of teeth on the ring gear. It is always expressed as a proportion and is a simple expression of gear speed reduction and torque multiplication.

To find an unknown ratio, make a chalk mark on a tire and on the driveshaft. Move the truck ahead (or back) slowly for one tire rotation and have an observer note the number of driveshaft rotations. Compare the number of turns to the possible ratios. You can also do this by jacking up both rear wheels and turning them by hand.

Suspension and Steering

FRONT SUSPENSION

Two wheel drive models use coil spring independent front suspension. A stabilizer (sway) bar is optional to minimize body lean and sway in curves. Four wheel drive models have a non-independent leaf spring front suspension. A stabilizer bar is standard for 1973–82. A steering linkage damper is standard on late models. Heavy duty shock absorbers, springs, and stabilizer bars have been optional for most models. Service procedures for the four wheel drive front drive axle are in Chapter 7.

Springs

1973 four wheel drive models have only one short front spring-to-frame rubber bumper on the right side. If you drive hard in rough terrain, there is a good chance of the front driveshaft moving up high enough to break the starter. The cure is to install new longer bumpers (no. 344717) on both sides. You will have to drill a hole for the left one.

REMOVAL AND INSTALLATION

CAUTION: *Springs, particularly coil springs, are under considerable tension. Be very careful when removing and installing* them; *they can exert enough force to cause very serious injuries.*

Two Wheel Drive

1. Raise the vehicle and support it under the frame so that the control arms will hang free.

2. Remove the lower shock absorber mounting bolt. Detach the stabilizer bar from the lower control arm.

3. Place a floor jack under the lower control arm cross-shaft.

CAUTION: *As a safety precaution, install a chain through the spring and the lower control arm.*

4. Raise the jack. This will remove the tension on the lower control arm so that the

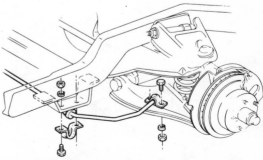

Two wheel drive front coil spring and stabilizer bar details

two U-bolts which secure the cross-shaft can be removed.

5. Lower the control arm *slowly* by releasing the floor jack to the point where the spring can be removed.

6. Remove the spring.

7. Place the spring on the control arm and then, using a jack, slowly raise the control arm. Use the safety chain as described in Step 3.

8. Place the control arm cross-shaft onto the crossmember and then install the U-bolts and the attaching nuts. Make certain that the indexing hole in the cross-shaft is lined up with the crossmember stud.

9. Torque the U-bolt nuts to 45 ft. lbs. through 1975, 85 ft. lbs. for 1976 and later models. Remove the safety chain.

10. Install the lower part of the shock absorber and the stabilizer bar.

11. Lower the vehicle.

Four Wheel Drive

1. Raise and support the truck under the front axle and frame so that the tension on the springs is relieved.

2. Remove the shackle upper retaining bolt and the front spring eye bolt.

3. Remove the spring-to-axle U-bolt nuts. Pull off the spring, the lower plate, and the spring pads.

4. Remove the shackle-to-spring bolt, bushings, and shackle.

To replace the bushing, place the spring onto a press or vise and press out the bushing. Press in the new bushing. The new bushing should protrude evenly on both sides of the spring.

5. Install the spring shackle bushings into

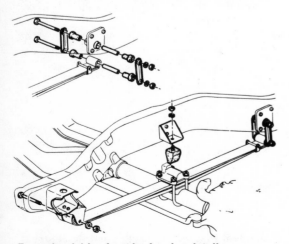

Four wheel drive front leaf spring details

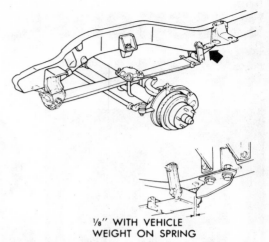

⅛″ WITH VEHICLE WEIGHT ON SPRING

1969–72 front spring shackle stop

the spring and then attach the shackle. Do not tighten the bolt.

6. Place the upper spring cushion onto the spring.

7. Place the front of the spring into the frame and install the bolt but do not tighten it.

8. Position the shackle bushing into the frame and attach the rear shackle but do not tighten it.

9. Install the lower spring pad and the spring retainer plate. Tighten the U-bolts to 150 ft. lbs. for 1973–82 models, 120 ft. lbs. for 1969–72.

10. Torque the rear spring shackle bolts and the rear eye bolts to 50 ft. lbs. and the front eye bolts to 90 ft. lbs.

11. Lower the vehicle.

If there is a rear shackle stop (1969–72), adjust the clearance between it and the spring eye to ⅛ in.

Shock Absorbers

The usual procedure for testing shock absorbers is to stand on the bumper at the end nearest the shock being tested and start the vehicle bouncing up and down. Step off; the vehicle should come to rest within one bounce cycle. Another good test is to drive the vehicle over a bumpy road. Bouncing over bumps is normal, but the shock absorbers should stop the bouncing, after the bump is passed, within one or two cycles.

REMOVAL AND INSTALLATION

The usual procedure is to replace shock absorbers in axle pairs, to provide equal damp-

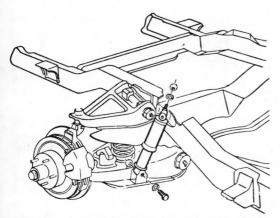

Two wheel drive front shock absorber details

ing. Heavy duty replacements are available for firmer control.

1. Raise and support the front axle as necessary.

2. Remove the bolt and nut from the lower shock end.

3. On two wheel drive original equipment shocks, remove the upper stud nut from inside the frame. Most aftermarket replacement two wheel drive shocks replace the original stud fixed to the top of the shock with a double ended stud; if you have these, you can just remove the outer nut. On four wheel drive shocks, remove the upper bolt and nut.

4. Purge the new shock of air by extending it in its normal position and compressing it while inverted. Do this several times. It is normal for there to be more resistance to extension than to compression.

5. Install the shock absorber. Tighten the two wheel drive upper stud nut (inside the frame) to 140 ft. lbs. and the four wheel drive upper bolt to 65 ft. lbs. Tighten the two wheel drive lower bolt to 75 ft. lbs. for 1969–72, and 60 ft. lbs. for 1973–82. Tighten the four

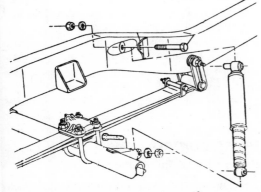

Four wheel drive front shock absorber details

wheel drive lower bolt to 65 ft. lb. You can tighten the two wheel drive outer top stud nut mentioned in Step 3 to about 60 ft. lbs.

Independent Front Suspension

Service procedures for the four wheel drive front drive axle are in Chapter 7.

BALL JOINTS

Inspection

Excessive ball joint wear will usually show up as wear on the inside of the front tires. Don't jump to conclusions; front end misalignment can give the same symptom.

1969–71 UPPER BALL JOINT

1. Raise and support the truck so that the control arms hang free.

2. Remove the wheel.

3. Support the lower control arm with a jackstand and disconnect the upper ball stud from the steering knuckle. Observe the Caution under Front Spring Removal and Installation.

4. Reinstall the nut on the ball stud and measure the torque required to rotate the stud. If the torque is not within 1–10 ft. lbs., replace the ball joint.

5. If no defects are evident, connect the steering knuckle to the upper stud and torque the nut to 50 ft. lbs. Tighten further to install the cotter pin, but don't exceed 90 ft. lbs.

1972–82 UPPER BALL JOINT

1. Perform Steps 1–2 of the 1969–71 inspection procedure.

2. The upper ball joint is spring-loaded in its socket. If it has any perceptible lateral shake or can be twisted in its socket, it should be replaced.

LOWER BALL JOINT

The lower ball joint gets the most wear due to the distribution of suspension load.

1. Support the weight of the control arm at the bottom of the tire.

2. Measure the distance between the tip of the ball joint stud and the tip of the grease fitting below the ball joint.

3. Move the support to the control arm and allow the wheel and tire to hang free. Measure the distance again. If the variation between the two measurements exceeds $3/32$ in. the ball joint should be replaced.

NOTE: *This is the manufacturer's recom-*

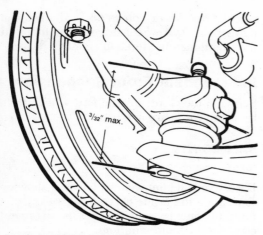

Lower ball joint inspection

mended wear limit. Your state inspection regulations may disagree.

Removal and Installation

NOTE: *Observe the Caution under Front Spring Removal and Installation when working with ball joints.*

LOWER BALL JOINT

1. Raise and support the truck. Support the lower control arm with a floor jack.
2. Remove the tire and wheel.
3. Remove the lower stud cotter pin and loosen, but do not remove, the stud nut.
4. Loosen the ball joint stud with a ball joint stud removal tool. It may be necessary to remove the brake caliper and wire it to the frame to gain enough clearance. Do not let the caliper hang by the hose.
5. When the stud is loose, remove the tool and ball stud nut.
6. Pull the brake disc and knuckle assembly up and off the ball stud and support the upper arm with a block of wood.

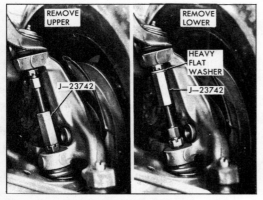

One type of ball joint removal tool

7. Remove the ball joint from the control arm with a ball joint removal tool. It must be pressed out.

To install:

8. Start the new ball joint into the control arm. Position the bleed vent in the rubber boot facing inward.
9. Seat the ball joint in the control arm. It must be pressed in.
10. Lower the upper arm and match the steering knuckle to the lower ball stud.
11. Install the brake caliper, if removed.
12. Install the ball stud nut and torque it to 90 ft. lbs. plus the additional torque necessary to align the cotter pin hole. Do not exceed 130 ft. lbs. or back the nut off to align the holes with the pin.
13. Install a new lube fitting and lubricate the new joint.
14. Install the tire and wheel.
15. Lower the truck.

UPPER BALL JOINT

1. Raise and support the truck.
2. Support the lower control arm with a floor jack.
3. Remove the cotter pin from the upper ball stud and loosen, but do not remove, the stud nut.
4. Using a ball joint stud removal tool, loosen the ball stud in the steering knuckle. When the stud is loose, remove the tool and the stud nut. It will be necessary to remove the brake caliper and wire it to the frame to gain clearance. Do not allow the caliper to hang by the hose.
5. Drill out the rivets. Remove the ball joint assembly.

To install:

6. Install the service ball joint, using the nuts supplied. Tighten the nuts to 45 ft. lbs.
7. Torque the ball stud nut to 50 ft. lbs. plus the additional torque required to align the cotter pin. Do not exceed 90 ft. lbs. and never back the nut off to align the pin.
8. Install a new cotter pin.
9. Install a new lube fitting and lubricate the new joint.
10. If removed, install the brake caliper.
11. Install the wheel and tire and lower the truck.

UPPER CONTROL ARM

Removal and Installation

1. Raise and support the truck on jackstands.

2. Support the lower control arm with a floor jack.

3. Remove the wheel and tire.

4. Remove the cotter pin from the upper control arm ball stud and loosen the stud nut one turn.

5. Loosen the upper control arm ball stud in the steering knuckle using a ball joint stud removal tool. Remove the nut from the ball stud and raise the upper arm to clear the steering knuckle. It will be necessary to remove the brake caliper and wire it to the frame to gain clearance.

6. Remove the nuts securing the control arm shaft to the frame and remove the control arm. Tape the shims and spacers together and tag for proper reassembly.

7. Installation is the reverse of removal. Place the control arm in position and install the nuts. Before tightening the nuts to 70 ft. lbs., insert the caster and camber shims in the same order as when removed. Have the front end alignment checked, and as necessary, adjusted.

LOWER CONTROL ARM

Removal and Installation

1. Raise and support the truck on jackstands.

2. Remove the spring. See Spring Removal and Installation.

3. Support the inboard end of the control arm after spring removal.

4. Remove the cotter pin from the lower ball stud and loosen the nut one turn.

5. Loosen the lower ball stud in the steering knuckle using a ball joint stud removal tool. When the stud is loose, remove the nut from the stud. It will be necessary to remove the brake caliper and wire it to the frame to gain clearance.

6. Remove the lower control arm.

7. Installation is the reverse of removal.

Front End Alignment

Caster and camber cannot be set or measured accurately without professional equipment. Toe-in can be adjusted with some degree of success without any special equipment.

CASTER ADJUSTMENT

Caster is the backward or forward tilt from the vertical of the steering knuckle centerline at the top, measured in degrees. A steering

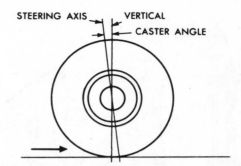

Front wheel caster angle

knuckle centerline tilted backward at the top has positive (+) caster, while one tilted forward has negative (−) caster. Most American passenger cars have negative or zero caster to reduce steering effort. Positive caster, as on the Blazer/Jimmy and most trucks, produces greater directional stability and requires greater steering effort, since it also increases the self-centering effect at the steering wheel.

Two Wheel Drive

No two wheel drive caster specifications are given, since the method for finding the recommended angle is rather complicated. It requires algebraically adding the angle of the frame at a specified point to the measured caster angle in order to obtain a corrected caster angle, measuring the distance between the bump stop bracket on the crossmember and the top of the lower control arm bumper, and checking the measurement on a chart or graph to find the recommended corrected caster angle.

Caster is adjusted by varying the numbers of shims on the bolts holding the upper control arm pivot shaft to the frame. The torque for the bolts is 70 ft. lbs.

Four Wheel Drive

Caster is fixed on four wheel drive models. If it varies significantly from specifications, the most likely cause is spring settling. About the only cure is to re-arch or replace the springs. Some truck alignment shops use tapered shims between the axle and the spring to make small caster corrections.

CAMBER ADJUSTMENT

Camber is the inward or outward tilt, measured in degrees, of the wheel at the top. A wheel tilted out at the top has positive (+) camber. A wheel tilted in has negative (−) camber. Camber has a great effect on tire wear.

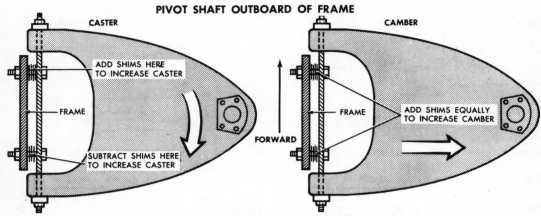

PIVOT SHAFT OUTBOARD OF FRAME

Two wheel drive caster and camber adjustments

Two Wheel Drive

No 1969–71 two wheel drive camber specifications are given, since the method for finding the recommended angle is rather complicated. It requires measuring the distance between the bump stop bracket on the crossmember and the top of the lower control arm bumper, and plotting the measurement on a graph to find the recommended camber angle. Specifications are given for 1972–82 models, since the earlier method is not required.

Camber is adjusted by varying equally the number of shims on the bolts holding the upper control arm pivot shaft to the frame. The torque for the bolts is 70 ft. lbs.

Four Wheel Drive

Camber is fixed on four wheel drive models. If it varies significantly from specifications, suspect steering knuckle ball joint wear. Another possibility is a bent axle tube, usually

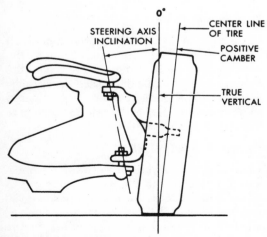

Front wheel camber angle

caused by those thrilling jumps. Bent axle tubes can be straightened, given the proper heavy equipment. A shop that handles truck frame straightening and alignment is the most likely place.

TOE-IN ADJUSTMENT

Toe-in is the amount, measured in inches, that the centerlines of the wheels are closer together at the front than at the rear. Virtually all cars, except some with front wheel drive, are set with toe-in. Some front wheel drive cars, and some four wheel drive trucks, require toe-out to prevent excessive toe-in under power.

NOTE: *Some alignment specialists set toe-in to the lower specified limit on vehicles with radial tires. The reason is that radial tires have less drag, and therefore a lesser tendency to toe-out at speed. By the same reasoning, off-road tires would require the upper limit of toe-in.*

Toe-in must be checked after caster and camber have been adjusted, but it can be adjusted without disturbing the other two settings. You can make this adjustment without special equipment, if you make careful measurements. The adjustment is made at the tie-rod sleeves. The wheels must be straight ahead.

1. Toe-in can be determined by measuring the distance between the centers of the tire treads, front and rear. If the tread pattern of your tires makes this impossible, you can measure between the edges of the wheel rims, but make sure to move the truck forward and measure in a couple of places to avoid errors caused by bent rims or wheel runout.

2. Loosen the clamp bolts on the tie-rod sleeves.

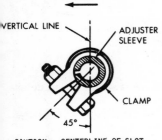

CAUTION: CLAMPS MUST BE
BETWEEN AND CLEAR OF DIMPLES
BEFORE TORQUING NUT.

ADJUSTER SLEEVE

CLAMPING INSTRUCTIONS FOR
ALL LIGHT TRUCKS.

A. All bolts must be installed in
   direction shown.
B. Rotate both inner and outer tie
   rod sockets rearward to limit of
   ball stud travel.
C. Position clamps within angles shown.
D. Tighten clamps.
E. With this same rearward rotation,
   all bolt centerlines must be
   between angles shown.

FWD

VERTICAL LINE

ADJUSTER
SLEEVE

CLAMP

45°

NOTE: IMPORTANT - SLOT
IN ADJUSTER SLEEVE
MUST NOT BE WITHIN
OPEN AREA OF CLAMP
JAWS OR CLOSER THAN
.10 TO THE EDGE OF
CLAMP JAW OPENING.
ROTATE CLAMP TO MEET
REQUIREMENTS WITHIN
PROPER POSITION AS SHOWN.

CAUTION: CENTERLINE OF SLOT
IN CLAMP MUST BE IN THIS
RANGE OF ADJUSTMENT.

Tie-rod sleeve clamp installation

Front End Alignment Specifications

Year	Model	Caster (deg) ▲	Camber (deg)	Toe-In (in.)
'69–'71	2WD	*	*	1/8–1/4
'72–'82	2WD	*	1/4	1/8–1/4
'69	4WD	3	1	3/32–3/16
'70	4WD	3¼	1	3/32–3/16
'71–'74	4WD	4	1½	1/8–1/4
'73–'74	Full time 4WD	4	1½	0
'75	4WD	4	1½	0
'76 thru mid-Jan.	4WD	4	1½	0
'76 from mid-Jan.	4WD	8	1½	0
'77–'78	4WD	8	1½	0
'79–'82	4WD	8	1	0①

*Specifications not given. See text for explanation.
▲All caster and camber figures are positive (+).
① '81–'82: 3/16″·

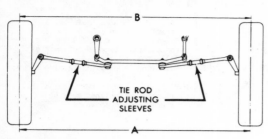

"B" IS LESS THAN "A" WHEN WHEELS TOE-IN

B

TIE ROD
ADJUSTING
SLEEVES

A

Toe-in adjustment

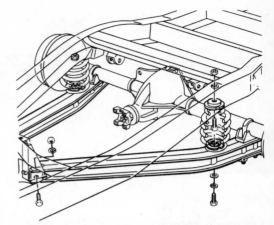

1969–72 two wheel drive rear coil spring details

3. Rotate the sleeves equally (in opposite directions) to obtain the correct measurement. If the sleeves are not adjusted equally, the steering wheel will be crooked.

NOTE: *If your steering wheel is already crooked, it can be straightened by turning the sleeves equally in the same direction.*

4. When the adjustment is complete, tighten the clamps.

REAR SUSPENSION

1969–72 two wheel drive models have coil spring rear suspension with the axle located by long control arms. All other models have leaf spring rear suspension. Staggered rear shock absorbers are used, 1973–82, to control axle hop on acceleration and braking. Heavy duty shock absorbers and springs have been available on most models.

Springs
REMOVAL AND INSTALLATION

CAUTION: *Springs, particularly coil springs, are under considerable tension. Be very careful when removing and installing them; they can exert enough force to cause very serious injuries.*

Coil Springs

1. Jack up the vehicle, supported at the frame. Position another jack under the control arm.

2. Remove the lower shock absorber bolt from its mounting on the lower control arm.

3. Remove the upper and lower clamps from the spring by releasing the lower bolt from the underside of the control arm and the upper bolt from inside the spring.

CAUTION: *Insert a safety chain through the spring and lower control arm.*

4. Lower the jack under the control arm

slowly until there is sufficient room to remove the spring.

To install the unit:

5. Place the spring clamp so that the end of the spring is within the area of the notch so that it will seat on the spring end without any hang-up. It will also align with the bolt hole in the control arm.

6. Position the clamp bolt with the washer up through the hole in the control arm and install the nut.

7. Place the upper clamp inside the spring and install the bolt and washer.

8. Raise the control arm and attach the shock absorber.

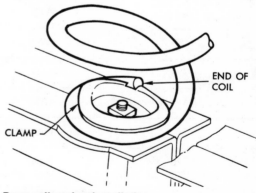

END OF
COIL

CLAMP

Rear coil spring installation

Leaf Springs

1. Raise the vehicle and support it so that there is no tension on the leaf spring assembly.

2. Loosen the spring-to-shackle retaining bolts. (Do not remove these bolts.)

3. Remove the securing bolts which attach the shackle to the spring hanger.

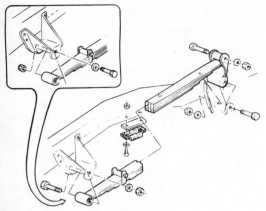

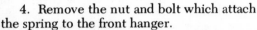

Typical rear leaf spring details

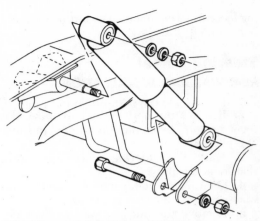

1969–72 rear shock absorber details

4. Remove the nut and bolt which attach the spring to the front hanger.

5. Remove the U-bolt nuts and remove the spring plate.

6. Pull the spring from the vehicle.

7. If the bushings need to be replaced, they must be pressed in and out.

8. Place the spring assembly onto the axle housing.

NOTE: *The shackle assembly must be attached to the rear spring eye before the rear shackle is installed.*

9. Position the spring retaining plate and the U-bolts (loosely).

10. Install the rear shackle bolt and nut, then the front eye bolt and nut. Tighten the bolts to 90 ft. lbs. for 1969–72, and 110 ft. lbs. for 1973–82.

NOTE: *Aftermarket kits, consisting of longer axle U-bolts and blocks to be placed between the spring and axle, are available to adjust the rear ride height. If this modification is carried to extremes, the front end caster angle and rear end stability will be affected.*

Shock Absorbers

See Front Shock Absorbers for information on testing.

REMOVAL AND INSTALLATION

The usual procedure is to replace shock absorbers in axle pairs, to provide equal damping. Heavy duty replacements are available for firmer control. Air adjustable shock absorbers can be used to maintain a level ride with heavy loads or when towing.

1. Raise and support the rear axle as necessary.

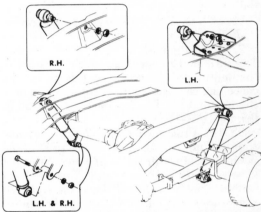

1973 and later staggered rear shock absorber details

2. If air shocks are installed, bleed the air and detach the lines.

3. Remove the nut and washer at the top.

4. Remove the nut, washer, and bolt at the bottom.

5. Purge the new shock of air by extending it in its normal position and compressing it while inverted. Do this several times. It is normal for there to be more resistance to extension than to compression.

6. Install the shock absorber. For 1969–72 models, tighten the nuts to 75 ft. lbs. for two wheel drive, and 65 ft. lbs. for four wheel drive. Tighten the upper nuts to 140 ft. lbs. for 1973–78 models and 150 ft. lbs. for 1979 and later models. Tighten the lower nuts to 115 ft. lbs. for all 1973 and later models.

STEERING

A common cause of excessive steering play on these trucks is the steering gear box coming loose from the frame. The torque for these bolts is 65 ft. lbs.

Steering Wheel

REMOVAL AND INSTALLATION

1. Disconnect the battery ground cable.
2. Remove the horn button. Remove the receiving cup, belleville washer, and bushing (if equipped).
3. Mark the steering wheel-to-steering shaft relationship.
4. On 1975 and later models, remove the snap-ring from the steering shaft.
5. Remove the nut and washer from the steering shaft.
6. Remove the steering wheel with a puller.

CAUTION: *Don't hammer on the steering shaft.*

7. Installation is the reverse of removal. The turn signal control assembly must be in the neutral position to prevent damaging the cancelling cam and control assembly. Tighten the nut to 40 ft. lbs. for 1969–72, and 30 ft. lbs. for 1973–82.

NOTE: *A steering wheel puller can be made by drilling two holes in a piece of steel the same distance apart as the two threaded holes in the steering wheel. Sometimes an old spring shackle will have the right dimensions. Drill another hole in the center. Place a center bolt with the head against the steering shaft and a nut against the bottom of the homemade puller bar. Thread the two outer bolts into the holes in the wheel. Unscrew the nut on the center bolt to draw the wheel off the shaft.*

One type of steering wheel puller

Turn Signal Switch

REPLACEMENT

1969–72

1. Disconnect the battery ground cable.
2. Remove the steering wheel, preload spring, and cancelling cam.
3. Remove the shift lever roll pin and shift lever (if applicable).
4. Remove the turn signal lever screw and the lever.
5. Push the hazard warning knob in. This must be done to avoid damaging the switch.
6. Disconnect the switch wire from the chassis harness located under the dash.
7. Remove the mast jacket upper bracket.
8. Remove the switch wiring cover from the column.
9. Unscrew the mounting screws and remove the switch, bearing housing, switch cover, and shift housing from the column.
10. Installation is the reverse of removal.

1973–82

1. Remove the steering wheel as previously outlined.
2. Remove the column to instrument panel trim cover. Loosen the three cover screws and lift the cover off the shaft. On 1976 and later models, place a screwdriver in the cover slot and pry out to free the cover.
3. The round lockplate must be pushed down to remove the wire snap-ring from the shaft. A special tool is available to do this. The tool is an inverted U-shape with a hole for the shaft. The shaft nut is used to force it down. Pry the wire snap-ring out of the shaft groove.
4. Remove the tool and lift the lockplate off the shaft.
5. Slip the cancelling cam, upper bearing preload spring, and thrust washer off the shaft.
6. Remove the turn signal lever screw and the lever. Push the flasher knob in and unscrew it.
7. Pull the switch connector out of the mast jacket and tape the upper part to facilitate switch removal. On tilt wheels, place the turn signal and shifter housing in the low position and remove the harness cover.
8. Remove the three switch mounting screws. Remove the switch by pulling it straight up while guiding the wiring harness cover through the column.
9. Install the replacement switch by working the connector and cover down

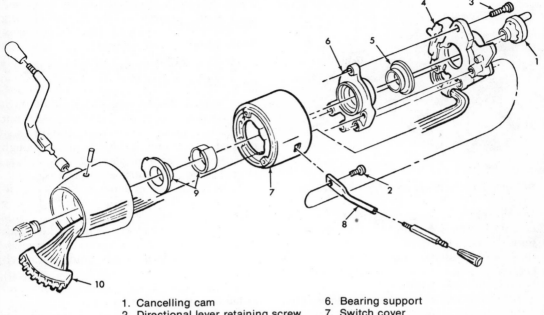

1. Cancelling cam
2. Directional lever retaining screw
3. Switch mounting screw
4. Switch
5. Upper bearing
6. Bearing support
7. Switch cover
8. Lever arm
9. Washer
10. Wiring connector

1969–72 turn signal switch details

through the housing and under the bracket. On tilt models, the connector is worked down through the housing, under the bracket, and then the cover is installed on the harness.

10. Install the switch mounting screws and the connector on the mast jacket bracket. Install the column to instrument panel trim plate.

11. Install the flasher knob and the turn signal lever.

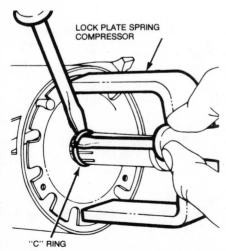

LOCK PLATE SPRING COMPRESSOR

"C" RING

Removing the lock plate and the snap ring

12. With the turn signal lever in neutral and the flasher knob out, slide the thrust washer, upper bearing pre-load spring, and cancelling cam onto the shaft.

13. Position the lockplate on the shaft and press it down until a new snap-ring can be inserted in the shaft groove.

14. Install the cover and the steering wheel.

Ignition Switch and Lock Cylinder

Removal and installation for the 1969–72 instrument panel mounted switch is in Chapter 5.

1973–78 LOCK CYLINDER REMOVAL AND INSTALLATION

The key and lock code numbers are kept in the records of the original selling dealer. This number enables a dealer to supply a new lock cylinder that will operate with the old key.

1. Remove steering wheel and turn signal switch as previously outlined.

NOTE: *It is not necessary to completely remove the turn signal switch. Pull the switch over the end of the shaft—no farther.*

2. Place lock cylinder in the Run position.

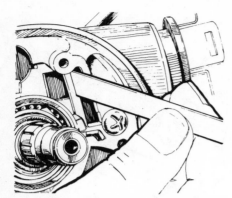

Removing the ignition lock cylinder—1973–78

3. Insert a small screwdriver into the rectangular column housing slot. Keeping the screwdriver to the right-side of the slot, break the housing flash loose and depress the spring latch at the lower end of the lock cylinder. Remove the lock cylinder.

NOTE: *When ordering a new lock cylinder, specify a cylinder assembly. This will save assembling the cylinder, washer, sleeve and adapter.*

4. To install, hold the lock cylinder sleeve and rotate the knob clockwise against the stop. Insert the cylinder into the housing, aligning the key and keyway. Hold a 0.070 in. drill bit between the lock bezel and housing. Rotate the cylinder counterclockwise, maintaining a light pressure until the drive section of the cylinder mates with the sector. Push in until the snap-ring pops into the grooves. Remove the bit. Check cylinder operation.

CAUTION: *The drill prevents forcing the lock cylinder inward beyond its normal position. The buzzer switch and spring latch*

can hold the lock cylinder in too far. Complete disassembly of the upper bearing housing is necessary to release an improperly installed lock cylinder.

1979–82 LOCK CYLINDER REMOVAL AND INSTALLATION

1. Remove the steering wheel and the turn signal switch as previously outlined. It is not necessary to completely remove the turn signal switch. Just pull the switch out far enough so it can hang out of the steering column shaft. Do not disconnect the wiring harness.

2. With the lock cylinder in the Run position, remove the lock cylinder and attaching screw and the cylinder.

3. To install, align the cylinder key with the keyway in the housing and rotate the key all the way clockwise while holding the cylinder body.

4. Insert the cylinder into the housing and install the attaching screw.

5. Install the turn signal switch and the steering wheel as previously outlined.

1973–82 IGNITION SWITCH REMOVAL AND INSTALLATION

The switch is on the steering column, behind the instrument panel.

1. Lower the steering column, making sure that it is supported.

CAUTION: *Extreme care is necessary to prevent damage to the collapsible column.*

2. Make sure the switch is in the Lock position. If the lock cylinder is out, pull the switch rod up to the stop, then go down one detent.

3. Remove the two screws and the switch.

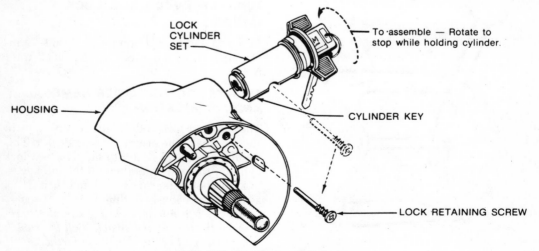

1979–82 lock cylinder replacement

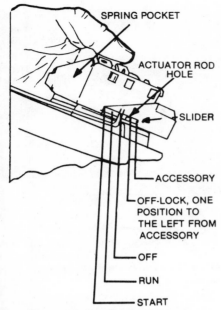

SPRING POCKET

ACTUATOR ROD HOLE

SLIDER

ACCESSORY

OFF-LOCK, ONE POSITION TO THE LEFT FROM ACCESSORY

OFF

RUN

START

1973 and later ignition switch details

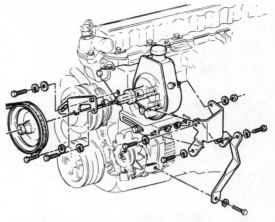

Typical 250 six cylinder power steering pump mounting details

4. Before installation, make sure the switch is in the Lock position. The switch can be moved to the Lock position using a screwdriver inserted into the locking rod slot.

5. Install the switch using the original screws.

CAUTION: *Use of screws that are too long could prevent the column from collapsing on impact.*

6. Replace the column.

Power Steering Pump

See Chapter 1 for fluid level checking and drive belt tension adjustment.

REMOVAL AND INSTALLATION

1. Disconnect the hoses at the pump. When the hoses are disconnected, secure the ends in a raised position to prevent leakage. Cap the ends of the hoses to prevent the entrance of dirt.

2. Cap the pump fittings.

3. Loosen the bracket-to-pump mounting nuts.

4. Remove the pump drive belt.

5. Remove the bracket-to-pump bolts and remove the pump from the truck.

6. Installation is the reverse of removal. Fill the reservoir and bleed the pump by turning the pulley counterclockwise (as viewed from the front) until bubbles stop forming. Bleed the system. Adjust the belt tension.

BLEEDING THE SYSTEM

1. Fill the reservoir to the proper level and let the fluid remain undisturbed for at least 2 minutes.

2. Start the engine and run it for only about 2 seconds.

3. Add fluid as necessary.

4. Repeat Steps 1–3 until the level remains constant.

5. Raise the front of the vehicle so that the front wheels are off the ground. Set the parking brake and block both rear wheels front and rear. Manual transmissions should be in Neutral; automatic transmissions should be in Park.

6. Start the engine and run it at approximately 1,500 rpm.

7. Turn the wheels (off the ground) to the right and left, lightly contacting the stops.

8. Add fluid as necessary.

9. Lower the vehicle and turn the wheels right and left on the ground.

10. Check the level and refill as necessary.

11. If the fluid is extremely foamy, let the truck stand for a few minutes with the engine off and repeat the above procedure. Check the belt tension and check for a bent or loose pulley. The pulley should not wobble with the engine running.

12. Check that no hoses are contacting any parts of the truck, particularly sheet metal.

13. Check the level and refill as necessary. This step and the next are very important. When filling, follow Steps 1–10 above.

14. Check for air in the fluid. Aerated fluid appears milky. If air is present, repeat the above operations. If it is obvious that the pump will not respond to bleeding after sev-

eral attempts, a pressure test may be required.

Tie Rod Ends
REMOVAL AND INSTALLATION

1. Raise the front of the truck and support it safely on jack stands.
2. Remove the tie rod end stud cotter pin and nut.
3. You can use a tie rod end ball joint removal tool to loosen the stud, or you can loosen it by tapping on the steering arm with a hammer while using a heavy hammer as a backup.
4. Remove the inner stud in the same way.
5. Loosen the tie rod adjuster sleeve clamp nuts.
6. Unscrew the tie rod end from the threaded sleeve. The threads may be left or right hand threads. Count the number of turns required to remove it.
7. To install, grease the threads and turn the new tie rod end in as many turns as were needed to remove it. This will give approximately correct toe-in. Tighten the clamp bolts.

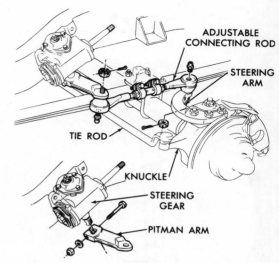

Typical four wheel drive steering linkage

8. Tighten the stud nuts to 45 ft. lbs. and install new cotter pins. You may tighten the nut to align the cotter pin, but don't loosen it.
9. Adjust the toe-in.

Brakes

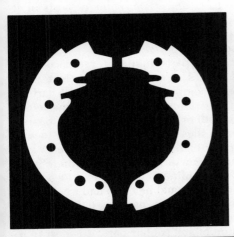

BRAKE SYSTEM

All models have a split hydraulic braking system. This system has separate hydraulic circuits for the front and rear brakes, using a master cylinder with separate reservoirs. If a wheel cylinder or brake line should fail in either circuit, the other two brakes will still work.

1969–70 models have 11 in. diameter front drum brakes of the duo-servo self-adjusting type. A vacuum power booster and wider front brakes (two wheel drive only) were optional. 1971–82 models have, as standard, 11.86 in. diameter front disc brakes with a vacuum power booster.

All models have drum rear brakes of the duo-servo self-adjusting type. These usually have finned drums for better cooling. Drum diameter is 11 in. for 1969–76 two wheel drive and 1969–74 four wheel drive models; 11.15 in. for the later models. The larger rear brakes were optional on 1974 four wheel drive models. The foot pedal parking brake works on the rear brakes.

All brakes on these trucks are self adjusting; there are no maintenance adjustments necessary except for the parking brake cable.

HYDRAULIC SYSTEM

Master Cylinder
REMOVAL AND INSTALLATION

1. Wipe off the master cylinder and its lines to remove excess dirt and then place cloths under the unit to absorb spilled fluid.
2. Remove the hydraulic lines from the master cylinder and plug them to prevent the entrance of foreign material.
3. Disconnect the brake pushrod from the brake pedal (non-power brakes).
4. Remove the attaching bolts and remove the master cylinder from the firewall or the brake booster.

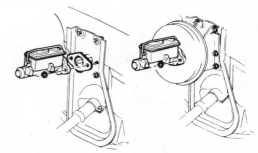

Typical master cylinder installations

5. Connect the non-power pushrod to the brake pedal with the pin and retainer.

6. Connect the brake lines and fill the master cylinder reservoirs to the proper level.

7. Bleed the brake system as outlined later in this section.

OVERHAUL

In most years, there are two sources for master cylinders, Delco-Moraine and Bendix. The Bendix unit can readily be identified by the external secondary stop bolt on the bottom, which is not present on the Delco-Moraine unit. Some early models use a Wagner unit which has the cover secured by a bolt. Master cylinders bearing identifying code letters should only be replaced with cylinders bearing the same code letters. Secondary pistons are also coded by rings or grooves on the shank or center section of the piston, and should only be replaced with pistons having the same code. The primary pistons also are of two types. One has a deep socket for the pushrod and the other has a very shallow socket. Be sure to replace pistons with identical parts. Failure to do this could result in a malfunction.

NOTE: *This is a tedious, time-consuming procedure. You can save yourself the trouble if you buy a rebuilt or new master cylinder.*

1. Remove the secondary piston stop screw at the bottom of the master cylinder front reservoir.

2. Position the master cylinder in a vise covering the jaws with cloth to prevent damage. (Do not tighten the vise too tightly.)

3. Remove the lock ring from the inside of the piston bore. Once this is done, the primary piston assembly may be removed.

4. The secondary piston, piston spring, and the retainer may be removed by blowing compressed air through the stop screw hole. Always use an old towel to catch the piston as it is forced from the cylinder. Do this very carefully as the piston sometimes comes out quite fast as a result of the high air pressure. If compressed air is not available, the piston may be removed with a small piece of wire. Bend the wire ¼ in. from the end into a right angle. Hook this end to the edge of the secondary piston and pull it from the bore. The brass tube fitting insert should not be removed unless it is being replaced.

5. Inspect the piston bore for corrosion or other obstructions. Make certain that the outer ports are clean and the fluid reservoirs are free of foreign matter. Check the by-pass and the compensating ports to see if they are clogged.

6. Remove the primary seal, seal protector, and secondary seals from the secondary piston.

NOTE: *Clean master cylinder parts in alcohol or brake fluid. Never use mineral-based cleaning solvents as these will destroy rubber parts.*

Clean all parts in denatured alcohol or brake fluid. Use a soft brush to clean metal parts and compressed air to dry all parts. If corrosion is found inside the housing, either crocus cloth or fine emery paper can be used to remove these deposits. Remember to wash all parts after this cleaning. Be sure to keep the parts clean until assembly. If there is any doubt of cleanliness, wash the part again. All rubber parts should be clean and free of fluid. Check each rubber part for cuts, nicks, or other damage. If there is any doubt as to the condition of any rubber part, it is best to replace it.

NOTE: *Since there are differences between master cylinders, it is important that the assemblies are identified correctly. There is a two-letter metal stamp located at the end of the master cylinder. The stamp indicates the displacement capabilities of the particular master cylinder. If the master cylinder is replaced, it must be replaced with a cylinder with the same markings.*

7. Install the new secondary piston assembly.

NOTE: *The seal which is nearest the flat end has its lips facing toward the flat end. On Delco units, the seal in the second groove has its lips facing toward the com-*

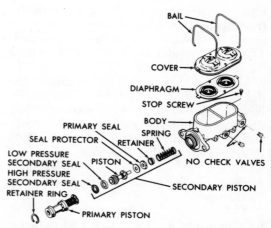

Exploded view of a typical master cylinder

pensating holes of the secondary piston. On Bendix units, the seal is an O-ring.

8. Install the new primary seal and seal protector over the end of the secondary piston opposite the secondary seals. It should be positioned so that the flat side of the seal seats against the flange of the piston with the compensating holes.

NOTE: *The seal protector isn't used on 1977 and later models.*

9. Install the complete primary piston assembly included in the repair kit.

10. Coat the master cylinder bore and the primary and secondary seals with brake fluid. Position the secondary seal spring retainer into the secondary piston spring.

11. Place the retainer and spring over the end of the secondary piston so that the retainer is placed inside the lips of the primary seal.

12. Seat the secondary piston. It may be necessary to manipulate the piston to get it to seat.

13. Position the master cylinder with the open end up and coat the primary and secondary seal on the primary piston with brake fluid. Push the primary piston into the bore of the master cylinder. Hold the piston and position the lock ring.

14. Still holding the piston down, install and tighten the stop screw to a torque of 25 to 40 in. lbs.

15. Install the reservoir cover and also the cover on the master cylinder and its retaining clip.

16. Bleed the master cylinder of air. Do this by positioning the cylinder with the front slightly down, filling it with brake fluid, and working the primary piston until all the bubbles in the expelled fluid are gone.

Combination Valve

This valve is used on all models with disc brakes (1971 and later). It is non-adjustable and non-serviceable. It can be found by following the lines from the master cylinder. The combination valve itself contains a metering valve that restricts flow to the front brakes until the rear brakes overcome the force of their retracting springs to prevent front brake lockup, a pressure differential warning switch which activates a warning light if either the front or rear hydraulic circuit is losing pressure, and a proportioning valve which limits hydraulic pressure to the rear brakes to prevent rear wheel lockup.

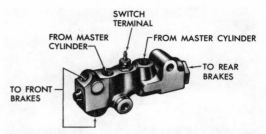

Brake combination valve used with disc brakes

The pressure differential warning switch will reset itself automatically when the brakes are used after a malfunction causing the warning light to go on has been corrected.

When the brake hydraulic system is bled of air, the metering valve pin on the end of the combination valve must be held in a slight amount to allow fluid flow to the front brakes.

Bleeding the Brakes

The purpose of bleeding the brakes is to expel air trapped in the hydraulic system. The system must be bled whenever the pedal feels spongy, indicating that compressible air has entered the system. It must also be bled whenever the system has been opened or leaking. You will need a helper for this job.

NOTE: *There are gadgets on the market to make it possible for one man to do this job. Usually they are a bleeder hose with a one-way check valve.*

Start with the wheel closest to the master cylinder and work out. With disc brakes, the metering valve pin on the end of the combination valve must be held in slightly to allow fluid flow to the front brakes.

1. Clean the bleeder screw at each wheel.

2. Attach a length of hose to the bleeder screw and submerge the end in a container of clean brake fluid.

3. Fill the master cylinder with brake fluid.

NOTE: *Brake fluid picks up moisture from the air. Don't leave the master cylinder or*

J-23709

To bleed the front disc brakes, you must hold in the metering valve pin on the end of the combination valve. Something similar to this special tool can be fabricated

Bleeding the front disc brakes

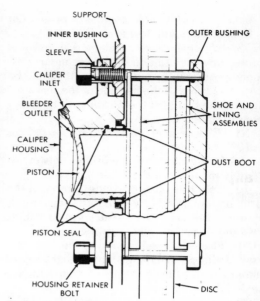

Disc brake details

the fluid container uncovered any longer than necessary. Never reuse brake fluid which has been taken from the brake lines. Always use new fluid. Also, be very careful not to spill any brake fluid on any painted surface. It eats paint.

Check the level often during bleeding.

4. Pump up the pedal and hold it.

5. Open the bleeder screw about ¾ turn. Have your helper press down on the pedal. Close the bleeder screw before the pedal reaches the end of its travel. Have your helper slowly release the pedal. Continue until no more air bubbles are forced out on application of the pedal.

6. Repeat the procedure on the remaining three brakes.

NOTE: *It sometimes helps to tap the disc brake caliper with a soft hammer while fluid is flowing when bleeding the front disc brakes.*

FRONT DISC BRAKES

Brake Pads

INSPECTION

Support the front suspension or axle on jack stands and remove the wheels. Look in at the ends of the caliper to check the lining thickness of the outer pad. Look through the inspection hole in the top of the caliper to check the thickness of the inner pad. Minimum acceptable pad thickness is $1/32$ in. from the rivet heads on original equipment riveted linings and $1/32$ in. lining thickness on bonded linings.

NOTE: *These manufacturer's specifications may not agree with your state inspection law.*

All original equipment pads are the riveted type; unless you want to remove the pads to measure the actual thickness from the rivet heads, you will have to make the limit for visual inspection $1/16$ in. or more. The same applies if you don't know what kind of lining you have. 1974 and later original equipment pads and GM replacement pads have an integral wear sensor. This is a spring steel tab on the rear edge of the inner pad which produces a squeal by rubbing against the rotor to warn that the pads have reached their wear limit.

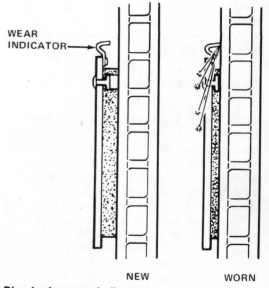

Disc brake wear indicators

CAUTION: *The squeal will eventually stop if the worn pads aren't replaced. Should this happen, replace the pads immediately to prevent expensive rotor (disc) damage.*

REPLACEMENT

The caliper has to be removed to replace the pads, so go on to that procedure. Skip steps 8–10, as there is no need to detach the brake line.

Caliper

REMOVAL AND INSTALLATION

1. Remove the cover on the master cylinder and remove enough fluid out of the reservoirs to bring the level to ⅓ full. This prevents spilling fluid when the piston is pushed back later. Discard the fluid.
2. Raise and support the vehicle. Remove the front wheels and tires.
3. Push the brake piston back into its bore using a C-clamp to pull the caliper outward.
4. Remove the two bolts which hold the caliper and then lift the caliper off the disc.
CAUTION: *Do not let the caliper assembly hang by the brake hose.*
5. Remove the inboard and outboard pads.
NOTE: *If the pads are to be reinstalled, mark them inside and outside.*
6. Remove the pad support spring from the piston.
7. Remove the two sleeves from the inside ears of the caliper and the four rubber bushings from the grooves in the caliper ears.

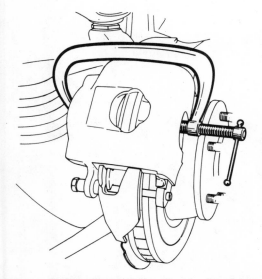

Using a C-clamp to seat the disc brake piston

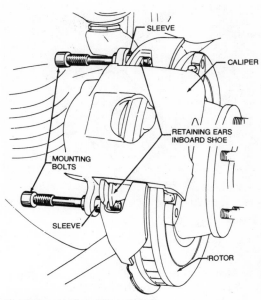

Front disc brake caliper details

8. Remove the hose from the steel brake line and tape the fittings to prevent foreign material from entering the line or the hoses.
9. Remove the retainer from the hose fitting.
10. Remove the hose from the frame bracket and pull off the caliper with the hose attached.
NOTE: *Check the inside of the caliper for fluid leakage; if there is any, the caliper should be overhauled.*
CAUTION: *Do not use compressed air to clean the inside of the caliper as this may unseat the dust boot.*
11. Connect the brake line to start reinstallation. Lubricate the sleeves, rubber bushings, bushing grooves, and the end of the mounting bolts using silicone lubricant.
12. Install new bushings in the caliper ears along with new sleeves. The sleeve should be replaced so that the end toward the shoe is flush with the machined surface of the ear.
13. Position the support spring and the inner pad into the center cavity of the piston. The outboard pad has ears which are bent over to keep the pad in position while the inboard pad has ears on the top end which fit over the caliper retaining bolts. A spring which is inside the brake piston holds the bottom edge of the inboard pad.
14. Push down on the inner pad until it lays flat against the caliper. It is important to push the piston all the way into the caliper if new linings are installed or the caliper will

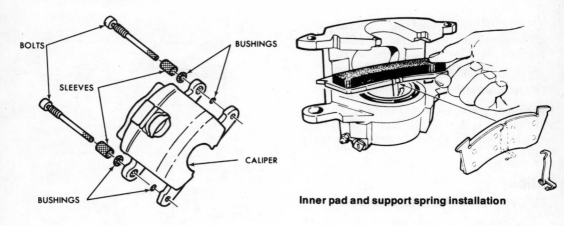

Inner pad and support spring installation

Caliper lubrication points

▓▓ LUBRICATE AREAS INDICATED

not fit over the rotor. The pad wear sensor must be to the rear of the vehicle.

15. Position the outboard pad with the ears of the shoes over the caliper ears and the tab at the bottom engaged in the caliper cutout.

16. With the two pads in position, place the caliper over the brake disc and align the holes in the caliper with those of the mounting bracket.

CAUTION: *Make certain that the brake hose is not twisted or kinked.*

17. Install the mounting bracket bolts through the sleeves in the inboard caliper ears and through the mounting bracket, making sure that the ends of the bolts pass under the retaining ears on the inboard pad. Tighten the bolts to 35 ft. lbs.

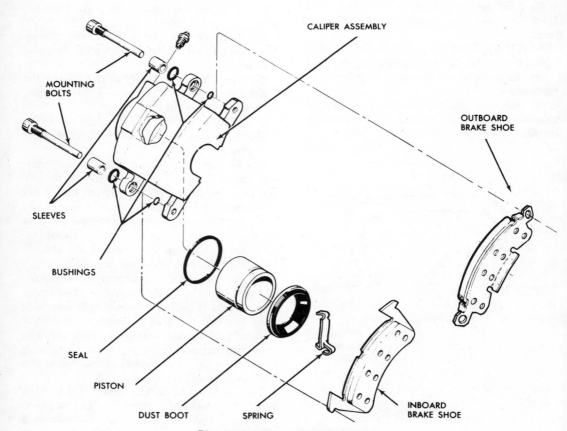

Disc brake caliper exploded view

18. Pump the brake pedal to seat the pads against the rotor. Don't do this unless both calipers are in place. Use a pair of channel lock pliers to bend over the upper ears of the outer pad so that it isn't loose.

19. Install the wheel and lower the truck.

20. Add fluid to the master cylinder reservoirs so that they are ¼ in. from the top.

21. Test the brake pedal by pumping it to obtain a "hard" pedal. Check the fluid level again and add fluid as necessary. Do not move the vehicle until a "hard" pedal is obtained.

OVERHAUL

Use only denatured alcohol or brake fluid to clean caliper parts. Never use any mineral based cleaning solvents such as gasoline or kerosene as they will deteriorate rubber parts.

1. Remove the caliper, clean it and place it on a clean work surface.

2. Remove the brake hose from the caliper and discard the copper gasket. Check the brake hose for cracks or deterioration. Replace the hose as necessary.

3. Drain the brake fluid from the caliper.

4. Pad the interior of the caliper with a shop towel and then apply compressed air to the caliper inlet hose.

WARNING: *Do not place your hands or fingers in front of the piston in an attempt to catch it. Use just enough air pressure to ease the piston out of the bore.*

An alternate method is to apply gentle pressure to the brake pedal with the brake line connected to the caliper.

5. Remove the piston dust boot by prying it out with a screwdriver. Use caution when performing this procedure.

6. Remove the piston seal from the caliper piston bore using a small piece of wood or plastic. DO NOT use any type of metal tool for this procedure.

7. Remove the bleeder valve from the caliper.

IMPORTANT: *Dust boot, piston seal, rubber bushings and sleeves are included in every rebuilding kit. These should be replaced at every caliper rebuild.*

8. Clean all parts and dry them completely, using compressed air if possible.

NOTE: *The use of lubricated shop air hoses may inject oil film into the assembly; use caution when using such hoses.*

9. Examine the mounting bolts for rust or corrosion. Replace them as necessary.

10. Examine the piston for scoring, nicks,

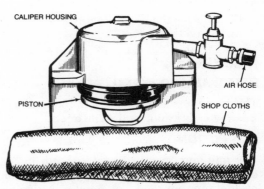

Using compressed air to remove the disc brake caliper piston. Always use a towel to catch the piston

or worn plating. If any of these conditions are present, replace the piston.

CAUTION: *Do not use any type of abrasive on the piston.*

11. Check the piston bore. Small defects can be removed with crocus cloth. Do not use emery cloth. If the bore cannot be cleaned in this manner, replace the caliper.

12. Lubricate the piston bore and the new piston seal with brake fluid. Place the seal in the caliper bore groove.

13. Lubricate the piston and position the new boot into the groove in the piston so that the fold faces the open end of the piston.

14. Place the piston into the caliper bore using caution not to unseat the seal. Force the piston to the bottom of the bore.

15. Place the dust boot in the caliper counterbore and seat the boot. Make sure that the boot is positioned correctly and evenly.

16. Install the brake hose in the caliper inlet using a new copper gasket.

NOTE: *The hose must be positioned in the caliper locating gate to assure proper positioning of the caliper.*

Caliper piston dust boot installation

17. Replace the bleeder screw.
18. Bleed the system.

Disc (Rotor)
REMOVAL AND INSTALLATION

This procedure is in Chapter 1, under Wheel Bearing Lubrication and Adjustment.

INSPECTION

The minimum wear thickness, 1.215 in., is cast into each disc hub. This is a minimum wear dimension and not a refinish dimension. If the thickness of the disc after refinishing will be 1.230 in. or less, it must be replaced. Refinishing is required whenever the disc surface shows scoring or severe rust scale. Scoring not deeper than .015 in. in depth can be corrected by refinishing.

NOTE: *Some discs have an anti-squeal groove. This should not be mistaken for scoring.*

REAR BRAKES

Drum
REMOVAL AND INSTALLATION

Drums on all models can be removed by raising the vehicle, removing the wheel lugs and the tire, and pulling the drum from the brake assembly. If the brake drums have been scored deeply, the brake adjuster must be backed off so that the brake shoes will retract from the drum. Some drums are retained by two screws to the hub, and can be removed after removing the screws.

The adjuster can be backed off by inserting a brake adjusting tool or screwdriver through the access hole provided. Hold the adjuster lever away from the starwheel; turn the starwheel. In some cases the access hole is in the brake drum. A metal cover plate is over the hole. This may be removed by using a hammer and chisel.

NOTE: *Make sure all metal particles are removed from the brake drum before reassembly.*

To install, reverse the removal procedure.

CAUTION: *Do not blow the brake dust out of the drums with compressed air. Powdered asbestos has been found to be a cancer-producing agent.*

INSPECTION
Lining

Remove the drum and inspect the lining thickness on both brake shoes. A front brake lining should be replaced if it is less than ⅛ in. thick at the lowest point on the brake shoe. The wear limit for rear brake linings is $1/16$.

NOTE: *Brake shoes should always be replaced in axle sets. The wear specifications given may disagree with your state inspection rules.*

Drum

When a drum is removed, it should be inspected for cracks, scores, or other imperfections. These must be corrected before the drum is replaced.

CAUTION: *If the drum is found to be cracked, replace it. Do not attempt to service a cracked drum.*

Minor drum score marks can be removed with fine emery cloth. Heavy score marks must be removed by "turning the drum." This is removing metal from the entire inner surface of the drum on a lathe in order to level the surface. Automotive machine shops and some large parts stores are equipped to perform this operation.

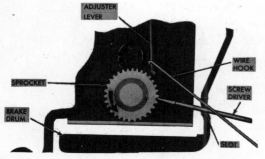

Backing off the brake adjuster to remove a worn drum

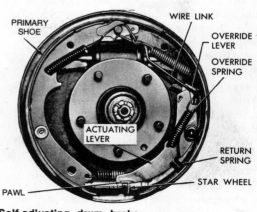

Self-adjusting drum brake

If the drum is not scored, it should be polished with fine emery cloth before replacement. If the drum is resurfaced, it should not be enlarged more than 0.060 in.

NOTE: *Your state inspection law may disagree with this specification.*

It is advisable, while the drums are off, to check them for out-of-round. An inside micrometer is necessary for an exact measurement; therefore unless this tool is available, the drums should be taken to a machine shop to be checked. Any drum which is more than 0.006 in. out-of-round will result in an inaccurate brake adjustment and other problems, and should be refinished or replaced.

NOTE: *Make all measurements at right angles to each other and at the open and closed edges of the drum machined surface.*

Shoes

REMOVAL AND INSTALLATION

1. Jack up and securely support the vehicle.

2. Loosen the parking brake equalizer enough to remove all tension on the brake cable (rear brakes only).

3. Remove the brake drums.

CAUTION: *The brake pedal must not be depressed while the drums are removed.*

4. Using a brake tool, remove the shoe springs. You can do this with ordinary tools, but it isn't easy.

5. Remove the self-adjuster actuator spring.

6. Remove the link from the secondary shoe by pulling it from the anchor pin.

7. Remove the hold-down pins. These are the brackets which run through the backing plate. They can be removed with a pair of pliers. Reach around the rear of the backing plate and hold the back of the pin. Turn the top of the pin retainer 45° with the pliers. This will align the elongated tang with the slot in the retainer. Be careful, as the pin is spring-loaded and may fly off when released. Use the same procedure for the other pin assembly.

8. Remove the adjuster actuator assembly.

NOTE: *Since the actuator, pivot, and override spring are considered an assembly it is not recommended that they be disassembled.*

9. Remove the shoes from the backing plate. Make sure that you have a secure grip

Removing the shoe springs

on the assembly as the bottom spring will still exert pressure on the shoes. Slowly let the tops of the shoes come together and the tension will decrease and the adjuster and spring may be removed.

NOTE: *If the linings are to be reused, mark them for identification.*

10. Remove the rear parking brake lever from the secondary shoe. Using a pair of pliers, pull back on the spring which surrounds the cable. At the same time, remove the cable from the notch in the shoe bracket. Make sure that the spring does not snap back or injury may result.

11. Use a cloth to remove dirt from the brake drum. Check the drums for scoring and cracks. Have the drums checked for out-of-round and service the drums as necessary.

12. Check the wheel cylincers by carefully

Removing the shoe hold-down pins

pulling the lower edges of the wheel cylinder boots away from the cylinders. If there is excessive leakage, the inside of the cylinder will be moist with fluid. If there is any leakage at all, a cylinder overhaul is in order. DO NOT delay, as a brake failure could result.

NOTE: *A small amount of fluid will be present to act as a lubricant for the wheel cylinder pistons.*

13. Check the flange plate, which is located around the axle, for leakage of differential lubricant. This condition cannot be overlooked as the lubricant will be absorbed into the brake linings and brake failure will result. Replace the seals as necessary. See Chapter 7 for details.

NOTE: *If new linings are being installed, check them against the old units for length and type.*

14. Check the new linings for imperfections.

CAUTION: *It is important to keep your hands free of dirt and grease when handling the brake shoes. Foreign matter will be absorbed into the linings and result in unpredictable braking.*

15. Lightly lubricate the parking brake cable and the end of the parking brake lever where it enters the shoe. Use high temperature waterproof grease or special brake lube.

16. Install the parking brake lever into the secondary shoe with the attaching bolt, spring washer, lockwasher, and nut. It is important that the lever move freely before the shoe is attached. Move the assembly and check for proper action.

17. Lubricate the adjusting screw and make sure that it works freely. Sometimes the adjusting screw will not move due to lack of lubricant or dirt contamination and the brakes will not adjust. In this calse, the adjuster should be disassembled, thoroughly cleaned, and lubricated before installation.

18. Connect the brake shoe spring to the bottom portion of both shoes. Make certain that the brake linings are installed to the correct manner, the primary and secondary shoe in the correct position. If you are not sure remove the other brake drum and check it.

19. Install the adjusting mechanism below the spring and separate the top of the shoes.

NOTE: *Make the following checks before installation;*

a. Be certain that the right-hand thread adjusting screw is on the left-hand side of the vehicle and the left-hand screw is on the right-hand side of the vehicle;

b. Make sure that the star adjuster is aligned with the adjusting hole.

c. The adjuster should be installed with the starwheel nearest the secondary shoe and the tension spring away from the adjusting mechanism;

d. If the original linings are being reused, put them back in their original locations.

20. Install the parking brake cable.

21. Position the primary shoe (the shoe with the short lining) first. Secure it with the hold-down pin and with its spring by pushing the pin through the back of the backing plate and, while holding it with one hand, install the spring and the retainer using a pair of needle-nose pliers. Install the adjuster actuator assembly.

22. Install the parking brake strut and the strut spring by pulling back the spring with pliers and engaging the end of the cable onto the brake strut and then releasing the spring.

23. Place the small metal guide plate over the anchor pin and position the self-adjuster wire cable eye.

CAUTION: *The wire should not be positioned with the conventional brake installation tool or damage will result. It should be positioned on the actuator assembly first and then placed over the anchor pin stud by hand with the adjuster assembly in full downward position.*

24. Install the actuator return spring. DO NOT pry the actuator lever to install the return spring. Position it using the end of a screwdriver or another suitable tool.

NOTE: *If the return springs are bent or in*

Brake backing plate lubrication points

Checking the actuator lever

any way distorted, they should be replaced.

25. Using the brake installation tool, place the brake return springs in position. Install the primary spring first over the anchor pin and then place the spring from the secondary shoe over the wire link end.

26. Pull the brake shoes away from the backing plate and apply a *thin* coat of high temperature, waterproof, grease or special brake lube to the brake shoe contact points.

CAUTION: *Only a small amount is necessary. Keep the lubricant away from the brake linings.*

27. Once the complete assembly has been installed, check the operation of the self-adjuster mechanism by moving the actuating lever by hand.

28. Adjust the brakes.

Drum installation

a. Turn the star adjuster until the drum slides over the brake shoes with only a slight drag. Remove the drum;

b. Turn the adjuster back 1¼ turns.

c. Install the drum and wheel and lower the vehicle;

NOTE: *If the adjusting hole in the drum has been punched out, make certain that the insert has been removed from the inside of the drum. Install a rubber hole cover to keep dirt out of the brake assembly. Also, be sure that the drums are installed in the same position as they were when removed—with the locating tang in line with the location hole in the axle shaft flange.*

d. Make the final adjustment by backing the vehicle and pumping the brakes until the self-adjusting mechanisms adjust to the proper level and the brake pedal reaches satisfactory height.

29. Adjusting the parking brake. Details are given later.

Wheel Cylinders
REMOVAL

1. Raise and support the axle.

2. Remove the wheel and tire.

3. Back off the brake adjustment if necessary and remove the drum.

4. Disconnect and plug the brake line.

5. Remove the brake shoe pull-back springs.

6. Remove the screws securing the wheel cylinder to the backing plate.

7. Disengage the wheel cylinder pushrods from the brake shoes and remove the wheel cylinder.

OVERHAUL

As with master cylinders, overhaul kits for wheel cylinders are readily available. When rebuilding and installing wheel cylinders, avoid getting any contaminants into the system. Always install clean, new high-quality brake fluid. If dirty or improper fluid has been used, it will be necessary to drain the entire system, flush the system with proper brake fluid, replace all rubber components, refill, and bleed the system.

1. Remove the rubber boots from the cylinder ends with pliers. Discard the boots.

2. Remove and discard the pistons and cups.

3. Wash the cylinder and metal parts in denatured alcohol or clean brake fluid.

CAUTION: *Never use a mineral-based sol-*

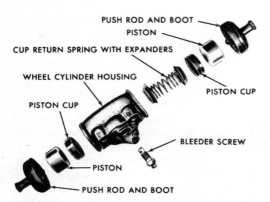

Exploded view of a typical drum brake wheel cylinder

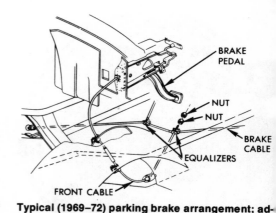

Typical (1969–72) parking brake arrangement; adjustment is made at the equalizer nut

vent such as gasoline, kerosene, or paint thinner for cleaning purposes. These solvents will swell rubber components and quickly deteriorate them.

4. Allow the parts to air dry or use compressed air. Do not use rags for cleaning since lint will remain in the cylinder bore.

5. Inspect the piston and replace it if it shows scratches.

6. Lubricate the cylinder bore and counterbore with clean brake fluid.

7. Install the rubber cups (flat side out) and then the pistons (flat side in).

8. Insert new boots into the counterbores by hand. Do not lubricate the boots.

INSTALLATION

1. Installation is the reverse of removal. Adjust the brakes and bleed the system.

Wheel Bearings

REMOVAL AND INSTALLATION, PACKING, ADJUSTMENT

All front wheel bearing service is covered in Chapter 1 under Wheel Bearing Lubrication and Adjustment. Rear wheel bearings are covered in Chapter 7.

PARKING BRAKE

ADJUSTMENT

Before attempting parking brake adjustment, make sure that the rear brakes are fully adjusted by making several stops in reverse.

1. Raise and support the rear axle. Release the parking brake.

2. Apply the pedal one click (four clicks for 1976–82).

3. Adjust the cable equalizer nut under the truck until a moderate drag can be felt when the rear wheels are turned forward.

4. Release the parking brake and check that there is no drag when the wheels are turned forward.

NOTE: *If the parking brake cable is replaced, prestretch it by applying the parking brake hard about three times before attempting adjustment.*

Body

10

You can repair most minor auto body damage yourself. Minor damage usually falls into one of several categories: (1) small scratches and dings in the paint that can be repaired without the use of body filler, (2) deep scratches and dents that require body filler, but do not require pulling, or hammering metal back into shape and (3) rust-out repairs. The repair sequences illustrated in this chapter are typical of these types of repairs. If you want to get involved in more complicated repairs including pulling or hammering sheet metal back into shape, you will probably need more detailed instructions. Chilton's *Minor Auto Body Repair, 2nd Edition* is a comprehensive guide to repairing auto body damage yourself.

TOOLS AND SUPPLIES

The list of tools and equipment you may need to fix minor body damage ranges from very basic hand tools to a wide assortment of specialized body tools. Most minor scratches, dings and rust holes can be fixed using an electric drill, wire wheel or grinder attachment, half-round plastic file, sanding block, various grades of sandpaper (#36, which is coarse through #600, which is fine) in both wet and dry types, auto body plastic,

primer, touch-up paint, spreaders, newspaper and masking tape.

Most manufacturers of auto body repair products began supplying materials to professionals. Their knowledge of the best, most-used products has been translated into body repair kits for the do-it-yourselfer. Kits are available from a number of manufacturers and contain the necessary materials in the required amounts for the repair identified on the package.

Kits are available for a wide variety of uses, including:

- Rusted out metal
- All purpose kit for dents and holes
- Dents and deep scratches
- Fiberglass repair kit
- Epoxy kit for restyling.

Kits offer the advantage of buying what you need for the job. There is little waste and little chance of materials going bad from not being used. The same manufacturers also merchandise all of the individual products used—spreaders, dent pullers, fiberglass cloth, polyester resin, cream hardener, body filler, body files, sandpaper, sanding discs and holders, primer, spray paint, etc.

CAUTION: *Most of the products you will be using contain harmful chemicals, so be extremely careful. Always read the complete label before opening the containers. When* *you put them away for future use, be sure they are out of children's reach!*

Most auto body repair kits contain all the materials you need to do the job right in the kit. So, if you have a small rust spot or dent you want to fix, check the contents of the kit before you run out and buy any additional tools.

ALIGNING BODY PANELS

Doors

There are several methods of adjusting doors. Your vehicle will probably use one of those illustrated.

Whenever a door is removed and is to be reinstalled, you should matchmark the position of the hinges on the door pillars. The holes of the hinges and/or the hinge attaching points are usually oversize to permit alignment of doors. The striker plate is also moveable, through oversize holes, permitting up-and-down, in-and-out and fore-and-aft movement. Fore-and-aft movement is made by adding or subtracting shims from behind the striker and pillar post. The striker should be adjusted so that the door closes fully and remains closed, yet enters the lock freely.

DOOR HINGES

Don't try to cover up poor door adjustment with a striker plate adjustment. The gap on each side of the door should be equal and uniform and there should be no metal-to-metal contact as the door is opened or closed.

1. Determine which hinge bolts must be loosened to move the door in the desired direction.

2. Loosen the hinge bolt(s) just enough to allow the door to be moved with a padded pry bar.

3. Move the door a small amount and check the fit, after tightening the bolts. Be sure that there is no bind or interference with adjacent panels.

4. Repeat this until the door is properly positioned, and tighten all the bolts securely.

Hood, Trunk or Tailgate

As with doors, the outline of hinges should be scribed before removal. The hood and trunk can be aligned by loosening the hinge bolts in their slotted mounting holes and moving the hood or trunk lid as necessary.

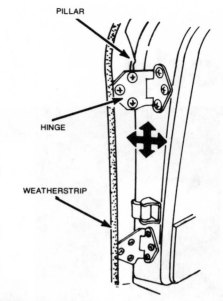

Door hinge adjustment

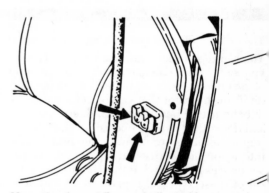

Move the door striker as indicated by arrows

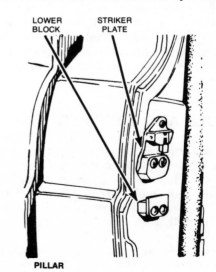

Striker plate and lower block

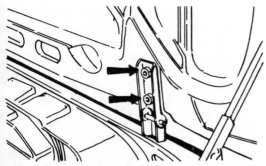

Loosen the hinge boots to permit fore-and-aft and horizontal adjustment

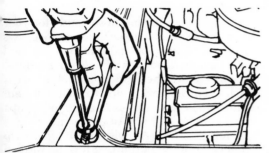

The hood is adjusted vertically by stop-screws at the front and/or rear

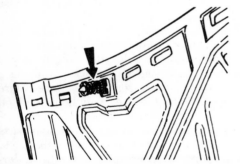

The hood pin can be adjusted for proper lock engagement

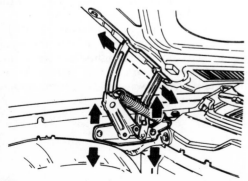

The height of the hood at the rear is adjusted by loosening the bolts that attach the hinge to the body and moving the hood up or down

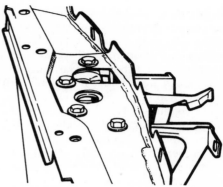

The base of the hood lock can also be repositioned slightly to give more positive lock engagement

The hood and trunk have adjustable catch locations to regulate lock engagement. Bumpers at the front and/or rear of the hood provide a vertical adjustment and the hood lockpin can be adjusted for proper engagement.

The tailgate on the station wagon can be adjusted by loosening the hinge bolts in their slotted mounting holes and moving the tailgate on its hinges. The latchplate and latch striker at the bottom of the tailgate opening can be adjusted to stop rattle. An adjustable bumper is located on each side.

RUST, UNDERCOATING, AND RUSTPROOFING

Rust

Rust is an electrochemical process. It works on ferrous metals (iron and steel) from the inside out due to exposure of unprotected surfaces to air and moisture. The possibility of rust exists practically nationwide—anywhere humidity, industrial pollution or chemical salts are present, rust can form. In coastal areas, the problem is high humidity and salt air; in snowy areas, the problem is chemical salt (de-icer) used to keep the roads clear, and in industrial areas, sulphur dioxide is present in the air from industrial pollution and is changed to sulphuric acid when it rains. The rusting process is accelerated by high temperatures, especially in snowy areas, when vehicles are driven over slushy roads and then left overnight in a heated garage.

Automotive styling also can be a contributor to rust formation. Spot welding of panels creates small pockets that trap moisture and form an environment for rust formation. Fortunately, auto manufacturers have been working hard to increase the corrosion protection of their products. Galvanized sheet metal enjoys much wider use, along with the increased use of plastic and various rust retardant coatings. Manufacturers are also designing out areas in the body where rust-forming moisture can collect.

To prevent rust, you must stop it before it gets started. On new vehicles, there are two ways to accomplish this.

First, the car or truck should be treated with a commercial rustproofing compound. There are many different brands of franchised rustproofers, but most processes involve spraying a waxy "self-healing" compound under the chassis, inside rocker panels, inside doors and fender liners and similar places where rust is likely to form. Prices for a quality rustproofing job range from $100–$250, depending on the area, the brand name and the size of the vehicle.

Ideally, the vehicle should be rustproofed as soon as possible following the purchase. The surfaces of the car or truck have begun to oxidize and deteriorate during shipping. In addition, the car may have sat on a dealer's lot or on a lot at the factory, and once the rust has progressed past the stage of light, powdery surface oxidation rustproofing is not likely to be worthwhile. Professional rustproofers feel that once rust has formed, rustproofing will simply seal in moisture already present. Most franchised rustproofing operations offer a 3–5 year warranty against rust-through, but will not support that warranty if the rustproofing is not applied within three months of the date of manufacture.

Undercoating should not be mistaken for rustproofing. Undercoating is a black, tarlike substance that is applied to the underside of a vehicle. Its basic function is to deaden noises that are transmitted from under the car. It simply cannot get into the crevices and seams where moisture tends to collect. In fact, it may clog up drainage holes and ventilation passages. Some undercoatings also tend to crack or peel with age and only create more moisture and corrosion attracting pockets.

The second thing you should do immediately after purchasing the car is apply a paint sealant. A sealant is a petroleum based product marketed under a wide variety of brand names. It has the same protective properties as a good wax, but bonds to the paint with a chemically inert layer that seals it from the air. If air can't get at the surface, oxidation cannot start.

The paint sealant kit consists of a base coat and a conditioning coat that should be applied every 6–8 months, depending on the manufacturer. The base coat must be applied before waxing, or the wax must first be removed.

Third, keep a garden hose handy for your car in winter. Use it a few times on nice days during the winter for underneath areas, and it will pay big dividends when spring arrives. Spraying under the fenders and other areas which even car washes don't reach will help remove road salt, dirt and other build-ups which help breed rust. Adjust the nozzle to a high-force spray. An old brush will help break up residue, permitting it to be washed away more easily.

It's a somewhat messy job, but worth it in the long run because rust often starts in those hidden areas.

At the same time, wash grime off the door sills and, more importantly, the under portions of the doors, plus the tailgate if you have a station wagon or truck. Applying a coat of wax to those areas at least once before and once during winter will help fend off rust.

When applying the wax to the under parts of the doors, you will note small drain holes. These holes often are plugged with undercoating or dirt. Make sure they are cleaned out to prevent water build-up inside the doors. A small punch or penknife will do the job.

Water from the high-pressure sprays in car washes sometimes can get into the housings for parking and taillights, so take a close look. If they contain water merely loosen the retaining screws and the water should run out.

Repairing Scratches and Small Dents

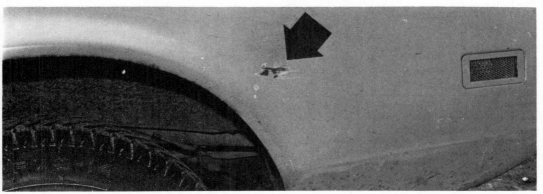

Step 1. This dent (arrow) is typical of a deep scratch or minor dent. If deep enough, the dent or scratch can be pulled out or hammered out from behind. In this case no straightening is necessary

Step 2. Using an 80-grit grinding disc on an electric drill grind the paint from the surrounding area down to bare metal. This will provide a rough surface for the body filler to grab

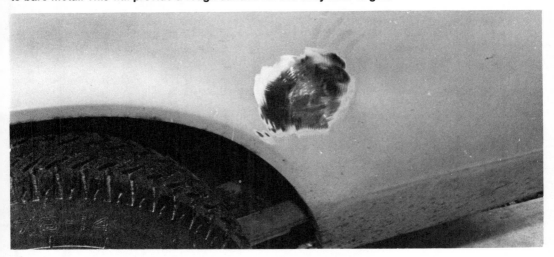

Step 3. The area should look like this when you're finished grinding

Step 4. Mix the body filler and cream hardener according to the directions

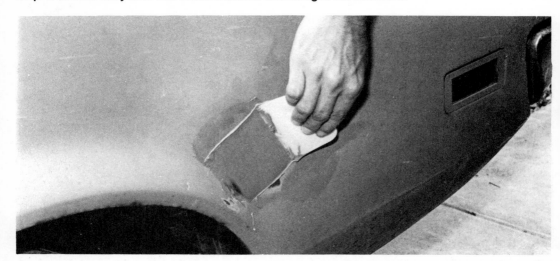

Step 5. Spread the body filler evenly over the entire area. Be sure to cover the area completely

Step 6. Let the body filler dry until the surface can just be scratched with your fingernail

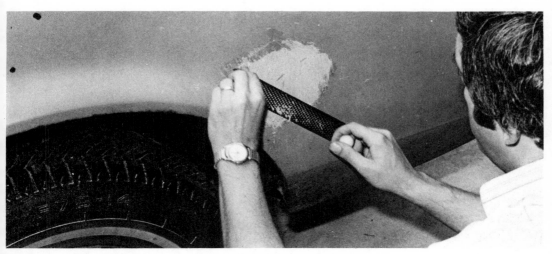

Step 7. Knock the high spots from the body filler with a body file

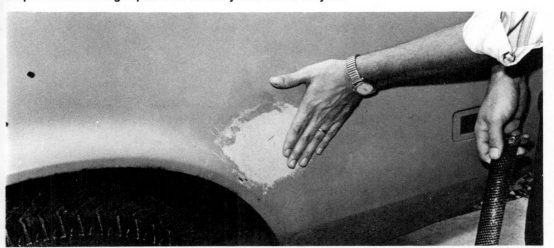

Step 8. Check frequently with the palm of your hand for high and low spots. If you wind up with low spots, you may have to apply another layer of filler

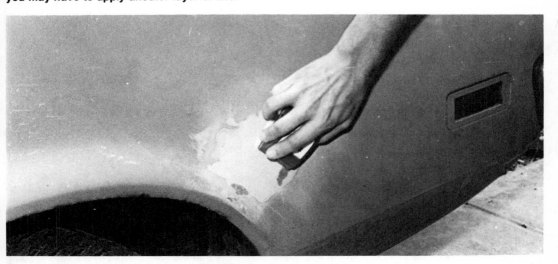

Step 9. Block sand the entire area with 320 grit paper

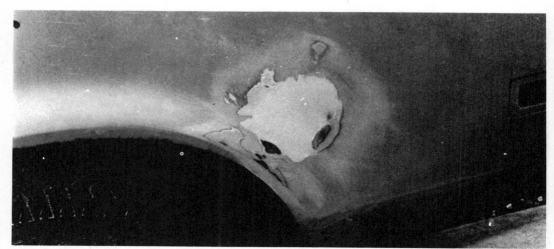

Step 10. When you're finished, the repair should look like this. Note the sand marks extending 2—3 inches out from the repaired area

Step 11. Prime the entire area with automotive primer

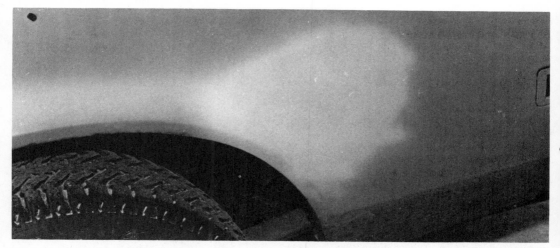

Step 12. The finished repair ready for the final paint coat. Note that the primer has covered the sanding marks (see Step 10). A repair of this size should be able to be spotpainted with good results

REPAIRING RUST HOLES

One thing you have to remember about rust: even if you grind away all the rusted metal in a panel, and repair the area with any of the kits available, *eventually* the rust will return. There are two reasons for this. One, rust is a chemical reaction that causes pressure under the repair from the inside out. That's how the blisters form. Two, the back side of the panel (and the repair) is wide open to moisture, and unpainted body filler acts like a sponge. That's why the best solution to rust problems is to remove the rusted panel and install a new one or have the rusted area cut out and a new piece of sheet metal welded in its place. The trouble with welding is the expense; sometimes it will cost more than the car or truck is worth.

One of the better solutions to do-it-yourself rust repair is the process using a fiberglass cloth repair kit (shown here). This will give a strong repair that resists cracking and moisture and is relatively easy to use. It can be used on large or small holes and also can be applied over contoured surfaces.

Step 1. Rust areas such as this are common and are easily fixed

Step 2. Grind away all traces of rust with a 24-grit grinding disc. Be sure to grind back 3—4 inches from the edge of the hole down to bare metal and be sure all traces of rust are removed

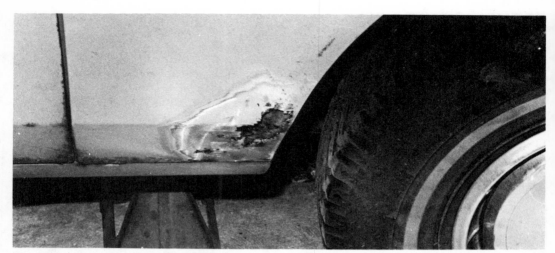

Step 3. Be sure all rust is removed from the edges of the metal. The edges must be ground back to un-rusted metal

Step 4. If you are going to use release film, cut a piece about 2″ larger than the area you have sanded. Place the film over the repair and mark the sanded area on the film. Avoid any unnecessary wrinkling of the film

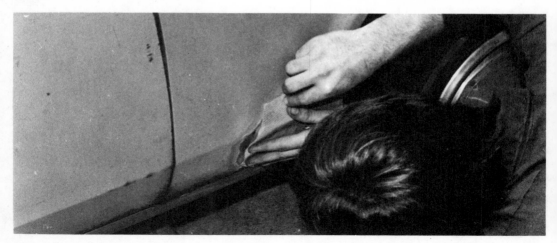

Step 5. Cut 2 pieces of fiberglass matte. One piece should be about 1″ smaller than the sanded area and the second piece should be 1″ smaller than the first. Use sharp scissors to avoid loose ends

Step 6. Check the dimensions of the release film and cloth by holding them up to the repair area

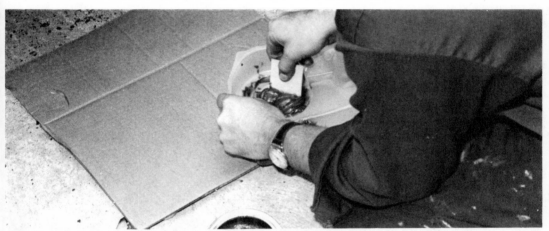

Step 7. Mix enough repair jelly and cream hardener in the mixing tray to saturate the fiberglass material or fill the repair area. Follow the directions on the container

Step 8. Lay the release sheet on a flat surface and spread an even layer of filler, large enough to cover the repair. Lay the smaller piece of fiberglass cloth in the center of the sheet and spread another layer of repair jelly over the fiberglass cloth. Repeat the operation for the larger piece of cloth. If the fiberglass cloth is not used, spread the repair jelly on the release film, concentrated in the middle of the repair

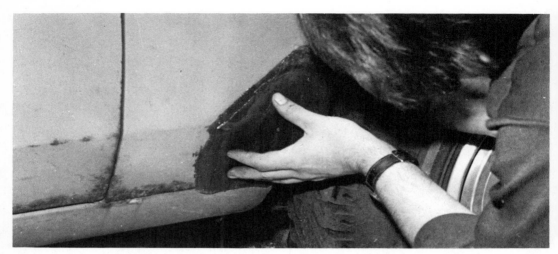

Step 9. Place the repair material over the repair area, with the release film facing outward

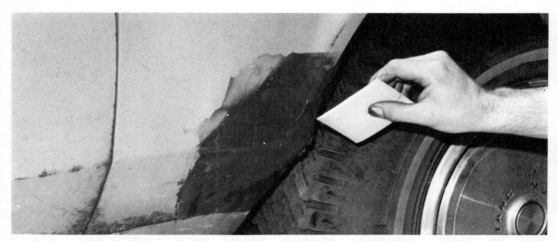

Step 10. Use a spreader and work from the center outward to smooth the material, following the body contours. Be sure to remove all air bubbles

Step 11. Wait until the repair has dried tack-free and peel off the release sheet. The ideal working temperature is 65—90° F. Cooler or warmer temperatures or high humidity may require additional curing time

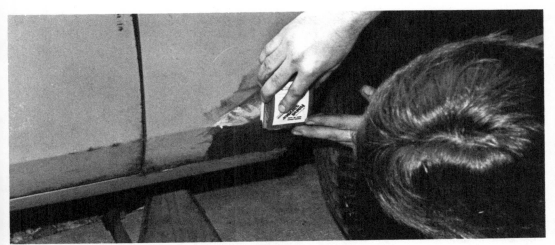

Step 12. Sand and feather-edge the entire area. The initial sanding can be done with a sanding disc on an electric drill if care is used. Finish the sanding with a block sander

Step 13. When the area is sanded smooth, mix some topcoat and hardener and apply it directly with a spreader. This will give a smooth finish and prevent the glass matte from showing through the paint

Step 14. Block sand the topcoat with finishing sandpaper

Step 15. To finish this repair, grind out the surface rust along the top edge of the rocker panel

Step 16. Mix some more repair jelly and cream hardener and apply it directly over the surface

Step 17. When it dries tack-free, block sand the surface smooth

Step 18. If necessary, mask off adjacent panels and spray the entire repair with primer. You are now ready for a color coat

AUTO BODY CARE

There are hundreds—maybe thousands—of products on the market, all designed to protect or aid your car's finish in some manner. There are as many different products as there are ways to use them, but they all have one thing in common—the surface must be clean.

Washing

The primary ingredient for washing your car is water, preferably "soft" water. In many areas of the country, the local water supply is "hard" containing many minerals. The little rings or film that is left on your car's surface after it has dried is the result of "hard" water.

Since you usually can't change the local water supply, the next best thing is to dry the surface before it has a chance to dry itself.

Into the water you usually add soap. Don't use detergents or common, coarse soaps. Your car's paint never truly dries out, but is always evaporating residual oils into the air. Harsh detergents will remove these oils, causing the paint to dry faster than normal. Instead use warm water and a non-detergent soap made especially for waxed surfaces or a liquid soap made for waxed surfaces or a liquid soap made for washing dishes by hand.

Other products that can be used on painted surfaces include baking soda or plain soda water for stubborn dirt.

Wash the car completely, starting at the top, and rinse it completely clean. Abrasive grit should be loaded off under water pressure; scrubbing grit off will scratch the finish. The best washing tool is a sponge, cleaning mitt or soft towel. Whichever you choose, replace it often as each tends to absorb grease and dirt.

Other ways to get a better wash include:

• Don't wash your car in the sun or when the finish is hot.

• Use water pressure to remove caked-on dirt.

• Remove tree-sap and bird effluence immediately. Such substances will eat through wax, polish and paint.

One of the best implements to dry your car is a turkish towel or an old, soft bath towel. Anything with a deep nap will hold any dirt in suspension and not grind it into the paint.

Harder cloths will only grind the grit into the paint making more scratches. Always start drying at the top, followed by the hood and trunk and sides. You'll find there's always more dirt near the rocker panels and wheelwells which will wind up on the rest of the car if you dry these areas first.

Cleaners, Waxes and Polishes

Before going any farther you should know the function of various products.

Cleaners—remove the top layer of dead pigment or paint.

Rubbing or polishing compounds—used to remove stubborn dirt, get rid of minor scratches, smooth away imperfections and partially restore badly weathered paint.

Polishes—contain no abrasives or waxes; they shine the paint by adding oils to the paint.

Waxes—are a protective coating for the polish.

CLEANERS AND COMPOUNDS

Before you apply any wax, you'll have to remove oxidation, road film and other types of pollutants that washing alone will not remove.

The paint on your car never dries completely. There are always residual oils evaporating from the paint into the air. When enough oils are present in the paint, it has a healthy shine (gloss). When too many oils evaporate the paint takes on a whitish cast known as oxidation. The idea of polishing and waxing is to keep enough oil present in the painted surface to prevent oxidation; but when it occurs, the only recourse is to remove the top layer of "dead" paint, exposing the healthy paint underneath.

Products to remove oxidation and road film are sold under a variety of generic names—polishes, cleaner, rubbing compound, cleaner/polish, polish/cleaner, self-polishing wax, pre-wax cleaner, finish restorer and many more. Regardless of name there are two types of cleaners—abrasive cleaners (sometimes called polishing or rubbing compounds) that remove oxidation by grinding away the top layer of "dead" paint, or chemical cleaners that dissolve the "dead" pigment, allowing it to be wiped away.

Abrasive cleaners, by their nature, leave thousands of minute scratches in the finish, which must be polished out later. These should only be used in extreme cases, but are usually the only thing to use on badly oxidized paint finishes. Chemical cleaners are much milder but are not strong enough for severe cases of oxidation or weathered paint.

The most popular cleaners are liquid or paste abrasive polishing and rubbing compounds. Polishing compounds have a finer abrasive grit for medium duty work. Rubbing compounds are a coarser abrasive and for heavy duty work. Unless you are familiar with how to use compounds, be very careful. Excessive rubbing with any type of compound or cleaner can grind right through the paint to primer or bare metal. Follow the directions on the container—depending on type, the cleaner may or may not be OK for your paint. For example, some cleaners are not formulated for acrylic lacquer finishes.

When a small area needs compounding or heavy polishing, it's best to do the job by hand. Some people prefer a powered buffer for large areas. Avoid cutting through the paint along styling edges on the body. Small, hand operations where the compound is applied and rubbed using cloth folded into a thick ball allow you to work in straight lines along such edges.

To avoid cutting through on the edges when using a power buffer, try masking tape. Just cover the edge with tape while using power. Then finish the job by hand with the tape removed. Even then work carefully. The paint tends to be a lot thinner along the sharp ridges stamped into the panels.

Whether compounding by machine or by hand, only work on a small area and apply the compound sparingly. If the materials are spread too thin, or allowed to sit too long, they dry out. Once dry they lose the ability to deliver a smooth, clean finish. Also, dried out polish tends to cause the buffer to stick in one spot. This in turn can burn or cut through the finish.

WAXES AND POLISHES

Your car's finish can be protected in a number of ways. A cleaner/wax or polish/cleaner followed by wax or variations of each all provide good results. The two-step approach (polish followed by wax) is probably slightly better but consumes more time and effort. Properly fed with oils, your paint should never need cleaning, but despite the best polishing job, it won't last unless it's protected with wax. Without wax, polish must be renewed at least once a month to prevent oxidation. Years ago (some still swear by it today), the best wax was made from the Brazilian palm, the Carnuba, favored for its vegetable base and high melting point. However, modern synthetic waxes are harder, which means they protect against moisture better, and chemically inert silicone is used for a long lasting protection. The only problem with silicone wax is that it penetrates all layers of paint. To repaint or touch up a panel or car protected by silicone wax, you have to completely strip the finish to avoid "fish-eyes."

Under normal conditions, silicone waxes will last 4–6 months, but you have to be careful of wax build-up from too much waxing. Too thick a coat of wax is just as bad as no wax at all; it stops the paint from breathing.

Combination cleaners/waxes have become popular lately because they remove the old layer of wax plus light oxidation, while putting on a fresh coat of wax at the same time. Some cleaners/waxes contain abrasive cleaners which require caution, although many cleaner/waxes use a chemical cleaner.

Applying Wax or Polish

You may view polishing and waxing your car as a pleasant way to spend an afternoon, or as a boring chore, but it has to be done to keep the paint on your car. Caring for the paint doesn't require special tools, but you should follow a few rules.

1. Use a good quality wax.

2. Before applying any wax or polish, be sure the surface is completely clean. Just because the car looks clean, doesn't mean it's ready for polish or wax.

3. If the finish on your car is weathered, dull, or oxidized, it will probably have to be compounded to remove the old or oxidized paint. If the paint is simply dulled from lack of care, one of the non-abrasive cleaners known as polishing compounds will do the trick. If the paint is severely scratched or really dull, you'll probably have to use a rubbing compound to prepare the finish for waxing. If you're not sure which one to use, use the polishing compound, since you can easily ruin the finish by using too strong a compound.

4. Don't apply wax, polish or compound in direct sunlight, even if the directions on the can say you can. Most waxes will not cure properly in bright sunlight and you'll probably end up with a blotchy looking finish.

5. Don't rub the wax off too soon. The result will be a wet, dull looking finish. Let the wax dry thoroughly before buffing it off.

6. A constant debate among car enthusiasts is how wax should be applied. Some maintain pastes or liquids should be applied in a circular motion, but body shop experts have long thought that this approach results in barely detectable circular abrasions, especially on cars that are waxed frequently. They

advise rubbing in straight lines, especially if any kind of cleaner is involved.

7. If an applicator is not supplied with the wax, use a piece of soft cheesecloth or very soft lint-free material. The same applies to buffing the surface.

SPECIAL SURFACES

One-step combination cleaner and wax formulas shouldn't be used on many of the special surfaces which abound on cars. The one-step materials contain abrasives to achieve a clean surface under the wax top coat. The abrasives are so mild that you could clean a car every week for a couple of years without fear of rubbing through the paint. But this same level of abrasiveness might, through repeated use, damage decals used for special trim effects. This includes wide stripes, wood-grain trim and other appliques.

Painted plastics must be cleaned with care. If a cleaner is too aggressive it will cut through the paint and expose the primer. If bright trim such as polished aluminum or chrome is painted, cleaning must be performed with even greater care. If rubbing compound is being used, it will cut faster than polish.

Abrasive cleaners will dull an acrylic finish. The best way to clean these newer finishes is with a non-abrasive liquid polish. Only dirt and oxidation, not paint, will be removed.

Taking a few minutes to read the instructions on the can of polish or wax will help prevent making serious mistakes. Not all preparations will work on all surfaces. And some are intended for power application while others will only work when applied by hand.

Don't get the idea that just pouring on some polish and then hitting it with a buffer will suffice. Power equipment speeds the operation. But it also adds a measure of risk. It's very easy to damage the finish if you use the wrong methods or materials.

Caring for Chrome

Read the label on the container. Many products are formulated specifically for chrome, but others contain abrasives that will scratch the chrome finish. If it isn't recommended for chrome, don't use it.

Never use steel wool or kitchen soap pads to clean chrome. Be careful not to get chrome cleaner on paint or interior vinyl surfaces. If you do, get it off immediately.

Troubleshooting

This section is designed to aid in the quick, accurate diagnosis of automotive problems. While automotive repairs can be made by many people, accurate troubleshooting is a rare skill for the amateur and professional alike.

In its simplest state, troubleshooting is an exercise in logic. It is essential to realize that an automobile is really composed of a series of systems. Some of these systems are interrelated; others are not. Automobiles operate within a framework of logical rules and physical laws, and the key to troubleshooting is a good understanding of all the automotive systems.

This section breaks the car or truck down into its component systems, allowing the problem to be isolated. The charts and diagnostic road maps list the most common problems and the most probable causes of trouble. Obviously it would be impossible to list every possible problem that could happen along with every possible cause, but it will locate MOST problems and eliminate a lot of unnecessary guesswork. The systematic format will locate problems within a given system, but, because many automotive systems are interrelated, the solution to your particular problem may be found in a number of systems on the car or truck.

USING THE TROUBLESHOOTING CHARTS

This book contains all of the specific information that the average do-it-yourself mechanic needs to repair and maintain his or her car or truck. The troubleshooting charts are designed to be used in conjunction with the specific procedures and information in the text. For instance, troubleshooting a point-type ignition system is fairly standard for all models, but you may be directed to the text to find procedures for troubleshooting an individual type of electronic ignition. You will also have to refer to the specification charts throughout the book for specifications applicable to your car or truck.

TOOLS AND EQUIPMENT

The tools illustrated in Chapter 1 (plus two more diagnostic pieces) will be adequate to troubleshoot most problems. The two other tools needed are a voltmeter and an ohmmeter. These can be purchased separately or in combination, known as a VOM meter.

In the event that other tools are required, they will be noted in the procedures.

Troubleshooting Engine Problems
See Chapters 2, 3, 4 for more information and service procedures.

Index to Systems

System	To Test	Group
Battery	Engine need not be running	1
Starting system	Engine need not be running	2
Primary electrical system	Engine need not be running	3
Secondary electrical system	Engine need not be running	4
Fuel system	Engine need not be running	5
Engine compression	Engine need not be running	6
Engine vacuum	Engine must be running	7
Secondary electrical system	Engine must be running	8
Valve train	Engine must be running	9
Exhaust system	Engine must be running	10
Cooling system	Engine must be running	11
Engine lubrication	Engine must be running	12

Index to Problems

Problem: Symptom	Begin at Specific Diagnosis, Number
Engine Won't Start:	
Starter doesn't turn	1.1, 2.1
Starter turns, engine doesn't	2.1
Starter turns engine very slowly	1.1, 2.4
Starter turns engine normally	3.1, 4.1
Starter turns engine very quickly	6.1
Engine fires intermittently	4.1
Engine fires consistently	5.1, 6.1
Engine Runs Poorly:	
Hard starting	3.1, 4.1, 5.1, 8.1
Rough idle	4.1, 5.1, 8.1
Stalling	3.1, 4.1, 5.1, 8.1
Engine dies at high speeds	4.1, 5.1
Hesitation (on acceleration from standing stop)	5.1, 8.1
Poor pickup	4.1, 5.1, 8.1
Lack of power	3.1, 4.1, 5.1, 8.1
Backfire through the carburetor	4.1, 8.1, 9.1
Backfire through the exhaust	4.1, 8.1, 9.1
Blue exhaust gases	6.1, 7.1
Black exhaust gases	5.1
Running on (after the ignition is shut off)	3.1, 8.1
Susceptible to moisture	4.1
Engine misfires under load	4.1, 7.1, 8.4, 9.1
Engine misfires at speed	4.1, 8.4
Engine misfires at idle	3.1, 4.1, 5.1, 7.1, 8.4

Sample Section

Test and Procedure	Results and Indications	Proceed to
4.1—Check for spark: Hold each spark plug wire approximately ¼″ from ground with gloves or a heavy, dry rag. Crank the engine and observe the spark.	If no spark is evident:	4.2
	If spark is good in some cases:	4.3
	If spark is good in all cases:	4.6

Specific Diagnosis

This section is arranged so that following each test, instructions are given to proceed to another, until a problem is diagnosed.

Section 1—Battery

Test and Procedure	Results and Indications	Proceed to
1.1—Inspect the battery visually for case condition (corrosion, cracks) and water level.	If case is cracked, replace battery:	**1.4**
	If the case is intact, remove corrosion with a solution of baking soda and water (**CAUTION**: *do not get the solution into the battery*), and fill with water:	**1.2**

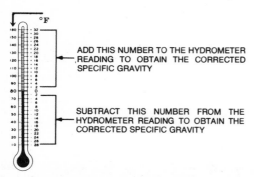

DIRT ON TOP OF BATTERY

CORROSION

PLUGGED VENT

LOOSE CABLE OR POSTS

CRACKS

LOW WATER LEVEL

Inspect the battery case

1.2—Check the battery cable connections: Insert a screwdriver between the battery post and the cable clamp. Turn the headlights on high beam, and observe them as the screwdriver is gently twisted to ensure good metal to metal contact.	If the lights brighten, remove and clean the clamp and post; coat the post with petroleum jelly, install and tighten the clamp:	**1.4**
	If no improvement is noted:	**1.3**

TESTING BATTERY CABLE CONNECTIONS USING A SCREWDRIVER

1.3—Test the state of charge of the battery using an individual cell tester or hydrometer.	If indicated, charge the battery. **NOTE:** *If no obvious reason exists for the low state of charge (i.e., battery age, prolonged storage), proceed to:*	**1.4**

°F

ADD THIS NUMBER TO THE HYDROMETER READING TO OBTAIN THE CORRECTED SPECIFIC GRAVITY

SUBTRACT THIS NUMBER FROM THE HYDROMETER READING TO OBTAIN THE CORRECTED SPECIFIC GRAVITY

Specific Gravity (@ 80° F.)

Minimum	Battery Charge
1.260	100% Charged
1.230	75% Charged
1.200	50% Charged
1.170	25% Charged
1.140	Very Little Power Left
1.110	Completely Discharged

The effects of temperature on battery specific gravity (left) and amount of battery charge in relation to specific gravity (right)

1.4—Visually inspect battery cables for cracking, bad connection to ground, or bad connection to starter.	If necessary, tighten connections or replace the cables:	
		2.1

Section 2—Starting System
See Chapter 3 for service procedures

Test and Procedure	Results and Indications	Proceed to

Note: Tests in Group 2 are performed with coil high tension lead disconnected to prevent accidental starting.

Test and Procedure	Results and Indications	Proceed to
2.1—Test the starter motor and solenoid: Connect a jumper from the battery post of the solenoid (or relay) to the starter post of the solenoid (or relay).	If starter turns the engine normally:	2.2
	If the starter buzzes, or turns the engine very slowly:	2.4
	If no response, replace the solenoid (or relay).	3.1
	If the starter turns, but the engine doesn't, ensure that the flywheel ring gear is intact. If the gear is undamaged, replace the starter drive.	3.1
2.2—Determine whether ignition override switches are functioning properly (clutch start switch, neutral safety switch), by connecting a jumper across the switch(es), and turning the ignition switch to "start".	If starter operates, adjust or replace switch:	3.1
	If the starter doesn't operate:	2.3
2.3—Check the ignition switch "start" position: Connect a 12V test lamp or voltmeter between the starter post of the solenoid (or relay) and ground. Turn the ignition switch to the "start" position, and jiggle the key.	If the lamp doesn't light or the meter needle doesn't move when the switch is turned, check the ignition switch for loose connections, cracked insulation, or broken wires. Repair or replace as necessary:	3.1
	If the lamp flickers or needle moves when the key is jiggled, replace the ignition switch.	3.3

Checking the ignition switch "start" position

STARTER RELAY (IF EQUIPPED)

Test and Procedure	Results and Indications	Proceed to
2.4—Remove and bench test the starter, according to specifications in the engine electrical section.	If the starter does not meet specifications, repair or replace as needed:	3.1
	If the starter is operating properly:	2.5
2.5—Determine whether the engine can turn freely: Remove the spark plugs, and check for water in the cylinders. Check for water on the dipstick, or oil in the radiator. Attempt to turn the engine using an 18″ flex drive and socket on the crankshaft pulley nut or bolt.	If the engine will turn freely only with the spark plugs out, and hydrostatic lock (water in the cylinders) is ruled out, check valve timing:	9.2
	If engine will not turn freely, and it is known that the clutch and transmission are free, the engine must be disassembled for further evaluation:	Chapter 3

Section 3—Primary Electrical System

Test and Procedure	Results and Indications	Proceed to
3.1—Check the ignition switch "on" position: Connect a jumper wire between the distributor side of the coil and ground, and a 12V test lamp between the switch side of the coil and ground. Remove the high tension lead from the coil. Turn the ignition switch on and jiggle the key.	If the lamp lights:	**3.2**
	If the lamp flickers when the key is jiggled, replace the ignition switch:	**3.3**
	If the lamp doesn't light, check for loose or open connections. If none are found, remove the ignition switch and check for continuity. If the switch is faulty, replace it:	**3.3**

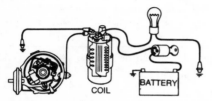

Checking the ignition switch "on" position

3.2—Check the ballast resistor or resistance wire for an open circuit, using an ohmmeter. See Chapter 3 for specific tests.	Replace the resistor or resistance wire if the resistance is zero. **NOTE:** *Some ignition systems have no ballast resistor.*	**3.3**

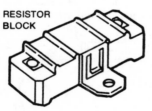

RESISTOR BLOCK

CALIBRATED RESISTANCE LEAD

Two types of resistors

3.3—On point-type ignition systems, visually inspect the breaker points for burning, pitting or excessive wear. Gray coloring of the point contact surfaces is normal. Rotate the crankshaft until the contact heel rests on a high point of the distributor cam and adjust the point gap to specifications. On electronic ignition models, remove the distributor cap and visually inspect the armature. Ensure that the armature pin is in place, and that the armature is on tight and rotates when the engine is cranked. Make sure there are no cracks, chips or rounded edges on the armature.	If the breaker points are intact, clean the contact surfaces with fine emery cloth, and adjust the point gap to specifications. If the points are worn, replace them. On electronic systems, replace any parts which appear defective. If condition persists:	**3.4**

Test and Procedure	Results and Indications	Proceed to
3.4—On point-type ignition systems, connect a dwell-meter between the distributor primary lead and ground. Crank the engine and observe the point dwell angle. On electronic ignition systems, conduct a stator (magnetic pickup assembly) test. See Chapter 3.	On point-type systems, adjust the dwell angle if necessary. **NOTE:** *Increasing the point gap decreases the dwell angle and vice-versa.*	**3.6**
	If the dwell meter shows little or no reading;	**3.5**
	On electronic ignition systems, if the stator is bad, replace the stator. If the stator is good, proceed to the other tests in Chapter 3.	

Dwell is a function of point gap

3.5—On the point-type ignition systems, check the condenser for short: connect an ohmeter across the condenser body and the pigtail lead.	If any reading other than infinite is noted, replace the condenser	**3.6**

OHMMETER

Checking the condenser for short

3.6—Test the coil primary resistance: On point-type ignition systems, connect an ohmmeter across the coil primary terminals, and read the resistance on the low scale. Note whether an external ballast resistor or resistance wire is used. On electronic ignition systems, test the coil primary resistance as in Chapter 3.	Point-type ignition coils utilizing ballast resistors or resistance wires should have approximately 1.0 ohms resistance. Coils with internal resistors should have approximately 4.0 ohms resistance. If values far from the above are noted, replace the coil.	**4.1**

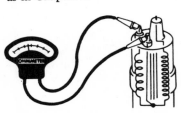

Check the coil primary resistance

Section 4—Secondary Electrical System
See Chapters 2–3 for service procedures

Test and Procedure	Results and Indications	Proceed to
4.1—Check for spark: Hold each spark plug wire approximately ¼" from ground with gloves or a heavy, dry rag. Crank the engine, and observe the spark.	If no spark is evident:	**4.2**
	If spark is good in some cylinders:	**4.3**
	If spark is good in all cylinders:	**4.6**

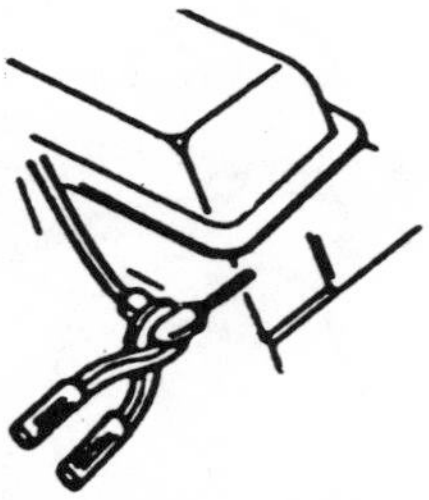

Check for spark at the plugs

4.2—Check for spark at the coil high tension lead: Remove the coil high tension lead from the distributor and position it approximately ¼" from ground. Crank the engine and observe spark. **CAUTION: This test should not be performed on engines equipped with electronic ignition.**	If the spark is good and consistent:	**4.3**
	If the spark is good but intermittent, test the primary electrical system starting at 3.3:	**3.3**
	If the spark is weak or non-existent, replace the coil high tension lead, clean and tighten all connections and retest. If no improvement is noted:	**4.4**
4.3—Visually inspect the distributor cap and rotor for burned or corroded contacts, cracks, carbon tracks, or moisture. Also check the fit of the rotor on the distributor shaft (where applicable).	If moisture is present, dry thoroughly, and retest per 4.1:	**4.1**
	If burned or excessively corroded contacts, cracks, or carbon tracks are noted, replace the defective part(s) and retest per 4.1:	**4.1**
	If the rotor and cap appear intact, or are only slightly corroded, clean the contacts thoroughly (including the cap towers and spark plug wire ends) and retest per 4.1:	
	If the spark is good in all cases:	**4.6**
	If the spark is poor in all cases:	**4.5**

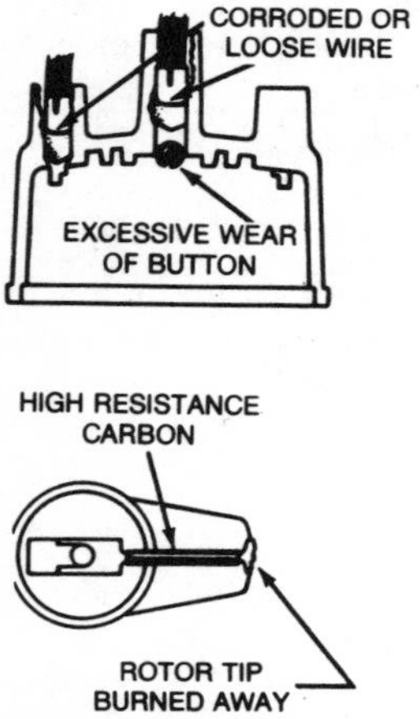

CORRODED OR
LOOSE WIRE

EXCESSIVE WEAR
OF BUTTON

HIGH RESISTANCE
CARBON

ROTOR TIP
BURNED AWAY

Inspect the distributor cap and rotor

| _Test and Procedure_ | _Results and Indications_ | _Proceed to_ |

4.4—Check the coil secondary resistance: On point-type systems connect an ohmmeter across the distributor side of the coil and the coil tower. Read the resistance on the high scale of the ohmmeter. On electronic ignition systems, see Chapter 3 for specific tests.

The resistance of a satisfactory coil should be between 4,000 and 10,000 ohms. If resistance is considerably higher (i.e., 40,000 ohms) replace the coil and retest per 4.1. **NOTE:** _This does not apply to high performance coils._

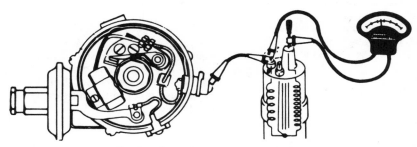

Testing the coil secondary resistance

4.5—Visually inspect the spark plug wires for cracking or brittleness. Ensure that no two wires are positioned so as to cause induction firing (adjacent and parallel). Remove each wire, one by one, and check resistance with an ohmmeter.

Replace any cracked or brittle wires. If any of the wires are defective, replace the entire set. Replace any wires with excessive resistance (over 8000 Ω per foot for suppression wire), and separate any wires that might cause induction firing.

4.6

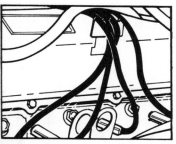

Misfiring can be the result of spark plug leads to adjacent, consecutively firing cylinders running parallel and too close together

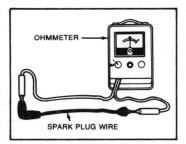

On point-type ignition systems, check the spark plug wires as shown. On electronic ignitions, do not remove the wire from the distributor cap terminal; instead, test through the cap

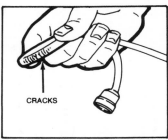

Spark plug wires can be checked visually by bending them in a loop over your finger. This will reveal any cracks, burned or broken insulation. Any wire with cracked insulation should be replaced

4.6—Remove the spark plugs, noting the cylinders from which they were removed, and evaluate according to the color photos in the middle of this book.

See following.

See following.

Test and Procedure	Results and Indications	Proceed to
4.7—Examine the location of all the plugs.	The following diagrams illustrate some of the conditions that the location of plugs will reveal.	**4.8**

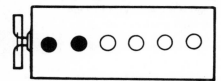

Two adjacent plugs are fouled in a 6-cylinder engine, 4-cylinder engine or either bank of a V-8. This is probably due to a blown head gasket between the two cylinders

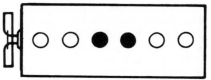

The two center plugs in a 6-cylinder engine are fouled. Raw fuel may be "boiled" out of the carburetor into the intake manifold after the engine is shut-off. Stop-start driving can also foul the center plugs, due to overly rich mixture. Proper float level, a new float needle and seat or use of an insulating spacer may help this problem

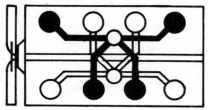

An unbalanced carburetor is indicated. Following the fuel flow on this particular design shows that the cylinders fed by the right-hand barrel are fouled from overly rich mixture, while the cylinders fed by the left-hand barrel are normal

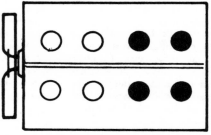

If the four rear plugs are overheated, a cooling system problem is suggested. A thorough cleaning of the cooling system may restore coolant circulation and cure the problem

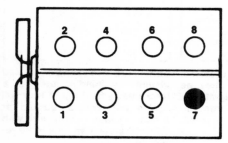

Finding one plug overheated may indicate an intake manifold leak near the affected cylinder. If the overheated plug is the second of two adjacent, consecutively firing plugs, it could be the result of ignition cross-firing. Separating the leads to these two plugs will eliminate cross-fire

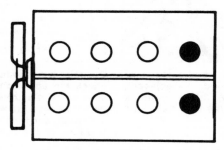

Occasionally, the two rear plugs in large, lightly used V-8's will become oil fouled. High oil consumption and smoky exhaust may also be noticed. It is probably due to plugged oil drain holes in the rear of the cylinder head, causing oil to be sucked in around the valve stems. This usually occurs in the rear cylinders first, because the engine slants that way

Test and Procedure	Results and Indications	Proceed to
4.8—Determine the static ignition timing. Using the crankshaft pulley timing marks as a guide, locate top dead center on the compression stroke of the number one cylinder.	The rotor should be pointing toward the No. 1 tower in the distributor cap, and, on electronic ignitions, the armature spoke for that cylinder should be lined up with the stator.	**4.8**
4.9—Check coil polarity: Connect a voltmeter negative lead to the coil high tension lead, and the positive lead to ground (**NOTE:** *Reverse the hook-up for positive ground systems*). Crank the engine momentarily.	If the voltmeter reads up-scale, the polarity is correct:	**5.1**
	If the voltmeter reads down-scale, reverse the coil polarity (switch the primary leads):	**5.1**
	Checking coil polarity	

Section 5—Fuel System
See Chapter 4 for service procedures

Test and Procedure	Results and Indications	Proceed to
5.1—Determine that the air filter is functioning efficiently: Hold paper elements up to a strong light, and attempt to see light through the filter.	Clean permanent air filters in solvent (or manufacturer's recommendation), and allow to dry. Replace paper elements through which light cannot be seen:	**5.2**
5.2—Determine whether a flooding condition exists: Flooding is identified by a strong gasoline odor, and excessive gasoline present in the throttle bore(s) of the carburetor.	If flooding is not evident:	**5.3**
	If flooding is evident, permit the gasoline to dry for a few moments and restart.	
	If flooding doesn't recur:	**5.7**
	If flooding is persistent:	**5.5**
	If the engine floods repeatedly, check the choke butterfly flap	
5.3—Check that fuel is reaching the carburetor: Detach the fuel line at the carburetor inlet. Hold the end of the line in a cup (not styrofoam), and crank the engine.	If fuel flows smoothly:	**5.7**
	If fuel doesn't flow (**NOTE:** *Make sure that there is fuel in the tank*), or flows erratically:	**5.4**
	Check the fuel pump by disconnecting the output line (fuel pump-to-carburetor) at the carburetor and operating the starter briefly	

Test and Procedure	Results and Indications	Proceed to
5.4—Test the fuel pump: Disconnect all fuel lines from the fuel pump. Hold a finger over the input fitting, crank the engine (with electric pump, turn the ignition or pump on); and feel for suction.	If suction is evident, blow out the fuel line to the tank with low pressure compressed air until bubbling is heard from the fuel filler neck. Also blow out the carburetor fuel line (both ends disconnected):	5.7
	If no suction is evident, replace or repair the fuel pump: NOTE: *Repeated oil fouling of the spark plugs, or a no-start condition, could be the result of a ruptured vacuum booster pump diaphragm, through which oil or gasoline is being drawn into the intake manifold (where applicable).*	5.7
5.5—Occasionally, small specks of dirt will clog the small jets and orifices in the carburetor. With the engine cold, hold a flat piece of wood or similar material over the carburetor, where possible, and crank the engine.	If the engine starts, but runs roughly the engine is probably not run enough. If the engine won't start:	5.9
5.6—Check the needle and seat: Tap the carburetor in the area of the needle and seat.	If flooding stops, a gasoline additive (e.g., Gumout) will often cure the problem:	5.7
	If flooding continues, check the fuel pump for excessive pressure at the carburetor (according to specifications). If the pressure is normal, the needle and seat must be removed and checked, and/or the float level adjusted:	5.7
5.7—Test the accelerator pump by looking into the throttle bores while operating the throttle.	If the accelerator pump appears to be operating normally:	5.8
	If the accelerator pump is not operating, the pump must be reconditioned. Where possible, service the pump with the carburetor(s) installed on the engine. If necessary, remove the carburetor. Prior to removal:	5.8

Check for gas at the carburetor by looking down the carburetor throat while someone moves the accelerator

5.8—Determine whether the carburetor main fuel system is functioning: Spray a commercial starting fluid into the carburetor while attempting to start the engine.	If the engine starts, runs for a few seconds, and dies:	5.9
	If the engine doesn't start:	6.1

Test and Procedure	Results and Indications	Proceed to
5.9—Uncommon fuel system malfunctions: See below:	If the problem is solved: If the problem remains, remove and recondition the carburetor.	**6.1**

Condition	Indication	Test	Prevailing Weather Conditions	Remedy
Vapor lock	Engine will not restart shortly after running.	Cool the components of the fuel system until the engine starts. Vapor lock can be cured faster by draping a wet cloth over a mechanical fuel pump.	Hot to very hot	Ensure that the exhaust manifold heat control valve is operating. Check with the vehicle manufacturer for the recommended solution to vapor lock on the model in question.
Carburetor icing	Engine will not idle, stalls at low speeds.	Visually inspect the throttle plate area of the throttle bores for frost.	High humidity, 32–40° F.	Ensure that the exhaust manifold heat control valve is operating, and that the intake manifold heat riser is not blocked.
Water in the fuel	Engine sputters and stalls; may not start.	Pump a small amount of fuel into a glass jar. Allow to stand, and inspect for droplets or a layer of water.	High humidity, extreme temperature changes.	For droplets, use one or two cans of commercial gas line anti-freeze. For a layer of water, the tank must be drained, and the fuel lines blown out with compressed air.

Section 6—Engine Compression
See Chapter 3 for service procedures

6.1—Test engine compression: Remove all spark plugs. Block the throttle wide open. Insert a compression gauge into a spark plug port, crank the engine to obtain the maximum reading, and record.	If compression is within limits on all cylinders:	**7.1**
	If gauge reading is extremely low on all cylinders:	**6.2**
	If gauge reading is low on one or two cylinders: (If gauge readings are identical and low on two or more adjacent cylinders, the head gasket must be replaced.)	**6.2**

Checking compression

6.2—Test engine compression (wet): Squirt approximately 30 cc. of engine oil into each cylinder, and retest per 6.1.	If the readings improve, worn or cracked rings or broken pistons are indicated:	**See Chapter 3**
	If the readings do not improve, burned or excessively carboned valves or a jumped timing chain are indicated: NOTE: *A jumped timing chain is often indicated by difficult cranking.*	**7.1**

Section 7—Engine Vacuum
See Chapter 3 for service procedures

Test and Procedure	Results and Indications	Proceed to
7.1—Attach a vacuum gauge to the intake manifold beyond the throttle plate. Start the engine, and observe the action of the needle over the range of engine speeds.	See below.	**See below**

INDICATION: normal engine in good condition

Proceed to: 8.1

Normal engine
Gauge reading: steady, from 17–22 in./Hg.

INDICATION: sticking valves or ignition miss

Proceed to: 9.1, 8.3

Sticking valves
Gauge reading: intermittent fluctuation at idle

INDICATION: late ignition or valve timing, low compression, stuck throttle valve, leaking carburetor or manifold gasket

Proceed to: 6.1

Incorrect valve timing
Gauge reading: low (10–15 in./Hg) but steady

INDICATION: improper carburetor adjustment or minor intake leak.

Proceed to: 7.2

Carburetor requires adjustment
Gauge reading: drifting needle

INDICATION: ignition miss, blown cylinder head gasket, leaking valve or weak valve spring

Proceed to: 8.3, 6.1

Blown head gasket
Gauge reading: needle fluctuates as engine speed increases

INDICATION: burnt valve or faulty valve clearance. Needle will fall when defective valve operates

Proceed to: 9.1

Burnt or leaking valves
Gauge reading: steady needle, but drops regularly

INDICATION: choked muffler, excessive back pressure in system

Proceed to: 10.1

Clogged exhaust system
Gauge reading: gradual drop in reading at idle

INDICATION: worn valve guides

Proceed to: 9.1

Worn valve guides
Gauge reading: needle vibrates excessively at idle but steadies as engine speed increases

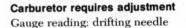

White pointer = steady gauge hand   Black pointer = fluctuating gauge hand

Test and Procedure	Results and Indications	Proceed to
7.2—Attach a vacuum gauge per 7.1, and test for an intake manifold leak. Squirt a small amount of oil around the intake manifold gaskets, carburetor gaskets, plugs and fittings. Observe the action of the vacuum gauge.	If the reading improves, replace the indicated gasket, or seal the indicated fitting or plug:	**8.1**
	If the reading remains low:	**7.3**
7.3—Test all vacuum hoses and accessories for leaks as described in 7.2. Also check the carburetor body (dashpots, automatic choke mechanism, throttle shafts) for leaks in the same manner.	If the reading improves, service or replace the offending part(s):	**8.1**
	If the reading remains low:	**6.1**

Section 8—Secondary Electrical System
See Chapter 2 for service procedures

Test and Procedure	Results and Indications	Proceed to
8.1—Remove the distributor cap and check to make sure that the rotor turns when the engine is cranked. Visually inspect the distributor components.	Clean, tighten or replace any components which appear defective.	**8.2**
8.2—Connect a timing light (per manufacturer's recommendation) and check the dynamic ignition timing. Disconnect and plug the vacuum hose(s) to the distributor if specified, start the engine, and observe the timing marks at the specified engine speed.	If the timing is not correct, adjust to specifications by rotating the distributor in the engine: (Advance timing by rotating distributor opposite normal direction of rotor rotation, retard timing by rotating distributor in same direction as rotor rotation.)	**8.3**
8.3—Check the operation of the distributor advance mechanism(s): To test the mechanical advance, disconnect the vacuum lines from the distributor advance unit and observe the timing marks with a timing light as the engine speed is increased from idle. If the mark moves smoothly, without hesitation, it may be assumed that the mechanical advance is functioning properly. To test vacuum advance and/or retard systems, alternately crimp and release the vacuum line, and observe the timing mark for movement. If movement is noted, the system is operating.	If the systems are functioning:	**8.4**
	If the systems are not functioning, remove the distributor, and test on a distributor tester:	**8.4**
8.4—Locate an ignition miss: With the engine running, remove each spark plug wire, one at a time, until one is found that doesn't cause the engine to roughen and slow down.	When the missing cylinder is identified:	**4.1**

Section 9—Valve Train
See Chapter 3 for service procedures

Test and Procedure	Results and Indications	Proceed to
9.1—Evaluate the valve train: Remove the valve cover, and ensure that the valves are adjusted to specifications. A mechanic's stethoscope may be used to aid in the diagnosis of the valve train. By pushing the probe on or near push rods or rockers, valve noise often can be isolated. A timing light also may be used to diagnose valve problems. Connect the light according to manufacturer's recommendations, and start the engine. Vary the firing moment of the light by increasing the engine speed (and therefore the ignition advance), and moving the trigger from cylinder to cylinder. Observe the movement of each valve.	Sticking valves or erratic valve train motion can be observed with the timing light. The cylinder head must be disassembled for repairs.	**See Chapter 3**
9.2—Check the valve timing: Locate top dead center of the No. 1 piston, and install a degree wheel or tape on the crankshaft pulley or damper with zero corresponding to an index mark on the engine. Rotate the crankshaft in its direction of rotation, and observe the opening of the No. 1 cylinder intake valve. The opening should correspond with the correct mark on the degree wheel according to specifications.	If the timing is not correct, the timing cover must be removed for further investigation.	**See Chapter 3**

Section 10—Exhaust System

Test and Procedure	Results and Indications	Proceed to
10.1—Determine whether the exhaust manifold heat control valve is operating: Operate the valve by hand to determine whether it is free to move. If the valve is free, run the engine to operating temperature and observe the action of the valve, to ensure that it is opening.	If the valve sticks, spray it with a suitable solvent, open and close the valve to free it, and retest.	
	If the valve functions properly:	10.2
	If the valve does not free, or does not operate, replace the valve:	10.2
10.2—Ensure that there are no exhaust restrictions: Visually inspect the exhaust system for kinks, dents, or crushing. Also note that gases are flowing freely from the tailpipe at all engine speeds, indicating no restriction in the muffler or resonator.	Replace any damaged portion of the system:	11.1

Section 11—Cooling System
See Chapter 3 for service procedures

Test and Procedure	Results and Indications	Proceed to
11.1—Visually inspect the fan belt for glazing, cracks, and fraying, and replace if necessary. Tighten the belt so that the longest span has approximately ½″ play at its midpoint under thumb pressure (see Chapter 1).	Replace or tighten the fan belt as necessary:	**11.2**

Checking belt tension

11.2—Check the fluid level of the cooling system.	If full or slightly low, fill as necessary:	**11.5**
	If extremely low:	**11.3**
11.3—Visually inspect the external portions of the cooling system (radiator, radiator hoses, thermostat elbow, water pump seals, heater hoses, etc.) for leaks. If none are found, pressurize the cooling system to 14–15 psi.	If cooling system holds the pressure:	**11.5**
	If cooling system loses pressure rapidly, reinspect external parts of the system for leaks under pressure. If none are found, check dipstick for coolant in crankcase. If no coolant is present, but pressure loss continues:	**11.4**
	If coolant is evident in crankcase, remove cylinder head(s), and check gasket(s). If gaskets are intact, block and cylinder head(s) should be checked for cracks or holes.	
	If the gasket(s) is blown, replace, and purge the crankcase of coolant: **NOTE:** *Occasionally, due to atmospheric and driving conditions, condensation of water can occur in the crankcase. This causes the oil to appear milky white. To remedy, run the engine until hot, and change the oil and oil filter.*	**12.6**
11.4—Check for combustion leaks into the cooling system: Pressurize the cooling system as above. Start the engine, and observe the pressure gauge. If the needle fluctuates, remove each spark plug wire, one at a time, noting which cylinder(s) reduce or eliminate the fluctuation.	Cylinders which reduce or eliminate the fluctuation, when the spark plug wire is removed, are leaking into the cooling system. Replace the head gasket on the affected cylinder bank(s).	

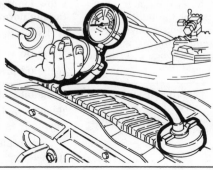

Pressurizing the cooling system

Test and Procedure	Results and Indications	Proceed to
11.5—Check the radiator pressure cap: Attach a radiator pressure tester to the radiator cap (wet the seal prior to installation). Quickly pump up the pressure, noting the point at which the cap releases.	If the cap releases within ± 1 psi of the specified rating, it is operating properly:	**11.6**
	If the cap releases at more than ± 1 psi of the specified rating, it should be replaced:	**11.6**

Checking radiator pressure cap

Test and Procedure	Results and Indications	Proceed to
11.6—Test the thermostat: Start the engine cold, remove the radiator cap, and insert a thermometer into the radiator. Allow the engine to idle. After a short while, there will be a sudden, rapid increase in coolant temperature. The temperature at which this sharp rise stops is the thermostat opening temperature.	If the thermostat opens at or about the specified temperature:	**11.7**
	If the temperature doesn't increase: (If the temperature increases slowly and gradually, replace the thermostat.)	**11.7**
11.7—Check the water pump: Remove the thermostat elbow and the thermostat, disconnect the coil high tension lead (to prevent starting), and crank the engine momentarily.	If coolant flows, replace the thermostat and retest per 11.6:	**11.6**
	If coolant doesn't flow, reverse flush the cooling system to alleviate any blockage that might exist. If system is not blocked, and coolant will not flow, replace the water pump.	

Section 12—Lubrication
See Chapter 3 for service procedures

Test and Procedure	Results and Indications	Proceed to
12.1—Check the oil pressure gauge or warning light: If the gauge shows low pressure, or the light is on for no obvious reason, remove the oil pressure sender. Install an accurate oil pressure gauge and run the engine momentarily.	If oil pressure builds normally, run engine for a few moments to determine that it is functioning normally, and replace the sender.	—
	If the pressure remains low:	**12.2**
	If the pressure surges:	**12.3**
	If the oil pressure is zero:	**12.3**
12.2—Visually inspect the oil: If the oil is watery or very thin, milky, or foamy, replace the oil and oil filter.	If the oil is normal:	**12.3**
	If after replacing oil the pressure remains low:	**12.3**
	If after replacing oil the pressure becomes normal:	—

Test and Procedure	Results and Indications	Proceed to
12.3—Inspect the oil pressure relief valve and spring, to ensure that it is not sticking or stuck. Remove and thoroughly clean the valve, spring, and the valve body.	If the oil pressure improves: If no improvement is noted:	— **12.4**
12.4—Check to ensure that the oil pump is not cavitating (sucking air instead of oil): See that the crankcase is neither over nor underfull, and that the pickup in the sump is in the proper position and free from sludge.	Fill or drain the crankcase to the proper capacity, and clean the pickup screen in solvent if necessary. If no improvement is noted:	**12.5**
12.5—Inspect the oil pump drive and the oil pump:	If the pump drive or the oil pump appear to be defective, service as necessary and retest per 12.1: If the pump drive and pump appear to be operating normally, the engine should be disassembled to determine where blockage exists:	**12.1** **See Chapter 3**
12.6—Purge the engine of ethylene glycol coolant: Completely drain the crankcase and the oil filter. Obtain a commercial butyl cellosolve base solvent, designated for this purpose, and follow the instructions precisely. Following this, install a new oil filter and refill the crankcase with the proper weight oil. The next oil and filter change should follow shortly thereafter (1000 miles).		

TROUBLESHOOTING EMISSION CONTROL SYSTEMS

See Chapter 4 for procedures applicable to individual emission control systems used on specific combinations of engine/transmission/model.

TROUBLESHOOTING THE CARBURETOR

See Chapter 4 for service procedures

Carburetor problems cannot be effectively isolated unless all other engine systems (particularly ignition and emission) are functioning properly and the engine is properly tuned.

Condition	*Possible Cause*
Engine cranks, but does not start	1. Improper starting procedure 2. No fuel in tank 3. Clogged fuel line or filter 4. Defective fuel pump 5. Choke valve not closing properly 6. Engine flooded 7. Choke valve not unloading 8. Throttle linkage not making full travel 9. Stuck needle or float 10. Leaking float needle or seat 11. Improper float adjustment
Engine stalls	1. Improperly adjusted idle speed or mixture **Engine hot** 2. Improperly adjusted dashpot 3. Defective or improperly adjusted solenoid 4. Incorrect fuel level in fuel bowl 5. Fuel pump pressure too high 6. Leaking float needle seat 7. Secondary throttle valve stuck open 8. Air or fuel leaks 9. Idle air bleeds plugged or missing 10. Idle passages plugged **Engine Cold** 11. Incorrectly adjusted choke 12. Improperly adjusted fast idle speed 13. Air leaks 14. Plugged idle or idle air passages 15. Stuck choke valve or binding linkage 16. Stuck secondary throttle valves 17. Engine flooding—high fuel level 18. Leaking or misaligned float
Engine hesitates on acceleration	1. Clogged fuel filter 2. Leaking fuel pump diaphragm 3. Low fuel pump pressure 4. Secondary throttle valves stuck, bent or misadjusted 5. Sticking or binding air valve 6. Defective accelerator pump 7. Vacuum leaks 8. Clogged air filter 9. Incorrect choke adjustment (engine cold)
Engine feels sluggish or flat on acceleration	1. Improperly adjusted idle speed or mixture 2. Clogged fuel filter 3. Defective accelerator pump 4. Dirty, plugged or incorrect main metering jets 5. Bent or sticking main metering rods 6. Sticking throttle valves 7. Stuck heat riser 8. Binding or stuck air valve 9. Dirty, plugged or incorrect secondary jets 10. Bent or sticking secondary metering rods. 11. Throttle body or manifold heat passages plugged 12. Improperly adjusted choke or choke vacuum break.
Carburetor floods	1. Defective fuel pump. Pressure too high. 2. Stuck choke valve 3. Dirty, worn or damaged float or needle valve/seat 4. Incorrect float/fuel level 5. Leaking float bowl

Condition	Possible Cause
Engine idles roughly and stalls	1. Incorrect idle speed 2. Clogged fuel filter 3. Dirt in fuel system or carburetor 4. Loose carburetor screws or attaching bolts 5. Broken carburetor gaskets 6. Air leaks 7. Dirty carburetor 8. Worn idle mixture needles 9. Throttle valves stuck open 10. Incorrectly adjusted float or fuel level 11. Clogged air filter
Engine runs unevenly or surges	1. Defective fuel pump 2. Dirty or clogged fuel filter 3. Plugged, loose or incorrect main metering jets or rods 4. Air leaks 5. Bent or sticking main metering rods 6. Stuck power piston 7. Incorrect float adjustment 8. Incorrect idle speed or mixture 9. Dirty or plugged idle system passages 10. Hard, brittle or broken gaskets 11. Loose attaching or mounting screws 12. Stuck or misaligned secondary throttle valves
Poor fuel economy	1. Poor driving habits 2. Stuck choke valve 3. Binding choke linkage 4. Stuck heat riser 5. Incorrect idle mixture 6. Defective accelerator pump 7. Air leaks 8. Plugged, loose or incorrect main metering jets 9. Improperly adjusted float or fuel level 10. Bent, misaligned or fuel-clogged float 11. Leaking float needle seat 12. Fuel leak 13. Accelerator pump discharge ball not seating properly 14. Incorrect main jets
Engine lacks high speed performance or power	1. Incorrect throttle linkage adjustment 2. Stuck or binding power piston 3. Defective accelerator pump 4. Air leaks 5. Incorrect float setting or fuel level 6. Dirty, plugged, worn or incorrect main metering jets or rods 7. Binding or sticking air valve 8. Brittle or cracked gaskets 9. Bent, incorrect or improperly adjusted secondary metering rods 10. Clogged fuel filter 11. Clogged air filter 12. Defective fuel pump

TROUBLESHOOTING FUEL INJECTION PROBLEMS

Each fuel injection system has its own unique components and test procedures, for which it is impossible to generalize. Refer to Chapter 4 of this Repair & Tune-Up Guide for specific test and repair procedures, if the vehicle is equipped with fuel injection.

TROUBLESHOOTING ELECTRICAL PROBLEMS

See Chapter 5 for service procedures

For any electrical system to operate, it must make a complete circuit. This simply means that the power flow from the battery must make a complete circle. When an electrical component is operating, power flows from the battery to the component, passes through the component causing it to perform its function (lighting a light bulb), and then returns to the battery through the ground of the circuit. This ground is usually (but not always) the metal part of the car or truck on which the electrical component is mounted.

Perhaps the easiest way to visualize this is to think of connecting a light bulb with two wires attached to it to the battery. If one of the two wires attached to the light bulb were attached to the negative post of the battery and the other were attached to the positive post of the battery, you would have a complete circuit. Current from the battery would flow to the light bulb, causing it to light, and return to the negative post of the battery.

The normal automotive circuit differs from this simple example in two ways. First, instead of having a return wire from the bulb to the battery, the light bulb returns the current to the battery through the chassis of the vehicle. Since the negative battery cable is attached to the chassis and the chassis is made of electrically conductive metal, the chassis of the vehicle can serve as a ground wire to complete the circuit. Secondly, most automotive circuits contain switches to turn components on and off as required.

Every complete circuit from a power source must include a component which is using the power from the power source. If you were to disconnect the light bulb from the wires and touch the two wires together (don't do this) the power supply wire to the component would be grounded before the normal ground connection for the circuit.

Because grounding a wire from a power source makes a complete circuit—less the required component to use the power—this phenomenon is called a short circuit. Common causes are: broken insulation (exposing the metal wire to a metal part of the car or truck), or a shorted switch.

Some electrical components which require a large amount of current to operate also have a relay in their circuit. Since these circuits carry a large amount of current, the thickness of the wire in the circuit (gauge size) is also greater. If this large wire were connected from the component to the control switch on the instrument panel, and then back to the component, a voltage drop would occur in the circuit. To prevent this potential drop in voltage, an electromagnetic switch (relay) is used. The large wires in the circuit are connected from the battery to one side of the relay, and from the opposite side of the relay to the component. The relay is normally open, preventing current from passing through the circuit. An additional, smaller, wire is connected from the relay to the control switch for the circuit. When the control switch is turned on, it grounds the smaller wire from the relay and completes the circuit. This closes the relay and allows current to flow from the battery to the component. The horn, headlight, and starter circuits are three which use relays.

It is possible for larger surges of current to pass through the electrical system of your car or truck. If this surge of current were to reach an electrical component, it could burn it out. To prevent this, fuses, circuit breakers or fusible links are connected into the current supply wires of most of the major electrical systems. When an electrical current of excessive power passes through the component's fuse, the fuse blows out and breaks the circuit, saving the component from destruction.

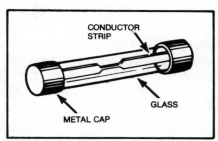

Typical automotive fuse

A circuit breaker is basically a self-repairing fuse. The circuit breaker opens the circuit the same way a fuse does. However, when either the short is removed from the circuit or the surge subsides, the circuit breaker resets itself and does not have to be replaced as a fuse does.

A fuse link is a wire that acts as a fuse. It is normally connected between the starter relay and the main wiring harness. This connection is usually under the hood. The fuse link (if installed) protects all the

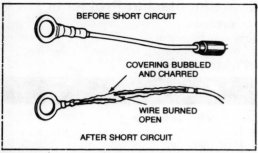

Most fusible links show a charred, melted insulation when they burn out

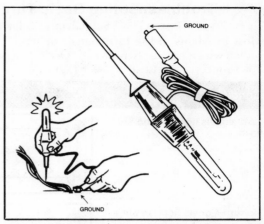

The test light will show the presence of current when touched to a hot wire and grounded at the other end

chassis electrical components, and is the probable cause of trouble when none of the electrical components function, unless the battery is disconnected or dead.

Electrical problems generally fall into one of three areas:

1. The component that is not functioning is not receiving current.

2. The component itself is not functioning.

3. The component is not properly grounded.

The electrical system can be checked with a test light and a jumper wire. A test light is a device that looks like a pointed screwdriver with a wire attached to it and has a light bulb in its handle. A jumper wire is a piece of insulated wire with an alligator clip attached to each end.

If a component is not working, you must follow a systematic plan to determine which of the three causes is the villain.

1. Turn on the switch that controls the inoperable component.

2. Disconnect the power supply wire from the component.

3. Attach the ground wire on the test light to a good metal ground.

4. Touch the probe end of the test light to the end of the power supply wire that was disconnected from the component. If the component is receiving current, the test light will go on.

NOTE: *Some components work only when the ignition switch is turned on.*

If the test light does not go on, then the problem is in the circuit between the battery and the component. This includes all the switches, fuses, and relays in the system. Follow the wire that runs back to the battery. The problem is an open circuit between the

battery and the component. If the fuse is blown and, when replaced, immediately blows again, there is a short circuit in the system which must be located and repaired. If there is a switch in the system, bypass it with a jumper wire. This is done by connecting one end of the jumper wire to the power supply wire into the switch and the other end of the jumper wire to the wire coming out of the switch. If the test light lights with the jumper wire installed, the switch or whatever was bypassed is defective.

NOTE: *Never substitute the jumper wire for the component, since it is required to use the power from the power source.*

5. If the bulb in the test light goes on, then the current is getting to the component that is not working. This eliminates the first of the three possible causes. Connect the power supply wire and connect a jumper wire from the component to a good metal ground. Do this with the switch which controls the component turned on, and also the ignition switch turned on if it is required for the component to work. If the component works with the jumper wire installed, then it has a bad ground. This is usually caused by the metal area on which the component mounts to the chassis being coated with some type of foreign matter.

6. If neither test located the source of the trouble, then the component itself is defective. Remember that for any electrical system to work, all connections must be clean and tight.

Troubleshooting Basic Turn Signal and Flasher Problems

See Chapter 5 for service procedures

Most problems in the turn signals or flasher system can be reduced to defective flashers or bulbs, which are easily replaced. Occasionally, the turn signal switch will prove defective.

F = Front   R = Rear   ● = Lights off   ○ = Lights on

Condition		Possible Cause
Turn signals light, but do not flash	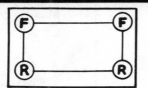	Defective flasher
No turn signals light on either side	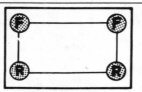	Blown fuse. Replace if defective. Defective flasher. Check by substitution. Open circuit, short circuit or poor ground.
Both turn signals on one side don't work	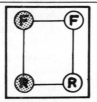	Bad bulbs. Bad ground in both (or either) housings.
One turn signal light on one side doesn't work	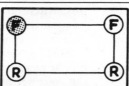	Defective bulb. Corrosion in socket. Clean contacts. Poor ground at socket.
Turn signal flashes too fast or too slowly	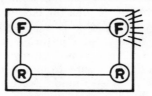	Check any bulb on the side flashing too fast. A heavy-duty bulb is probably installed in place of a regular bulb. Check the bulb flashing too slowly. A standard bulb was probably installed in place of a heavy-duty bulb. Loose connections or corrosion at the bulb socket.
Indicator lights don't work in either direction		Check if the turn signals are working. Check the dash indicator lights. Check the flasher by substitution.
One indicator light doesn't light		On systems with one dash indicator: See if the lights work on the same side. Often the filaments have been reversed in systems combining stoplights with taillights and turn signals. Check the flasher by substitution. On systems with two indicators: Check the bulbs on the same side. Check the indicator light bulb. Check the flasher by substitution.

Troubleshooting Lighting Problems
See Chapter 5 for service procedures

Condition	Possible Cause
One or more lights don't work, but others do	1. Defective bulb(s) 2. Blown fuse(s) 3. Dirty fuse clips or light sockets 4. Poor ground circuit
Lights burn out quickly	1. Incorrect voltage regulator setting or defective regulator 2. Poor battery/alternator connections
Lights go dim	1. Low/discharged battery 2. Alternator not charging 3. Corroded sockets or connections 4. Low voltage output
Lights flicker	1. Loose connection 2. Poor ground. (Run ground wire from light housing to frame) 3. Circuit breaker operating (short circuit)
Lights "flare"—Some flare is normal on acceleration—If excessive, see "Lights Burn Out Quickly"	High voltage setting
Lights glare—approaching drivers are blinded	1. Lights adjusted too high 2. Rear springs or shocks sagging 3. Rear tires soft

Troubleshooting Dash Gauge Problems

Most problems can be traced to a defective sending unit or faulty wiring. Occasionally, the gauge itself is at fault. See Chapter 5 for service procedures.

Condition	Possible Cause

COOLANT TEMPERATURE GAUGE

Gauge reads erratically or not at all	1. Loose or dirty connections 2. Defective sending unit. 3. Defective gauge. To test a bi-metal gauge, remove the wire from the sending unit. Ground the wire for an instant. If the gauge registers, replace the sending unit. To test a magnetic gauge, disconnect the wire at the sending unit. With ignition ON gauge should register COLD. Ground the wire; gauge should register HOT.

AMMETER GAUGE—TURN HEADLIGHTS ON (DO NOT START ENGINE). NOTE REACTION

Ammeter shows charge Ammeter shows discharge Ammeter does not move	1. Connections reversed on gauge 2. Ammeter is OK 3. Loose connections or faulty wiring 4. Defective gauge

Condition	Possible Cause

OIL PRESSURE GAUGE

Condition	Possible Cause
Gauge does not register or is inaccurate	1. On mechanical gauge, Bourdon tube may be bent or kinked. 2. Low oil pressure. Remove sending unit. Idle the engine briefly. If no oil flows from sending unit hole, problem is in engine. 3. Defective gauge. Remove the wire from the sending unit and ground it for an instant with the ignition ON. A good gauge will go to the top of the scale. 4. Defective wiring. Check the wiring to the gauge. If it's OK and the gauge doesn't register when grounded, replace the gauge. 5. Defective sending unit.

ALL GAUGES

Condition	Possible Cause
All gauges do not operate All gauges read low or erratically All gauges pegged	1. Blown fuse 2. Defective instrument regulator 3. Defective or dirty instrument voltage regulator 4. Loss of ground between instrument voltage regulator and frame 5. Defective instrument regulator

WARNING LIGHTS

Condition	Possible Cause
Light(s) do not come on when ignition is ON, but engine is not started Light comes on with engine running	1. Defective bulb 2. Defective wire 3. Defective sending unit. Disconnect the wire from the sending unit and ground it. Replace the sending unit if the light comes on with the ignition ON. 4. Problem in individual system 5. Defective sending unit

Troubleshooting Clutch Problems

It is false economy to replace individual clutch components. The pressure plate, clutch plate and throwout bearing should be replaced as a set, and the flywheel face inspected, whenever the clutch is overhauled. See Chapter 6 for service procedures.

Condition	Possible Cause
Clutch chatter	1. Grease on driven plate (disc) facing 2. Binding clutch linkage or cable 3. Loose, damaged facings on driven plate (disc) 4. Engine mounts loose 5. Incorrect height adjustment of pressure plate release levers 6. Clutch housing or housing to transmission adapter misalignment 7. Loose driven plate hub
Clutch grabbing	1. Oil, grease on driven plate (disc) facing 2. Broken pressure plate 3. Warped or binding driven plate. Driven plate binding on clutch shaft
Clutch slips	1. Lack of lubrication in clutch linkage or cable (linkage or cable binds, causes incomplete engagement) 2. Incorrect pedal, or linkage adjustment 3. Broken pressure plate springs 4. Weak pressure plate springs 5. Grease on driven plate facings (disc)

Troubleshooting Clutch Problems (cont.)

Condition	Possible Cause
Incomplete clutch release	1. Incorrect pedal or linkage adjustment or linkage or cable binding 2. Incorrect height adjustment on pressure plate release levers 3. Loose, broken facings on driven plate (disc) 4. Bent, dished, warped driven plate caused by overheating
Grinding, whirring grating noise when pedal is depressed	1. Worn or defective throwout bearing 2. Starter drive teeth contacting flywheel ring gear teeth. Look for milled or polished teeth on ring gear.
Squeal, howl, trumpeting noise when pedal is being released (occurs during first inch to inch and one-half of pedal travel)	Pilot bushing worn or lack of lubricant. If bushing appears OK, polish bushing with emery cloth, soak lube wick in oil, lube bushing with oil, apply film of chassis grease to clutch shaft pilot hub, reassemble. NOTE: Bushing wear may be due to misalignment of clutch housing or housing to transmission adapter
Vibration or clutch pedal pulsation with clutch disengaged (pedal fully depressed)	1. Worn or defective engine transmission mounts 2. Flywheel run out. (Flywheel run out at face not to exceed 0.005") 3. Damaged or defective clutch components

Troubleshooting Manual Transmission Problems
See Chapter 6 for service procedures

Condition	Possible Cause
Transmission jumps out of gear	1. Misalignment of transmission case or clutch housing. 2. Worn pilot bearing in crankshaft. 3. Bent transmission shaft. 4. Worn high speed sliding gear. 5. Worn teeth or end-play in clutch shaft. 6. Insufficient spring tension on shifter rail plunger. 7. Bent or loose shifter fork. 8. Gears not engaging completely. 9. Loose or worn bearings on clutch shaft or mainshaft. 10. Worn gear teeth. 11. Worn or damaged detent balls.
Transmission sticks in gear	1. Clutch not releasing fully. 2. Burred or battered teeth on clutch shaft, or sliding sleeve. 3. Burred or battered transmission mainshaft. 4. Frozen synchronizing clutch. 5. Stuck shifter rail plunger. 6. Gearshift lever twisting and binding shifter rail. 7. Battered teeth on high speed sliding gear or on sleeve. 8. Improper lubrication, or lack of lubrication. 9. Corroded transmission parts. 10. Defective mainshaft pilot bearing. 11. Locked gear bearings will give same effect as stuck in gear.
Transmission gears will not synchronize	1. Binding pilot bearing on mainshaft, will synchronize in high gear only. 2. Clutch not releasing fully. 3. Detent spring weak or broken. 4. Weak or broken springs under balls in sliding gear sleeve. 5. Binding bearing on clutch shaft, or binding countershaft. 6. Binding pilot bearing in crankshaft. 7. Badly worn gear teeth. 8. Improper lubrication. 9. Constant mesh gear not turning freely on transmission mainshaft. Will synchronize in that gear only.

Condition	Possible Cause
Gears spinning when shifting into gear from neutral	1. Clutch not releasing fully. 2. In some cases an extremely light lubricant in transmission will cause gears to continue to spin for a short time after clutch is released. 3. Binding pilot bearing in crankshaft.
Transmission noisy in all gears	1. Insufficient lubricant, or improper lubricant. 2. Worn countergear bearings. 3. Worn or damaged main drive gear or countergear. 4. Damaged main drive gear or mainshaft bearings. 5. Worn or damaged countergear anti-lash plate.
Transmission noisy in neutral only	1. Damaged main drive gear bearing. 2. Damaged or loose mainshaft pilot bearing. 3. Worn or damaged countergear anti-lash plate. 4. Worn countergear bearings.
Transmission noisy in one gear only	1. Damaged or worn constant mesh gears. 2. Worn or damaged countergear bearings. 3. Damaged or worn synchronizer.
Transmission noisy in reverse only	1. Worn or damaged reverse idler gear or idler bushing. 2. Worn or damaged mainshaft reverse gear. 3. Worn or damaged reverse countergear. 4. Damaged shift mechanism.

TROUBLESHOOTING AUTOMATIC TRANSMISSION PROBLEMS

Keeping alert to changes in the operating characteristics of the transmission (changing shift points, noises, etc.) can prevent small problems from becoming large ones. If the problem cannot be traced to loose bolts, fluid level, misadjusted linkage, clogged filters or similar problems, you should probably seek professional service.

Transmission Fluid Indications

The appearance and odor of the transmission fluid can give valuable clues to the overall condition of the transmission. Always note the appearance of the fluid when you check the fluid level or change the fluid. Rub a small amount of fluid between your fingers to feel for grit and smell the fluid on the dipstick.

If the fluid appears:	It indicates:
Clear and red colored	Normal operation
Discolored (extremely dark red or brownish) or smells burned	Band or clutch pack failure, usually caused by an overheated transmission. Hauling very heavy loads with insufficient power or failure to change the fluid often result in overheating. Do not confuse this appearance with newer fluids that have a darker red color and a strong odor (though not a burned odor).
Foamy or aerated (light in color and full of bubbles)	1. The level is too high (gear train is churning oil) 2. An internal air leak (air is mixing with the fluid). Have the transmission checked professionally.
Solid residue in the fluid	Defective bands, clutch pack or bearings. Bits of band material or metal abrasives are clinging to the dipstick. Have the transmission checked professionally.
Varnish coating on the dipstick	The transmission fluid is overheating

TROUBLESHOOTING DRIVE AXLE PROBLEMS

First, determine when the noise is most noticeable.

Drive Noise: Produced under vehicle acceleration.

Coast Noise: Produced while coasting with a closed throttle.

Float Noise: Occurs while maintaining constant speed (just enough to keep speed constant) on a level road.

External Noise Elimination

It is advisable to make a thorough road test to determine whether the noise originates in the rear axle or whether it originates from the tires, engine, transmission, wheel bearings or road surface. Noise originating from other places cannot be corrected by servicing the rear axle.

ROAD NOISE

Brick or rough surfaced concrete roads produce noises that seem to come from the rear axle. Road noise is usually identical in Drive or Coast and driving on a different type of road will tell whether the road is the problem.

TIRE NOISE

Tire noise can be mistaken as rear axle noise, even though the tires on the front are at fault. Snow tread and mud tread tires or tires worn unevenly will frequently cause vibrations which seem to originate elsewhere; *temporarily, and for test purposes only,* inflate the tires to 40–50 lbs. This will significantly alter the noise produced by the tires, but will not alter noise from the rear axle. Noises from the rear axle will normally cease at speeds below 30 mph on coast, while tire noise will continue at lower tone as speed is decreased. The rear axle noise will usually change from drive conditions to coast conditions, while tire noise will not. Do not forget to lower the tire pressure to normal after the test is complete.

ENGINE/TRANSMISSION NOISE

Determine at what speed the noise is most pronounced, then stop in a quiet place. With the transmission in Neutral, run the engine through speeds corresponding to road speeds where the noise was noticed. Noises produced with the vehicle standing still are coming from the engine or transmission.

FRONT WHEEL BEARINGS

Front wheel bearing noises, sometimes confused with rear axle noises, will not change when comparing drive and coast conditions. While holding the speed steady, lightly apply the footbrake. This will often cause wheel bearing noise to lessen, as some of the weight is taken off the bearing. Front wheel bearings are easily checked by jacking up the wheels and spinning the wheels. Shaking the wheels will also determine if the wheel bearings are excessively loose.

REAR AXLE NOISES

Eliminating other possible sources can narrow the cause to the rear axle, which normally produces noise from worn gears or bearings. Gear noises tend to peak in a narrow speed range, while bearing noises will usually vary in pitch with engine speeds.

Noise Diagnosis

The Noise Is:	Most Probably Produced By:
1. Identical under Drive or Coast	Road surface, tires or front wheel bearings
2. Different depending on road surface	Road surface or tires
3. Lower as speed is lowered	Tires
4. Similar when standing or moving	Engine or transmission
5. A vibration	Unbalanced tires, rear wheel bearing, unbalanced driveshaft or worn U-joint
6. A knock or click about every two tire revolutions	Rear wheel bearing
7. Most pronounced on turns	Damaged differential gears
8. A steady low-pitched whirring or scraping, starting at low speeds	Damaged or worn pinion bearing
9. A chattering vibration on turns	Wrong differential lubricant or worn clutch plates (limited slip rear axle)
10. Noticed only in Drive, Coast or Float conditions	Worn ring gear and/or pinion gear

Troubleshooting Steering & Suspension Problems

Condition	Possible Cause
Hard steering (wheel is hard to turn)	1. Improper tire pressure 2. Loose or glazed pump drive belt 3. Low or incorrect fluid 4. Loose, bent or poorly lubricated front end parts 5. Improper front end alignment (excessive caster) 6. Bind in steering column or linkage 7. Kinked hydraulic hose 8. Air in hydraulic system 9. Low pump output or leaks in system 10. Obstruction in lines 11. Pump valves sticking or out of adjustment 12. Incorrect wheel alignment
Loose steering (too much play in steering wheel)	1. Loose wheel bearings 2. Faulty shocks 3. Worn linkage or suspension components 4. Loose steering gear mounting or linkage points 5. Steering mechanism worn or improperly adjusted 6. Valve spool improperly adjusted 7. Worn ball joints, tie-rod ends, etc.
Veers or wanders (pulls to one side with hands off steering wheel)	1. Improper tire pressure 2. Improper front end alignment 3. Dragging or improperly adjusted brakes 4. Bent frame 5. Improper rear end alignment 6. Faulty shocks or springs 7. Loose or bent front end components 8. Play in Pitman arm 9. Steering gear mountings loose 10. Loose wheel bearings 11. Binding Pitman arm 12. Spool valve sticking or improperly adjusted 13. Worn ball joints
Wheel oscillation or vibration transmitted through steering wheel	1. Low or uneven tire pressure 2. Loose wheel bearings 3. Improper front end alignment 4. Bent spindle 5. Worn, bent or broken front end components 6. Tires out of round or out of balance 7. Excessive lateral runout in disc brake rotor 8. Loose or bent shock absorber or strut
Noises (see also "Troubleshooting Drive Axle Problems")	1. Loose belts 2. Low fluid, air in system 3. Foreign matter in system 4. Improper lubrication 5. Interference or chafing in linkage 6. Steering gear mountings loose 7. Incorrect adjustment or wear in gear box 8. Faulty valves or wear in pump 9. Kinked hydraulic lines 10. Worn wheel bearings
Poor return of steering	1. Over-inflated tires 2. Improperly aligned front end (excessive caster) 3. Binding in steering column 4. No lubrication in front end 5. Steering gear adjusted too tight
Uneven tire wear (see "How To Read Tire Wear")	1. Incorrect tire pressure 2. Improperly aligned front end 3. Tires out-of-balance 4. Bent or worn suspension parts

HOW TO READ TIRE WEAR

The way your tires wear is a good indicator of other parts of the suspension. Abnormal wear patterns are often caused by the need for simple tire maintenance, or for front end alignment.

Excessive wear at the center of the tread indicates that the air pressure in the tire is consistently too high. The tire is riding on the center of the tread and wearing it prematurely. Occasionally, this wear pattern can result from outrageously wide tires on narrow rims. The cure for this is to replace either the tires or the wheels.

This type of wear usually results from consistent under-inflation. When a tire is under-inflated, there is too much contact with the road by the outer treads, which wear prematurely. When this type of wear occurs, and the tire pressure is known to be consistently correct, a bent or worn steering component or the need for wheel alignment could be indicated.

Feathering is a condition when the edge of each tread rib develops a slightly rounded edge on one side and a sharp edge on the other. By running your hand over the tire, you can usually feel the sharper edges before you'll be able to see them. The most common causes of feathering are incorrect toe-in setting or deteriorated bushings in the front suspension.

When an inner or outer rib wears faster than the rest of the tire, the need for wheel alignment is indicated. There is excessive camber in the front suspension, caus- ing the wheel to lean too much putting excessive load on one side of the tire. Misalignment could also be due to sagging springs, worn ball joints, or worn control arm bushings. Be sure the vehicle is loaded the way it's nor- mally driven when you have the wheels aligned.

Cups or scalloped dips appearing around the edge of the tread almost always indicate worn (sometimes bent) sus- pension parts. Adjustment of wheel alignment alone will seldom cure the problem. Any worn component that connects the wheel to the suspension can cause this type of wear. Occasionally, wheels that are out of balance will wear like this, but wheel imbalance usually shows up as bald spots between the outside edges and center of the tread.

Second-rib wear is usually found only in radial tires, and appears where the steel belts end in relation to the tread. It can be kept to a minimum by paying careful attention to tire pressure and frequently rotating the tires. This is often considered normal wear but excessive amounts indi- cate that the tires are too wide for the wheels.

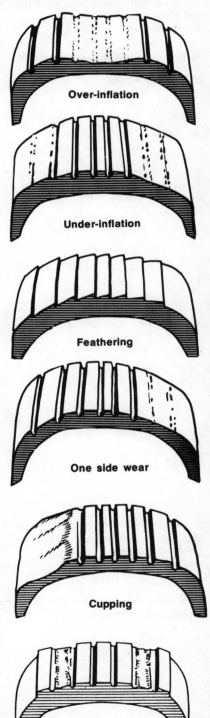

Over-inflation

Under-inflation

Feathering

One side wear

Cupping

Second-rib wear

Troubleshooting Disc Brake Problems

Condition	Possible Cause
Noise—groan—brake noise emanating when slowly releasing brakes (creep-groan)	Not detrimental to function of disc brakes—no corrective action required. (This noise may be eliminated by slightly increasing or decreasing brake pedal efforts.)
Rattle—brake noise or rattle emanating at low speeds on rough roads, (front wheels only).	1. Shoe anti-rattle spring missing or not properly positioned. 2. Excessive clearance between shoe and caliper. 3. Soft or broken caliper seals. 4. Deformed or misaligned disc. 5. Loose caliper.
Scraping	1. Mounting bolts too long. 2. Loose wheel bearings. 3. Bent, loose, or misaligned splash shield.
Front brakes heat up during driving and fail to release	1. Operator riding brake pedal. 2. Stop light switch improperly adjusted. 3. Sticking pedal linkage. 4. Frozen or seized piston. 5. Residual pressure valve in master cylinder. 6. Power brake malfunction. 7. Proportioning valve malfunction.
Leaky brake caliper	1. Damaged or worn caliper piston seal. 2. Scores or corrosion on surface of cylinder bore.
Grabbing or uneven brake action— Brakes pull to one side	1. Causes listed under "Brakes Pull". 2. Power brake malfunction. 3. Low fluid level in master cylinder. 4. Air in hydraulic system. 5. Brake fluid, oil or grease on linings. 6. Unmatched linings. 7. Distorted brake pads. 8. Frozen or seized pistons. 9. Incorrect tire pressure. 10. Front end out of alignment. 11. Broken rear spring. 12. Brake caliper pistons sticking. 13. Restricted hose or line. 14. Caliper not in proper alignment to braking disc. 15. Stuck or malfunctioning metering valve. 16. Soft or broken caliper seals. 17. Loose caliper.
Brake pedal can be depressed without braking effect	1. Air in hydraulic system or improper bleeding procedure. 2. Leak past primary cup in master cylinder. 3. Leak in system. 4. Rear brakes out of adjustment. 5. Bleeder screw open.
Excessive pedal travel	1. Air, leak, or insufficient fluid in system or caliper. 2. Warped or excessively tapered shoe and lining assembly. 3. Excessive disc runout. 4. Rear brake adjustment required. 5. Loose wheel bearing adjustment. 6. Damaged caliper piston seal. 7. Improper brake fluid (boil). 8. Power brake malfunction. 9. Weak or soft hoses.

Troubleshooting Disc Brake Problems (cont.)

Condition	Possible Cause
Brake roughness or chatter (pedal pumping)	1. Excessive thickness variation of braking disc. 2. Excessive lateral runout of braking disc. 3. Rear brake drums out-of-round. 4. Excessive front bearing clearance.
Excessive pedal effort	1. Brake fluid, oil or grease on linings. 2. Incorrect lining. 3. Frozen or seized pistons. 4. Power brake malfunction. 5. Kinked or collapsed hose or line. 6. Stuck metering valve. 7. Scored caliper or master cylinder bore. 8. Seized caliper pistons.
Brake pedal fades (pedal travel increases with foot on brake)	1. Rough master cylinder or caliper bore. 2. Loose or broken hydraulic lines/connections. 3. Air in hydraulic system. 4. Fluid level low. 5. Weak or soft hoses. 6. Inferior quality brake shoes or fluid. 7. Worn master cylinder piston cups or seals.

Troubleshooting Drum Brakes

Condition	Possible Cause
Pedal goes to floor	1. Fluid low in reservoir. 2. Air in hydraulic system. 3. Improperly adjusted brake. 4. Leaking wheel cylinders. 5. Loose or broken brake lines. 6. Leaking or worn master cylinder. 7. Excessively worn brake lining.
Spongy brake pedal	1. Air in hydraulic system. 2. Improper brake fluid (low boiling point). 3. Excessively worn or cracked brake drums. 4. Broken pedal pivot bushing.
Brakes pulling	1. Contaminated lining. 2. Front end out of alignment. 3. Incorrect brake adjustment. 4. Unmatched brake lining. 5. Brake drums out of round. 6. Brake shoes distorted. 7. Restricted brake hose or line. 8. Broken rear spring. 9. Worn brake linings. 10. Uneven lining wear. 11. Glazed brake lining. 12. Excessive brake lining dust. 13. Heat spotted brake drums. 14. Weak brake return springs. 15. Faulty automatic adjusters. 16. Low or incorrect tire pressure.

Condition	Possible Cause
Squealing brakes	1. Glazed brake lining. 2. Saturated brake lining. 3. Weak or broken brake shoe retaining spring. 4. Broken or weak brake shoe return spring. 5. Incorrect brake lining. 6. Distorted brake shoes. 7. Bent support plate. 8. Dust in brakes or scored brake drums. 9. Linings worn below limit. 10. Uneven brake lining wear. 11. Heat spotted brake drums.
Chirping brakes	1. Out of round drum or eccentric axle flange pilot.
Dragging brakes	1. Incorrect wheel or parking brake adjustment. 2. Parking brakes engaged or improperly adjusted. 3. Weak or broken brake shoe return spring. 4. Brake pedal binding. 5. Master cylinder cup sticking. 6. Obstructed master cylinder relief port. 7. Saturated brake lining. 8. Bent or out of round brake drum. 9. Contaminated or improper brake fluid. 10. Sticking wheel cylinder pistons. 11. Driver riding brake pedal. 12. Defective proportioning valve. 13. Insufficient brake shoe lubricant.
Hard pedal	1. Brake booster inoperative. 2. Incorrect brake lining. 3. Restricted brake line or hose. 4. Frozen brake pedal linkage. 5. Stuck wheel cylinder. 6. Binding pedal linkage. 7. Faulty proportioning valve.
Wheel locks	1. Contaminated brake lining. 2. Loose or torn brake lining. 3. Wheel cylinder cups sticking. 4. Incorrect wheel bearing adjustment. 5. Faulty proportioning valve.
Brakes fade (high speed)	1. Incorrect lining. 2. Overheated brake drums. 3. Incorrect brake fluid (low boiling temperature). 4. Saturated brake lining. 5. Leak in hydraulic system. 6. Faulty automatic adjusters.
Pedal pulsates	1. Bent or out of round brake drum.
Brake chatter and shoe knock	1. Out of round brake drum. 2. Loose support plate. 3. Bent support plate. 4. Distorted brake shoes. 5. Machine grooves in contact face of brake drum (Shoe Knock). 6. Contaminated brake lining. 7. Missing or loose components. 8. Incorrect lining material. 9. Out-of-round brake drums. 10. Heat spotted or scored brake drums. 11. Out-of-balance wheels.

Troubleshooting Drum Brakes (cont.)

Condition	Possible Cause
Brakes do not self adjust	1. Adjuster screw frozen in thread. 2. Adjuster screw corroded at thrust washer. 3. Adjuster lever does not engage star wheel. 4. Adjuster installed on wrong wheel.
Brake light glows	1. Leak in the hydraulic system. 2. Air in the system. 3. Improperly adjusted master cylinder pushrod. 4. Uneven lining wear. 5. Failure to center combination valve or proportioning valve.

Appendix

General Conversion Table

Multiply by	To convert	To	
2.54	Inches	Centimeters	.3937
30.48	Feet	Centimeters	.0328
.914	Yards	Meters	1.094
1.609	Miles	Kilometers	.621
6.45	Square inches	Square cm.	.155
.836	Square yards	Square meters	1.196
16.39	Cubic inches	Cubic cm.	.061
28.3	Cubic feet	Liters	.0353
.4536	Pounds	Kilograms	2.2045
3.785	Gallons	Liters	.264
.068	Lbs./sq. in. (psi)	Atmospheres	14.7
.138	Foot pounds	Kg. m.	7.23
1.014	H.P. (DIN)	H.P. (SAE)	.9861
—	To obtain	From	Multiply by

Note: 1 cm. equals 10 mm.; 1 mm. equals .0394".

Conversion—Common Fractions to Decimals and Millimeters

Common Fractions	Decimal Fractions	Millimeters (approx.)	Common Fractions	Decimal Fractions	Millimeters (approx.)	Common Fractions	Decimal Fractions	Millimeters (approx.)
1/128	.008	0.20	11/32	.344	8.73	43/64	.672	17.07
1/64	.016	0.40	23/64	.359	9.13	11/16	.688	17.46
1/32	.031	0.79	3/8	.375	9.53	45/64	.703	17.86
3/64	.047	1.19	25/64	.391	9.92	23/32	.719	18.26
1/16	.063	1.59	13/32	.406	10.32	47/64	.734	18.65
5/64	.078	1.98	27/64	.422	10.72	3/4	.750	19.05
3/32	.094	2.38	7/16	.438	11.11	49/64	.766	19.45
7/64	.109	2.78	29/64	.453	11.51	25/32	.781	19.84
1/8	.125	3.18	15/32	.469	11.91	51/64	.797	20.24
9/64	.141	3.57	31/64	.484	12.30	13/16	.813	20.64
5/32	.156	3.97	1/2	.500	12.70	53/64	.828	21.03
11/64	.172	4.37	33/64	.516	13.10	27/32	.844	21.43
3/16	.188	4.76	17/32	.531	13.49	55/64	.859	21.83
13/64	.203	5.16	35/64	.547	13.89	7/8	.875	22.23
7/32	.219	5.56	9/16	.563	14.29	57/64	.891	22.62
15/64	.234	5.95	37/64	.578	14.68	29/32	.906	23.02
1/4	.250	6.35	19/32	.594	15.08	59/64	.922	23.42
17/64	.266	6.75	39/64	.609	15.48	15/16	.938	23.81
9/32	.281	7.14	5/8	.625	15.88	61/64	.953	24.21
19/64	.297	7.54	41/64	.641	16.27	31/32	.969	24.61
5/16	.313	7.94	21/32	.656	16.67	63/64	.984	25.00
21/64	.328	8.33						

Conversion—Millimeters to Decimal Inches

mm	inches	mm	inches	mm	inches	mm	inches	mm	inches
1	.039 370	31	1.220 470	61	2.401 570	91	3.582 670	210	8.267 700
2	.078 740	32	1.259 840	62	2.440 940	92	3.622 040	220	8.661 400
3	.118 110	33	1.299 210	63	2.480 310	93	3.661 410	230	9.055 100
4	.157 480	34	1.338 580	64	2.519 680	94	3.700 780	240	9.448 800
5	.196 850	35	1.377 949	65	2.559 050	95	3.740 150	250	9.842 500
6	.236 220	36	1.417 319	66	2.598 420	96	3.779 520	260	10.236 200
7	.275 590	37	1.456 689	67	2.637 790	97	3.818 890	270	10.629 900
8	.314 960	38	1.496 050	68	2.677 160	98	3.858 260	280	11.032 600
9	.354 330	39	1.535 430	69	2.716 530	99	3.897 630	290	11.417 300
10	.393 700	40	1.574 800	70	2.755 900	100	3.937 000	300	11.811 000
11	.433 070	41	1.614 170	71	2.795 270	105	4.133 848	310	12.204 700
12	.472 440	42	1.653 540	72	2.834 640	110	4.330 700	320	12.598 400
13	.511 810	43	1.692 910	73	2.874 010	115	4.527 550	330	12.992 100
14	.551 180	44	1.732 280	74	2.913 380	120	4.724 400	340	13.385 800
15	.590 550	45	1.771 650	75	2.952 750	125	4.921 250	350	13.779 500
16	.629 920	46	1.811 020	76	2.992 120	130	5.118 100	360	14.173 200
17	.669 290	47	1.850 390	77	3.031 490	135	5.314 950	370	14.566 900
18	.708 660	48	1.889 760	78	3.070 860	140	5.511 800	380	14.960 600
19	.748 030	49	1.929 130	79	3.110 230	145	5.708 650	390	15.354 300
20	.787 400	50	1.968 500	80	3.149 600	150	5.905 500	400	15.748 000
21	.826 770	51	2.007 870	81	3.188 970	155	6.102 350	500	19.685 000
22	.866 140	52	2.047 240	82	3.228 340	160	6.299 200	600	23.622 000
23	.905 510	53	2.086 610	83	3.267 710	165	6.496 050	700	27.559 000
24	.944 880	54	2.125 980	84	3.307 080	170	6.692 900	800	31.496 000
25	.984 250	55	2.165 350	85	3.346 450	175	6.889 750	900	35.433 000
26	1.023 620	56	2.204 720	86	3.385 820	180	7.086 600	1000	39.370 000
27	1.062 990	57	2.244 090	87	3.425 190	185	7.283 450	2000	78.740 000
28	1.102 360	58	2.283 460	88	3.464 560	190	7.480 300	3000	118.110 000
29	1.141 730	59	2.322 830	89	3.503 903	195	7.677 150	4000	157.480 000
30	1.181 100	60	2.362 200	90	3.543 300	200	7.874 000	5000	196.850 000

To change decimal millimeters to decimal inches, position the decimal point where desired on either side of the millimeter measurement shown and reset the inches decimal by the same number of digits in the same direction. For example, to convert 0.001 mm to decimal inches, reset the decimal behind the 1 mm (shown on the chart) to 0.001; change the decimal inch equivalent (0.039″ shown) to 0.000039″.

Tap Drill Sizes

Screw & Tap Size	National Fine or S.A.E. Threads Per Inch	Use Drill Number
No. 5	44	37
No. 6	40	33
No. 8	36	29
No. 10	32	21
No. 12	28	15
1/4	28	3
5/16	24	1
3/8	24	Q
7/16	20	W
1/2	20	29/64
9/16	18	33/64
5/8	18	37/64
3/4	16	11/16
7/8	14	13/16
1 1/8	12	1 3/64
1 1/4	12	1 11/64
1 1/2	12	1 27/64

Tap Drill Sizes

Screw & Tap Size	National Coarse or U.S.S. Threads Per Inch	Use Drill Number
No. 5	40	39
No. 6	32	36
No. 8	32	29
No. 10	24	25
No. 12	24	17
1/4	20	8
5/16	18	F
3/8	16	5/16
7/16	14	U
1/2	13	27/64
9/16	12	31/64
5/8	11	17/32
3/4	10	21/32
7/8	9	49/64
1	8	7/8
1 1/8	7	63/64
1 1/4	7	1 7/64
1 1/2	6	1 11/32

Decimal Equivalent Size of the Number Drills

Drill No.	Decimal Equivalent	Drill No.	Decimal Equivalent	Drill No.	Decimal Equivalent
80	.0135	53	.0595	26	.1470
79	.0145	52	.0635	25	.1495
78	.0160	51	.0670	24	.1520
77	.0180	50	.0700	23	.1540
76	.0200	49	.0730	22	.1570
75	.0210	48	.0760	21	.1590
74	.0225	47	.0785	20	.1610
73	.0240	46	.0810	19	.1660
72	.0250	45	.0820	18	.1695
71	.0260	44	.0860	17	.1730
70	.0280	43	.0890	16	.1770
69	.0292	42	.0935	15	.1800
68	.0310	41	.0960	14	.1820
67	.0320	40	.0980	13	.1850
66	.0330	39	.0995	12	.1890
65	.0350	38	.1015	11	.1910
64	.0360	37	.1040	10	.1935
63	.0370	36	.1065	9	.1960
62	.0380	35	.1100	8	.1990
61	.0390	34	.1110	7	.2010
60	.0400	33	.1130	6	.2040
59	.0410	32	.1160	5	.2055
58	.0420	31	.1200	4	.2090
57	.0430	30	.1285	3	.2130
56	.0465	29	.1360	2	.2210
55	.0520	28	.1405	1	.2280
54	.0550	27	.1440		

Decimal Equivalent Size of the Letter Drills

Letter Drill	Decimal Equivalent	Letter Drill	Decimal Equivalent	Letter Drill	Decimal Equivalent
A	.234	J	.277	S	.348
B	.238	K	.281	T	.358
C	.242	L	.290	U	.368
D	.246	M	.295	V	.377
E	.250	N	.302	W	.386
F	.257	O	.316	X	.397
G	.261	P	.323	Y	.404
H	.266	Q	.332	Z	.413
I	.272	R	.339		

Anti-Freeze Chart

Temperatures Shown in Degrees Fahrenheit +32 is Freezing

Cooling System Capacity Quarts	Quarts of ETHYLENE GLYCOL Needed for Protection to Temperatures Shown Below													
	1	2	3	4	5	6	7	8	9	10	11	12	13	14
10	+24°	+16°	+ 4°	−12°	−34°	−62°								
11	+25	+18	+ 8	− 6	−23	−47								
12	+26	+19	+10	0	−15	−34	−57°							
13	+27	+21	+13	+ 3	− 9	−25	−45							
14			+15	+ 6	− 5	−18	−34							
15			+16	+ 8	0	−12	−26							
16			+17	+10	+ 2	− 8	−19	−34	−52°					
17			+18	+12	+ 5	− 4	−14	−27	−42					
18			+19	+14	+ 7	0	−10	−21	−34	−50°				
19			+20	+15	+ 9	+ 2	− 7	−16	−28	−42				
20				+16	+10	+ 4	− 3	−12	−22	−34	−48°			
21				+17	+12	+ 6	0	− 9	−17	−28	−41			
22				+18	+13	+ 8	+ 2	− 6	−14	−23	−34	−47°		
23				+19	+14	+ 9	+ 4	− 3	−10	−19	−29	−40		
24				+19	+15	+10	+ 5	0	− 8	−15	−23	−34	−46°	
25				+20	+16	+12	+ 7	+ 1	− 5	−12	−20	−29	−40	−50°
26					+17	+13	+ 8	+ 3	− 3	− 9	−16	−25	−34	−44
27					+18	+14	+ 9	+ 5	− 1	− 7	−13	−21	−29	−39
28					+18	+15	+10	+ 6	+ 1	− 5	−11	−18	−25	−34
29					+19	+16	+12	+ 7	+ 2	− 3	− 8	−15	−22	−29
30					+20	+17	+13	+ 8	+ 4	− 1	− 6	−12	−18	−25

For capacities over 30 quarts divide true capacity by 3. Find quarts Anti-Freeze for the ⅓ and multiply by 3 for quarts to add.

For capacities under 10 quarts multiply true capacity by 3. Find quarts Anti-Freeze for the tripled volume and divide by 3 for quarts to add.

To Increase the Freezing Protection of Anti-Freeze Solutions Already Installed

Cooling System Capacity Quarts	Number of Quarts of ETHYLENE GLYCOL Anti-Freeze Required to Increase Protection													
	From +20° F. to					From +10° F. to					From 0° F. to			
	0°	−10°	−20°	−30°	−40°	0°	−10°	−20°	−30°	−40°	−10°	−20°	−30°	−40°
10	1¾	2¼	3	3½	3¾	¾	1½	2¼	2¾	3¼	¾	1½	2	2½
12	2	2¾	3½	4	4½	1	1¾	2½	3¼	3¾	1	1¾	2½	3¼
14	2¼	3¼	4	4¾	5½	1¼	2	3	3¾	4½	1	2	3	3½
16	2½	3½	4½	5¼	6	1¼	2½	3½	4¼	5¼	1¼	2¼	3¼	4
18	3	4	5	6	7	1½	2¾	4	5	5¾	1½	2½	3¾	4¾
20	3¼	4½	5¾	6¾	7½	1¾	3	4¼	5½	6½	1½	2¾	4¼	5¼
22	3½	5	6¼	7¼	8¼	1¾	3¼	4¾	6	7¼	1¾	3¼	4½	5½
24	4	5½	7	8	9	2	3½	5	6½	7½	1¾	3½	5	6
26	4¼	6	7½	8¾	10	2	4	5½	7	8¼	2	3¾	5½	6¾
28	4½	6¼	8	9½	10½	2¼	4¼	6	7½	9	2	4	5¾	7¼
30	5	6¾	8½	10	11½	2½	4½	6½	8	9½	2¼	4¼	6¼	7¾

Test radiator solution with proper hydrometer. Determine from the table the number of quarts of solution to be drawn off from a full cooling system and replace with undiluted anti-freeze, to give the desired increased protection. For example, to increase protection of a 22-quart cooling system containing Ethylene Glycol (permanent type) anti-freeze, from +20° F. to −20° F. will require the replacement of 6¼ quarts of solution with undiluted anti-freeze.

Index

Chilton's Repair & Tune-Up Guides

The complete line covers domestic cars, imports, trucks, vans, RV's and 4-wheel drive vehicles.

BOOK CODE	TITLE	BOOK CODE	TITLE
#7199	AMC 75-82; all models inc. Eagle	#6937	Granada 75-80
#7163	Aries 81-82	#5905	GTO 68-73
#7032	Arrow Pick-Up 79-81	#5821	GTX 68-73
#6637	Aspen 76-80	#6980	Honda 73-82
#5902	Audi 70-73	#6845	Horizon 78-82
#7028	Audi 4000/5000 77-81	#5912	International Scout 67-73
#6337	Audi Fox 73-75	#5998	Jaguar 69-74
#5807	Barracuda 65-72	#7136	Jeep CJ 1945-81
#6931	Blazer 69-82	#6739	Jeep Wagoneer, Commando, Cherokee 66-79
#5576	BMW 59-70	#6962	Jetta 1980
#6844	BMW 70-79	#6931	Jimmy 69-82
#5821	Belvedere 68-73	#7059	J-2000 1982
#7027	Bobcat	#5905	Le Mans 68-73
#7045	Camaro 67-81	#7055	Lynx 81-82 inc. EXP & LN-7
#6695	Capri 70-77	#6634	Maverick 70-77
#6963	Capri 79-82	#6981	Mazda 71-82
#7059	Cavalier 1982	#7031	Mazda RX-7 79-81
#5807	Challenger 65-72	#6065	Mercedes-Benz 59-70
#7037	Challenger (Import) 71-81	#5907	Mercedes-Benz 68-73
#7041	Champ 78-81	#6809	Mercedes-Benz 74-79
#6316	Charger 71-75	#7128	Mercury 68-71 all full sized models
#7162	Chevette 76-82 inc. diesel	#6696	Mercury Mid-Size 71-81 inc. T-Bird,
#7135	Chevrolet 68-81 all full size models		Montego & Cougar
#6936	Chevrolet/GMC Pick-Ups 70-82	#6780	MG 61-81
#6930	Chevrolet/GMC Vans 67-82	#6973	Monarch 75-80
#7051	Chevy Luv 72-81 inc. 4wd	#6542	Mustang 65-73
#7056	Chevy Mid-Size 64-82 inc. El Camino,	#6812	Mustang II 74-78
	Chevelle, Laguna, Malibu & Monte Carlo	#6963	Mustang 79-82
#6841	Chevy II 62-79	#6841	Nova 69-79
#7059	Cimarron 1982	#7049	Omega 81-82
#7049	Citation 80-81	#6845	Omni 78-82
#7037	Colt 71-81	#5792	Opel 64-70
#6634	Comet 70-77	#6575	Opel 71-75
#6316	Coronet 71-75	#5982	Peugeot 70-74
#6691	Corvair 60-69 inc. Turbo	#7049	Phoenix 81-82
#6576	Corvette 53-62	#7027	Pinto 71-80
#6843	Corvette 63-82	#6552	Plymouth 68-76 full sized models
#6933	Cutlass 70-82	#6934	Plymouth Vans 67-82
#6324	Dart 68-76	#5822	Porche 69-73
#6962	Dasher 74-80	#7048	Porche 924 & 928 76-81 inc. Turbo
#5790	Datsun 61-72	#6962	Rabbit 75-80
#7196	Datsun F10, 310, Nissan Stanza 77-82	#6331	Ramcharger/Trail Duster 74-75
#7170	Datsun 200SX, 510, 610, 710, 810 73-82	#7163	Reliant 81-82
#7197	Datsun 210 and 1200 73-82	#5821	Roadrunner 68-73
#6932	Datsun Z & ZX 70-82	#5988	Saab 69-75
#7050	Datsun Pick-Ups 70-81 inc. 4wd	#7041	Sapporo 78-81
#6324	Demon 68-76	#5821	Satellite 68-73
#6554	Dodge 68-77 all full sized models	#6962	Scirocco 75-80
#6486	Dodge Charger 67-70	#7059	Skyhawk 1982
#6934	Dodge Vans 67-82	#7049	Skylark 80-81
#6326	Duster 68-76	#6982	Subaru 70-82
#7055	Escort 81-82 inc. EXP & LN-7	#5905	Tempest 68-73
#6320	Fairlane 62-75	#6320	Torino 62-75
#6965	Fairmont 78-80	#5795	Toyota 66-70
#6485	Fiat 64-70	#7043	Toyota Celica & Supra 71-81
#7042	Fiat 69-81	#7036	Toyota Corolla, Carina, Tercel, Starlet 70-81
#6846	Fiesta 78-80	#7044	Toyota Corona, Cressida, Crown, Mark II 70-81
#7046	Firebird 67-81	#7035	Toyota Pick-Ups 70-81
#7059	Firenza 1982	#5910	Triumph 69-73
#7128	Ford 68-81 all full sized models	#7162	T-1000 1982
#7140	Ford Bronco 66-81	#6326	Valiant 68-76
#6983	Ford Courier 72-80	#5796	Volkswagen 49-71
#6696	Ford Mid-Size 71-78 inc. Torino,	#6837	Volkswagen 70-81
	Gran Torino, Ranchero, Elite & LTD II	#6637	Volaré 76-80
#6913	Ford Pick-Ups 65-82 inc. 4wd	#6529	Volvo 56-69
#6849	Ford Vans 61-82	#7040	Volvo 70-80
#6935	GM Sub-compact 71-81 inc. Vega,	#6965	Zephyr 78-80
	Monza, Astre, Sunbird, Starfire & Skyhawk		

Chilton's Repair & Tune-Up Guides are available at your local retailer or by mailing a check or money order for **$9.95** plus **$1.00** to cover postage and handling to:

Chilton Book Company
Dept. DM
Radnor, PA 19089

NOTE: When ordering be sure to include your name & address, book code & title.